INDIGENOUS LEGAL JUDGMENTS

This book is a collection of key legal decisions affecting Indigenous Australians, which have been re-imagined so as to be inclusive of Indigenous people's stories, historical experience, perspectives, and world views.

In this groundbreaking work, Indigenous and non-Indigenous scholars have collaborated to rewrite 16 key decisions. Spanning from 1889 to 2017, the judgments reflect the trajectory of Indigenous people's engagements with Australian law. The collection includes decisions that laid the foundation for the wrongful application of terra nullius and the long disavowal of native title. Contributors have also challenged narrow judicial interpretations of native title, which have denied recognition to Indigenous people who suffered the prolonged impacts of dispossession. Exciting new voices have reclaimed Australian law to deliver justice to the Stolen Generations and to families who have experienced institutional and police racism. Contributors have shown how judicial officers can use their power to challenge systemic racism and tell the stories of Indigenous people who have been dehumanised by the criminal justice system.

The new judgments are characterised by intersectional perspectives which draw on postcolonial, critical race and whiteness theories. Several scholars have chosen to operate within the parameters of legal doctrine. Some have imagined new truth-telling forums, highlighting the strength and creative resistance of Indigenous people to oppression and exclusion. Others have rejected the possibility that the legal system, which has been integral to settler-colonialism, can ever deliver meaningful justice to Indigenous people.

Heather Douglas is a Professor at the Melbourne Law School, The University of Melbourne.

Nicole Watson is a Munanjali and Birri Gubba woman from south-east Queensland. Nicole is an Associate Professor and Director of the Academic Unit, Nura Gili Centre for Indigenous Programs, University of New South Wales.

INDIGENOUS LEGAL JUDGMENTS

Bringing Indigenous Voices into Judicial Decision Making

Edited by Nicole Watson and Heather Douglas

Routledge
Taylor & Francis Group
LONDON AND NEW YORK

First published 2021
by Routledge
2 Park Square, Milton Park, Abingdon, Oxon OX14 4RN

and by Routledge
605 Third Avenue, New York, NY 10158

Routledge is an imprint of the Taylor & Francis Group, an informa business

British Library Cataloguing-in-Publication Data
A catalogue record for this book is available from the British Library

Library of Congress Cataloging-in-Publication Data
Names: Watson, Nicole, 1973- editor. | Douglas, Heather, editor.
Title: Indigenous legal judgments: bringing indigenous voices into judicial decision making / edited by Nicole Watson and Heather Douglas.
Description: Abingdon, Oxon; New York, NY: Routledge, 2021. | Includes bibliographical references and index.
Identifiers: LCCN 2020057510 (print) | LCCN 2020057511 (ebook) | ISBN 9781032004815 (hardback) | ISBN 9780367467456 (paperback) | ISBN 9781003174349 (ebook)
Subjects: LCSH: Aboriginal Australians–Legal status, laws, etc.–Cases. | Torres Strait Islanders–Legal status, laws, etc.–Cases. | Indigenous peoples–Legal status, laws, etc.–Australia–Cases.
Classification: LCC KU519.I64 I533 2021 (print) | LCC KU519.I64 (ebook) | DDC 342.9408/72–dc23
LC record available at https://lccn.loc.gov/2020057510
LC ebook record available at https://lccn.loc.gov/2020057511

ISBN: 978-1-032-00481-5 (hbk)
ISBN: 978-0-367-46745-6 (pbk)
ISBN: 978-1-003-17434-9 (ebk)

Typeset in Bembo
by Deanta Global Publishing Services, Chennai, India

This book is dedicated to the memory of Sam Watson.

CONTENTS

FIGURES

CONTRIBUTORS

Debbie Bargallie is a descendent of the Kamilaroi and Wonnarua peoples and a Senior Research Fellow at the Griffith Institute for Educational Research, Griffith University. Debbie was the recipient of the prestigious Stanner Award in 2019 and is the author of *Unmasking the Racial Contract: Indigenous Voices on Racism in the Australian Public Service* (2020) published by Aboriginal Studies Press.

Narelle Bedford is an Assistant Professor at the Faculty of Law, Bond University. Narelle's mum is Jackie Bedford from the Yuin people of South Coast NSW, who spent most of her life living in and serving the Tharawal community.

Larissa Behrendt is a Eualeyai/Kamillaroi woman and a Distinguished Professor of Law and Director of Research, Jumbunna Institute for Indigenous Education and Research, University of Technology Sydney.

Peter Billings is a Professor at the School of Law, The University of Queensland.

Trudie Broderick is a Birri Gubba/Barbadian woman born and raised in Meanjin. Trudie is a PhD candidate with the School of Law at the University of Queensland and a Poche Scholar.

Marcelle Burns is a Gomeroi-Kamilaroi First Nations woman and a Lecturer at the School of Law, University of New England.

Jonathan Crowe is a Professor of Law at Bond University.

Roshan de Silva-Wijeyeratne is a member of the Edinburgh Centre for Constitutional Law at the University of Edinburgh, and an Advisory Board Member for the Centre on Human Rights in Conflict, University of East London. He graduated from the School of Oriental and African Studies (University of London) and has published extensively on the colonial/postcolonial legal history of South and Southeast Asia. Roshan is currently working on a co-edited collection on the transformative relationship between state, religion and culture in South, Southeast Asia and Australasia.

Heather Douglas is a Professor at the Melbourne Law School, The University of Melbourne.

Kirsten Gray is a Yuwaalaraay/Muruwari woman and lawyer.

Dani Larkin is a Bunjalung/Kungarykany woman and Deputy Director of the Indigenous Law Centre, University of New South Wales.

Taryn Lee is a Yawuru woman and holds a Bachelor of Laws, a Graduate Diploma in Legal Practice, a Master's in Human Rights, and an Executive Master's in Business Administration.

Terri Libesman is an Associate Professor at the University of Technology Sydney, Faculty of Law.

Heron Loban is a Torres Strait Islander woman. She is a Senior Lecturer at the School of Humanities, Languages, and Social Sciences, Griffith University.

Virginia Marshall is a Wiradjuri Nyemba woman and Inaugural Indigenous Postdoctoral Fellow with the Australian National University's School of Regulation and Global Governance and the Fenner School of Environment and Society, and Principal Solicitor at Triple BL Legal. She is the author of the award-winning book, *Overturning Aqua Nullius: Securing Aboriginal Water Rights* (2017) published by Aboriginal Studies Press.

Hannah McGlade is a Noongar woman and Associate Professor at Curtin University in the School of Law. She is also a member of the UN Permanent Forum for Indigenous Issues, where she promotes Indigenous people's human rights.

Tanya Mitchell is a Senior Lecturer at the University of Sydney Law School.

Osca Monaghan is a non-binary, mixed-race, Guugu Yimithirr lawyer with the Aboriginal Legal Service. They are a criminal defence lawyer, but their research interests are rooted primarily in decolonial and Indigenous legal and political thought.

Jennifer Nielsen is an Associate Professor in Law and Justice, Faculty of Business, Law and Arts, Southern Cross University. She is a socio-legal scholar with expertise in critical race and whiteness theory, and race discrimination at work.

Suvendrini Perera is a John Curtin Distinguished Professor at the School of Media, Culture, and Creative Arts, Curtin University.

Amanda Porter is a proud descendant (through her mother's family) of the Brinja clan of the Yuin Nation in South Coast NSW. She is a Senior Lecturer at the Law School, Melbourne University.

Zoe Rathus is a Senior Lecturer at the Law School, Griffith University , with previous experience in the community legal centre and domestic violence sectors.

Simon Rice is Kim Santow Professor of Law and Social Justice, University of Sydney Law School.

Keryn Ruska is a Noonuccal woman and a solicitor at the Caxton Legal Centre, with previous experience in the government and academia.

Mary Spiers Williams descends from First Peoples of the Sydney sandstone basin north into Darkenjung Country, Anglo-Celtic first coloniser-settlers, and other immigrant-settlers. She is the Sub Dean of Indigenous Studies in the College of Arts and Social Sciences at the Australian National University.

Eddie Synot is a Wamba Wamba First Nations person. He is a Research Associate at the Indigenous Law Centre, University of New South Wales, and a PhD candidate at Griffith University.

Nicole Watson is a Munanjali and Birri Gubba woman from south-east Queensland. Nicole is an Associate Professor and Director of the Academic Unit, Nura Gili Centre for Indigenous Programs, University of New South Wales.

Alison Whittaker is a Gomeroi legal academic and writer. She is a Senior Researcher at the Jumbunna Institute for Indigenous Education and Research and author of the award-winning book *BLAKWORK* (2018) published by Magabala Books.

Deenorah Yellub is a Goemulaig, Mualaig woman, raised on Mabuiag Island, Zenadh Kes (Torres Strait). She is a Senior In-house Legal Counsel at the Queensland Law Society.

Simon Young is a Professor at the University of Southern Queensland's School of Law and Centre for Heritage and Culture, an Adjunct Professor at the University of Western Australia, and an External Fellow of the University of Queensland's Centre for Public, International, and Comparative Law.

FOREWORD BY MEGAN DAVIS

As a young Aboriginal law student studying at the University of Queensland, an Indigenous Legal Judgments collection would have done much to make me feel more welcome and less excluded from the 'law'. I studied in the immediate post-*Mabo* aftermath. I distinctly remember a distinguished professor at my law school at the University of Queensland saying 'five cents for native title is five cents too much'. A collection like this would have given much solace to a Queensland Aboriginal kid—a legatee of the reserve system—whose experience of the law was more of oppression than redemption. It would have validated the emotions and thoughts I had as a student as we studied 'the rule of law' or read legal theory and philosophy about 'social justice'.

When I see the welcoming arms of the Australian legal profession to Indigenous law students and law graduates today, I am relieved and happy that they will not have to experience the kind of intellectual loneliness Aboriginal lawyers like myself did. I am no fan of Reconciliation Action Plans or performative rituals of Acknowledgment of Country, particularly by property lawyers, but on the other hand it is not hostile to the place of Indigenous peoples and Indigenous culture as it once was.

The Indigenous judgments enterprise though is much more than a source of comfort and intellectual and cultural strength for Indigenous law students. It will be a resource for the entire legal profession, the first of its kind. The legal profession is increasingly open to the experiences and knowledge of First Nations peoples. Yet we are still, by and large, subjects of, reformers of, students of, the law. We have much representation and experience as parliamentary authors of the law but little as judgment writers and judicial decision-makers.

This collection does what the feminist law judgment-writing project has done for feminism and the law and that is to amplify the Indigenous Voice in the law. For those of us First Nations lawyers who grew up on country or in Aboriginal communities, the multitude of seminal judgments read as a student or lawyer were baffling in their poor or erroneous comprehension of Aboriginal law and culture. The erasure of our culture, our songs, our dance, our being. Many of us have rewritten those judgments in our heads. And in our minds at night, as we wind down and permit the reflections of the day to wash over us, puzzled by a judgment, we have rewritten findings and conclusions in our heads with the lens of our women, our cultural authority, our incarcerated men and women, our ancestors, our voiceless, our disenfranchised, our dispossessed. This collection does this in fact.

And through this exercise, and through these chapters, we empower our people. It is an expression of self-determination. In these pages you will find some of the very best First Nations legal minds and emerging jurists are published. Co-editor Associate Professor Nicole Watson is a Munanjali and Birri Gubba lawyer who has devoted much of her practice to combating racism and injustice. Nicole, also a UQ law alumni, is the daughter of one of Queensland's most revered Aboriginal leaders, Sam Watson, who taught so many of us young law students something law school forgot, and that is the way civic action can change the world. Similarly another chapter and judgment is co-authored by Dr Dani Larkin, a Bundjalung public lawyer and the great-granddaughter of Jack Patten. Like her great-grandfather she is forging a career seized with fighting for the civil and political rights of our people. There are also Aboriginal lawyers who are not academics but who practice, such as the esteemed Noonuccal lawyer, Keryn Ruska, who is one of the leading family law and social justice practitioners in Australia today. The variety of voices in this collection, including non-Indigenous brothers and sisters, give great nuance and depth to the collection but also gravity to the endeavour of Indigenous judgments and decision-making.

Divided thematically into five parts—sovereignty, land and sea Country, racism and discrimination, family and identity, criminalisation and criminal neglect—the collection traverses a diverse range of judgments. From major constitutional decisions such as *Kartinyeri v Commonwealth* to the influential historical judgment *Cooper v Stuart*, the multitude of authors deliver a fascinating array of approaches to rewriting a judgment. From resistance and non-judgment writing and critical race theory to delivering a judgment as the Makarrata Commission, a public institution contemplated by the Uluru Statement from the Heart (as Wamba Wamba lawyer Eddie Synot's incredible judgment does), to judgments that contemplate a future treaty and a Republic, each judgment reimagines the world of the past or imagines our future. Each judgment takes the reader on a challenging journey of writing and rewriting the world around us.

I was on the Referendum Council, whose work led to the Uluru Statement from the Heart being issued at Uluru in May 2017. As a constitutional lawyer, I designed the regional deliberative dialogues that informed the national constitutional convention. In each dialogue we taught delegates civics and legal education, primarily public law, to enable discussion and debate on complex constitutional proposals. However, the most influential driver of participation was the primary message of the dialogues: law reform is about imagination.

We conveyed to each dialogue that law reform requires you to suspend your disbelief that the world cannot change. Law reform requires you to imagine that the world *can* change. It requires a leap of faith that the institutions built to deliver the change can deliver, even those institutions that have let down our people and abandoned our people. The consensus outcome at the national constitutional convention, despite all the tensions and disagreements on recognition and reform, is a tribute to the power of imagination.

Despite all the anger at the Commonwealth government and the unfairness of the Commonwealth Indigenous Advancement Strategy and the flawed 'Recognise' campaign propagating symbolic recognition over substantive, our people were able to put their frustration to one side and imagine that *their* world can be a better place. And they asked for a Voice. This is an extraordinary statement. And this collection too is extraordinary because it gives Voice; it gives voice to Indigenous ways of rethinking the law and rethinking the world. I am so immensely proud to endorse this collection to you and the Australian legal profession, under the sage leadership of Nicole Watson and Heather Douglas.

Professor Megan Davis BA LLB GDLP LLM PHD
Balnaves Chair in Constitutional Law.
Pro Vice Chancellor Indigenous and Professor of Law, UNSW Law.
Honorary Professor of Law, Melbourne Law School, The University of Melbourne.
Acting Commissioner, New South Wales Land and Environment Court.
Vice Chair and expert member, United Nations Expert Mechanism on the Rights of Indigenous Peoples, UN Human Rights Council, UN Geneva.
Commissioner, Australian Rugby League Commission.

ACKNOWLEDGMENTS

This project would not have been possible without the support of the Australian Research Council ('ARC').[1] We express our gratitude for the ARC's Discovery Indigenous scheme and acknowledge its important role in supporting Aboriginal and Torres Strait Islander research. We would also like to thank all of the authors who produced thought-provoking and inspiring pieces for this collection. Their efforts are all the more impressive when one considers that this collection was produced during a global pandemic that coincided with immense change in the higher education sector.

Although academics spend a great deal of their professional lives engrossed in writing, few of us had any experience of judgment writing prior to this project. In order to prepare ourselves for this daunting task, we convened two rounds of workshops in February 2019 and February 2020. We are grateful to Sarah Bradley AO and the Honourable Justice Rachel Pepper for sharing their insights into judgment writing at the first round of workshops. We would also like to thank the Honourable Sally Brown AM for her inspiring contribution to the second round of workshops.

The workshops would not have run so smoothly without the assistance of our colleagues who are responsible for organising the events that are crucial to our work as academics. We would like to thank Jane Gay at the University of Queensland Law School and Carla Viola and Simran Singh at the University of Sydney Law School for their logistical support. We would also like to thank Julia Robertson, Research Manager, University of Sydney Law School, for her ongoing support of this project.

We would like to thank our colleagues who reviewed the commentaries and judgments, namely, Renata Alexander, Rick Bigwood, Peter Billings, Beverley Brown, Sally Brown AM, Deborah Curran, John Eldridge, Lee Godden, Tim Goodwin, Kirsty Gover, Susan Harris-Rimmer, Jonathan Hunyor, Coel Kirkby,

Dylan Lino, Melissa Lucashenko, Graeme Orr, Justice Anthe Philippides, Alexander Reilly, Daryle Rigney, Jacinta Ruru, Vicki Sentas, Peta Stephenson, Anita Stuhmcke, Maureen Tehan, Prue Vines, Tamara Walsh, and Simon Young.

Completing this manuscript was an onerous task, which would have been so much more arduous without the commitment of our incredible research assistant Sarah Kendall. We would also like to acknowledge Kathy Frankland of Community and Personal Histories, Queensland Department of Aboriginal and Torres Strait Islander Partnerships, for her assistance in piecing together the life of Eliza Woree in Chapter 11. We also thank our editor, Colin Perrin, at Routledge for his faith in the project.

Finally, we would like to thank our loved ones who supported us throughout this project. Nicole would like to thank her husband, Russell, for his love and encouragement. She would also like to thank her late father, Sam Watson, who was an early and enthusiastic supporter of this project. Heather would like to thank her partner Paul for his love and support.

Note

1 The editors are the recipients of a Discovery (Indigenous) grant and Dr Watson holds a Discovery Australian Aboriginal and Torres Strait Islander Award ('Bringing Indigenous Voices into Judicial Decision Making' IN18000021).

1

INTRODUCTION

Nicole Watson and Heather Douglas[1]

Indigenous people have often been objects of rather than voices heard in judicial narratives and decisions. In this new and original collection, 16 key Australian judgments[2] have been rewritten in order to be inclusive of Indigenous peoples' histories, experiential knowledge, and world views. Each judgment is preceded by a short commentary that places the case in its social, policy, and legal context, explains the judgment being rewritten, and explains what the rewritten judgment does differently. Judgment writers were given the option of working within legal doctrine or inventing a new method operating outside of legal doctrine to give voice to Indigenous people. This approach recognised the reality that many Indigenous people live under both the laws of the Australian state and the distinct laws and lore of their own communities. It also allowed for the exploration of the possibilities, limits, and implications of introducing an Indigenous voice to judging and the potential for a new and distinct perspective to reimagine justice through an Indigenous lens.

The collection includes decisions spanning over 150 years, from 1889 to 2017. The new judgments are characterised by intersectional perspectives which draw on postcolonial, critical race and whiteness theories. In this introduction, we outline the project inspiration and then discuss the approach of the writers and their experience of the rewriting process. We have arranged the cases in this collection into five overlapping and interrelated themes. These themes and the judgments that have been rewritten for this collection will be briefly discussed in this chapter, placing them within the story of Aboriginal and Torres Strait Islander peoples' engagement with Australian law.

Project inspiration

The project draws its inspiration from the emergence of feminist judgment-writing projects around the world, beginning in Canada[3] and subsequently taken up in the United Kingdom,[4] Australia,[5] New Zealand,[6] and the USA.[7] Other projects have applied a similar method of reimagining judgments, for example, in relation to children's rights,[8] the environment,[9] and international law.[10]

In particular, this collection has drawn inspiration from a handful of judgments in previous projects that have been rewritten in an Indigenous voice. For example, the Women's Court of Canada[11] reconsidered the Federal Government's decision to exclude Indigenous women from negotiations on the right to self-government in *Native Women's Association of Canada v Canada*.[12] In the Australian Feminist Judgments project, three Indigenous women took different approaches in rewriting judgments. The Tanganekald Meintangk Boandik scholar, Irene Watson, was asked to rewrite the decision, *Kartinyeri v Commonwealth*.[13] Professor Watson responded with an essay explaining why it was necessary for her to speak from a position of Indigenous sovereignty, and thus impossible to take on the persona of a judge in the Australian legal system whose very existence denied that sovereignty.[14]

The Torres Strait Islander scholar Heron Loban, who has family connections to Mabuiag and Boigu, rewrote the decision, *Australian Consumer and Competition Commission (ACCC) v Keshow*.[15] In that case, the respondent, Keshow, entered into unscrupulous financial transactions with Indigenous women in remote communities. Loban's objective in rewriting the judgment of *ACCC v Keshow* was to ensure that the Indigenous women complainants had a voice.[16] She achieved this goal by creating the fictitious role of the Indigenous judge, who, as a matter of practice, is included in the resolution of all matters in the Federal Court that concern Indigenous parties.

The Munanjali and Birri Gubba scholar, Nicole Watson, revisited the decision, *Tuckiar v R*.[17] Tuckiar, a Yolngu man, was convicted of the murder of a police officer in 1933. The High Court quashed Tuckiar's conviction because he had been denied a fair trial. Watson provided great scope for optimism about the possibility of writing judgments with an Indigenous voice in her futuristic reimagining of this case.[18] She envisioned a treaty had been concluded between Aboriginal and Torres Strait Islander nations and the Republic of Australia. Under the treaty, a First Nations Court of Australia was established to revisit past decisions and find justice.

Finally, the New Zealand Feminist Judgments project included six judgments that applied a '*mana wahine*' approach, that is, an approach that placed Maori women and their concerns at the centre.[19] Elements of a *mana wahine* framework include: making Maori ways of life visible in the text, identification of rights and obligations sourced in Maori law, consideration of the realities of Maori life in the application of legal tests, and paying respect to Maori values and principles.[20] This framework was applied to cases concerning the administration of social security legislation,[21] legislation banning prisoners from voting in general elections,[22] Maori fishing rights,[23] Maori land law,[24] criminal law,[25] and sentencing.[26] The range of approaches to rewriting and reimagining these cases underscores the diversity of Indigenous voices.

Writers' approaches and experiences

Each judgment in this collection is accompanied by a commentary that explains the facts of the case being rewritten, the issues involved, the original decision(s) made in the case, and what the rewritten judgment does differently. Indigenous academics and practitioners are the primary writers of each decision and they are often teamed with a non-Indigenous writing partner. Most of the contributions, both judgments and commentaries, are co-authored. For many of the cases, the co-authors are both Indigenous and non-Indigenous. These partnerships show how Indigenous and non-Indigenous people can work together in a respectful way to promote the rights of Aboriginal and Torres Strait Islander people through legal judgment.

Two rounds of workshops were held in Sydney and Brisbane with the contributors and others who were supportive of the project. At the first workshops, participants had the opportunity to hear from current and retired judges about the audience for judgments, how to construct a judgment, the use of contextual and extrinsic materials, and the use of judicial notice. There was also an opportunity for judgment and commentary writers to introduce the case they planned to rewrite and talk to the group about the importance of the case selected. The second round of workshops provided an opportunity for judgment and commentary writers to present their drafts, receive feedback from other participants, and discuss and debrief about the rewriting experience.

For many participants, the experience of revisiting the facts of the judgment and 'unpacking' them was one of the most challenging aspects of the writing process, but also one of the most valuable. Some participants identified that reconstructing facts through Indigenous eyes provided an opportunity to learn about not just what was said, but also what was missing in the original judgments and, therefore, whose stories were privileged. The rewriting process often exposed assumptions about the concept of 'relevance', the notion of 'expertise', and the choices made about which evidence is highlighted in judgments. For several participants, the rewriting process underscored the political aspects of cases and affirmed that legal interpretation is a political exercise undertaken, overwhelmingly, by privileged white men who bring their biases to the task. It is notable that in Australia, the judiciary is still mainly composed of white men.[27] In contrast, there are fewer than ten Aboriginal or Torres Strait Islander judges and magistrates presiding in Australian courts.[28] In response to these gaps and interpretive choices, some used the rewriting process as an opportunity to resurrect the missing stories of Aboriginal people and Torres Strait Islanders or tell them in a new way. In this sense, rewriting judgments can be understood as a way of making meaning or 'storying'.[29] Such efforts also suggest that the privileged white men who are at the helm of the judiciary can do more to incorporate the voices of Indigenous parties and witnesses in their judgments.

Several participants found that the writing process revealed the limitations of the common law. Some participants made comments reminiscent of Audre Lorde's declaration that 'the master's tools will never dismantle the master's house'.[30] Some participants also expressed concerns about how Aboriginal and Torres Strait Islander people could engage in the space of colonial law and write in a way that did not give colonial law absolute power.[31] One writer asked whether, in demonstrating the possibility of rewriting a judgment within the boundaries set by the common law, the author was shoring up the law's jurisdictional power and limiting critique. As the Gomeroi scholar, Alison Whittaker, observes in her note explaining why she wrote a poem for this collection, 'It's easy to reveal the structural racism of settler law—it's very hard to imagine a way out of it that doesn't replicate that structure'.[32] In her early work, Carol Smart made a similar point, noting that 'it is a dilemma that all radical movements face, namely the problem of challenging a form of power without accepting its own terms of reference and hence losing the battle before it has begun'.[33] It may be that the limitations of the judicial role also placed a significant constraint on the participants. In assuming the office of the judge, perhaps some felt constrained to adhere to certain formal and stylistic conventions limiting their ability to dismantle the 'master's house'. It is possible that if the task were different—for example to write new legislation or to prepare a constitution—participants would have felt they had more flexibility to enact change.[34]

For many of the writers, trauma was close to their lives and writing the judgments was an emotional exercise. The task of rewriting was reminiscent of the ordeal of law school[35] for several writers. Some recalled that at law school they were taught that judges were invested with greater authority than the Aboriginal and Torres Strait Islander parties and communities involved in the cases they read, something that had never made sense to them. Some writers chose to rewrite cases to which they had a close personal or familial connection and felt a solemn obligation to honour those who were denied justice. Even in the absence of such connections, authors felt a sense of cultural responsibility to the people who were involved in the case.

Many of the writers analysed the lived experience of Indigenous peoples, which encompassed the lingering and multi-faceted impacts of child removal policies and systemic racism in the legal system. They also made visible Indigenous perspectives of history and acknowledged monumental acts of resistance, such as the Aboriginal Tent Embassy. In this respect, they subscribed to practices shared by Indigenous scholars throughout the academy, irrespective of disciplinary background.

Notably, many of the judgment writers reflected on their standpoint in rewriting their judgments. Professor Aileen Morton-Robinson and Professor Martin Nakata have identified that it is common among Indigenous scholars to recognise and speak to their standpoint.[36] Indigenous standpoint theory postulates that knowledge is moulded by power relations. The knowledge systems of powerful groups are omnipresent. While subordinated groups in society are familiar with such systems, they also draw upon their own perspectives.[37] Indigenous standpoint theory provides a foundation for scholars to analyse everyday Indigenous experiences that would otherwise be invisible to dominant knowledge systems. Dr Louise Phillips and Ngugi Wakka Wakka scholar, Professor Tracey Bunda, suggest that speaking to one's standpoint is both a way of naming oneself in Aboriginal epistemological practice and also indirectly acknowledges feminist theory 'as a source of standpoint methodology'.[38]

There is one final point to be considered in relation to the contributors' approaches, which concerns the use of language. In Australia, there is a diversity of opinion concerning the appropriateness of terms such as 'Indigenous', 'Aboriginal and Torres Strait Islander', and more recently, 'First Nations'. There are also different approaches to the use of 'people'. While some continue to use 'people' in the singular, others have adopted 'peoples' in order to reflect the diversity of Aboriginal and Torres Strait Islander nations. Some reject all such terms as colonial constructs,[39] and instead define their identity by reference to their Country. Prior to the arrival of the British, the continent now known as Australia was divided into a tapestry of over 500 nations. Today, it is still a common practice among Indigenous people to introduce oneself by reference to the Country to which one belongs. It is not the place of this collection to take a position on such complex and nuanced debates. We merely acknowledge that the diversity of opinion concerning terminology finds resonance in the different conventions adopted by the contributors.

The judgments in Australian law

Australia inherited an English common law tradition and this is reflected in many of its legal principles. However, distinctive features shape contemporary legal decision making and some of these features are strongly linked to Aboriginal and Torres Strait Islander peoples' engagement with this system. It is impossible in a brief introduction such as this to explore all of the key turning points in the history of Aboriginal and Torres Strait Islander peoples' interactions with the Australian legal system. We have arranged the cases in this collection into five overlapping and interrelated themes. We use these themes in this introduction to signpost some of the important moments in the complex story of Aboriginal and Torres Strait Islander peoples' engagement with Australian law and we place the judgments in this collection in that story.

Part I: Sovereignty

Indigenous people in Australia have never ceded their sovereignty,[40] yet calls for the Australian legal system to recognise Indigenous sovereignty have consistently been ignored or rejected. In May 2017, an important convention took place at Uluru in the centre of Australia. Through the convention, 250 Indigenous leaders worked together to prepare the Uluru Statement.[41] The Uluru Statement sets out that:

> Our Aboriginal and Torres Strait Islander tribes were the first sovereign Nations of the Australian continent and its adjacent islands, and possessed it under our own laws and customs...[sovereignty] has never been ceded or extinguished, and co-exists with the sovereignty of the Crown.

The Uluru Statement calls for:

> the establishment of a First Nations Voice enshrined in the Constitution. Makarrata is the culmination of our agenda: *the coming together after a struggle*. It captures our aspirations for a fair and truthful relationship with the people of Australia and a better future for our children based on justice and self-determination.
>
> We seek a Makarrata Commission[42] to supervise a process of agreement-making between governments and First Nations and truth-telling about our history.[43]

The presentation of the Uluru Statement has escalated the call for a referendum to bring change to the *Australian Constitution* to enable the creation of an Aboriginal and Torres Strait Islander Voice to the Parliament. The Cobble Cobble scholar, Professor Megan Davis, has said there continues to be 'a great chasm between what the Australian state wants for Indigenous people and what Indigenous people seek'.[44] To date movements towards a referendum have been fraught with obstacles.

There have been many previous efforts by Aboriginal people and Torres Strait Islanders to gain recognition of their sovereignty and calls for constitutional recognition of Indigenous peoples are not new. In 2010, the Australian Government established an Expert Panel on Constitutional Recognition of Indigenous Australians.[45] The panel undertook wide-ranging consultation to build consensus on the recognition of Indigenous people in the Constitution. While the Expert Panel didn't endorse it, many Aboriginal and Torres Strait Islander people who spoke to the Expert Panel called for the constitutional recognition of Aboriginal sovereignty.[46] The Expert Panel reported in 2012 and made a number of recommendations for constitutional reform,[47] none of which were ultimately implemented.

Using the constitutional reform process has been just one approach to seeking recognition of sovereignty. Over 100 years ago, the question of Indigenous people's rights to their land was considered by the Privy Council in *Cooper v Stuart*.[48] In this case, the Privy Council drew on English legal principles, articulated by Blackstone in 1765,[49] to determine that Australia was a 'settled' colony and thus there could be no recognition of a title to land that pre-dated the arrival of the British. According to the Privy Council, New South Wales was regarded as 'a tract of territory, practically unoccupied, without settled inhabitants or settled land, at the time when it was peacefully annexed to the British dominions'.[50] The legal fiction of terra nullius (in Latin, 'nobody's land') encapsulated in *Cooper v Stuart* became a legal foundation in Australia that was difficult for the Australian common law to reject. The Wamba Wamba scholar, Eddie Synot, and Roshan de Silva-Wijeyeratne reconsider *Cooper v Stuart* in Chapter 3. They imagine that there has been a successful referendum to implement a First Nations Voice. In this context, the Makarrata Commission has been established and an aspect of the Commission's work is a program called the 'Research Partnership', which is a process of truth-telling. They also identify the legislative and structural reforms necessary to review *Cooper v Stuart*.

Another historical flashpoint on the sovereignty question was when, in 1963, the Yolngu people of North-East Arnhem Land presented bark petitions to the Australian Parliament, protesting the excision of land from the reserve where they lived and the granting of a mining lease to Nabalco over their Country.[51] The Yolngu people claimed that they had a proprietary interest in the communal lands and that the lands were held by local clans on the Gove Peninsula, notwithstanding Nabalco's 42-year bauxite mining lease over the area. In *Millirpum v Nabalco Pty Ltd*,[52] the Yolngu people sought a declaration that they were entitled to the land based on a common law claim of Aboriginal title. In deciding the case against the Yolngu people, Blackburn J found that the Yolngu people had 'a subtle and elaborate system highly adapted to the country in which the people led their lives, which provided a stable order of society and was remarkably free from the vagaries of personal whim or influence'.[53] However, the Yolngu people's relationships with their Country did not give rise to any proprietary interest. We begin this collection in Chapter 2 with Osca Monaghan's rethinking of *Millirpum v Nabalco Pty Ltd*. Monaghan, a Guugu Yimithirr lawyer, sets a tone that is echoed by many writers in this collection. Ultimately, Monaghan finds that writing within the law is to acquiesce to the settler legal order and thus writing an Indigenous judgment within Australian law is an impossibility.

Although many Indigenous people question the legitimacy of Australian law, they have often used that law in their efforts towards recognition of their sovereignty. In 1988, Denis Walker tested recognition through the criminal legal process. Walker was charged with offences under the *Crimes Act 1900* (NSW) and refused to enter a plea. He argued that the Commonwealth and State Parliaments lacked the power to enact legislation affecting Indigenous people without their request and consent. Walker's argument was that both before and after 1770, when Captain Cook recorded his sighting of Point Lookout and other features of the east coast landscape,[54] his people, the Noonuccal, inhabited North Stradbroke Island and possessed a system of government and laws. Before his trial, Walker applied for special leave to appeal to the High Court where he, unsuccessfully, pursued the lack of jurisdiction claim. Drawing inspiration from Lon Fuller's

1949 article, 'The Case of the Speluncean Explorers',[55] the Yuin scholar, Amanda Porter, and Tanya Mitchell (in Chapter 4) create three judges who take different approaches in rewriting the High Court's decision. Their approach highlights the problems with writing an Indigenous judgment within the settler-colonial legal system and shows the diversity of voices of Indigenous judges. Like other contributions in this collection, the authors also provide a more detailed account of the complex life and achievements of the central person in the case, in this instance, Denis Walker.

Part II: Land and sea Country

For Indigenous people, sovereignty and rights to land and sea are intrinsically interrelated. While we recognise this, we have grouped three cases under the heading 'Land and sea Country' in order to explore further the deep connection between Indigenous people and their Country.[56] With each passing year, new evidence demonstrates a yet longer time that Aboriginal people have been living on the Australian continent. Archaeological evidence demonstrates the presence of Indigenous people for at least 65,000 years. Indigenous people in Australia had also established trade links with other countries[57] well before the Europeans arrived in Sydney Cove in 1788 to establish a penal colony.[58] The denial of Aboriginal people's connection to land has been a central feature of their oppression.[59] Throughout the 19th and 20th centuries, Aboriginal people were massacred in their thousands, herded like animals off their lands into reserves and missions, and forced to work in domestic placements and cattle stations often far from their homelands.[60]

Indigenous people have consistently demanded legal recognition of their enduring relationships with their lands. Such demands were overlooked by generations of Australia's political leaders, including the late Prime Minister, William McMahon. In his Australia Day statement in 1972, McMahon rejected calls by Indigenous leaders for the creation of land rights, out of fear that such reforms would jeopardise the security of existing land titles.[61] In response, four young Koori men, Michael Anderson, Tony Coorey, Billy Craigie, and Bertie Williams, established the Aboriginal Tent Embassy outside Australia's Parliament House,[62] with only a beach umbrella and placards. The Embassy originally symbolised the struggle for land rights, but it came to represent Aboriginal political rights more generally.[63] Fifty years later, land remains a central aspect of the push by Aboriginal people and Torres Strait Islanders towards greater recognition of their rights.

The 1992 decision of the High Court in *Mabo v Queensland (No 2)* ('*Mabo (No 2)*')[64] was another watershed moment in Australian history.[65] In *Mabo (No 2)*, the plaintiffs, Eddie Koiki Mabo, Reverend David Passi, Sam Passi, James Rice, and Celuia Mapo Sale, sought declarations that the Meriam people were entitled to the Murray Islands in the Torres Strait 'as owners; as possessors; as occupiers; or as persons entitled to use and enjoy the Islands'.[66] Ultimately, the majority of the High Court recognised a form of title to land that it called 'native title'. Native title was defined by reference to the traditional 'laws and customs' of Aboriginal and Torres Strait Islander peoples. Native title survived as a burden on the Crown's radical title and was subject to extinguishment by the sovereign.[67] The majority of the Court was satisfied that the plaintiffs had maintained their connection to their land and that their native title had not been extinguished by legislation or any other executive actions inconsistent with their title.[68]

After *Mabo (No 2)*, many speculated on the broader implications of the High Court's recognition of the Murray Islanders' native title to their lands,[69] and generally the jurisdiction of Australian law. Native title law has become a discrete area of study, research, and legal practice. The *Mabo (No 2)* case was followed by discrete legislation,[70] the development of a specialist native title tribunal,[71] and a flourishing case law.[72] However, many have been disappointed by the restrictive approach taken to the *Mabo (No 2)* decision in subsequent judgments.[73]

One of the issues confronting Indigenous groups seeking recognition of their native title has been proving the continuity of their connection to land in the face of non-Indigenous settlement—including urbanisation and farming. When members of the Yorta Yorta Aboriginal Community applied to the Federal Court for recognition of their native title to land and waters along and around the Murray and Goulburn Rivers, Olney J found that '[t]he tide of history ha[d] indeed washed away any real acknowledgment of their traditional laws and any real observance of their traditional customs'.[74] The High Court subsequently dismissed the appeal of the Yorta Yorta community against the judgment of the Federal Court.[75] In her rewriting of the case (in Chapter 6), Gomeroi-Kamilaroi scholar, Marcelle Burns, finds in favour of the Yorta Yorta people and focuses on the Yorta Yorta peoples' perspective and survival of their 'custodial ethic'. As Simon Young notes in the commentary, the reimagined judgment reconceptualises the challenge for the court as being reframed to recognise 'adaptation and resilience' rather than 'measuring cultural erosion'.[76]

The extent of extinguishment of native title rights was central to the decision in *Akiba on behalf of the Torres Strait Regional Seas Claim Group v Commonwealth* ('*Akiba*').[77] In this case, the High Court considered whether fisheries legislation extinguished commercial fishing rights or merely regulated the exercise of these rights. The High Court held that the right to commercially fish was supported by the native title right to take for any purpose, and the right had not been extinguished by fisheries legislation.[78] The judgment was described as 'signalling new respect' for First Peoples' custodianship of land and waters.[79] However, as part of the original *Akiba* case, the applicants also claimed that reciprocal rights between people in different societies within the Torres Strait should be recognised. In Chapter 7, the Wiradjuri Nyemba scholar, Virginia Marshall, rewrites the decision in order to include reciprocal rights among those recognised as falling within the applicant's native title. In her accompanying commentary, the Gomeroi scholar, Alison Whittaker, describes Marshall's approach as a 'challenge' to settler law's tendency to compartmentalise Country across 'multiple axes'. In Marshall's reimagined judgment, reciprocal rights are acknowledged as integral to Torres Strait Islander peoples' laws, customs, and traditions, and as such, cannot be severed from those that were recognised in the original decision.

The *Native Title Act 1993* (Cth) belongs to a body of Commonwealth legislation that Indigenous peoples have utilised in order to protect their relationships with Country and preserve the integrity of an ancient heritage that is inextricably tied to the land. Within this suite of legislation is the *Aboriginal and Torres Strait Islander Heritage Protection Act 1984* (Cth). In common with the former, the latter has revealed fundamental conflicts between the Australian and Indigenous legal systems. This clash was brought into stark relief in *Tickner v Chapman* (1995) 57 FCR 451 (the '*Kumarangk Case*').

The *Kumarangk Case* concerned judicial review of a ministerial declaration made pursuant to the *Aboriginal and Torres Strait Islander Heritage Protection Act 1984* (Cth) which prohibited the construction of a bridge to Kumarangk, also known as Hindmarsh Island. Kumarangk falls within the lands and waters of the Ngarrindjeri Nation and is of profound cultural significance. The Federal Court determined that the Minister's decision was invalid on a number of grounds, including his failure to personally consider confidential information provided by Ngarrindjeri women concerning their cultural and religious beliefs which, under Ngarrindjeri law, could not be disclosed to men. The decision was upheld on appeal to the Full Court. In Chapter 5, Narelle Bedford, whose mother hails from the Yuin people of South Coast NSW, and Peter Billings have approached the decision with a view to bringing Ngarrindjeri perspectives to the centre. They have also incorporated greater reference to pertinent socio-legal resources that existed at the time of the Full Court's decision, such as the draft *United Nations Declaration on the Rights of Indigenous Peoples*.

Part III: Racism and discrimination

National and international pressure was building throughout the late 1950s and early 1960s for change to the way that Aboriginal and Torres Strait Islander peoples' affairs were governed. The Federal Council for Aboriginal Advancement ('FCAA') was founded in 1958 with the aim of achieving equal citizenship rights for Aboriginal people.[80] While Australia was prospering through the 1950s, various reports detailed the high levels of malnutrition and disease common among Aboriginal people.[81] In 1965, a group of students, including Charlie Perkins, undertook the 'Freedom Ride' along the NSW coast to draw attention to the terrible conditions faced by many Aboriginal people.[82] These pressures resulted in Australia's Prime Minister, Harold Holt, signing the *International Convention on the Elimination of All Forms of Racial Discrimination* in 1966, but more was needed.[83]

The original drafting of the *Australian Constitution* excluded Aboriginal and Torres Strait Islander people from its purview. Section 51(xxvi) of the Constitution, the 'race power', gave the Commonwealth Parliament power to make laws with respect to 'the people of any race, other than the aboriginal race in any State, for whom it [was] deemed necessary to make special laws'. Section 127 of the Constitution read, '[i]n reckoning the numbers of people of the Commonwealth, or of a State or part of the Commonwealth, aboriginal natives shall not be counted'. The effect of the exclusion in s 51(xxvi) was that Aboriginal people's affairs was primarily a state responsibility.[84] This had led to a patchwork of inconsistent, discriminatory, and oppressive approaches, such as the 'protection' legislation that created a form of wardship applicable only to Indigenous people, and later, the assimilation policy that sought to absorb Indigenous people into the mainstream population. For many Aboriginal people, campaigning for a referendum to amend the Constitution so that the Commonwealth could assume responsibility for Aboriginal affairs became central to their lives.[85] Between 1962 and 1964, more than 50 petitions were sent to the federal government seeking changes to the Constitution that pressed for the deletion of 'other than the aboriginal race in any State' from s 51(xxvi) and the repeal of s 127.[86] In 1967, the referendum took place, with no opposition to the 'yes' case from either side of politics. Ninety per cent of Australian people voted 'yes' to the proposed changes to the Constitution.[87] The 1967 referendum was important as it excised the racist references from the Constitution, but this did not equate to constitutional recognition of Indigenous peoples, or deal with racial discrimination experienced by individuals in their daily lives.[88]

It would have been inconceivable to the activists who gave so much to the 'yes' campaign that the Commonwealth would use its new power to enact laws that were detrimental to Indigenous people. This raises the question—in interpreting the 'race power' should the views of those who fought for constitutional change in 1967 be taken into account? In their revision of *Kartinyeri v Commonwealth* [1998] HCA 22 (Chapter 8), the Eualeyai/Kamillaroi scholar, Professor Larissa Behrendt, and Yawuru lawyer, Taryn Lee, answer that question in the affirmative. They also argue that in interpreting the 'race power', consideration should be given to international human rights norms. Finally, the authors assume the existence of fiduciary obligations owed by the Commonwealth to Indigenous peoples, borne out of their unique historical relationship.

Other political efforts have attempted to address issues of racial discrimination in Australia. In 1973, the Whitlam government removed race as a criterion in Australia's immigration policy and two years later introduced the *Racial Discrimination Act 1975* (Cth) ('RDA'). Noel Pearson has described the RDA as 'akin to the Civil Rights Act 1964 in the US'.[89] While the RDA has had important practical outcomes for some Aboriginal and Torres Strait Islander people, it has also resulted in unintended applications and often been used as a political football. In particular, s 18C of the RDA, which makes it unlawful to do an act that is likely to 'offend, insult, humiliate or intimidate' another or a group of people on the basis of their race, has long been targeted by conservative commentators as a dangerous constraint on the exercise of freedom of speech. Such sentiments were amplified in the aftermath of *Eatock v Bolt* [2011] FCA 1103 ('*Eatock v Bolt*'). In that case, prominent Indigenous people were targeted in a series of articles written by the conservative commentator, Andrew Bolt. In the articles, Bolt criticised the individuals, some of whom were of fair complexion, for identifying with their Indigenous heritage and questioned the propriety of their motivations for doing so. The Federal Court found that Bolt and his publisher had contravened s 18C.[90] However, the penalties imposed were slight. No orders were made for the payment of damages or even the proffering of an apology.

In her reconsideration of *Eatock v Bolt* in Chapter 10, the Gomeroi scholar, Alison Whittaker, grappled with the burden of 'unwanted complicity' in a legal system that, for the most part, reinforces the structure that is colonisation. Her response was a poem consisting of three-word phrases that most frequently appeared in the judgment of Bromberg J. In his accompanying commentary, Simon Rice describes the poem as a critique of not only judicial decision making in racial vilification cases, but also racial vilification laws. This chapter aims to show that over time, the noble aspirations of such laws have lost meaning so that they have become mere words on a page.

State-based legislative efforts have also been introduced to address racial discrimination. However, these are seldom used by Aboriginal and Torres Strait Islander people and when they are, they are rarely successful.[91] The inability of such legislation to respond to anything other than overt forms of racial discrimination was highlighted in the decision, *Commissioner of Corrective Services v Aldridge (No 2)*.[92] Mr Aldridge was a senior Aboriginal member of the New South Wales Department of Corrective Services and was responsible for overseeing the Department's implementation of the recommendations of the Royal Commission into Aboriginal Deaths in Custody. Mr Aldridge made a complaint of racial discrimination in the workplace under the *Anti-Discrimination Act 1977* (NSW). Mr Aldridge had been verbally abused by the Assistant Commissioner, and later, he was removed from his position. Mr Aldridge's complaint was upheld by the Administrative Decisions Tribunal, whose decision was overturned by the Administrative Decisions Tribunal Appeal Panel ('Appeal Panel'). In Chapter 9, the Kamilaroi and Wonnarua scholar, Debbie Bargallie, and Jennifer Nielsen have reimagined the Appeal Panel's decision by centring Mr Aldridge's voice and reinterpreting the facts in light of his lived experience of racism. In the new judgment, the evidence is also contextualised by the institutional culture of the Department, a place where racism was normalised. Bargallie and Nielsen conclude that the totality of the evidence supported the inference that Mr Aldridge had been treated less favourably than his white colleagues because of his race.

Part IV: Family and identity

Throughout the 19th century and the first half of the 20th century, Aboriginal people were subject to harsh protectionist legislation and later, assimilationist regimes. A patchwork of laws across the country governed where Aboriginal people could live and work and who they could marry.[93] Some Aboriginal people, who were able to prove that they had assimilated, were exempt from the legislation. Tragically, those who secured their freedom on this basis were thereafter precluded from maintaining ties with their families.[94] Various governments employed white protectors, and patrol officers were tasked with ensuring the safety of their Aboriginal wards.[95] However, the story on the ground was that Aboriginal people were subjected to arbitrary rules and their children were routinely removed from their care and placed in often brutal and neglectful institutions far from Country.[96] As many as one in three children were removed from their families during this period.[97]

Munanjali and Birri Gubba scholar, Nicole Watson, and Trudie Broderick explore this part of Australia's history in Chapter 11, reconsidering *Dempsey v Rigg*.[98] Isaac Rigg was charged with the offence of unlawfully employing an Aboriginal person under the provisions of the *Aboriginals Protection and Restriction of the Sale of Opium Act 1897* (Qld). Rigg had employed an Aboriginal woman, Eliza Woree, to perform domestic chores in his home. As he had not obtained a permit to do so, Rigg was liable under the Act. While Eliza Woree is actually the person at the centre of *Dempsey v Rigg*, we learn little about her from the original case. Nicole Watson creates a First Nations Court of Australia in order to imagine Eliza Woree's story.

The last of the protectionist legislation was not dismantled in Australia until the 1960s.[99] In 1995, the Commonwealth Attorney-General, Michael Lavarch, requested the Human Rights and Equal Opportunity Commission to inquire into the removal of Aboriginal and Torres Strait Islander children from their families. The commissioners conducted their Inquiry over two years and spoke to hundreds of Indigenous people affected by the forced removals. The Inquiry's report, *Bringing Them Home*,[100] sets out in its introduction:

> Grief and loss are the predominant themes of this report. Tenacity and survival is also acknowledged...For individuals, their removal as children and the abuse they experienced at the hands of the authorities or their delegates have permanently scarred their lives. The harm continues in later generations, affecting their children and grandchildren.[101]

Those removed from their families under these regimes are now known as the 'Stolen Generations'. *Bringing Them Home* recommended that reparation, including monetary compensation, be made to all who suffered because of the forcible removal policies, in recognition of the 'gross violations of human rights'.[102] It also recommended that a national compensation fund be established; a recommendation that is yet to be implemented.

In the absence of a national compensation regime, some members of the Stolen Generations have been compelled to seek relief through litigation, a lengthy and perilous journey that is often fruitless. It was not until the decision, *South Australia v Lampard-Trevorrow* [2010] SASC 56, that a member of the Stolen Generations succeeded in securing damages for harms suffered as a result of child removal. Bruce Trevorrow was only 13 months old when he was taken, in the absence of legal justification, from the love and care of his family. He later sued the state of South Australia for negligence, false imprisonment, misfeasance in public office, breach of fiduciary duty, and breach of procedural fairness. Mr Trevorrow was successful at first instance. On appeal to the Full Court of the Supreme Court of South Australia, the trial judge's findings were upheld, bar false imprisonment and breach of fiduciary duty.

In her reimagined judgment, in Chapter 12, the Muruwari and Yuwaalaraay lawyer, Kirsten Gray, upholds the trial judge's finding of false imprisonment. Throughout her judgment, Gray reveals the pervasive influence of racism upon both the policy of child removal and the actions of those who deprived Mr Trevorrow of the affection of his family. In her accompanying commentary, Terri Libesman reminds us of the important role played by intentional torts such as false imprisonment in protecting citizens from the abuse of power by the executive.

The legacies of the Stolen Generations continue to impact Aboriginal and Torres Strait Islander families.[103] Indigenous children are eight times more likely than other children to have contact with child protection services and seven times more likely to be the subject of a substantiated complaint than other children.[104] Tragically, Aboriginal and Torres Strait Islander children are nearly ten times more likely to live in state-supervised out-of-home care than other children.[105] Legislation across Australia, including the federal family law legislation,[106] requires state child protection agencies to prioritise placements with kin and support efforts to ensure that Aboriginal and Torres Strait Islander children maintain their cultural connections.[107] White legal frameworks are, however, often ill-equipped to recognise and accommodate the cultural connections of Aboriginal and Torres Strait Islander families, particularly those who live in urban communities. This was highlighted in *Backford v Backford* [2017] FamCAFC 1 ('*Backford*').

Backford was a complex parenting case concerning an Aboriginal mother, an Aboriginal father, a non-Aboriginal father, and five children. Ultimately, the Family Court made orders for the children to be placed with their respective fathers and for them to have limited visiting time with their mother. In approaching the decision, the Noonuccal lawyer, Keryn Ruska, and Zoe Rathus have written, in Chapter 13, that the trial judge, lawyers, and family report writer all acknowledged the mother's Indigenous identity and heritage. Yet between them they 'failed to facilitate its meaningful presence' in either the evidence or the decision. In their imagined appellate judgment, Ruska and Rathus allow the mother's appeal and express the hope that at the re-hearing there will be an updated family report which will elucidate the mother's cultural connections and the rights of the children to enjoy that crucial part of their identity.

Part V: Criminalisation and criminal neglect

Australia has a shocking record of locking up Indigenous people. According to statistics, Indigenous Australians are the most imprisoned people in the world.[108]

In 2020, Aboriginal and Torres Strait Islander adults were around 12 times more likely than other adults to be imprisoned.[109] More concerning still, over half of the children in youth detention at any time in Australia are Aboriginal or Torres Strait Islander youth.[110] Aboriginal and Torres Strait Islander young people are 21 times more likely to be incarcerated than other children.[111] Pat Dodson has said, 'For the vast bulk of our people the legal system is not a trusted instrument of justice—it is a feared and despised processing plant that propels the most vulnerable and disabled of our people towards a broken, bleak future'.[112] He observed that 'accepting the status quo permits the criminal justice system to suck us up like a vacuum cleaner and deposit us like waste in custodial institutions'.[113]

Recent figures show that the proportion of Aboriginal and Torres Strait Islander women who are incarcerated compared to non-Indigenous women is particularly stark. Aboriginal women make up around three per cent of the Australian female population but 30 per cent of the women's prison population.[114] Furthermore, Aboriginal and Torres Strait Islander women in custody are likely to leave behind dependent children, to have experienced high rates of domestic violence, sexual assault, mental health disorders, and homelessness, and to be members of the Stolen Generations.[115] In their rewriting of *Roach v Electoral Commissioner* (2007) 233 CLR 162 in Chapter 14, Bunjalung woman, Dani Larkin, and Jonathan Crowe draw attention to these issues. They tell Vicki Roach's compelling story, engaging with it to argue that any exclusion of prisoners from the franchise is disproportionate and therefore constitutionally invalid.

There have been successive studies and recommendations for reforms to address the overrepresentation of Indigenous people in custody.[116] One of the tragic issues associated with incarceration is the risk of a premature and lonely death in a prison or watch-house cell. The most important inquiry to explore this issue was the Royal Commission into Aboriginal Deaths in Custody ('RCIADIC').[117] In 1987, a Royal Commission was appointed to investigate the deaths of 99 Aboriginal people who had died in custody from 1980 to 1989. In relation to the deceased, the RCIADIC found that 'facts associated in every case with their Aboriginality played a significant and in most cases dominant role in their being in custody and dying in custody'.[118] The Commission's *National Report*[119] stated that 'too many Aboriginal people are in custody too often'.[120] While the recommendations led to a plethora of procedural and policy reforms relating to arrest, remand, and incarceration practices across Australia, they have not stemmed the loss of life. A recent report found that 441 Aboriginal and Torres Strait Islander people have died in custody since 1991.[121] Around one-third of these deaths were by hanging.[122] Recent analysis suggests that the failure of police watch-houses, prisons, and hospitals to follow their own procedures, provide adequate medical care, and manage mental health issues appropriately contributed to the deaths.[123] But despite the warnings of the RCIADIC report 30 years ago, there are still too many Indigenous people in custody.

A Coronial Inquest is required whenever a person dies in custody. For the families of Aboriginal and Torres Strait Islander people who have died in custody, the coroner's investigation provides them with an opportunity to be heard and for the story of the death of their loved one to be told in a public forum.[124] While the task of the coroner is to investigate the circumstances of the death and determine why it happened, as Alison Whittaker observes, the language used by the coroner in making his or her findings is important,[125] especially regarding how responsibility for the death is described.

In her rewriting of the *Report of the Inquest into the Death of Miss Dhu* (Perth, 16 December 2016) in Chapter 17, Noongar woman, Hannah McGlade, speaks directly to Ms Dhu's people and highlights the racism inherent in the treatment of Ms Dhu by police officers, doctors, and nurses who failed to hear or take seriously Ms Dhu's cries of pain which preceded her death. Both McGlade's rewritten report and the commentary prepared by Suvendrini Perera highlight the lack of accountability of those who failed to take care of Ms Dhu.

Racist police views of Indigenous people and attendant discriminatory approaches to policing often result in a failure by individual officers to follow police procedures and execute their duties appropriately. These failures have contributed to many deaths of Aboriginal and Torres Strait Islander people in custody.[126] The lack of accountability for these failures is well-known.[127] Racist policing practices and the lack of police accountability for the harms caused extend beyond the custody context. Torres Strait Islander woman, Heron Loban, and Heather Douglas document the case of the sinking of the *Malu Sara* in the Torres Strait, where five Torres Strait Islander lives were lost. While the coroner found that the police officer in charge of the search and rescue operation failed to carry out his duties responsibly, he decided not to send information to the Director of Public Prosecutions for possible criminal investigation and refused to provide reasons for the decision. In Chapter 15, Loban and Douglas reimagine *Nona and Ahmat v Barnes* [2012] QCA 346 by back-dating and applying the *Human Rights Act 2019* (Qld), finding that the coroner should have provided reasons for his decision. To make the judgment accessible to Torres Strait Islander people, Torres Strait Islander lawyer, Deenorah Yellub, provides a translation of the judgment orders in the Kala Lagau Ya language of Mabuiag Island in the Torres Strait.

Mary Spiers Williams, who descends from First Peoples of the Sydney sandstone basin, tackles the problem of racism embedded in the processes and culture of the criminal legal system and considers how it contributes to the injustices experienced by the Aboriginal and Torres Strait Islander people who disproportionately come within its purview. In her reimagining of the sentencing appeal in *Bugmy v The Queen* (2013) 302 ALR 192 in Chapter 16, Spiers Williams recognises the ongoing impact of colonisation, the reality of systemic discrimination against Indigenous peoples in Australia, and the nexus of these to the criminalisation of Aboriginal people. She suggests that the intermediate Court's failure in *Bugmy v The Queen* to recognise structural discrimination against Indigenous people may raise a legitimate apprehension of bias against First Peoples. She also recognises her duty as a judge of the High Court to not only reflect on her own standpoints but also to repudiate racial discrimination.

Since we started writing this introduction, there have been five Aboriginal deaths in custody. Most recently, Aunty Sherry Fisher-Tilberoo died in a cell in a Brisbane watch-house. The police officers who were responsible for her care had not checked on Aunty Sherry Fisher-Tilberoo for more than six hours. The 'Black Lives Matter' campaign, which began in the USA, has become enlivened in Australia. Nerita Waight, the co-chair of the National Aboriginal and Torres Strait Islander Legal Services, recently said, 'Our people are dying in custody every few weeks—this is a national emergency and we demand urgent national leadership'.[128] She said that Black Lives Matter is not a slogan, 'this is a movement which will not end until there is justice for every family'.[129]

Conclusion

As this introduction shows, Aboriginal and Torres Strait Islander people have used the law creatively to try to achieve their goals. But the law has often operated, and continues to operate, as an oppressive tool. This collection shows the myriad ways that we might see justice through an Indigenous lens. We hope the chapters that follow will find their way into legal education, training, and practice, and help to create a new generation of legal scholars, lawyers, and jurists who will prise open spaces for the inclusion of Indigenous peoples' stories in legal decision making.

Notes

1 We thank Dr Dylan Lino for comments and feedback on an earlier version of this introduction.
2 One of the judgments, *Cooper v Stuart* (1889) 14 App Cas 286, involved parties based in Australia but was ultimately decided by the Privy Council in the United Kingdom. Until 1986 when the *Australia Act 1986* (Cth and UK) was introduced, litigants could bypass the High Court by appealing from State Supreme Courts to the Privy Council. See Murray Gleeson, 'The Privy Council—An Australian Perspective' in Hugh Dillon (ed), *Advocacy and Judging: Selected Papers of Murray Gleeson* (Federation Press, 2017) 146.
3 'The Women's Court of Canada' (2006) <http://www.womenscourt.ca/>.
4 Rosemary Hunter, Clare McGlynn and Erica Rackley (eds), *Feminist Judgments: From Theory to Practice* (Hart, 2010); Sharon Cowan, Chloe Kennedy and Vanessa Munro (eds), *Scottish Feminist Judgments: (Re)Creating Law from the Outside In* (Hart, 2019); Mairead Enright, Julie McCandless and Aoife O'Donoghue (eds), *Northern/Irish Feminist Judgment: Judges' Troubles and the Gendered Politics of Identity* (Hart, 2017).
5 Heather Douglas et al. (eds), *Australian Feminist Judgments: Righting and Re-writing Law* (Hart, 2014).
6 Elisabeth McDonald et al. (eds), *Feminist Judgments of Aotearoa New Zealand-Te Rino: A Two Stranded Rope* (Hart, 2017).
7 Kathryn Stanchi, Linda Berger, and Bridget Crawford (eds), *Feminist Judgments: Rewritten Opinions of the United States Supreme Court* (Cambridge University Press, 2016).
8 Helen Stalford, Kathryn Hollingsworth, and Stephen Gilmore (eds), *Rewriting Children's Rights Judgments: From Academic Vision to New Practice* (Hart, 2017).

9 Nicole Rogers and Michelle Maloney (eds), *Law as if Earth Really Mattered: The Wild Law Judgment Project* (Routledge, 2017).
10 Loveday Hodson and Troy Lavers (eds), *Feminist Judgments in International Law* (Hart, 2019).
11 The Women's Court of Canada is a project bringing together academics, activists, and litigators to rewrite the Canadian Charter equality cases: see Diana Majury, 'Introducing the Women's Court of Canada' (2006) 18(1) *Canadian Journal of Women and the Law* 1.
12 Mary Eberts, Sharon McIvor, and Teressa Nahanee, '*Native Women's Association of Canada v Canada*' (2006) 18(1) *Canadian Journal of Women and the Law* 67.
13 (1998) 195 CLR 337.
14 Irene Watson, 'First Nations Stories, Grandmother's Law: Too Many Stories to Tell' in Douglas et al. (n 5) 46.
15 [2005] FCA 558.
16 Heron Loban, '*ACCC v Keshow* [2005] FCA 558' in Douglas et al. (n 5) 180.
17 (1934) 52 CLR 335.
18 Nicole Watson, 'In the Matter of Djappari (Tuckiar) [2035] FNCA 1' in Douglas et al. (n 5) 442.
19 McDonald et al. (n 6) 42.
20 Ibid., 44.
21 Mãmari Stephens, '*Ruka v Department of Social Welfare* [1997] 1 NZLR 154' in McDonald et al. (n 6) 94.
22 Mihiata Pirini and Lisa Yarwood, '*Taylor v Attorney-General* [2015] NZHC 1706' in McDonald et al. (n 6) 62.
23 Emma Gattey, '*Waipapakura v Hempton* (1914) 33 NZLR 1065' in McDonald et al. (n 6) 354.
24 Kerensa Johnston and Mariah Hori Te Pa, '*Bruce v Edwards* [2002] NZCA 294' in McDonald et al. (n 6) 336.
25 Khylee Quince and Julia Tolmie, '*Police v Kawiti* [2000] 1 NZLR 117' in McDonald et al. (n 6) 489.
26 Valmaine Toki, '*R v Shashana Lee Te Tomo* [2012] 2 NZHC 71' in McDonald et al. (n 6) 522.
27 Francesca Bartlett and Heather Douglas, '"Benchmarking" A Supreme Court and Federal Court Judge in Australia' (2018) 8(9) *Oñati Socio-Legal Series* 1355.
28 As there are so few, we name them here. Local Court New South Wales: Pat O'Shane 1986–2013. Magistrates Court Western Australia: Sue Gordon from 1988, David Maclean from 2018, Andrew Matthews and Gavin MacLean from 2020. Magistrates Court Queensland: Jacqui Payne from 1999, Zac Sarra from 1999, Catherine Pirie from 2000, James Morton from 2017. Magistrates Court of Victoria: Rose Falla from 2013. Australian Capital Territory Magistrates Court: Louise Taylor from 2018. Federal Circuit Court: Matthew Myers from 2012. District Court of New South Wales: Judge Bob Bellear, 1996–2005. District Court of Queensland: Nathan Jarro from 2018.
29 Louise Phillips and Tracey Bunda, *Research Through, With and As Storying* (Routledge, 2018) 7.
30 Audre Lorde, *Sister Outsider: Essays and Speeches* (The Crossing Press, 1984) 110.
31 Watson (n 14). See also Irene Watson, *Aboriginal Peoples, Colonialism and International Law: Raw Law* (Routledge, 2014).
32 Alison Whittaker, 'A Note' in ch 10 of this collection.
33 Carol Smart, *Feminism and the Power of Law* (Routledge, 1989) 5.
34 We thank Dr Dylan Lino for making this suggestion. We note that some of the 'judgments' in this collection take a different path: see e.g. ch 6.
35 See generally Asmi Wood and Nicole Watson, 'Mirror, Mirror on the Wall, Who is the Fairest of Them All?' (2018) 28(2) *Legal Education Review* 1.

36 Aileen Moreton-Robinson, 'Towards an Australian Indigenous Women's Standpoint Theory: A Methodological Tool' (2013) 28(78) *Australian Feminist Studies* 331; Martin Nakata, *Disciplining the Savages: Savaging the Disciplines* (Aboriginal Studies Press, 2007).
37 Yin Paradies, 'Whither Standpoint Theory in a Post-Truth World?' (2018) 10(2) *Cosmopolitan Civil Societies: An Interdisciplinary Journal* 120.
38 Phillips and Bunda (n 29) 11.
39 Sarah Maddison, *Black Politics* (Allen & Unwin, 2009) 103.
40 Irene Watson, 'The Future Is Our Past: We Once Were Sovereign and We Still Are' (2012) 8(3) *Indigenous Law Bulletin* 12.
41 Dani Larkin and Kate Galloway, 'Uluru Statement from the Heart: Australian Public Law Pluralism' (2018) 30(2) *Bond Law Review* 335; Gabrielle Appleby and Megan Davis, 'The Uluru Statement and the Promises of Truth' (2018) 49 *Australian Historical Studies* 501.
42 Makarrata is a Yolngu term that means a coming together after a struggle.
43 From the Heart, 'The Uluru Statement' (2017) <https://fromtheheart.com.au/uluru-statement/the-statement/>.
44 Megan Davis, 'Australia's Reconciliation Process and Its International Context: Recognition and the Health and Well-being of Australia's Aboriginal and Torres Strait Islander Peoples' (2015) 18(2) *Indigenous Law Bulletin* 56, 62.
45 Julia Gillard MP (Prime Minister), Robert McClelland MP (Attorney-General) and Jenny Macklin MP, 'Expert Panel on Constitutional Recognition of Indigenous Australians Appointed' (Media Release, 23 December 2010) <https://formerministers.dss.gov.au/13957/expert-panel-on-constitutional-recognition-of-indigenous-australians-appointed/>.
46 Expert Panel on Constitutional Recognition of Indigenous Australians, *Recognising Aboriginal and Torres Strait Islander Peoples in the Constitution: Report of the Expert Panel* (Report, January 2012).
47 Ibid.
48 (1889) 14 App Cas 286.
49 William Blackstone, *Commentaries on the Laws of England* (Clarendon Press, 1765) vol 1, 107.
50 *Cooper v Stuart* (1889) 14 App Cas 286, 291.
51 The petitions are cared for by the Department of the House of Representatives. See Australian Institute of Aboriginal and Torres Strait Islander Studies, 'Yirrkala Bark Petitions 1963' (2020) <https://aiatsis.gov.au/collections/collections-online/digitised-collections/yirrkala-bark-petitions-1963>.
52 (1971) 17 FLR 141.
53 Ibid., 267.
54 Marion Diamond, 'Stradbroke: A Brief History' (2012) 7(1) *Fryer Folios* 13; Faith Walker, 'Useful and Profitable: History and Race Relations at the Myora Aboriginal Mission, Stradbroke Island, Australia, 1892–1940' (1998) 1(1) *Memoirs of the Queensland Museum, Cultural Heritage Series* 137, 440.
55 Lon Fuller, 'The Case of the Speluncean Explorers' (1949) 62(4) *Harvard Law Review* 616.
56 Underlining this connection we note it is also highlighted in *Cooper v Stuart* (1889) 14 App Cas 286 and *Millirpum v Nabalco Pty Ltd* (1971) 17 FLR 141, discussed in the previous section.
57 Marshall Clark and Sally K May (eds), *Macassan History and Heritage* (ANU Press, 2013).
58 Grace Karskens, *The Colony: A History of Early Australia* (Allen & Unwin, 2010).
59 Michael Dodson and Lisa Strelein, 'Australia's Nation-Building: Renegotiating the Relationship between Indigenous Peoples and the State' (2001) 24(3) *University of New South Wales Law Journal* 826, 828.

60 Megan Davis, 'Closing the Gap on Indigenous Disadvantage: A Trajectory of Indigenous Inequality in Australia' (2015) Winter/Spring *Georgetown Journal of International Affairs* 34, 35–7.
61 Scott Robinson, 'The Aboriginal Embassy: An Account of the Protests of 1972' in Gary Foley, Andrew Schaap and Edwina Howell (eds), *The Aboriginal Tent Embassy: Sovereignty, Black Power, Land Rights and the State* (Routledge, 2014) 3, 4.
62 Johanna Perheentupa, *Redfern Aboriginal Activism in the 1970s* (Aboriginal Studies Press, 2020) 1.
63 John Chesterman, *Civil Rights: How Indigenous Australians won Formal Equality* (University of Queensland Press, 2005) 95–6.
64 *Mabo v Queensland (No 2)* (1992) 175 CLR 1 ('*Mabo [No 2]*').
65 Many scholars have provided detailed histories of the case. See e.g. Nonie Sharp, *No Ordinary Judgment: Mabo, the Murray Islanders' Land Case* (Aboriginal Studies Press, 1996).
66 *Mabo (No 2)* (1992) 175 CLR 1, 2. See also David Ritter, 'The "Rejection of Terra Nullius" in Mabo: A Critical Analysis' (1996) 18(1) *Sydney Law Review* 5.
67 *Mabo (No 2)* (1992) 175 CLR 1, 69.
68 Ibid., 216. Note that the Queensland Government made a strong effort to obstruct the claim: see *Mabo v Queensland* (1992) 175 CLR 1.
69 Indeed, Denis Walker drew upon *Mabo (No 2)* in his claim that he was not subject to the jurisdiction of NSW criminal law, but Mason CJ rejected this claim.
70 *Native Title Act 1993* (Cth).
71 The National Native Title Tribunal: see <http://www.nntt.gov.au/Pages/Home-Page.aspx>.
72 Sean Brennan et al. (eds), *Native Title from Mabo to Akiba: A Vehicle for Change and Empowerment* (Federation Press, 2015).
73 Simon Young, *The Trouble with Tradition: Native Title and Cultural Change* (Federation Press, 2008).
74 *Members of the Yorta Yorta Aboriginal Community v Victoria* [1998] FCA 1606, [129].
75 *Members of the Yorta Yorta Aboriginal Community v Victoria* [2002] HCA 58.
76 Simon Young, 'Commentary', ch 6 of this collection.
77 (2013) 250 CLR 209.
78 Lauren Butterly, 'Changing Tack: Akiba and the Way Forward for Indigenous Governance of Sea Country' (2013) 17(1) *Australian Indigenous Law Reporter* 2.
79 Simon Young, 'The Increments of Justice: Exploring the Outer Reach of Akiba's Edge towards Native Title "Ownership"' (2019) 42(3) *University of New South Wales Law Journal* 825.
80 Faith Bandler, *Turning the Tide: A Personal History of the Federal Council for the Advancement of Aborigines and Torres Strait Islanders* (Aboriginal Studies Press, 1989).
81 See e.g. William Grayden's report released in 1957. See generally Pamela McGrath and David Brooks, 'Their Darkest Hour: The Films and Photographs of William Grayden and the History of the "Warburton Range Controversy" of 1957' (2010) 34 *Aboriginal History* 115.
82 Charles Perkins, *A Bastard Like Me* (Ure Smith, 1975).
83 Our analysis here is necessarily over-simplified. For a more thorough analysis see Chesterman (n 63) and Jennifer Clark, '"The Wind of Change" in Australia: Aborigines and the International Politics of Race 1960–1972' (1998) 20(1) *The International History Review* 89.
84 See Dylan Lino, *Constitutional Recognition: First Peoples and the Australian Settler State* (Federation Press, 2018) 133–4. Lino explores these issues in detail and observes: 'the provision appears to have reflected a view of the framers that, unlike the affairs of non-white migrants, whose threatening influx was of the utmost national concern, the affairs of Indigenous people, widely believed to be an unthreatening "doomed race", were to remain primarily a State responsibility'. Lino notes that

prior to constitutional reform, the Commonwealth did exercise some powers over Indigenous peoples after federation.

85 Jackie Huggins, 'The 1967 Referendum Four Decades Later' (2007) 19(3) *The Sydney Papers* 1, iv–9.

86 Bain Attwood and Andrew Markus, *The 1967 Referendum: Race, Power and the Australian Constitution* (Aboriginal Studies Press, 2007).

87 For further information and resources see National Museum of Australia, 'Referendum, 1957–67' (2020) <https://www.nma.gov.au/explore/features/indigenous-rights/civil-rights/referendum>.

88 As outlined in the previous section. Hence, the campaign for recognition continues to the present day, manifest in platforms such as the Uluru Statement.

89 Noel Pearson, 'The Reward for Public Life is Public Progress: An Appreciation of the Public Life of the Hon EG Whitlam AC QC Prime Minister 1972–1975' (Speech, Whitlam Oration, Whitlam Institute, University of Western Sydney, 13 November 2013) 4.

90 Katharine Gelber and Luke McNamara, 'Freedom of Speech and Racial Vilification in Australia: "The Bolt Case" in Public Discourse' (2013) 48 *Australian Journal of Political Science* 470.

91 Debbie Bargallie, *Unmasking the Racial Contract: Indigenous Voices on Racism in the Australian Public Service* (Aboriginal Studies Press, 2020); Jennifer Nielsen, 'Whiteness and Anti-Discrimination Law – It's in the Design' (2008) 3(2) *ACRAWSA e-journal*.

92 [2002] NSWADTAP 6.

93 For an analysis of the different state protection regimes see John Chesterman and Brian Galligan, *Citizens without Rights* (Cambridge University Press, 1997).

94 John Summers, *The Parliament of the Commonwealth of Australia and Indigenous Peoples 1901–1967* (Research Paper No 10, 2000-01). See also *Namatjira v Raabe* (1959) 100 CLR 664 for a discussion of this issue. Albert Namatjira was an Aboriginal man and not a ward. However, he shared alcohol with a nephew who was a ward and, as a result, he was charged with a criminal offence.

95 Stephen Gray, *The Protectors: A Journey through Whitefella Past* (Allen & Unwin, 2011).

96 These regimes are documented in Australian Human Rights Commission, *Bringing Them Home: Report of the National Inquiry into the Separation of Aboriginal and Torres Strait Islander Children from Their Families* (Report, April 1997) ch 2 ('*Bringing Them Home Report*').

97 Ibid., 31.

98 (1914) St R Qd 245.

99 *Bringing Them Home Report* (n 96) 220.

100 Ibid.

101 Ibid., 4.

102 Ibid., 245.

103 Shurlee Swain, *History of Inquiries Reviewing Institutions Providing Care for Children* (Report, 2014) 156.

104 Australian Institute of Health and Welfare, *Child Protection in Australia 2017–18* (Report, 2019) 17, 30.

105 Kyllie Cripps and Julian Laurens, 'The Protection of Cultural Identity in Aboriginal and Torres Strait Islander Children Exiting from Statutory Out of Home Care Via Permanent Care Orders: Further Observations on the Risk of Cultural Disconnection to Inform a Policy and Legislative Reform Framework' (2016) 19 *Australian Indigenous Law Review* 70.

106 *Family Law Act 1975* (Cth) s 60CC.

107 Kyllie Cripps and Julian Laurens, 'Protecting Indigenous Children's Familial and Cultural Connections: Reflections on Recent Amendments to the *Care and Protection Act 2007* (NT)' (2015) 8 *Indigenous Law Bulletin* 12.

108 Thalia Anthony, 'Fact Check Q&A: Are Indigenous Australians the Most Incarcerated People on Earth?' *The Conversation* (online, 6 June 2017) <https://

theconversation.com/factcheck-qanda-are-indigenous-australians-the-most-incarcerated-people-on-earth-78528>.
109 Australian Bureau of Statistics, 'Corrective Services, Australia' (17 September 2020) <https://www.abs.gov.au/statistics/people/crime-and-justice/corrective-services-australia/latest-release>.
110 Australian Institute of Health and Welfare, *Youth Detention Population in Australia* (Australian Government, 2019) 2, 11–3.
111 Ibid., 13.
112 Patrick Dodson, '25 Years on from the Royal Commission into Aboriginal Deaths in Custody Recommendations' (2016) 8(23) *Indigenous Law Bulletin* 24, 27.
113 Ibid., 29.
114 Australian Law Reform Commission, *Pathways to Justice: Inquiry into the Incarceration Rate of Aboriginal and Torres Strait Islander Peoples* (Report No 133, 2018) 22.
115 Eileen Baldry and Ruth McCausland, 'Mother Seeking Safe Home: Aboriginal Women Post-Release' (2009) 21(2) *Current Issues in Criminal Justice* 288, 290.
116 Australian Law Reform Commission (n 115).
117 Elliott Johnston, *National Report, Royal Commission into Aboriginal Deaths in Custody* (Australian Government Publishing Service, 1991).
118 Ibid., 1.
119 Ibid.
120 Ibid., vol 1 [13.3].
121 Lorena Allam, 'National Emergency: Urgent Leadership Needed after Fifth Aboriginal Death in Custody Since June' *The Guardian* (online, 20 September 2020) <https://www.theguardian.com/australia-news/2020/sep/20/national-emergency-urgent-leadership-needed-after-fifth-aboriginal-death-in-custody-since-june>. Indigenous people are now less likely to die in custody than non-Indigenous people; however, 20 per cent of deaths in police custody are Aboriginal and Torres Strait Islander people: Alexandra Gannoni and Samantha Bricknell, *Indigenous Deaths in Custody: 25 Years Since the Royal Commission into Aboriginal Deaths in Custody* (Australian Government, 2019) 11.
122 Gannoni and Bricknell (n 121) 9.
123 In conjunction with the Jumbunna Institute for Indigenous Education and Research, University of Technology Sydney (UTS), Guardian Australia has developed a database of Indigenous deaths in custody and their causes: 'Deaths Inside: Indigenous Deaths in Custody 2020' *The Guardian* (online, 5 June 2020) <https://www.theguardian.com/australia-news/ng-interactive/2018/aug/28/deaths-inside-indigenous-australian-deaths-in-custody>.
124 Raymond Brazil, 'Respecting the Dead Protecting the Living' (2008) 12 *Australian Indigenous Law Reporter* 45, 51.
125 Alison Whittaker, '"Dragged Like a Dead Kangaroo": Why Language Matters for Deaths in Custody' *The Guardian* (online, 8 September 2018) <https://www.theguardian.com/commentisfree/2018/sep/07/dragged-like-a-dead-kangaroo-why-language-matters-for-deaths-in-custod>.
126 A recent report claims that police and medical centres failed to follow their own procedures in 41 per cent of Indigenous deaths in custody: Lorena Allam, Calla Wahlquist and Nick Evershed, 'Aboriginal Deaths in Custody: 434 Have Died Since 1991, New Data Shows' *The Guardian* (online, 6 June 2020) <https://www.theguardian.com/australia-news/2020/jun/06/aboriginal-deaths-in-custody-434-have-died-since-1991-new-data-shows>.
127 Amanda Porter, 'Riotous or Righteous Behaviour? Representations of Subaltern Resistance in the Australian Mainstream Media' (2015) 26(3) *Current Issues in Criminal Justice* 289.
128 Allam (n 121).
129 Ibid.

PART I

Sovereignty

2

MILIRRPUM v NABALCO PTY LTD (1971) 17 FLR 141

MILIRRPUM .... PLAINTIFFS;

AND

NABALCO PTY LTD .... DEFENDANT;

AND

COMMONWEALTH .... DEFENDANT;

(1971) 17 FLR 141

Native title—Proof of relationship of Aboriginal people with land—Communal native title.

Osca Monaghan

Indigenous judging

I have been asked to perform the role of an Indigenous judge in the matter of *Milirrpum v Nabalco Pty Ltd* (1971) 17 FLR 141 ('*Milirrpum v Nabalco*'). In order to discharge the functions of an Indigenous judge, it is first necessary to determine the scope and content of that role within the parameters of this project. The requirement that the judgment take place within the confines of the colonial legal system poses an immediate problem that is not easily overcome; the obvious question at the outset must be whether it is even possible to occupy the role of an Indigenous judge whilst applying colonial law.

Subjectivity in the settler colony

I begin from the premise that 'Indigenous' is a political category that gains its coherence only in the context of ongoing colonial power.[1] To be 'Indigenous' is to be constituted in the colonial relation—and it is to be in resistance to colonial power. It is precisely this political dimension to Indigenous identity that enables the strategic deployment of the concept. Brendan Hokowhitu (Ngäti Pukenga) expresses the political and symbolic reification entailed within 'Indigenous' and the related rationale justifying its strategic deployment:

> The one consistency across Indigenous contexts is that colonization effected the annexation of Indigenous lands and attempted to destroy Indigenous epistemologies via 'civilization' and then assimilation. The pan-Indigenous movement is (if there is such a thing), as a consequence, based on the common sharing of the anguish and loss of colonization that, in turn, has created a generalizable Indigenous ontology and taxonomy. That is, several strategically essentialized cultural pillars, including land, language, and culture, have risen from the ashes of the colonial taxonomic meltdowns, which Indigenous peoples have strategically employed to gain at least some foothold of agency.[2]

What is evident is that the 'coloniser/colonised binary…still tithes Indigenous ontology to "being colonized"'.[3] This entrapment has been expressed as a 'double bind'[4] and has the potential to be both epistemic and ontological[5]—though the nature and extent of the entrapment are still being explored. For some, there is an avenue out of the dialectic established by this imposed binary through, for instance, a 'resurgent politics of recognition premised on self-actualization, direct action, and the resurgence of cultural practices'.[6] Other Indigenous thinkers, however, locate the dominant modes of Indigenous resistance (and the counter-resistances they provoke) squarely within the production of settler-colonial subjectivities and the broader project of modernity. This ensures our continued entrapment within the colonial bind,[7] neither in spite of our resistance, nor because of it, but instead because both our resistance and the settler state's counter-resistances are dynamics framed by 'modernity's tradition of dissent'.[8]

The entrapment created by the coloniser/colonised binary has a duality that ensures that although the entrapment is asymmetrically experienced, it encloses the settler's range of movements as well. This offers little comfort in the way of the material and everyday, but to the extent that the primary goal of the settler-colonial project is the naturalisation—or nativisation—of the settler colony, then the dynamic gestured at above also ensures that the project is incapable of completion. As I have argued elsewhere,[9] the:

> 'nativisation' or 'indigenisation' of the settler state...remains an essential element of settler colonial desires. The terms denote not just a displacing or replacing desire, but...a desire for an *originary authority* that dissipates Indigenous claims to sovereignty and territory.[10]

The naturalisation of the settler colony is not merely complete when the settler's presence on Indigenous lands is both legal and morally legitimate (and thus 'incontestable'[11]), but when the settler state is able to claim the *originary authority* of an 'Indigenous settler' or of a 'nativised settler state'. This desire can never be fully realised whilst Indigenous people exist as the holders of specific rights and demands—even if these demands themselves originate within and are 'framed by modernity's tradition of dissent'.[12]

The foregoing makes clear that the Indigenous sits in opposition to the settler-colonial. The 'Indigenous' component of the impugned 'Indigenous judge' necessitates a resistant and critical distance from colonial power. The question now becomes: can the 'judging' component be recuperated for the purposes of Indigenous resistance, or is it too firmly imbricated within colonial power?

Colonial law

Whilst some have suggested that one of the benefits conferred by colonisation is the 'legacy of legality [and] the rule of law',[13] in truth the law both legitimates and facilitates the violence of colonisation. It is more accurate to describe the law—as Martin Chanock does—as the 'cutting edge of colonialism...a weapon...an instrument of the power of the alien state and part of the process of coercion'.[14] Rather than an imperial 'gift' to the 'savage',[15] or a key component of a 'civilising mission',[16] the law was (is) integral to the exploitation and domination of coloniser over colonised. As 'a process in which one society endeavoured to rule and to transform another',[17] colonialism introduced systems of courts and policing, 'arrayed beside the mission, the school, the store, and the local government office' to enforce 'compliance to a new political order and...to impose a new culture'.[18] The transformative impact of Western law introduced 'a new way of conceptualising relationships and powers',[19] both between colonisers and colonised, between the colonised themselves, and between the colonised and the natural world.[20]

Colonial—or Western—law is not merely implicated in the settler-colonial project; it is one among a suite of technologies that deploy settler-colonial power. Given this context, it is no longer striking to assert the particularity of Western law, which is the 'creation of a particular set of historical and political realities and of a particular mind-set or world view'.[21] Or, said with more specificity: that colonial law rests on a 'hegemonic, positivist and raced view of the world, with the planet as a commodity'.[22] It is also no longer controversial to place this particularity within its political project, as Kenneth B Nunn asserts:

> Law is a Eurocentric enterprise...that attempts to promote European values and interests at the expense of all others. Law carries out a Eurocentric program as it organizes [sic] and directs culture. Law does this by reinforcing a Eurocentric way of thinking, promoting Eurocentric values and affirming—indeed celebrating—the Eurocentric cultural experience.[23]

As part of its Eurocentric paradigm, the law's deeply raced character cannot be overstated. Much has been written about the 'profound interchange'[24] of meaning between race and the law in Western/colonial legal systems, and particularly as they have been developed in settler-colonial contexts.[25] In societies built upon a racial hierarchy, this profound interchange permeates because the law develops in tandem with other 'process[es] of colonial state-building'.[26] This is particularly evident in the context of criminal law,[27] but, relevant to the case of *Milirrpum*, is also obvious in the property law context.[28] The ideological scaffolding underpinning all property laws in Australia is the belief in the superiority of Western ways of being in relation to the land. The very insistence on the deployment of the colonial concepts of dispossession, possession, alienability, title, exclusivity, etc. points to a particularly limited, legalistic, and commodified view of the earth. Furthermore, these concepts have been developed in ways that ensure the *dispossession* of Indigenous peoples, secure *possession* for settlers or those who will *alienate* 'their lands' by exchanging *title* and *excluding* others in defence of their title. The very meaning of these terms developed to further the settler-colonial project.[29]

The (settler-)colonial state was (and is) produced through a 'politics of legal ordering',[30] wherein 'the structural relation of one legal authority to another' remains contested.[31] This contestation plays out differently in different contexts, but in all of them, the colonial law facilitates the imposition of settler control over Indigenous peoples.[32] Settler-colonialism can be understood as a protracted dispute over the character and constitution of political authority,[33] as the colonisers seek to enforce political, legal, and social dominance and control. Historically, this enforcement was uneven, resulting in a de facto legal pluralism that made some concessions to nearby Indigenous peoples as a means of easing inter-group conflict.[34] This was the case in New South Wales, where 'a tentative, "weak" pluralism' that allowed Indigenous people to resolve their own internal disputes outside of the colonial system was in operation for the first few decades of British settlement.[35] This legal pluralism was short-lived, however—to be replaced by a more uniform enforcement of settler authority,[36] directed at strengthening the colonial legal regime.[37] As settler-colonial studies scholars have demonstrated,[38] solidifying the colonial regime required, if not the physical 'elimination of the Native, then the "elimination" of Indigenous political difference'.[39] As Strakosch and Macoun emphasise, the elimination of Indigenous difference can take many forms:

> by physically eliminating Indigenous peoples; by severing their physical connections to lands that lie at the heart of their political systems; by breaking down families and communities; by drawing Indigenous politics into the state and reforming them; and by entering into explicit contractual exchanges (such as treaties) which publicly erase the political distinctions between coloniser and colonised.[40]

From the foregoing, it is no great leap—and I do not think it is controversial either[41]—to say that, in the settler-colonial context, the law is a tool of settler-colonial power, and that it is in service to the always present settler-colonial project. This is the case even when it takes the appearance of cultural accommodation or safety, and it is the case even when it attempts to absorb Indigenous means of resolving disputes into its existing processes. I am here primarily gesturing to the increased push to appropriate Indigenous knowledges and embed them within the colonial legal system's overarching framework in the form of Indigenous sentencing courts, or in the form of formal recognition of customary law. Although such manoeuvres may bring about some benefits,[42] they nonetheless represent a 'drawing' in and 'reformation' of 'Indigenous politics into the state', and so, they may also serve the additional function of assimilation and elimination.

It is somewhat customary to contrast Indigenous and colonial legal systems to highlight their incommensurability.[43] But, I do not find that to be the relevant consideration for our present purpose. Instead, we must insist always on an interrogation of power and jurisdiction. Even if colonial and Indigenous legal systems were compatible or reconcilable with each other, the contestation over legal ordering remains. Shiri Pasternak reminds us that '[d]ecolonising law means deconstructing the state's grounds to inaugurate law on lands acquired through colonial settlement'.[44] So, for the purposes of deciding whether we can recuperate colonial law for the purpose of Indigenous judging, our question is whether it is possible to do that work using the colonial legal system. This question will no doubt be met by a variety of responses but, for my part, I believe that while short- and medium-term political and material gains may be realised through the marshalling of—and/or reformation of—the colonial legal system, that legal system is nonetheless contrary to longer-term and more radical decolonial desires.

Pragmatics, politics, and a decolonising legal theory

At this juncture, it is perhaps important to emphasise that the position I have come to is not only political or strategic (i.e. that I believe that Indigenous emancipatory goals are not able to be served 'by the master's tools'[45]). Although my position *is* political in that sense, it *also* encompasses a more fundamental belief that it is not possible to be in resistance to colonial power whilst *exercising* colonial power through colonial laws. In saying this, I am not speaking to questions of identity. If our conversation were primarily concerned with identity,

I would have to concede that one can be both Indigenous and exercise colonial power—colonial power exists and operates on and through multiple fronts, and Indigenous people can (and do) exercise and embody it. But if our *politic* is directed towards Indigenous liberation then our politic must resist colonial power wherever it is identified.

To reiterate, I do believe that short-, medium-, and even some longer-term Indigenous political and material gains can be realised by working within the confines of the colonial legal system. These gains are important for securing an Indigenous future that continues to be threatened by ongoing colonial violence. This, however, produces a tension because ultimately this work runs the risk of undercutting broader Indigenous liberationist goals. We must be aware that:

> sometimes the governing paradigms which have structured all of our lives are so powerful that we can think we are doing progressive work, dismantling the structures of racism and other oppressions, when in fact we are reinforcing the paradigms.[46]

It is therefore crucial that we ask in what way a given practice or manoeuvre is structured by settler-colonialism so that we are not co-opted 'into becoming instruments of [our] own dispossession'.[47] This relocates our attention to the structural nature of settler-colonialism, which directs our attention to the fundamental questions of jurisdiction, sovereignty, and authority. When viewed against these questions, it is evident that mere recalibration through increased Indigenous participation, and even Indigenous self-management within the frameworks imposed by the settler state, serve only to entrench Indigenous subjugation to the colonial order.

In order to find space to imagine decolonisation and Indigenous liberation, I find it necessary to turn away from the question of what an Indigenous judge would find possible within the confines of a persistently colonising legal system. In this, I agree with the main thrust of Irene Watson's contribution to the Australian Feminist Judgments Project, when she notes that:

> the rewriting of the judgment of *Kartinyeri* in accordance with the methodology of this project would not prise open places for Nunga women because the rewriting needs to be done from 'another place', outside the jurisdiction of the Australian common law and the sovereignty of the Australian state.[48]

To my mind, this place 'outside' the colonial legal system is brought into being when we take seriously the task of thinking through and imagining and enacting 'other ways of living justly together'.[49] For some, this opening up of places outside the colonial legal system emerges primarily in the context of Indigenous resurgence.[50] While this is certainly true, I do not believe it provides a complete avenue out of the colonial bind, and does not itself direct us towards a decolonial future. In order to do that, we must engage in the contestation of legal ordering—although the way we do this ought not to be done in the coloniser's courts or on their terms.

To my mind, the structural realities of the settler-colonial relation ensure that it is not possible to side-step these issues by begging recourse to pragmatics—or consideration of the short-term material gains that might be secured. If our commitment is to disrupting the colonial bind in order to imagine avenues of escape, then the question is not whether short- or medium-term gains can be realised by leaning on (or working within) a legal system fundamentally designed to negate broader Indigenous claims to liberation and sovereignty. A pragmatic approach asks one to begin where one finds oneself, but the work of decolonisation must begin in the imagination and requires a commitment to a utopianism that a pragmatic politic would reject as impossible. In the words of the anarchists, 'another world is possible', and it is in its imaginings that we must begin.

In thinking through the decolonial question, I always begin with Tuck and Yang's assertion that 'decolonization is not a metaphor'.[51] As they argue, it is not reducible to a broader social justice politic. Decolonisation must be thought through in terms of its colonial specifications. Colonialism is an all-encompassing project; it is simultaneously a land-centred endeavour that assembles a totalising apparatus of state power to 'order the relationships between particular peoples, lands, the "natural world," and civilization',[52] and an endeavour that targets the hearts and minds of both settlers and Indigenous peoples in order to convince both of its own legitimacy.[53] The colonial apparatus enforced its order of the world through the imposition of specific forms of 'sexuality, legality, raciality, language, religion and property'.[54] Decolonisation, then, is 'the intelligent, calculated, and active resistance to the forces of colonialism that perpetuate the subjugation and/or exploitation of our minds, bodies, and lands, and it is engaged for the ultimate purpose of overturning the colonial structure and realizing Indigenous liberation'.[55]

For all Indigenous people—and I suspect for many settlers also—the questions that are raised when we ask how we can live together on more just terms are deeply personal. I certainly do not have answers, only a sense that there are different questions we need to be collectively asking. I am suspicious of the potential for Indigenous counter-hegemonic discourses to, themselves, become hegemonic,[56] and I am suspicious also of any tendency towards reducing all decolonial manoeuvres to an Indigenous renaissance. To draw on Brendan Hokowhitu again, he reminds us that:

> [s]imply being Indigenous, or adhering to 'traditional' cultural practices, or even resisting the neo-colonial state does not naturalise a sovereign space located beyond the postcolonial complex.…Too often in Indigenous studies we fall into a coloniser/colonised binary, which debilitates our ability to see the density of the postcolonial complex. Too often Indigenous studies

> scholars envisage Indigenous acts as inherently sovereign acts against an omnipresent hegemonic colonial state.[57]

While it is 'easy to romantically imagine neo-Indigenous cultural formations unsettling the national narrative',[58] we should not assume that such cultural formations are inherently unsettling[59] given both the plasticity and productivity of settler-colonialism. In other words, settler colonialism 'produces forms of indigeneity complicit with its agenda'[60] and is able to adapt (often via appropriation and/or accommodation) in response to more resistant expressions.

There are obvious questions that follow or persist in light of the above—around culture, tradition, practice, authenticity, and resistance. But I am not sure they need to be resolved in order to make decolonial manoeuvres. I return always to the fundamentals of settler-colonialism: as a contest over legal ordering and legitimacy, we can always start by asking what ideological territory we cede. And, as Kent McNeil reminds us, 'the legality of settler state sovereignty is a relative matter that depends on which legal orders are chosen to determine legality: settler legal orders or indigenous legal orders'.[61] I think it is a mistake to acquiesce to the former.

Notes

1 Taiaiake Alfred and Jeff Corntassel, 'Being Indigenous: Resurgences against Contemporary Colonialism' (2005) 40(4) *Government and Opposition* 597; Hokulani K Aikau et al., 'Indigenous Feminisms Roundtable' (2015) 36(3) *Frontiers: A Journal of Women Studies* 84, 86, 106; Linda Tuhiwai Smith, *Decolonising Methodologies: Research and Indigenous Peoples* (Zed Books, 1st ed, 1999) 7.

2 Brendan Hokowhitu, 'Monster: Post-Indigenous Studies' in Aileen Moreton-Robinson (ed), *Critical Indigenous Studies: Engagements in First World Locations* (University of Arizona Press, 2016), 83, 85 ('Monster').

3 Ibid., 89.

4 Francis Ludlow et al., 'The Double Binds of Indigeneity and Indigenous Resistance' (2016) 5 *Humanities* 53, drawing on Gregory Bateson's work on the concept of the double-bind: Gregory Bateson, *Steps to an Ecology of Mind* (Ballantine Books, 1972) 201, 241.

5 See e.g. Hokowhitu, 'Monster' (n 2); Ludlow et al. (n 4); Tania M Li, 'Articulating Indigenous Identity in Indonesia: Resource Politics and the Tribal Slot' (2000) 42 *Comparative Studies in Society and History* 149; Frank Hirtz, 'It Takes Modern Means to be Traditional: On Recognising Indigenous Cultural Communities in the Philippines' (2003) 34 *Development and Change* 887.

6 Glen Coulthard, *Red Skin, White Masks* (University of Minnesota Press, 2014) 24.

7 Hokowhitu, 'Monster' (n 2) 91.

8 Ibid., 90.

9 Oscar Monaghan, 'Dual Imperatives: Decolonising the Queer and Queering the Decolonial' in Dino Hodge (ed), *Colouring the Rainbow: Blak, Queer and Trans Perspectives* (Wakefield Press, 2015) 195.

10 Ibid., 198.

11 Scott Lauria Morgensen, *Spaces between Us* (University of Minnesota Press, 2011) 16.

12 Hokowhitu, 'Monster' (n 2) 90.

13 Martin Chanock, *Law, Custom and Social Order: The Colonial Experience in Malawi and Zambia* (Cambridge University Press, 1985) 5.
14 Ibid., 4.
15 Peter Fitzpatrick, 'Custom as Imperialism' in J M Abun-Nasr and U Spellenbert (eds), *Law and Identity in Africa*, quoted in Sally Engle Merry, 'Law and Colonialism' (1991) 25(4) *Law & Society Review* 889, 890.
16 Philip Darby, *The Three Faces of Imperialism* (Yale University Press, 1987).
17 Merry (n 15).
18 Ibid.
19 Chanock (n 13) 4.
20 Ibid.
21 Kenneth B Nunn, 'Law as a Eurocentric Enterprise' (1997) 15 *Law & Inequality* 323, 325.
22 Irene Watson, *Aboriginal Peoples, Colonialism and International Law: Raw Law* (Routledge, 2015) 1.
23 Nunn (n 21) 328.
24 Dorothy E Roberts, 'Deviance, Resistance, and Love' (1994) *Utah Law Review* 179, 181 ('Deviance'), citing Dorothy E Roberts 'Crime, Race and Reproduction' (1993) 67(6) *Tulane Law Review* 1945.
25 See e.g. Natsu Taylor Saito, 'Race and Decolonization: Whiteness as Property in the American Settler Colonial Project' (2015) 31 *Harvard Journal on Racial & Ethnic Justice* 31; Brenna Bhandar, *Colonial Lives of Property: Law, Land, and Racial Regimes of Ownership* (Duke University Press, 2018); Julie Evans, 'Where Lawlessness is Law: The Settler-Colonial Frontier as a Legal Space of Violence' (2009) 30(1) *The Australian Feminist Law Journal* 3.
26 Amanda Nettelbeck and Russell Smandych, 'Policing Indigenous Peoples on Two Colonial Frontiers: Australia's Mounted Police and Canada's North-West Mounted Police' (2010) 43(2) *Australian and New Zealand Journal of Criminology* 356. See also Harry Blagg, *Crime, Aboriginality and the Decolonisation of Justice* (Hawkins Press, 2008); Jen Preston, 'Neoliberal Settler Colonialism, Canada and the Tar Sands' (2013) 55(2) *Race and Class* 42.
27 See e.g. Roberts, 'Deviance' (n 24) 181; Roberts, 'Crime, Race and Reproduction' (n 24); Nettelbeck and Smandych, (n 26) 358; Dorothy E Roberts, 'Constructing a Criminal Justice System Free of Racial Bias: An Abolitionist Framework' (2007) 39(1) *Columbia Human Rights Law Review* 261.
28 See e.g. Alberto Lopez, Alfred Brophy, and Kali Murray, *Integrating Spaces: Property Law and Race* (Wolters Kluwer, 2011).
29 Whether these concepts can themselves be rehabilitated for different ends would to some, perhaps, be the material point. To my mind, however, that question needlessly accepts the parameters of the colonial mindset. Whilst I'm *certain* there is space within colonial legal systems to carve out space within which some Indigenous goals may be realised, what ideological ground would be ceded in the process and what broader emancipatory horizons do we lose as a result?
30 Lauren Benton, *Law and Colonial Cultures: Legal Regimes in World History, 1400–1900* (Cambridge University Press, 2002) 253.
31 Ibid., 2.
32 Ibid.
33 Ibid.
34 Ibid., 167.
35 Ibid.
36 Ibid.
37 Ibid.
38 Lorenzo Veracini, 'Settler Colonialism and Decolonisation' (2007) 6(2) *Borderlands e-Journal*; Patrick Wolfe, 'Settler Colonialism and the Elimination of the Native' (2006) 8(4) *Journal of Genocide Research* 387.

39 Wolfe (n 38).
40 Elizabeth Strakosch and Alissa Macoun, 'The Vanishing Endpoint of Settler Colonialism' (2012) 37–38 *Arena* 40, 45, quoted in Juan Tauri, 'Criminal Justice in Contemporary Settler Colonialism' (2014) 8(1) *African Journal of Criminology and Justice Studies* 20, 22–3.
41 Cf. Mark McMillan, 'Holding on to the "Hope of Law"' (2014) 16(2) *Flinders Law Journal* 251.
42 See e.g. Ivan Potas et al., *Circle Sentencing in New South Wales: A Review and Evaluation* (Monograph No 22, October 2003).
43 See e.g. Watson (n 22); Taiaiake Alfred, *Peace, Power, Righteousness: An Indigenous Manifesto* (Oxford University Press, 1999); Ambelin Kwaymullina and Blaze Kwaymullina, 'Learning to Read the Signs: Law in an Indigenous Reality' (2010) 34(2) *Journal of Australian Studies* 195.
44 Shiri Pasternak, 'Jurisdiction and Settler Colonialism: Where Do Laws Meet?' (2014) 29(2) *Canadian Journal of Law and Society* 145, 146.
45 See Audre Lorde, 'The Master's Tools Will Never Dismantle the Master's House' in Cherríe Moraga and Gloria E Anzaldúa (eds), *This Bridge Called My Back: Writings by Radical Women of Color* (Sixth Printing, 2nd ed, 1983) 98 (comments made at 'The Personal and the Political Panel', Second Sex Conference, 29 October 1979).
46 Here, I am guided especially by Trina Grillo, 'Anti-Essentialism and Intersectionality: Tools to Dismantle the Master's House' (1995) 10 *Berkley Women's Law Journal* 17.
47 Glen Coulthard, a scholar from the Yellowknives Dene First Nation, succinctly describes the ruling logic of settler-colonialism as a kind of '*governmentality*': 'A relatively diffuse set of governing relations that operate through a circumscribed mode of recognition that structurally ensures continued access to Indigenous peoples' land and resources by producing neocolonial subjectivities that coopt [sic] Indigenous people into becoming instruments of their own dispossession' (Coulthard [n 6] 156).
48 Irene Watson, 'First Nations Stories, Grandmother's Law' in Heather Douglas et al. (eds), *Australian Feminist Judgments: Righting and Re-writing Law* (Hart Publishing, 2014) 46, 53.
49 Julie Evans et al., 'Sovereignty: Frontiers of Possibility' in Julie Evans et al. (eds), *Sovereignty: Frontiers of Possibility* (University of Hawai'i Press, 2013) 1, quoting Wendy Brown, 'Learning to Love Again: An Interview with Wendy Brown' (2006) 6 *Contretemps* 27.
50 See e.g. Coulthard (n 6); Leanne Simpson, *Dancing on Our Turtle's Back* (Arbeiter Ring Publishing, 2012); Alfred (n 43).
51 Eve Tuck and K Wayne Yang, 'Decolonization is Not a Metaphor' (2012) 1(1) *Decolonization: Indigeneity, Education & Society* 1.
52 Ibid., 21.
53 Albert Memmi expresses this idea clearly when he says, 'In order for the colonizer to be the complete master, it is not enough for him to be so in actual fact, he must also believe in its legitimacy. In order for that legitimacy to be complete, it is not enough for the colonized to be a slave, he must also accept his role', quoted by Waziyatawin Angela Wilson and Michael Yellow Bird, 'Beginning Decolonization' in Waziyatawin Angela Wilson and Michael Yellow Bird (eds), *For Indigenous Eyes Only: A Decolonization Handbook* (School of American Research Press, 2005) 2–3.
54 Tuck and Yang (n 51).
55 Waziyatawin Angela Wilson and Michael Yellow Bird, *For Indigenous Eyes Only: A Decolonization Handbook* (School of American Research Press, 2005) 5, cited in Wanda D McAslin and Denise C Breton, 'Justice as Healing: Going Outside the Colonizers' Cage' in Norman K Denzin, Yvonna S Lincoln, and Linda Tuhiwai Smith (eds), *Handbook of Critical and Indigenous Methodologies* (Sage Publications, 2008) 511.
56 For a discussion see Chris Andersen and Brendan Hokowhitu, 'Whiteness: Naivety, Void and Control' (2007) 8 *Junctures* 39. In particular: 'as indigenous renaissances are emboldened, as they create momentum, the reaction/resistance to the singular

universalising discourses of the coloniser reflects their anti-pluralism. Counter-hegemonic discourses can, if they are monolithic, become hegemonic in themselves. It seems to me that many indigenous people, often those in vanguard positions, constantly engage with and validate the delimiting and hegemonic notion of "authenticity" to the detriment, I believe, of cultural vitality. It is as if the will to power inherently needs the will to unify. I choose to not construct mauri (life-force) in this way' (at 43).

57 Brendan Hokowhitu, 'Producing Elite Indigenous Masculinities' (2012) 2(2) *Settler Colonial Studies* 23, 44, 45.

58 Ibid., 42.

59 Ibid., 44. Hokowhitu contrasts this with Bruyneel's understanding of Indigenous cultural formations as resistance in Kevin Bruyneel, *The Third Space of Sovereignty* (University of Minnesota Press, 2007): see especially xvii.

60 Hokowhitu (n 57) 45.

61 Kent McNeil, 'Indigenous Land Rights and Self-Government: Inseparable Entitlements' in Lisa Ford and Tim Rowse (eds), *Between Indigenous and Settler Governance* (Routledge, 2012) 135.

3

COOPER v STUART (1889) 14 App Cas 286

Constitutional Foundations: The Persistent Myth of *Cooper v Stuart*

Eddie Synot and Roshan de Silva-Wijeyeratne

Why review *Cooper v Stuart*?

We have chosen to review the Privy Council opinion of *Cooper v Stuart*[1] because of the case's continuing influence on Australia's constitutional framework. *Cooper v Stuart* remains important, despite having been overturned by *Mabo v Queensland (No 2)* ('*Mabo (No 2)*'),[2] because of the Privy Council's justification for the application of English common law to the colony of New South Wales.[3] The Privy Council's explanation, which rested on NSW being a 'tract of territory practically unoccupied, without settled inhabitants or settled law', stood as the legal authority for Australian nationhood for over a century.[4] This became known as the 'enlarged notion of terra nullius', a process that Brennan J explained in *Mabo (No 2)* as resulting in the 'parcel by parcel' dispossession of First Nations which 'underwrote the development of the nation'.[5] This explanation also helped prefigure the circumstances in which the Australian state, including the *Australian Constitution*, developed without legitimate consideration for the rights of First Nations.[6]

Many have addressed the extent to which terra nullius was inappropriately applied to Australia.[7] Rather than revisit this, we are interested in the case's social history and why the political expediencies of colonial society, as read through *Cooper v Stuart*, have helped create a narrow constitutional system incapable of adequately addressing First Nations' claims. This inability necessitates an alternative approach to solutions from within the law: the need to find political solutions outside of the strictly juridical. This means rather than rewrite *Cooper v Stuart*, we have provided a commentary on the social history of the case and its impact on Australian constitutionalism. We then end this commentary by discussing a Makarrata Commission as proposed by the Uluru Statement from the Heart.[8] The Makarrata Commission is imagined as a constitutional reform that would address the founding silence of Australian constitutionalism, as read through *Cooper v Stuart*, that has denied First Nations. The Makarrata Commission would provide the transformative solutions required to move Indigenous and non-Indigenous relations beyond the narrow offerings of Australia's juridical system.

We take our cue from Brennan J's observation that it was the performative logic of sovereign power that systematically dispossessed First Nations as colonial settlement expanded. As Andrew Fitzmaurice observed in the aftermath of *Mabo (No 2)*, the dispossession of First Nations, according to critics of juridical accounts, 'occurred through myriad different processes and events in everyday life and not through a body of legal and philosophical writings and court judgements completely removed from the colonial frontier'.[9] We don't add to a historiography of dispossession that reduces 'dispossession' to a singular legal event that abstracts the 'eventness' of dispossession from its social anchoring. Rather, we situate *Cooper v Stuart* in its social context as an example of that 'parcel by parcel' dispossession, while looking to solutions that embrace the 'myriad different processes and events' that informed the case and extend beyond the courtroom.

The facts of *Cooper v Stuart*

Cooper v Stuart forms part of the ad hoc application of imperial constitutional law to retrospectively justify British jurisdiction over colonial possessions. On appeal from the Supreme Court of New South Wales ('NSWSC'), the Privy Council had to determine the validity of NSW re-claiming ten acres of land, the power for which was contained within an original 1823 grant by the governor, Sir Thomas Brisbane.[10] The grant for 1,400 acres was made to William Hutchinson within the Sydney region, an area that now encompasses Waterloo and Alexandria. Hutchinson was an early business partner of the Coopers and the grant in question passed to the Coopers and became part of their estate by the 1880s.

The 1823 grant contained a 'reservation' allowing NSW to claw back ten acres for public purposes. It was this power, gazetted by Governor Augustus Loftus on 14 November 1882[11] for a public park in the industrial areas of Waterloo and Alexandria, that the Coopers challenged.[12] The Coopers claimed the reservation in 1882 was void on the grounds of repugnancy and that it was in violation of the rule against perpetuities. Both arguments were rejected by the NSWSC. The Privy Council upheld the decision of the NSWSC holding that the rule against perpetuities did not apply to the Crown as it did to private individuals.[13]

Creating an empty land

The Privy Council's finding required assessing the extent to which English law applied to NSW, including when and how it had entered NSW. When doing so, Lord Watson (for the Council) explained:

> There is a great difference between the case of a Colony acquired by conquest or cession, in which there is an established system of law, and that of a Colony which consisted of a tract of territory practically unoccupied, without settled inhabitants or settled law, at the time when it was peacefully annexed to the British dominions. The Colony of New South Wales belongs to the latter class.[14]

Lord Watson's statement, at the highest level of judicial authority, was effectively that NSW had been terra nullius or, in the language of the common law, acquired by 'peaceful settlement'. While notable advocates for First Nations' rights existed at the time of the judgment, the Privy Council's failure to regard First Nations as existing cemented, at least formally, Australian legal foundations as being derived from the British having *occupied* and *settled* an otherwise empty land.[15] Lord Watson's assertions were not so straightforward, however. Lord Watson's determination was based on his *own* interpretation of Sir William Blackstone's *Commentaries* regarding the applicability of English law to newly acquired territories.[16] The problem for many is that Lord Watson took liberties with the definitions of 'practically unoccupied' and 'settled', resulting in an expansion of the applicability of occupation and settlement to lands legitimately occupied and possessed by peoples that colonial authorities otherwise characterised as being incapable of occupation and possession.[17] These events remain important to the constitutional framework of Australia because had the rights of First Nations been recognised, and had NSW been considered to have been acquired by *conquest* or *cession* rather than having been *settled*, the British, according to imperial law and practice, *technically* should have recognised and enforced First Nations' rights.[18]

The impact on Australian jurisprudence

Cooper v Stuart reflected dominant Victorian attitudes towards First Nations.[19] But these attitudes, based as they were in the reality of a colonial society that had progressed without legitimate recognition of First Nations, were not representative of prevailing international law principles and practices at the time—or now—of acquiring new territories that, if applied differently, should have meant the protection and enforcement of First Nations' rights to their lands.[20] It was not until 1992, just over 100 years following *Cooper v Stuart*, and another one hundred following the landing of the First Fleet on Eora Country at Sydney Cove in 1788, that terra nullius was overturned. Yet this overturning was not as complete as claimed, resulting in what Daniel Lavery has described as the 'troubling doctrinal paradox' at the core of Australian legal foundations.[21]

The doctrinal paradox results from the fact that while *Mabo (No 2)* overturned assumptions that didn't recognise First Nations' beneficial property interests in common law, Brennan J's leading judgment otherwise maintained the 'enlarged notion of terra nullius' as justification for the Crown's 'radical title' over the Australian continent by maintaining the settlement justification for British acquisition. For Lavery, not only was Brennan J's interpretation of the authorities he relied on incorrect,[22] but his Honour's characterisation of 'an enlarged notion of terra nullius' to explain the British Crown's settlement (not conquest) of the Australian continent had the result of continuing to characterise First Nations as 'backward peoples'. Furthermore, Brennan J's reasoning compounded the different development of Australian jurisprudence to all other imperial constitutional law applications relating to the acquisition of new territories and the pre-existing rights of Indigenous peoples.[23]

The result of this further expansion and application of terra nullius in *Mabo (No 2)*, following that which had already occurred in *Cooper v Stuart*, continues to deny First Nations in Australia. It limits the ability of the law to adequately address First Nations' claims by denying those claims beyond limited rights to common law native title and by refusing to hear questions of the sovereign foundation of the Australian state. Lavery explains:

> while an enlarged notion of terra nullius was condemned from the property law perspective in Mabo [No 2], paradoxically the territorial sovereignty of the modern Australian nation-state rests on this selfsame enlarged notion of terra nullius—one which treats its Indigenous peoples as 'backward'.[24]

By doing so, *Mabo (No 2)* has maintained the 'enlarged notion of terra nullius' as the authorising ground of the Australian nation. Questions of this renewed foundation and its implications for First Nations' claims, a foundation which is the result of a British 'act of state' that claimed NSW, were, as matters of international law, deemed beyond the jurisdiction of 'municipal courts' by *Mabo (No 2)*.[25] By denying competence to hear First Nations' questions of that foundation, and refusing recognition beyond common law native title so as not to 'fracture the skeleton of principle which gives the body of our law its shape and internal consistency',[26] the High Court, despite claiming to cleanse the common law, left terra nullius (as an incident of international law) in place—the latter only within the jurisdiction of Parliament to alter. As Merete Borch explains, following her detailed review of terra nullius and its impact on Australian law, this has become 'a problem which can only be addressed by a mobilisation of the political will to negotiate'.[27]

While *Mabo (No 2)* pierced the myth of a continent existing 'practically unoccupied, without settled inhabitants or settled law', the High Court only went so far, offering (retrospectively) in its place a vulnerable native title susceptible to extinguishment by the Crown, difficult to prove, and largely without remedy for loss.[28] In Peter Fitzpatrick's summary of Brennan J's contradictions, echoing Lavery's explanation of the doctrinal paradox, the High Court concluded that the:

> rights and privileges conferred by native title were unaffected by the Crown's acquisition of radical title, but the acquisition of sovereignty exposed native title to extinguishment by a valid exercise of sovereign power inconsistent with the continued right to enjoy native title.[29]

Ultimately, the High Court protected its own sovereign authority at the expense of First Nations under the disguise of recognition. Indeed, the High Court evaded the question of sovereignty in terms that echoed Hans Kelsen's observations on the origins of law—if one looks too hard, one may find nothing there because the foundation is always extra-legal.[30] Effectively, concerns as to whether the High Court *is* or *isn't* competent to hear claims regarding the sovereign foundation of the Australian state become obsolete when we understand that the origin or foundation of the law is always *political* and is continuously renewed by decisions such as *Mabo (No 2)*, and as such, requires a political act in response to achieve its reform. It is only when these political acts are re-imagined and legitimated as objectively legal and detached from the context in which they are born, which may very well be their place in a legal order when considering the *Australian Constitution* does provide a political mechanism for its own amendment,[31] that the problem of the law's existence *as it is* in the face of an assertion of *what it should be* can be dismissed as something extra-legal. This is especially the case with regard to law's own founding authority, as the majority in *Mabo (No 2)* effectively did by passing the contentious issue of sovereignty back to the legislature.[32] Of course, the problem for First Nations throughout Australian history is that both the political and legal institutions of Australian society have been problematic, at best, avenues of reform.

The society of *Cooper v Stuart*

The 1880s were a period of continuing reform in NSW.[33] In particular, domestic and imperial federation were among the many causes in which Sir Daniel Cooper of *Cooper v Stuart* was active.[34] This period was also crucial for the working classes of Waterloo and Alexandria. Animosity toward absentee landowners, including the Coopers, grew due to a perceived lack of contribution to the welfare of the colony while they drew large incomes from estates amassed from free land grants.[35] This was a challenging period for First Nations also. Victorian protection legislation was introduced in 1869 that also affected NSW, especially the border regions.[36] Frontier conflict, continuing in other regions of Australia, had largely ceased in NSW by this time. However, First Nations in NSW were increasingly affected by successive administrative actions aimed at 'neglected children'—the first NSW 'Protection Act' having been implemented in 1909.[37] This Act was the culmination of changes that had formally begun in 1883 (but stretching back decades) when Colonial Secretary and Premier Alexander Stuart, the nominal respondent in *Cooper v Stuart*, established the NSW Board for the Protection of Aborigines ('the Protection Board').[38] The Protection Board was established to assist with managing the Maloga (later Cummeragunja), Warangesda, and La Perouse communities. Reports from the private Association for the Protection of Aborigines, which advocated for the assimilation and protection of First Nations, also informed Stuart's decision to establish the Aborigines Protection Board in 1883.[39]

Much of the 'parcel by parcel' dispossession that Brennan J noted in *Mabo (No 2)* was completed in NSW by this time. Rather, the focus of this period was on 'protection' aimed at facilitating the expected dying out and 'ultimate absorption' of First Nations.[40] But the social history of this period also demonstrates that knowledge of First Nations was more widespread in NSW than would appear when reading Lord Watson's account. The problem, however, was the form of this knowledge, expressed as it was by characterising First Nations as absent, or as belonging to the past. It did not matter that First Nations existed as they did; their existence, and their future, as Stuart claimed when establishing the Protection Board, required a 'more systematic and enlightened treatment' but only so that the 'blessing of civilization' could be bestowed on a remnant people whose time had passed.[41]

From convicts to wool barons

The Cooper story is also a product of its time. Made wealthy by their landholdings and interests that expanded from flour-milling and merchandising to banking, the Coopers became part of the colonial elite within two generations of the first Cooper being transported to NSW in the 1810s.[42] Represented in NSW by his son William, Sir Daniel Cooper spent most of the latter half of the 19th century in England. Illustrative of the Coopers' vast yet waning influence in the face of a changing colonial society, Cooper was the first speaker of the New South Wales Legislative Assembly ('NSWLA') in 1856 and a contemporary of Sir Charles Cowper and Sir Henry Parkes, acting also in various public positions of esteem including as Agent General for NSW.[43] Sir Daniel Cooper's uncle—also named Daniel—was a business partner of William Hutchinson, the recipient of the 1823 grant.[44] Both Hutchinson and the earlier Cooper had been transported to NSW as convicts.[45] As emancipists, both earned favour with successive governors, amassing large land grants and occupying various positions of authority. The 1823 grant in question, made at the beginning of an expansive period of colonial expansion and land development between the 1820s and 1850s,[46] passed to the Coopers as a result of their business dealings with Hutchinson, becoming part of their larger estate which included Captain John Piper's land at Rose Bay.[47] It was at Rose Bay, on Gadigal and Birrabirragal Country of the Dharug nation, that the latter Cooper built the Point Piper mansion 'Woollahra House' in 1856.[48] During this period Cooper was knighted in 1857, made Baronet of Woollahra in 1863, Knight Commander of St Michael and St George in 1880, and member of the Knight Grand Cross of the Order of St Michael and St George in 1888.[49]

The Coopers' social position, although waning, provided an obvious advantage to their claims. Illustrative of this was an article published by the *Freeman's Journal* on 22 August 1885 titled 'The Coopers Again'.[50] The *Freeman's Journal* characterised the Coopers' objection to the resumption of ten acres as 'an example of what a school-boy would term "cool cheek"...the old, old case of the Cooper family standing in the way of public interest'.[51] Debate similar to this sentiment was recorded regularly in the NSWLA. The differing positions of those against and in support of the Coopers seemingly reflected struggles to find a regulatory and social response to a changing society where expansive estates held by individual families were becoming obsolete. These estates became enmeshed in complex issues due to having been leased and sub-leased on multiple terms to multiple agents, causing a bureaucratic mess of conflicting rights and interests, somewhat akin to the uncertainty of title generated by the preponderance of old system land in the colony of South Australia.[52]

One of the strongest criticisms of the Coopers was that they had 'become possessed of their vast wealth, not by hard work as ordinary mortals do, but by lavishly generous Crown grants'.[53] That the Coopers also benefited from public works on land they had received for free further infuriated detractors. James McGowen, representing Redfern from 1891–1917 and Premier of NSW from 1910–1913, persistently voiced this criticism.[54] The *Freeman's Journal* echoed McGowen, claiming that 'unearned increment [had] swelled [the Coopers'] wealth' as a result of public works completed as the city spread, enabling the Coopers to profit from further subdividing and leasing their land.[55] McGowen emphasised also how there existed no remedy against the government or the Coopers for leaseholders locked in iniquitous agreements, a situation made worse due to the Coopers' indifference to '[a]ll that [had] gone to improve the value of this leasehold property', improvements paid for by a public purse 'wrung in the shape of taxation from these poor people'.[56]

The Coopers had defenders too. Arthur Bruce Smith, representing Gundagai from 1882–1884, Glebe from 1889–1894, and inaugural member for Parkes in the Australian Parliament, was an ardent advocate of the Coopers. Bruce Smith claimed the Coopers' wealth was the result of prudent judgment, not free land grants. Bruce Smith asked:

> If we are going to tax those who foresaw what was coming on the results of their judgment, what are we going to do with regard to those whose enterprise was equally patriotic, but who had not the same good fortune?[57]

Bruce Smith's stance reflected his political ideology that favoured a limited state while rewarding individuals for hard work, as detailed in his 1887 book *Liberty and Liberalism*, a defence of Adam Smith's economic and philosophical principles as applied to NSW.[58] Furthering his defence, Bruce Smith claimed the Coopers' land was only that which '[a]ny one could buy' and that the Coopers should not be penalised because they had 'the judgement to foresee the future of that particular part of the surroundings of Sydney'.[59] Seemingly, Bruce Smith was unaware, or perhaps wilfully unaware, of the patronage that had allowed people, including the Coopers and others of 'good judgement', to realise their fortunes.

The *Freeman's Journal* tied these criticisms, in the face of defences such as those from Bruce Smith, and the broader social milieu together, making final reference to the Coopers' power and influence. 'Hitherto, owing to their wealth and power', claimed the *Freeman's Journal*, 'they have managed to get compensations for invasions of supposed rights...no other individual in the community could have got'[60]—recognitions and compensations to which First Nations have never been entitled either. On the origin of their wealth, however, the historical record is clear on at least some of the Coopers' holdings, including the 1823 grant. The State Library of New South Wales ('NSWSL') holds records of many of these, including two grants dated 22 March 1836 for 1,130 acres to Daniel Cooper and Solomon Levey and another dated 4 June 1845 for 200 acres to Daniel Cooper. Both grants honoured promises made by former governors despite the practice of free land grants having ceased in 1831, and both passed to Sir Daniel Cooper from his uncle Daniel.[61]

Grants such as these were instruments of that 'parcel by parcel' dispossession described by Brennan J.[62] Authorised by the Crown's assumption of authority over First Nations' territory, these practices were justified by characterising First Nations as 'backward peoples' without rights. Something of a paradox underpins this justification in that the meta-legal grounds of authorisation for dispossession are silent until retrospectively (re)discovered in *Cooper v Stuart*. The case makes clear that colonial authorities did not promulgate any legal doctrine to legitimise dispossession as a matter of either international or domestic common law. However, doctrinal denial of First Nations' rights would not have appeared necessary to the colonists, because, as addressed, First Nations were characterised by the colonists as intrinsically barbarous, without any interest in land.

Friends of the governor

Governor Lachlan Macquarie is key to this overarching narrative of colonial progress authorised by dispossession. Governor from 1810 to 1821, Macquarie's transformation of NSW from a penal colony to a flourishing commercial society through land grants, commerce, and settlements provided the opportunity and reward that led to the kind of wealth that families such as the Coopers amassed.[63] This earlier period presented violent challenges for First Nations as part of the continuing frontier conflicts of NSW, challenges unlike those faced in NSW during the 1880s.[64] Similar tensions existed across the 70 years that connected both Macquarie and Stuart towards First Nations. Macquarie's

Native Institution was set up in 1814 and was informed by similar attitudes to Stuart's establishment of the Protection Board in 1883.[65] Both institutions aimed at the elevation of First Nations into civilisation; both targeted First Nations' children to do so. While Stuart's practices were not as viscerally violent as Macquarie's, they were nonetheless informed by similar beliefs in the fundamental inferiority of First Nations, a core doctrine of the development of Australian nationhood that informed any consideration or dismissal of First Nations.

Macquarie's administration was notorious for its bureaucratic and militaristic nature, but this character was also key to its success following the turmoil of Governor Bligh's administration and the Rum Rebellion.[66] Macquarie's governance was balanced, however, through an administration that cultivated a close network of emancipists that included Hutchinson and the earlier Cooper.[67] Although this network was not entirely celebrated, free settlers and colonial authorities such as the Colonial Secretary, Earl Bathurst, had long been pursuing an inquiry into the penal colonies, citing dismay at Macquarie's administration and cultivation of emancipists.[68] Bathurst was concerned, among other things, with Macquarie's arbitrary rule over free settlers beyond the authority of his commission. Perhaps most crucially, however, Bathurst feared Macquarie's administration was undermining transportation as a deterrent and was contrary to the founding intention of 'settlements in New Holland' as 'Receptacles for Offenders'.[69] According to Bathurst, Macquarie's duty was foremost to 'a system of just discipline, as may render Transportation an Object of serious Apprehension'.[70]

Hutchinson, the original grant holder of the 1823 grant, was a key beneficiary of the types of practices that Bathurst was targeting. Hutchinson, after previously being transported for stealing, came to occupy key positions within Macquarie's administration including Principal Superintendent of Convicts and Public Works.[71] These positions enabled Hutchinson and others to accumulate considerable wealth and influence in NSW, especially through control over the allocation of convict labour.[72] After years of agitation, however, Macquarie's administration eventually came under review when Bathurst got his wish of a commission of inquiry, appointing John Bigge to inquire into the administration of NSW in 1819.[73] James Dennis, former military man and amateur historian whose writing in 1937 was illustrative of a national effort to produce a proud history of Australian nationhood, was scathing of Bathurst's criticisms and the report's reception in London.[74] Writing of Macquarie as a hero for contemporary Australia, Dennis claimed the accusations against Macquarie were embellished, and that Macquarie was not the autocrat he had been made out to be. Rather, Macquarie was a heroic humanitarian who cared about 'the people' and had attempted to challenge old-world interests that Bathurst represented.[75] For Dennis, Macquarie demonstrated 'humanity' and concern for land as the 'heritage of future generations', ensuring no single class would be able to lock up the land as had happened under the Enclosure Acts in Britain.[76]

What is clear for our purposes, however, is that Macquarie's concern for the 'heritage of the people' is a contradiction in terms when considering the fact of First Nations' dispossession. Macquarie persistently made large land grants to his network, as did his successor Thomas Brisbane. Concern with such patronage contributed to Viscount Goderich's instructions to cease free grants of land in 1831.[77] Some of Hutchinson's own grants were received in this manner from Brisbane following Macquarie having advocated for them in a letter to Brisbane, a letter that included the encouragement of the continued patronage of emancipists such as Hutchinson.[78] For the social history of *Cooper v Stuart*, this clamour for land represents the instrumentalisation of claims about the non-existence of First Nations and their resulting dispossession made by the likes of Macquarie, Lord Watson, and Stuart. Far from being detached from the fate of a dying race, these daily acts of dispossession made up the 'parcel by parcel' dispossession of First Nations which 'underwrote the development of the nation'.

Reviewing *Cooper v Stuart*

First Nations are still affected by the retrospective justification of their dispossession as terra nullius. This is perhaps nowhere more evident than it is in the 'skeletal' structure Brennan J placed in the path of further recognition, a limit most recently affirmed by the High Court in *Love v Commonwealth*.[79] This leaves a question as to how to review *Cooper v Stuart*. We gave consideration to rewriting the case according to international law at the time of the 1823 grant, the 1889 decision, and as it stands now, as has been argued by many commentators.[80] We believe this is problematic, however, because among other reasons, Indigenous peoples in other British colonies were violently dispossessed despite acknowledgment of their rights through instruments such as treaties.[81] It stands to reason, however, that even an alternative application of the law, or the existence of original agreements, cannot account for what escapes and authorises the law, and arguably may not have produced a situation any different to that currently faced by First Nations.

Our approach has been to step outside of these limitations by imagining a Makarrata Commission that would supervise agreement-making and truth-telling between Indigenous and non-Indigenous Australians. Much has happened since the Uluru Statement from the Heart was issued to the Australian people in 2017. Neither these events nor the specific reform of a First Nations Voice is the focus of this commentary, however. Rather, our review of *Cooper v Stuart* imagines the development of the Makarrata Commission following a successful referendum to implement a First Nations Voice.[82] We imagine a program called the Research Partnership as a process of truth-telling as part of the Makarrata Commission. The Research Partnership would provide the resources required to enable a successful and self-determined process of agreement-making and truth-telling to revisit both the political and legal foundations of the Australian state that rest at the core of disputes between Indigenous and non-Indigenous

Australians. The required legislative reforms to achieve this re-founding have also been envisaged; they include the following:

- The First Nations Voice, Chapter 9, s 129 of the *Australian Constitution* (amendment to the *Australian Constitution* to provide for the First Nations Voice);[83]
- *Constitution Alteration (First Nations Voice) Act 2021* (Cth) (enabling legislation for referendum to change the *Australian Constitution*);
- *Makarrata Commission Act 2022* (Cth) (enabling legislation);
- *First Nations Voice Act 2022* (Cth) (enabling legislation for First Nations Voice as a statutory and self-determining representative body);
- *Makarrata Commission and Associated Programs Regulation 2022* (Cth) (regulations to enable the Makarrata Commission); and
- Council of Australian Governments ('COAG') *Makarrata Commission Agreement 2022* (Cth) (agreements to ensure cooperation on agreement-making and truth-telling).

Notes

1 *Cooper v Stuart* (1889) 14 App Cas 286.
2 *Mabo v Queensland (No 2)* (1992) 175 CLR 1 ('*Mabo (No 2)*').
3 *Cooper v Stuart* (1889) 14 App Cas 286.
4 Ibid., 5.
5 *Mabo (No 2)* (1992) 175 CLR 1, 69.
6 *Australian Constitution Act 1900* (Imp) 63 & 64 Vict, c 12, s 9 ('*Australian Constitution*').
7 See e.g. Nii Lante Wallace-Bruce, 'Two Hundred Years On: A Reexamination of the Acquisition of Australia' (1989) 19 *Georgia Journal of International & Comparative Law* 87; Gerry Simpson, '*Mabo*, International Law, *Terra Nullius* and the Stories of Settlement: An Unresolved Jurisprudence' (1993) 19 *Melbourne University Law Review* 195; David Ritter, 'The "Rejection of *Terra Nullius*" in Mabo: A Critical Analysis' (1996) 18(1) *Sydney Law Review* 5; Samantha Hepburn, 'Disinterested Truth: Legitimation of the Doctrine of Tenure Post-*Mabo*' (2005) 29 *Melbourne University Law Review* 1, 5; Andrew Fitzmaurice, 'The Genealogy of Terra Nullius' (2007) 38(129) *Australian Historical Studies* 1.
8 'Makarrata' is a Yolngu word describing a constitutional process that translates to a 'coming together after struggle'. The Uluru Statement from the Heart called for a First Nations Voice enshrined in the Australian Constitution and a Makarrata Commission to supervise agreement-making and truth-telling. Commonwealth of Australia, *Final Report of the Referendum Council* (Referendum Council Report, 2017).
9 Fitzmaurice (n 7) 1.
10 *Cooper v Stuart* (1886) 7 LR (NSW) Eq 1.
11 New South Wales, *Government Gazette,* No 452, 14 November 1882, 5893.
12 The park remains today as Alexandria Park, Sydney, NSW.
13 *Cooper v Stuart* (1889) 14 App Cas 286.
14 Ibid., 5.
15 For supportive views of First Nations during this era see Saliha Belmessous, 'The Tradition of Treaty Making in Australian History' in Saliha Belmessous (ed), *Empire by Treaty* (Oxford University Press, 2015) 186, 195–202.
16 See e.g. William Blackstone, *Commentaries on the Laws of England*, Wilfrid Prest (ed) (Oxford University Press, 2016) 68–82.
17 See e.g. Thalia Anthony, 'Blackstone on Colonialism: Australian Judicial Interpretations' in Wilfrid Prest (ed), *Blackstone and His Commentaries: Biography, Law,*

History (Hart, 2009) 129; Daniel Lavery, '"Not Purely of Law"—The Doctrine of Backward Peoples in *Milirrpum*' (2017) 23 *James Cook Law Review* 53, 71.

18 See Wallace-Bruce (n 7) and Lavery (n 17) for a comprehensive review of these points.

19 The reach of these attitudes is evident in the *Report from the Select Committee on Aborigines (British Settlements)* (House of Commons Paper No 425, Session 1837), 125–6. The Select Committee claimed the 'aborigines of New Holland' were of 'the most degraded of the human race' and that the 'territorial rights of the natives were not considered' because the 'barbarous state of these people' meant they were 'so entirely destitute...of the rudest forms of civil polity, that their claims, whether as sovereigns or proprietors of the soil, have been utterly disregarded'. Note also those that advocated for First Nations irrespective of these attitudes detailed in Belmessous (n 15).

20 Wallace-Bruce (n 7); Hepburn (n 7). See Belmessous (n 15) for a detailed account of debate in the colonies of South Australia and Western Australia as to whether it was individual land holders or colonial authorities that were responsible for compensating First Nations and how these arguments lost out to the 'expediency' of imperial life. The excuse that too much had progressed to rectify the position of First Nations is echoed throughout Australian history, especially in juridical responses to the position of land tenure. See e.g. *Mabo (No 2)* (1992) 175 CLR 1.

21 Daniel Lavery, 'No Decorous Veil: The Continuing Reliance on an Enlarged Terra Nullius Notion in *Mabo [No 2]*' (2019) 43(1) *Melbourne University Law Review* 233, 247–58.

22 Ibid., 242–7.

23 Ibid., 252–8.

24 Ibid., 237.

25 *Mabo (No 2)* (1992) 175 CLR 1, 32; Lavery (n 21) 238.

26 *Mabo (No 2)* (1992) 175 CLR 1, 29. See also Penny Pether, 'Principles or Skeletons? *Mabo* and the Discursive Constitution of the Australian Nation' (1998) 4(1) *Law Text Culture* 115.

27 Merete Borch, 'Rethinking the Origins of *Terra Nullius*' (2001) 32 (117) *Australian Historical Studies* 222, 239.

28 See e.g. *Members of the Yorta Yorta Aboriginal Community v Victoria* (2002) 214 CLR 422; see also Alexander Reilly, 'How *Mabo* Helps Us Forget' (2006) 6 *Macquarie Law Journal* 25, 26.

29 Peter Fitzpatrick, '"No Higher Duty": *Mabo* and the Failure of Legal Foundation' (2002) 13 *Law and Critique* 233, 234–5.

30 See e.g. Hans Kelsen, *Pure Theory of Law*, ed Max Knight (The Lawbook Exchange, 2005) 218. Kelsen specifically separates out the 'ethical-political' functions of laws from the question of the foundation of a validly positive law.

31 *Australian Constitution* s 128.

32 *Mabo (No 2)* (1992) 175 CLR 1, 48.

33 See e.g. Stuart Macintyre and Sean Sclamer, 'Colonial States and Civil Society, 1860–90' in Stuart Macintyre and Alison Bashford (eds), *The Cambridge History of Australia: Volume I, Indigenous and Colonial Australia* (Cambridge University Press, 2013) 189.

34 Daniel Cooper, *Federal British Empire the Best Defence of the Mother Country and Her Colonies* (William Ridgeway, 1880); State Library of NSW, Mitchell Library, 042/P208, 2243626.

35 New South Wales, *Parliamentary Debates*, Legislative Assembly, 18 December 1879, 717–8 (John McElhone, MLA); New South Wales, *Parliamentary Debates,* Legislative Assembly, 5 May 1886, 1719 (Joseph Creer, MLA); New South Wales, *Parliamentary Debates*, Legislative Assembly, 11 November 1902, 4327 (Arthur Griffith, MLA).

36 *Aborigines Protection Act 1869* (Vic).

37 *The Aborigines Protection Act 1909* (NSW) became the statutory enactment of the New South Wales Board for the Protection of Aborigines, previously set up in 1883.

38 New South Wales Legislative Assembly, *Protection of the Aborigines* (Minute of Colonial Secretary, Minute No. M18452/2, 26 February 1883).

39 Ibid., 4–17.
40 See e.g. John Chesterman and Heather Douglas, '"Their Ultimate Absorption": Assimilation in 1930s Australia' (2004) 81 *Journal of Australian Studies* 47; Lauren Benton, Adam Clulow and Bain Attwood (eds), *Protection and Empire: A Global History* (Cambridge University Press, 2018).
41 New South Wales Legislative Assembly, *Protection of the Aborigines* (n 38) 2.
42 'Sir Daniel Cooper', *Australian Town and Country Journal* (Sydney, 28 January 1888) 34; 'Daniel Cooper', *Sydney Mail and New South Wales Advertiser* (Sydney, 16 May 1906); AW Martin, 'Sir Daniel Cooper, 1821–1902' *Australian Dictionary of Biography*, Volume 3 (Melbourne University Press, 1969).
43 AW Martin (n 42).
44 Their business 'Hutchinson, Terry & Co', also known as the 'Waterloo Co', was used by the Coopers to expand their land holdings: JW Davidson, 'Daniel Cooper 1785–1853', *Australian Dictionary of Biography,* Volume 1 (Melbourne University Press, 1966).
45 Ibid.; Paul Edwin Le Roy, 'William Hutchinson 1772–1846', *Australian Dictionary of Biography*, Volume 1 (Melbourne University Press, 1966).
46 See e.g. Lisa Ford and David Andrew Roberts, 'Expansion, 1820–1850' in Stuart Macintyre and Alison Bashford (eds), *The Cambridge History of Australia: Volume I, Indigenous and Colonial Australia* (Cambridge University Press, 2013) 121.
47 State Library of NSW, Mitchell Library, 'Sir Daniel Cooper 1857–1902' MLMSS 1847 1(1). The conveyance of the property in 1825 from Hutchinson to Daniel Cooper and Solomon Levey is listed as received on trust by Sir Daniel Cooper from the earlier Cooper in 1852: William Cooper, 'Received the Undermentioned Deeds and Papers…' (13 July 1876), State Library of NSW, Mitchell Library, 'Papers Relating to Properties and Business Activities Connected to Daniel Cooper, Solomon Levey, Sir Daniel Cooper and Others, 1813–1948', MLMSS 10350, 2(8).
48 The former gatehouse of Woollahra House is now the Rose Bay police station. 'Woollahra House—Laying the Foundation Stone', *Empire* (Sydney, 15 December 1856) 4; State Library of NSW, Mitchell Library, 'The Monthly Record of Eminent Men: Sir Daniel Cooper, Bart., G.C.M.G., George Potter, 1890' A923.29/C.
49 State Library of NSW (n 48) item 8, item 11 and item 13.
50 'The Cooper's Again', *Freeman's Journal* (Sydney, 22 August 1885) 12.
51 Ibid.
52 New South Wales, *Parliamentary Debates*, Legislative Assembly, 3 December 1902, 5051–6.
53 'The Cooper's Again' (n 50).
54 New South Wales, *Parliamentary Debates*, Legislative Assembly, 5 September 1895, 533 (James McGowen, MLA).
55 'The Cooper's Again' (n 50).
56 New South Wales, *Parliamentary Debates*, Legislative Assembly, 5 September 1895, 5056 (James McGowen, MLA).
57 New South Wales, *Parliamentary Debates*, Legislative Assembly, 20 May 1890, 525 (Arthur Bruce Smith, MLA).
58 Arthur Bruce Smith, *Liberty and Liberalism* (Centre for Independent Studies, 2005).
59 Ibid.
60 'The Cooper's Again' (n 50).
61 State Library of NSW, Mitchell Library, 'Papers Relating to Properties and Business Activities Connected to Daniel Cooper, Solomon Levey, Sir Daniel Cooper and Others, 1813–1948', MLMSS 10350, 1(8), Series 01, Ref 9632345. Free land grants ended following instructions from Viscount Goderich dated 9 January 1831: *Historical Records of Australia* (Series I, Volume XVI) 19.
62 *Mabo (No 2)* (1992) 175 CLR 1, 69.
63 See e.g. Mary Casey, 'Remaking Britain: Establishing British Identity and Power at Sydney Cove, 1788–1821' (2006) 24 *Australasian Historical Archaeology* 87; Ian Stuart, 'Macquarie and the Towns' (2019) 105(1) *JRAHS* 26.

64 See e.g. Lisa Ford, *Settler Sovereignty: Jurisdiction and Indigenous People in Australia, 1788–1836* (Harvard University Press, 2010) 74; Stephen Gapps, *The Sydney Wars* (NewSouth, 2018).
65 See e.g. Kay Anderson and Colin Perrin, 'Beyond Savagery: The Limits of Australian "Aboriginalism"' (2008) 14(2) *Cultural Studies Review* 147, 157–8; Rachel Standfield, 'The Parramatta Maori Seminary and the Education of Indigenous Peoples in Early Colonial New South Wales' (2012) 41(2) *History of Education Review* 119.
66 See e.g. Alan Atkinson, 'The Little Revolution in New South Wales, 1808' (1990) XII(I) *The International History Review* 65; John Ritchie, 'Macquarie's Style of Governing' (1990) 3(1) *Bulletin of the Centre for Tasmanian Historical Studies* 52.
67 See e.g. Marion Phillips, *A Colonial Autocracy: New South Wales under Governor Macquarie, 1810–1821* (PS King & Son, 1909); JM Bennett, 'The Day of Retribution—Commissioner Bigge's Inquiries in Colonial New South Wales' (1971) 15(2) *The American Journal of Legal History* 85.
68 Bennett (n 67) 88.
69 House of Commons, *Report of the Commissioner of Inquiry into the State of the Colony of New South Wales* (19 June 1822); *Historical Records of Australia*, (Series I, Volume X) 2, 'Enclosure No 2, Earl Bathurst to Mr Commissioner Bigge' 4.
70 *Historical Records of Australia* (n 69) 4–5.
71 Paul Edwin Le Roy (n 45); 'To the Editor of the Australian', *Australian* (Sydney, 21 July 1825). One of the many records detailing Macquarie and Hutchinson's relationship is a letter dated 1 June 1820 promising land to Hutchinson—such promises were relied upon to claim land even after the practice of free grants had ceased in 1831. See also State Records of NSW, *Colonial Secretary's Papers, 1788–1856* (Main Series of Letters Received 1788–1826) 359.
72 See e.g. David Andrew Roberts, '"The Valley of Swells" "Special" or "Educated" Convicts on the Wellington Valley Settlement' (2006) 3(1) *History Australia* 11.1; Leanne Johns and Pierre van der Eng, 'Networks and Business Development: Convict Businesspeople in Australia, 1817–24' (2010) 52(5) *Business History* 812.
73 *Historical Records of Australia* (n 69) 2.
74 James Dennis, 'Bigge versus Macquarie' (1937) 23(6) *Royal Australian Historical Society* 411. For a more contemporary review of Macquarie's governance see Harry Dillon and Peter Butler, *Macquarie: From Colony to Country* (Penguin Random House Australia, 2010).
75 Dennis (n 74) 421–2.
76 Ibid., 431.
77 *Historical Records of Australia* (n 61) 19.
78 State Records of NSW, *Colonial Secretary's Papers, 1788–1856* (Special Bundles 1794–1825) 355.
79 *Love v Commonwealth* [2020] HCA 3. While the High Court was split 4–3 in *Love* as to whether an Aboriginal person could be considered 'alien' for the purposes of s 51(xix) of the *Australian Constitution* ('the aliens power'), all seven of the separately issued judgments were unanimous in their affirming of *Mabo (No 2)* regarding the question of sovereignty.
80 See e.g. Lavery (n 21).
81 See e.g. Alexandria Harmon (ed), *The Power of Promises: Rethinking Indian Treaties in the Pacific Northwest* (University of Washington Press, 2008); John Borrows and Michael Coyle (eds), *The Right Relationship: Reimagining the Implementation of Historical Treaties* (University of Toronto Press, 2017).
82 *Australian Constitution* ch VIII s 128 requires a 'majority of the States' and 'a majority of the electors voting' to approve any amendment at referendum.
83 This is based on the example proposed by Pat Anderson et al., Submission No 479 to the Joint Select Committee, *Joint Select Committee on Constitutional Recognition Relating to Aboriginal and Torres Strait Islander Peoples* (3 November 2018) 6.

MAKARRATA COMMISSION

'Coming together after struggle'

The Commission to oversee agreement-making and truth-telling between First Nations and Australian governments, institutions, individuals, and other organisations.

RESEARCH PARTNERSHIP

Chapter IV, 'Research Partnership', *Makarrata Commission Act 2022* (Cth)

SERIES	First Nations Sovereignty and Political Governance
TITLE	*What Is the Research Partnership?*
DATE	26 January 2022
REFERENCE	ISPG/1/2022
VERSION	1.0
AUTHORITY	The First Nations Voice, Chapter 9, s 109 of the *Australian Constitution* *Constitution Alteration (First Nations Voice) Act 2021* (Cth) ('*Referendum Act*') *Makarrata Commission Act 2022* (Cth) ('*Makarrata Act*') *First Nations Voice Act 2022* (Cth) ('*Voice Act*') *Makarrata Commission and Associated Programs Regulation 2022* (Cth) ('*Makarrata Regulations*') Council of Australian Governments ('COAG') Makarrata Commission Agreement 2022 (Cth) ('COAG Makarrata Agreement')

1. **THE MAKARRATA COMMISSION**
   The Makarrata Commission ('the Commission') was established by authority of the First Nations Voice (*Australian Constitution* s 109) and the *Makarrata Act* to supervise agreement-making and truth-telling between First Nations and Australian governments, institutions, individuals, and other organisations. The Commission reports to the First Nations Voice.

2. **THE RESEARCH PARTNERSHIP**
   The Research Partnership ('RP') aids the Commission and community partners ('CP') to achieve truthful relationships based on justice and self-determination. The RP's object is to support the Commission's mandated agenda of (1) supervising agreement-making between First Nations, governments, and other relevant parties and (2) truth-telling.

   2.1 **Community partners**

   2.1.1 The RP relationship with CPs is ongoing.

2.1.2 Obligations and responsibilities of the RP and CPs are ongoing according to the objects of the Commission and individual community partnership agreements.

2.2 **Data sovereignty**

2.2.1 The data produced by the RP does not belong to the RP. The data remains the property of the individual, organisation, or CP involved, with custodianship entrusted to the Commission.

2.2.2 The RP has ongoing obligations and responsibilities to the custodianship of data on behalf of CPs who maintain ownership and control over agreed matters relating to that data, including but not limited to its gathering, production, storage, accessibility, and dissemination.

2.3 **Responsibilities and obligations**

2.3.1 The RP has responsibilities and obligations toward gathering, production, storage, accessibility, and dissemination of data that are informed by its guiding principles (Part 3 of the *Makarrata Act*, Schedule 1 of the *Makarrata Regulations*, Item 4 of this brief).

2.3.2 The RP has responsibilities and obligations towards CPs that are informed by its guiding principles as set out in the *Makarrata Act* and individual partnership agreements.

2.3.3 The RP's obligations and responsibilities are set out in the *Makarrata Regulation* (Schedule 2) and are further subject to individual CP agreements entered into.

2.4 **Research coordination**

2.4.1 The RP coordinates research initiatives between CPs and other entities that may be identified from time to time during the unique RP including data and resources under custody of the Commonwealth, State, and Territory authorities, local government, non-governmental organisations, private entities, and others as they become apparent throughout the life of the unique RP.

2.4.2 The Commission has powers under the *Makarrata Act* (Part 2) and its relevant delegated regulations to compel public and private entities to provide data and information in their custody and to cooperate with the research information and data gathering objectives and requests of the RP, CPs, and Commission.

3. **PURPOSE OF INFORMATION AND DATA**

3.1 The RP provides research training and resources in partnership with CPs to gather, produce, store, access, and disseminate research information and data required to enable agreement-making between First Nations, governments, and other relevant parties and for truth-telling.

3.2 **Research information and data availability**

3.2.1 Research data gathered and produced by the RP may include, but is not limited to, historical research, archival research and documents, family and genealogical research, knowledge and capacity building, legal and political information, health research and information, and other research and information gathering, production, storage, and dissemination-related activities relevant to and as directed by the Commission and the RP.

3.3 **Resources and training**

3.3.1 The RP provides resources and training for the development of research capabilities of CPs and to establish durable and accessible forms of information storage and data sovereignty that are community-controlled and owned.

4. **GUIDING PRINCIPLES**

4.1 The RP must ensure all work undertaken is completed according to the standards of justice and self-determination as mandated by the *Voice Act* (Part 1) and the *Makarrata Act* (Part 1), and as negotiated with individual CPs.

4.2 The guiding principles are taken from the Uluru Statement from the Heart as reported in the Final Report of the Referendum Council 2017.

4.3 The Uluru Statement from the Heart is recognised as a foundational constitutional document by the *Referendum Act* (Part 1), the successful referendum in 2021, and both the *Voice Act* (Part 1) and *Makarrata Act* (Part 1).

4.4 The guiding principles of the Uluru Statement from the Heart are:

4.4.1 Does not diminish Aboriginal sovereignty and Torres Strait Islander sovereignty;

4.4.2 Involves substantive, structural reform;

4.4.3 Advances self-determination and the standards established under the *United Nations Declaration on the Rights of Indigenous Peoples*;

4.4.4 Recognises the status and rights of First Nations;

4.4.5 Tells the truth of history;

4.4.6 Does not foreclose on future advancement;

4.4.7 Does not waste the opportunity of reform;

4.4.8 Provides a mechanism for First Nations agreement-making;

4.4.9 Has the support of First Nations; and

4.4.10 Does not interfere with positive legal arrangements.

5. **FIRST NATIONS' SOVEREIGNTY AND POLITICAL GOVERNANCE**

5.1 The First Nations' sovereignty and political governance ('FNSPG') series informs and provides resources and capacity development for First Nations, CPs, and other community partners to understand the history and development of First Nations' sovereignty and political governance.

5.2 The FNSPG series is aimed at providing the research information, data, and capacities specifically required by First Nations to enter into just and self-determining agreements and truth-telling practices. This includes research information and data on why and how First Nations' rights as political and cultural entities were denied, research information and data to establish contemporary First Nations' claims, and capacity and resource development to enable First Nations to be empowered through their own sovereignty and political governance.

4

WALKER v NEW SOUTH WALES [1994] HCA 64

Commentary: *Walker v New South Wales* [1994] HCA 64

Tanya Mitchell and Amanda Porter

> And don't say you as individuals aren't responsible for it; you pay taxes to your police forces, your legislators and your courts do the dirty work for you. So don't say you haven't got a hand in this, you helped pay for this coming down on us.[1]
>
> The truth is that we were here before the British. The truth is that we hold sovereignty and dominion over these lands. The truth is that there've been genocide and multiple crimes against humanity and massacres committed on this land that haven't been brought to justice.[2]
>
> It is a basic principle that all people should stand equal before the law. A construction which results in different criminal sanctions applying to different persons for the same conduct offends that basic principle...And just as all persons in the country enjoy the benefits of domestic laws from which they are not expressly excluded, so also must they accept the burdens those laws impose. The presumption applies with added force in the case of the criminal law, which is inherently universal in its operation, and whose aims would otherwise be frustrated.[3]

Introduction

Denis Walker, a member of the Noonuccal Nation and a proud Murri Aboriginal man, was a legal strategist, philosopher, freedom fighter, and fearless sovereignty activist. Between 1988 and 1999, he brought three test cases before the courts on Aboriginal and Torres Strait Islander peoples and the jurisdiction of criminal law. The first of these cases, *R v Walker*,[4] preceded *Mabo No 2* ('*Mabo*'),[5] and two more followed it: *Walker v New South Wales*[6] ('*Walker*') and *Walker v Speechley*.[7] Scholars have analysed these cases in detail,[8] so we offer only a brief synopsis before shifting the focus to the man behind the case.

Denis Walker[9] brought the case of *Walker* in 1994, two years after the High Court handed down its landmark decision *Mabo* in which it declared that the doctrine of terra nullius was not a part of the common law of Australia. Elimination of terra nullius enabled the High Court to hold that native title had survived colonisation. *Mabo* ignited hope for Aboriginal and Torres Strait Islander peoples that other forms of Aboriginal customary law may also have survived colonisation. In *Walker*, Denis Walker tested this possibility in relation to criminal law.

The case came before the Lismore District Court in relation to charges arising from an incident in Nimbin in northern New South Wales (NSW). Mr Walker was attempting to stop some redevelopment work being carried out by Lismore Council on a sacred site which, Mr Walker pointed out, was within the lands of the Bandjalung Nation.[10] He was defending an Aboriginal burial site.[11] In relation to this incident, he was charged with two criminal offences: maliciously discharging a loaded firearm with intent to resist lawful arrest (punishable by 14 years' penal servitude)[12] and assaulting police (punishable by five years' imprisonment).[13] The victim was a non-Indigenous police officer. The police were called and there was an altercation between Mr Walker and the police officer, resulting in Mr Walker being charged with the two offences.

Mr Walker's case was listed for trial in the Lismore District Court but before the trial began, he filed a claim in the High Court arguing that the common law and statutory laws do not apply to Aboriginal people without their consent.[14] The state of New South Wales brought an application requesting that the High Court dismiss Mr Walker's statement of claim on the basis that it did not plead a reasonable cause of action. The application was not heard in open court—instead, Mason CJ dealt with it in chambers.

In *Walker*, where his reasons were reported, Mason CJ made a determination regarding the reception of English law into the colony of New South Wales:

> Even if it be assumed that the customary criminal law of Aboriginal people survived British settlement, it was extinguished by the passage of criminal statutes of general application. In *Mabo (No. 2)*, the Court held that there was no inconsistency between native title being held by people of Aboriginal descent and the underlying radical title being vested in the Crown. There is no analogy with the criminal law. English criminal law did not, and Australian criminal law does not, accommodate an alternative body of law operating alongside it.[15]

Mason CJ held that the claim that the common law and statute law do not apply to Aboriginal people without their consent 'amount[s] to the contention that a new source of sovereignty resides in the Aboriginal people',[16] but noted that *Mabo* rejected that suggestion.[17] His Honour applied the principle set out by Gibbs J in *Coe v Commonwealth*.[18] In that case, the plaintiff made a claim of Aboriginal sovereignty over Australia, but Gibbs J held that 'the aboriginal people are subject to the laws of the Commonwealth and of the States or Territories in which they respectively reside'.[19] After his claim was dismissed in the High Court, Mr Walker returned to the Lismore District Court where he was found guilty by a jury and sentenced to three years' imprisonment with a non-parole period of 12 months.[20]

The Indigenist judgment

Drawing inspiration from Lon Fuller's 1949 article, 'The Case of the Speluncean Explorers',[21] our three judges take different approaches to Mr Walker's claim to demonstrate the challenges, while at the same time acknowledging the difficulties, shortcomings, and frustrations, of attempting to write an 'Indigenist judgment'[22] within the confines and constraints of the settler-colonial legal system. It is also a starting point for exploring the complicity we felt as fictional judges within this settler-colonial legal system. This discomfort stemmed in part from directly profiting from a legal industry that is built off Blak death and suffering. As Alison Whittaker observes, 'the settler justice system is nothing but a long queue of First Nations women holding photos of their dead kids'.[23]

A second and related purpose and rationale of the split judgment is to both explore and demonstrate the spectrum of Indigenist jurisprudence.

The judgment imagines an application for leave to appeal from Mason CJ's dismissal of Mr Walker's statement of claim. Three judges hear the application and each of them grants leave to appeal, ordering that the matter be heard by the full court of the High Court, though each adopts a uniquely 'Indigenist' line of reasoning.

Righteous J adopts an approach which might be characterised as formal and positivist. She is working within doctrine but pushes back on key components of it, such as the impact of criminal law on Aboriginal and Torres Strait Islander peoples. She feels trapped between High Court pronouncements of the common law and indisputable evidence of the sovereignty of the Bundjalung Nation. Recognition of this fact leads her to the conclusion that '[a]t the heart of this case hence lies a conflict of laws dilemma'.

Breckenridge J takes the natural law approach. She argues that the NSW law is so unjust that it should not be applied and construes Mr Walker's actions as civil disobedience, akin to a right to protest. Specifically, Breckenridge J cites the obiter comments of Murphy J in *Neal*[24] regarding the right of citizens to be 'agitators'. In that case, Murphy J said in relation to an Aboriginal offender who was appealing his sentence:

> If he is an agitator, he is in good company. Many of the great religious and political figures of history have been agitators, and human progress owes much to the efforts of these and the many who are unknown.[25]

Pragmatico J takes an approach that accommodates the fact of legal pluralism in Australia. Through this lens, she argues that common law can and should recognise Indigenous law-making power over events occurring on Indigenous land. The central issue here is one of jurisdiction. Walker has consented to be bound by Bundjalung law (personal) and was on Bundjalung land (territorial) so the question of which law applies is a matter for the Bundjalung Nation and NSW to work out in accordance with conflicts of law rules.

While the judgments present three possible ways of resolving the legal questions, this commentary focuses on the man who brought this fight to the High Court on no less than three occasions.

Denis Walker: brief portrait of a legal strategist, philosopher, and freedom fighter

Denis Walker (1947–2017), known later in his life as Bejam Kunmunara Jarlow Nunukel Kabool, was a Noonuccal man from Minjerribah-Moorgumpin, or what is known to the Crown as Stradbroke Island, Queensland. He was a prominent Aboriginal activist who committed his entire life to Aboriginal sovereignty and civil rights movements. Known for his central role in the land rights movements of the 1970s, Walker was a co-founder of the Brisbane Chapter of the Australian Black Panther Party (in February 1972; see Figure 4.1) and played a central role in the establishment of the first Aboriginal Medical Service and Aboriginal Legal Service in Brisbane, services which continue to operate today. His political activism and involvement with the Aboriginal Black Panther Movement brought him into contact with the aggressive policing and overzealous surveillance of the Australian Security Intelligence Organisation (ASIO), notably during the now notorious covert action program from 1969–1975, which deliberately targeted Black Panther Party members and monitored their daily actions.[26]

In addition to his contributions to community and political activism, Denis Walker also led a series of practical interventions within the criminal jurisdiction. One of the founding pillars of the Aboriginal Legal Service, for example, was to provide a defence mechanism for police brutality and initially included 'pig patrols' to monitor police encounters with the Aboriginal community in housing estates and other public areas. As described at the beginning of this chapter, Denis Walker also spearheaded three test cases on Aboriginal people and Torres Strait Islanders and the criminal jurisdiction: *R v Walker*,[28] *Walker v New South Wales*[29] (the subject of this chapter) and *Walker v Speechley*.[30] We hope that this judgment and commentary go some way in commencing to document the late Mr Walker's gargantuan contribution to activism, community, and social justice from the mid-1960s to 2017, both in Brisbane, nationally, and internationally. It is our hope that more Australian legal commentary begins to document and take seriously the contribution of agitators like the late Denis Walker and many other unsung heroes in Aboriginal history and the present.

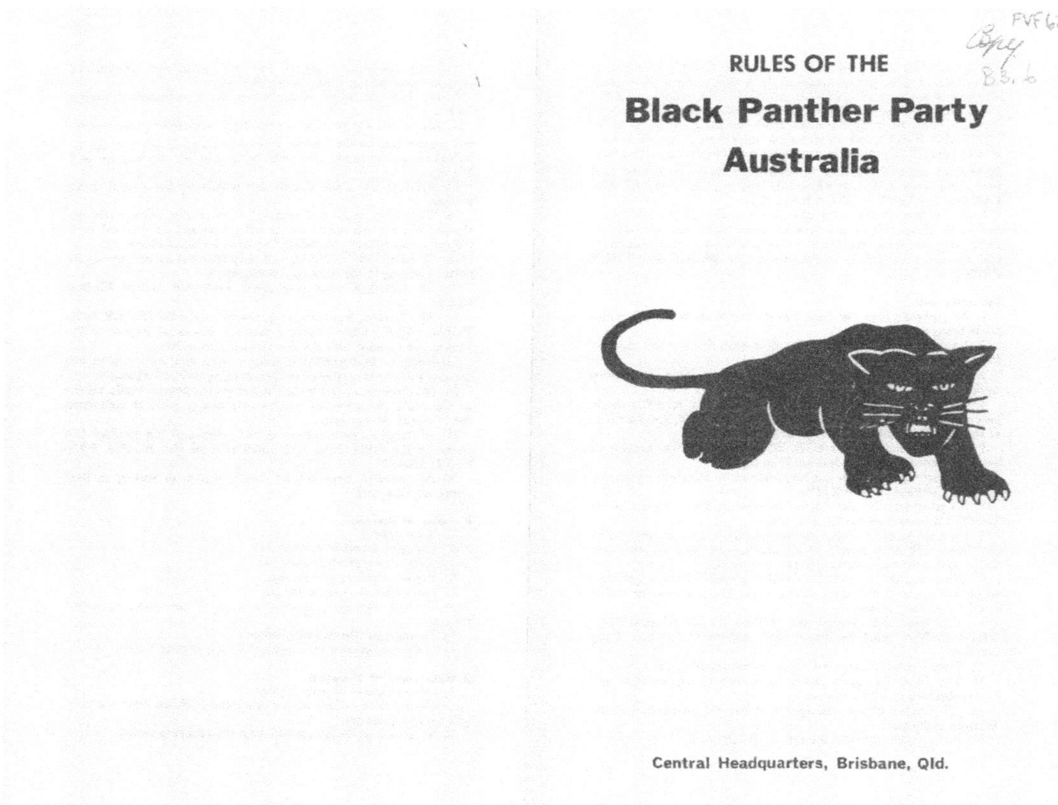

FIGURE 4.1 (a–d) The original manifesto of the Brisbane chapter of the Black Panther Party, officially released on 24 February 1972.[27]

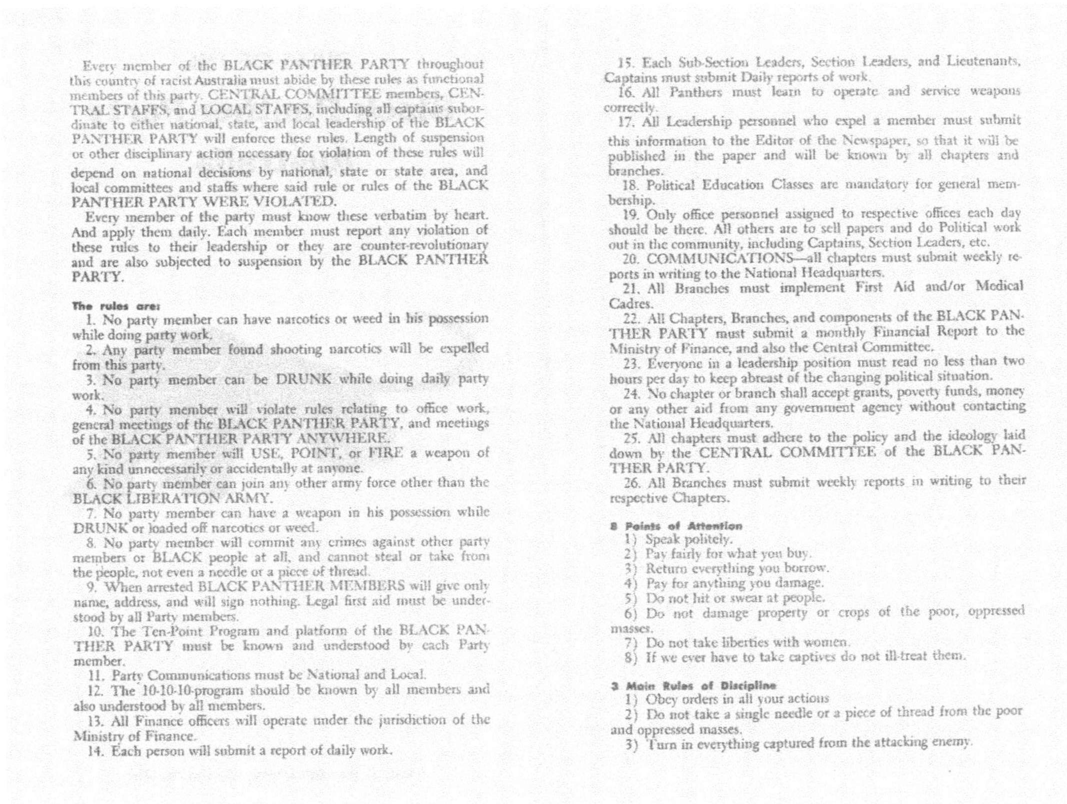

Every member of the BLACK PANTHER PARTY throughout this country of racist Australia must abide by these rules as functional members of this party. CENTRAL COMMITTEE members, CENTRAL STAFFS, and LOCAL STAFFS, including all captains subordinate to either national, state, and local leadership of the BLACK PANTHER PARTY will enforce these rules. Length of suspension or other disciplinary action necessary for violation of these rules will depend on national decisions by national, state or state area, and local committees and staffs where said rule or rules of the BLACK PANTHER PARTY WERE VIOLATED.

Every member of the party must know these verbatim by heart. And apply them daily. Each member must report any violation of these rules to their leadership or they are counter-revolutionary and are also subjected to suspension by the BLACK PANTHER PARTY.

The rules are:

1. No party member can have narcotics or weed in his possession while doing party work.
2. Any party member found shooting narcotics will be expelled from this party.
3. No party member can be DRUNK while doing daily party work.
4. No party member will violate rules relating to office work, general meetings of the BLACK PANTHER PARTY, and meetings of the BLACK PANTHER PARTY ANYWHERE.
5. No party member will USE, POINT, or FIRE a weapon of any kind unnecessarily or accidentally at anyone.
6. No party member can join any other army force other than the BLACK LIBERATION ARMY.
7. No party member can have a weapon in his possession while DRUNK or loaded off narcotics or weed.
8. No party member will commit any crimes against other party members or BLACK people at all, and cannot steal or take from the people, not even a needle or a piece of thread.
9. When arrested BLACK PANTHER MEMBERS will give only name, address, and will sign nothing. Legal first aid must be understood by all Party members.
10. The Ten-Point Program and platform of the BLACK PANTHER PARTY must be known and understood by each Party member.
11. Party Communications must be National and Local.
12. The 10-10-10-program should be known by all members and also understood by all members.
13. All Finance officers will operate under the jurisdiction of the Ministry of Finance.
14. Each person will submit a report of daily work.
15. Each Sub-Section Leaders, Section Leaders, and Lieutenants, Captains must submit Daily reports of work.
16. All Panthers must learn to operate and service weapons correctly.
17. All Leadership personnel who expel a member must submit this information to the Editor of the Newspaper, so that it will be published in the paper and will be known by all chapters and branches.
18. Political Education Classes are mandatory for general membership.
19. Only office personnel assigned to respective offices each day should be there. All others are to sell papers and do Political work out in the community, including Captains, Section Leaders, etc.
20. COMMUNICATIONS—all chapters must submit weekly reports in writing to the National Headquarters.
21. All Branches must implement First Aid and/or Medical Cadres.
22. All Chapters, Branches, and components of the BLACK PANTHER PARTY must submit a monthly Financial Report to the Ministry of Finance, and also the Central Committee.
23. Everyone in a leadership position must read no less than two hours per day to keep abreast of the changing political situation.
24. No chapter or branch shall accept grants, poverty funds, money or any other aid from any government agency without contacting the National Headquarters.
25. All chapters must adhere to the policy and the ideology laid down by the CENTRAL COMMITTEE of the BLACK PANTHER PARTY.
26. All Branches must submit weekly reports in writing to their respective Chapters.

8 Points of Attention

1) Speak politely.
2) Pay fairly for what you buy.
3) Return everything you borrow.
4) Pay for anything you damage.
5) Do not hit or swear at people.
6) Do not damage property or crops of the poor, oppressed masses.
7) Do not take liberties with women.
8) If we ever have to take captives do not ill-treat them.

3 Main Rules of Discipline

1) Obey orders in all your actions
2) Do not take a single needle or a piece of thread from the poor and oppressed masses.
3) Turn in everything captured from the attacking enemy.

FIGURE 4.1 Continued

January 1972

Black Panther Party Australia

PLATFORM AND PROGRAM

What we want
What we believe

1. We want freedom. We want power to determine the destiny of our Black Community. We believe that Black people will not be free until we are able to determine our destiny.

2. We want full employment for our people.
We believe that the federal government is responsible and obligated to give every man employment or a guaranteed income. We believe that if the white Australian businessmen will not give full employment, then the means of production should be taken from the businessman and placed in the community so that the people of the community can organise and employ all of its people and give a high standard of living.

3. We want an end to the robbery by the white man of our Black Community.
We believe that this racist Government has robbed us and now we are demanding restitution for the armed robbery of our land, which is the social, culture and economic base of any people. We will accept land and mineral rights for the existing black communities, and monary restitution for those dispossessed victims. The Germans are now aiding the Jews in Israel for the genocide and the Jewish people. The Germans murdered 6 million Jews. The Australian racist has taken part in the slaughter of over a quarter of a million Black People (This entails 75% of the total population and the total genocide of Tasmanian Blacks). We feel that as the number of Jews murdered represented only a small portion of the Jewish population as compared with the significant attempted genocide of the black people of this country, we feel that it is a modest demand that we make.

4. We want decent housing, fit for shelter of human beings.
We believe that if the white landlords will not give decent housing to our black community, then the housing and the land should be made into cooperatives so that our community, with government aid, can build and make decent housing for its people.

5. We want education for our people that exposes the true nature of this decadent Australian society. We want education that teaches us our true history and our role in the present-day society. We believe in an educational system that will give to our people a knowledge of self. If a man does not have knowledge of himself and his position in society and the world, then he has little chance to relate to anything else.

FIGURE 4.1 Continued

6. We want all black men to be exempt from military service. We believe that Black people should not be forced to fight in the military service to defend a racist government that does not protect us. We will not fight and kill other people of colour in the world who, like black people, are well victimized by the white racist government of Australia. We will protect ourselves from the force and violence of the racist police and the racist military, by whatever means necessary.

7. We want an immediate end to POLICE BRUTALITY, MURDER & RAPE OF BLACK people. We believe we can end police brutality in our black community from racist police oppression and brutality. There is a need to make policemen out of the "Pigs" that are presently acting as law enforcement agencies. It's only way that this can be done is to give the communities control of the POLICE. Without this the "PIGS" will continue to be used as tools of the Fascists system. When the Government becomes a law breaker the people must become the law-enforcer.

8. We want freedom for all black men held in federal, state, county and city prisons and jails.
We believe that all black people shoudl be released from the many jails and prisons because they have not received a fair and impartial trail.

9. We want all black people when brought to trial to be tried in court by a jury of their peer group or people from their black communities.
We believe that the courts should follow the Law. The Law gives a man the right to be tried by his peer group. A peer is a person from a similar economic social, religious, geographical, environmental, historical and racial back-ground. To do this the court will be forced to select a jury from the black community from which the black defendant came. We have been, and are being tried by all-white juries that have understanding of the "average reasoning man" of the black community.

10. We want land, bread, housing, education, clothing, justice and peace. And as our major political objective, a United Nations-supervised plediscite to be held throughout the black colony in which only balck colonial subjects will be allowed to participate, for the purpose of determining the will of black people as to their national destiny. When, in the course of human events, it becomes necessary for one people to dissolve the political bands which have which have connected them with another, and to assume, among the powers of the earth, the separate and equal station to which the laws of nature and nature's God entitle them, a decent respect to the opinions of mankind requiries that they should declare the causes which impel them to the separation. We hold these truths to be self-evident, that all men are created equal; that they are endowed by their Creator with certain unalienable rights; that among these are life, liberty, and the pursuit of happiness. That, to secure these rights, from the consent of the governed; that, whenever any form of government becomes destructive of these ends, it is the right of the people to alter or to abolish it, and to institute a new government, laying its foundation on such principles, and most likely to effect their safety and happiness. Prudence, indeed will dictate that governments long established should not be all changed for light and transient causes; and, accordingly, suffer, while evils are sufferable, than to right themselves by abolishing the forms to which they are accustomed. But when a long train of abuses and usurpations, pursing invariably the same object, evinces a design to reduce them under absolute despotism, it is their right, it is their duty, to throw off such government, and to provide new guards for their future security.

. . . .

FIGURE 4.1 Continued

Notes

1 Denis Walker, 'Invasion Day Rally' (Speech, Brisbane, 26 January 2008) <https://speakola.com/ideas/tag/DENNIS+WALKER>.

2 Murrumu Walubara Yidinji, as cited in Paul Daley, 'The Man Who Renounced Australia', *The Guardian* (Sydney, 26 August 2014) <https://www.theguardian.com/world/postcolonial/2014/aug/26/-sp-the-man-who-renounced-australia>.

3 *Walker v New South Wales* [1994] HCA 64, [5] ('*Walker*').
4 (1989) 2 Qd R 79.
5 *Mabo v Queensland (No 2)* (1992) 175 CLR 1 ('*Mabo*').
6 [1994] HCA 64.
7 *Walker v Speechley*, S133/1997 (17 August 1998) High Court of Australia Transcripts.
8 See, e.g., Heather Douglas and Mark Finnane, *Indigenous Crime and Settler Law: White Sovereignty after Empire* (Palgrave, 2012) Ch 6.
9 In his later years, Denis rejected this name and reportedly preferred to go by the name Bejam Kunmunara Jarlow Nunukel Kabool.
10 *R v Walker* (New South Wales Court of Criminal Appeal, Gleeson CJ, Allen J, and Barr AJ, unreported, 20 November 1995) 2.
11 Malcolm Brown, *Heart of Gold: The Life of Benevolent Solicitor Bruce Miles OAM* (Bruce Miles Foundation, 2006) 160.
12 *Crimes Act 1900* (NSW) s 33A.
13 Ibid., 58.
14 *Walker* [1994] HCA 64, [1].
15 Ibid., [6].
16 Ibid., [2].
17 Ibid.
18 (1979) 24 ALR 118 ('*Coe*').
19 Ibid., 129.
20 *R v Walker* (New South Wales Court of Criminal Appeal, Gleeson CJ, Allen J, and Barr AJ, unreported, 20 November 1995) 1.
21 Lon Fuller, 'The Case of the Speluncean Explorers' (1949) 62(4) *Harvard Law Review* 616. In that article, Fuller uses different approaches to judgment writing, for example, formalist/positivist, purposive, and natural law/justice, to expose the subjectivities (such as class and status) involved in judicial decision making.
22 We use the term Indigenist in line with the use of critical Indigenous scholars, especially Lester-Irabinna Rigney, who coined the term. See generally, Lester-Irabinna Rigney, 'Internationalization of an Indigenous Anticolonial Cultural Critique of Research Methodologies: A Guide to Indigenist Research Methodology and Its Principles' (1999) 14(2) *Wicazo Sa Review* 109.
23 @AJ_Whittaker (Alison Whittaker) (Twitter, 22 November 2019, 3:56pm, <https://twitter.com/AJ_Whittaker/status/1197755685708021760>.
24 *Neal v The Queen* (1982) 149 CLR 305.
25 Ibid., 316.
26 Gary Foley, 'Black Power in Redfern 1968–1972' (5 October 2001) <http://vuir.vu.edu.au/27009/1/Black%20power%20in%20Redfern%201968-1972.pdf>.
27 Source: Denis Walker, *Black Panther Party Australia, Brisbane Chapter, Manifesto Number Two* (release date: 24 February 1972).
28 (1989) 2 Qd R 79.
29 [1994] HCA 64.
30 *Walker v Speechley*, S133/1997 (17 August 1998) High Court of Australia Transcripts.

DENIS WALKER .... PLAINTIFF;

AND

NEW SOUTH WALES .... DEFENDANT;

[1994] HCA 64

Constitutional law—Aboriginal and Torres Strait Islander peoples—Criminal law—Whether Aboriginal law survived colonisation—Application of state statutes to Aboriginal and Torres Strait Islander peoples.

[1] RIGHTEOUS J.[1] This case involves a statement of claim brought by the plaintiff, Mr Denis Walker. Mr Walker is a citizen of the Noonuccal Nation and a proud Murri Aboriginal man. He is also recognised by the jurisdiction vested within this court, and despite his protests to the contrary, as a citizen of Australia.

[2] The case involves accusations of criminal activity which allegedly took place when Mr Walker was physically located within the unceded Bundjalung territory, or what is known to the Crown as 'Nimbin' on the far north coast of New South Wales. More specifically, the dispute took place on a sacred site within this particular location.

[3] This matter is an application for leave to appeal from Mason CJ sitting in chambers as a single judge of the High Court of Australia.[2] In that case, Mason CJ held that the statement of claim did not give rise to a reasonable cause of action and should be dismissed. The plaintiff's statement of claim reads as follows:

i. The matter is one within the original jurisdiction of the High Court as it is a matter involving a state and a resident of another state.
ii. Walker is an Aboriginal person, a member of the Noonuccal Nation, whose traditional lands are on the area referred to as Stradbroke Island in the state of Queensland.
iii. Walker has been charged with an offence under the laws of New South Wales. This offence allegedly occurred at the town of Nimbin in the state of New South Wales, which is located on the traditional territory or Country of the Bundjalung Sovereign First Nation peoples.
iv. By acts of state in 1788, 1829, and 1887, the lands now known as Australia were subjugated by the British Crown.
v. The peoples who were then living in the lands now known as Australia ('Aboriginal people') had organised systems of law and custom to

govern relations between individuals, between individuals and the group, and between groups.

vi. Laws relating to relations between individuals, including violence, and the behaviour of persons from different tribes when on the land of other tribes formed an integral part of the legal systems of the Aboriginal people.

vii. Aboriginal people continued to practise their laws and customs at the time Australia was subjugated and continue to do so.

viii. To the extent that laws of the British Crown and its successors have superseded the laws and customs of the Aboriginal people, they are only valid to the degree that they have been accepted by the Aboriginal people on whose land they purport to operate.

ix. The Parliaments of the Commonwealth of Australia and of the States and Territories lack the power to legislate in a manner affecting Aboriginal people without the request and consent of the Aboriginal people.

x. Further and alternatively, if the Parliament of the Commonwealth or of a State or Territory legislates in a manner affecting Aboriginal people, the law in so far as it relates to Aboriginal people is of no effect until it is adopted by the Aboriginal people whom, or whose land, it purports to effect.

[4] By this statement of claim, the plaintiff accepts that he has been charged with an offence against the laws of the state of New South Wales, an offence which allegedly occurred in 'Nimbin' in the language of this court. The plaintiff, Mr Walker, seeks declarations that the laws do not apply to him because they are not laws enforceable in the fora of the Bundjalung Sovereign First Nation. Mr Walker asserts that as a Noonuccal man acting under the authority of Bundjalung Elders, Bundjalung lore has primary, concurrent, or exclusive jurisdiction over the matter at hand. The defendant, the state of New South Wales, brought an application by summons that the plaintiff's action be dismissed or alternatively stayed under Order 26, rule 18 of the High Court Rules.[3] These orders provide that 'the Court or a Justice may order a pleading to be struck out on the ground that it does not disclose a reasonable cause of action or answer'.[4]

[5] The question which arises is whether Aboriginal lore—specifically, Bundjalung lore—is something which can be recognised by the common law and which continues to this day, in the same way that *Mabo v Queensland (No 2)*[5] ('*Mabo*') decided that the law of the Meriam people relating to land tenure continues to exist and is capable of being recognised within Australian courts as native title,[6] and as is similarly the case with respect to *inter se* rights such as marriage, succession, and inheritance.[7]

[6] The incident before the court allegedly took place within the territorial boundaries of the Bundjalung Nation. The Bundjalung Nation is located to the south of what is now referred to as the 'Clarence River', where it

shares borders with the Yaegl Nation and Gumbayngirr Nation in the south, extending west to the Ngarabal Nation. It extends to the north where it shares a border with the Yuggera and Barrunggam Nations. It is a nation which is home to a proud community and a proud tradition of lore, language, and customs which extends back over 65,000 years.

[7] In terms of the legislative competency of the Parliaments of the Commonwealth and New South Wales, the matter, at least on its surface, seems clear. The legislature of New South Wales has power to make laws for 'the peace, welfare and good government' of New South Wales.[8] This includes the power to make laws relating to the regulation of crimes. The township of Nimbin falls within the geographical jurisdiction of the state of New South Wales. Similarly, this court simultaneously recognises the legal personality known as 'Denis Walker' as an Australian citizen, notwithstanding the fact that he is a citizen of the Noonucal Nation and similarly notwithstanding his subjective understanding of his identity, having repeatedly and publicly renounced his Australian identity on numerous occasions.[9]

[8] I take on notice the findings and recommendations of the Australian Law Reform Commission's report, *Recognition of Aboriginal Customary Laws*,[10] which outlined the significance of Aboriginal lore and the implications for the operation of the criminal jurisdiction. Second and equally, I take on notice the findings of the national report of the *Royal Commission into Aboriginal Deaths in Custody*[11] which documents the contemporary issues of disproportionate rates of incarceration and cultural genocide which Aboriginal and Torres Strait Islander peoples face as a matter of commonplace regularity. It is important to acknowledge equally that the settler-colonial law—and particularly criminal jurisdiction—is genocidal in its ongoing impact on Aboriginal and Torres Strait Islander communities. In this regard, I note these appalling statistics and the Parliament's inaction on the recommendations of the *Royal Commission into Aboriginal Deaths in Custody* and the report, *Recognition of Aboriginal Customary Laws*, among other national reports and inquiries.

[9] However, I also note Mason CJ's *ratio* concerning the fundamental importance of equality before the law with respect to criminal jurisdiction. I agree with Mason CJ that it is a basic principle that all people should stand equal before the law and that this is especially important with respect to criminal law, which is inherently universal in its operation.

[10] For these and other reasons as stated above, I am not satisfied with the ease with which Mason CJ rejects the statement of claim from this court. Given the serious nature of these issues, which go to the heart of our nation and politics, I grant leave to appeal and order that this matter be heard by a full court.

[11] Breckenridge J. I agree with the outcome Righteous J has arrived at but by way of a slightly different reasoning.

[12] Mr Walker has allegedly committed offences under the laws of the state of New South Wales. For myself, the legal issue of much greater significance

is that this case concerns issues of natural justice and conflict of laws. As Righteous J set out in her judgment above, the incident took place on Bundjalung territory but involves a Noonucal man for alleged offences against the state of New South Wales. As a Bundjalung judge, writing this judgment has been considerably challenging.

[13] The legal issues in this case concern the application of criminal laws to Aboriginal and Torres Strait Islander peoples. It defies logic, morals, and ethics that such matters be decided by a single judge before the High Court of Australia and based on inadequate evidence. In light of the continued devastation wrought by criminal law upon Aboriginal peoples, Mr Walker's actions are justified, indeed dignified. In the words of Murphy J's statement in *Neal v The Queen* (1982),[12] Mr Walker is 'an agitator':

> That Mr. Neal was an "agitator" or stirrer in the magistrate's view obviously contributed to the severe penalty. If he is an agitator, he is in good company. Many of the great religious and political figures of history have been agitators, and human progress owes much to the efforts of these and the many who are unknown. As Wilde aptly pointed out in *The Soul of Man under Socialism*, "Agitators are a set of interfering, meddling people, who come down to some perfectly contented class of the community and sow the seeds of discontent amongst them. That is the reason why agitators are so absolutely necessary. Without them, in our incomplete state, there would be no advance towards civilisation." Mr. Neal is entitled to be an agitator.[13]

Importantly, and as Murphy J lamented in that decision, 'agitators' deserve the protection of the Australian legal system.

[14] I would grant leave to appeal and order that this matter be retried by a full court of the High Court. I request that all Bundjalung Elders be able to join the new proceedings as friends of the court.

[15] PRAGMATICO J. I agree with the outcome reached by Righteous and Breckenridge JJ and only wish to add the following.

[16] I draw attention to the fact, first and foremost, that Mr Walker was defending a sacred site which was located on the unceded sovereign territory of the Bundjalung Nation.

[17] I accept that Mr Walker was defending this site and that as an Aboriginal man he ought to be entitled to such a defence in relation to charges arising in criminal law.

[18] The leading precedents around issues of legal recognition of Aboriginal and Torres Strait Islander legal systems are the cases of *Mabo* and *Coe v Commonwealth*[14] ('*Coe*'). The question in *Mabo* was which law governs *land*. The question in *Coe* was which law governs *people*. Gibbs J stated that 'the aboriginal [sic] people are subject to the laws of the Commonwealth and of the States or Territories in which they respectively reside'.[15]

[19] The mainstream courts have consistently viewed criminal law as qualitatively different from property law. This is because, so the argument goes, it applies to persons rather than land, and is inherently universal in its operation. It derives directly from the law-making power of the sovereign government and the common law does not permit the existence of a parallel law-making power. Deane and Gaudron JJ mention criminal law in *Mabo*, but in the limited sense of crimes relating to land, such as 'alleged larceny of produce or trespass after a purported termination of the title by the Crown'.[16] Brennan J did not comment on the application of criminal law with respect to Aboriginal and Torres Strait Islander peoples.[17] However, as Griffith CJ noted in *Quan Yick v Hinds*:[18] 'It has never been doubted that the general provisions of the criminal law were introduced by the [*Australian Courts Act* 1828 (Cth)]'.[19] Thus, the argument goes, criminal law has applied to all subjects of the Crown, which includes Aboriginal and Torres Strait Islander peoples, since 1828.

[20] Though these matters are complex, the Australian settler-colonial legal system has, on numerous occasions, acknowledged the continued practice of customary Aboriginal criminal law and taken it into account on bail, sentencing, and even the determination of criminal liability.[20]

[21] In excising the concept of terra nullius from the common law in *Mabo*, Brennan J said: 'The fiction by which the rights and interests of indigenous inhabitants in land were treated as non-existent was justified by a policy which has no place in the contemporary law of this country'.[21] Deane and Gaudron JJ used stronger language to expose the injustice wrought by the disjuncture between theory and practice: 'The acts and events by which that dispossession in legal theory was carried into practical effect constitute the darkest aspect of the history of this nation'.[22]

[22] It is now time for this court to excise the fiction that there is no parallel sovereign law-making power in Australia and that customary Aboriginal criminal law is not 'recognised or given effect by the colonial legal system'.[23] To borrow the words of Davies, '[w]ith the decline of nation states as the locus of political and legal power, it seems inevitable that traditional state-centred [formal legalism] must give way to a different paradigm which recognizes the plurality of law'.[24]

[23] Counsel for the plaintiff stated in oral submissions that the claim before the court 'is not a claim of sovereignty', but the statement of claim presupposes that there are two sovereign law-making powers that purport to exercise jurisdiction over Mr Walker. The plaintiff contends firstly, in his statement of claim, that the 'Parliaments of the Commonwealth of Australia and the States and Territories lack the power to legislate in a manner affecting aboriginal people without the request and consent of aboriginal people'. This proposition necessarily challenges the jurisdiction of settler-colonial legislation over Aboriginal peoples. Secondly, the plaintiff contended in oral submissions that Aboriginal customary law has survived colonisation in the same

way in which native title has survived colonisation as recognised in *Mabo* and has been recognised by common law. Paragraph viii of the statement of claim reads '[t]o the extent that laws of the British Crown and its successors have superseded the laws and customs of the Aboriginal people they are only valid to the degree that they have been accepted by the Aboriginal people on whose land they purport to operate'. Counsel for the plaintiff said in oral submissions, '[t]he only question [this case] concerns is the law that applies to a person who is purported to be charged with offences against the *Crimes Act 1900* (NSW)'. This is a claim of jurisdiction by a parallel sovereign law-making power. Taking the Aboriginal law-making power as a starting point, instead of that of the settler-colonial state, the claim could be recast as follows: '[t]o the extent that laws of the British Crown and its successors have superseded the laws and customs of the Aboriginal people, they are only valid to the degree that they have been recognised by the law of Aboriginal people exercising jurisdiction over Noonuccal territory or Noonuccal persons'.

[24] In my view, for the reasons given, the statement of claim gives rise to complex issues which deserve a hearing on the merits by the full court of the High Court. Accordingly, the defendant's application that the statement of claim be struck out must be rejected. I would grant leave to appeal and refer the matter to the full court of the High Court.

Orders

1. That leave to appeal be granted.
2. That the matter be referred to the full court for a re-hearing on the merits.
3. That, in the interests of ascertaining a true account of events and achieving a fair trial, the parties to the incident giving rise to the criminal charges be allowed the opportunity to recount their understanding of events.
4. That the Elders of the Bundjalung Nation be allowed to give expert evidence about the site Mr Walker was protecting.

Notes

1 Amanda Porter and Tanya Mitchell.
2 *Walker v New South Wales* [1994] HCA 64.
3 *High Court Rules* Order 26, r 18, as repealed by *High Court Rules 2004* (Cth).
4 Ibid.
5 *Mabo v Queensland (No 2)* (1992) 175 CLR 1 ('*Mabo*').
6 Ibid.
7 See Australian Law Reform Commission, *Recognition of Aboriginal Customary Laws* (Report No 31, June 1986). The authors would like to thank Kirsty Gover for this observation.
8 *Constitution Act 1902* No 32 (NSW) s 5.
9 Mr Walker has famously renounced his Australian citizenship on many occasions. The court notes that he has never applied for and does not hold an Australian passport.

10 Australian Law Reform Commission (n 7).
11 Elliott Johnston, *National Report of the Royal Commission into Aboriginal Deaths in Custody* (Australian Government Publishing Service, 1991).
12 *Neal v The Queen* (1982) 149 CLR 305.
13 Ibid., 316–7.
14 (1979) 24 ALR 118 ('*Coe*').
15 Ibid., 129.
16 *Mabo* (1992) 175 CLR 1, 94.
17 Ibid., 34.
18 (1905) 2 CLR 345.
19 Ibid., 359.
20 See Heather Douglas and Mark Finnane, *Indigenous Crime and Settler Law: White Sovereignty after Empire* (Palgrave, 2012) Ch 6.
21 *Mabo* (1992) 175 CLR 1, 42.
22 Ibid., 109.
23 Margaret Davies, 'Legal Pluralism' in Peter Cane and Herbert M Kritzer (eds), *The Oxford Handbook of Empirical Legal Research* (Oxford University Press, 2010) 805, 819.
24 Ibid., 825.

PART II

Land and sea Country

5

TICKNER v CHAPMAN (1995) 57 FCR 451

FIGURE 5.1 Stop the Bridge: Respect and Protect Kumarangk/Hindmarsh Island, 1994.

Commentary: *Tickner v Chapman* (1995) 57 FCR 451

Narelle Bedford and Peter Billings

Background

What does procedural justice entail when culturally sensitive information is relevant to administrative decision making? Essentially, this was the question arising in judicial review proceedings concerning a heritage declaration by the Commonwealth Minister for Aboriginal and Torres Strait Islander Affairs, Robert Tickner. The effect of Tickner's decision—pursuant to the *Aboriginal and Torres Strait Islander Heritage Protection Act 1984* (Cth) ('*HPA*')—was to protect Aboriginal heritage by prohibiting the development of a bridge and buildings on Kumarangk, land of the Ngarrindjeri Nation (also known as Hindmarsh Island in South Australia).

In February 1995, the Federal Court held that Tickner's decision was unlawful (a) because of inadequate public notice and (b) by virtue of the Minister failing to afford sufficient personal 'consideration' of representations (sacred information supplied by certain Ngarrindjeri women) before issuing the declaration.[1] The Full Court of the Federal Court (FCAFC) upheld the decision of the trial judge in December 1995.[2]

The FCAFC deemed the public notice was inadequate in terms of, inter alia, its geographic specificity. Yet, as Mathews J stated subsequently, 'it is inimical to Aboriginal culture to single out a small discrete piece of land and say that this will be the area desecrated. For the land is, to them, a single and indivisible part of their culture'.[3] However, the clear terms of the *HPA* precluded the option of respecting this more encompassing and indissoluble conception of land.

The FCAFC also decided that there was a lack of active intellectual consideration of the Ngarrindjeri women's confidential submissions. Arguably, the FCAFC imposed an unduly burdensome responsibility on the Minister in the circumstances. We suggest that, in this respect, the *HPA* was open to a less formal interpretation in order to reconcile Aboriginal tradition and beliefs with the statute and its underlying remedial and protective purposes.

Another provocative feature of the *HPA* that we allude to in our judgment is the use of broad ministerial discretion as the main technique for heritage protection. The condition for *ministerial satisfaction* that a 'specified area' is one that 'is a significant Aboriginal area' (per s 10 [1][b]), prompted Irene Watson to observe that the Act

> provides for the protection of Aboriginal sites, objects and remains but at the same time the minister responsible retains the power to authorise their destruction. This is an example of giving with one hand and taking back with the other. [4]

The *Kumarangk Case* became notorious for the phrase 'secret women's business' which related to confidential beliefs that its proponents—particular Ngarrindjeri women—did not want publicly disclosed. This dispute prompted rancorous debates in the political and public domain about fabricated evidence and spawned extensive litigation,[5] including the subsequent *Kartinyeri* case.[6] Writing after the publication of the Full Court's judgment and two related reports—the Royal Commission report (SA)[7] and the *Mathews Report*[8]—Hillary Charlesworth opined that the saga 'will surely enter Australian folklore as one of the most complex, and litigated, of disputes'.[9] It all suggested 'major flaws in the Australian legal system with respect to protection of Indigenous heritage'.[10] Equally, other scholars have carefully argued that the *HPA* inadequately protects Aboriginal heritage.[11] Certainly, the *Kumarangk Case* revealed how promoting procedural justice principles to benefit the wider community can frustrate statutory objectives, cause injustice for particular Indigenous peoples, and undermine their human rights.

The new joint judgment

Under s 14 of the *Federal Court Act 1976* (Cth), the FCAFC can be constituted as three or more judges sitting together. Re-imagining the *Kumarangk* decision as a Full Court constituted by five judges is, we think, an effective way of signalling the importance of the issues arising. This approach allowed us to incorporate the reasoning of the original judges at trial and appellate levels, and it meant we were restricted to legal authorities extant in 1995. In crafting the new judgment, we were also constrained by the supervisory nature of judicial review and the clear language of the *HPA*. Supervising the legality of administrative action does not invite commentary on the wisdom of policy choices nor extend to rewriting legislation.

In writing purposefully to foreground Indigenous perspectives, we make a humble attempt to redress the loss of agency[12] and damage incurred by the Ngarrindjeri People, specifically the women, throughout the entire process of the dispute. Even the case name—*Tickner v Chapman* —focuses attention on two white males and renders the Ngarrindjeri applicants invisible. Yet preservation and protection of their ancient and continuing cultural heritage were at the heart of the matter.

A deliberate decision was made to include references to a wider range of socio-legal materials than quoted in the original decision. For example, we refer to the draft *Declaration of the Rights of Indigenous Peoples*[13] and related UN documentation as resources available to the Full Court in 1995. Equally distinctive is our contextual use of comparative law, which was employed to convey emerging judicial techniques employed in legal proceedings involving and impacting Indigenous peoples in Canada and New Zealand.

We acknowledge Irene Watson and Larissa Behrendt as influential Indigenous voices inspiring our judgment.[14]

Notes

1 *Chapman v Tickner* (1995) 55 FCR 316, 371, 373.
2 *Tickner v Chapman* (1995) 57 FCR 451 ('*Kumarangk Case*').
3 Jane Mathews, *Commonwealth Hindmarsh Island Report* (Report, 27 June 1996) 191 ('*Mathews Report*').
4 Irene Watson, 'Aboriginal(ising) International Law and Other Centres of Power' (2011) 20(3) *Griffith Law Review* 619, 622.
5 See e.g. *Chapman v Luminis Pty Ltd (No 4)* [2001] 123 FCR 62, dismissing the Chapmans' damages claim.
6 *Kartinyeri v Commonwealth* (1998) 195 CLR 337. See also Chapter 8 of this collection.
7 I E Stevens, *Report of the Hindmarsh Island Bridge Royal Commission* (Report, June 1996). The Royal Commission found that there had been a fabrication of secret 'women's business'. Cf. *Chapman v Luminis Pty Ltd (No 4)* [2001] 123 FCR 62, 115.
8 *Mathews Report* (n 3). Justice Matthews was appointed by the Federal Government to prepare a report (under HPA s 10) in respect of a second heritage protection application, submitted on 19 December 1995, that was intended to overcome *Tickner v Chapman* (1995) 57 FCR 451. As a result of *Wilson v Minister for Aboriginal and Torres Strait Islander Affairs* (1996) 189 CLR 1, the *Mathews Report* could not be used to inform the declaratory decision. The Reporter's role was constitutionally incompatible with performance of judicial functions or judicial responsibilities.
9 Hillary Charlesworth, '"Little Boxes": A Review of the Commonwealth Hindmarsh Island Report by Justice Jane Mathews' (1997) 3(90) *Aboriginal Law Bulletin* 19, 19.
10 Ibid.
11 See e.g. Maureen Tehan, 'To Be or Not to Be (Property): Anglo-Australian Law and the Search for Protection of Indigenous Cultural Heritage' (1996) 15(2) *University of Tasmania Law Review* 267; Joanna Bourke, 'Women's Business: Sex, Secrets and the Hindmarsh Island Affair' (1997) 20(2) *University of New South Wales Law Journal* 333.
12 Alexander Reilly, 'Finding an Indigenous Perspective in Administrative Law' (2009) 19(2) *Legal Education Review* 271, 289, noting 'the Ngarrindjeri experienced a certain loss of autonomy by engaging in the administrative law process...as some of their cultural beliefs were exposed and their community divided'.
13 *United Nations Declaration on the Rights of Indigenous Peoples*, GA Res 61/295, UN Doc A/RES/61/295 (2 October 2007).
14 See Larissa Behrendt, 'No One Can Own the Land' (1994) 1(1) *Australian Journal of Human Rights* 43; Irene Watson, 'Indigenous Peoples' Law-Ways: Survival against the Colonial State' (1997) 8(1) *Australian Feminist Law Journal* 39.

The Kumarangk Case

TICKNER .... PLAINTIFFS;

AND

CHAPMAN .... DEFENDANTS;

(1995) 57 FCR 451

Administrative law—Judicial review—Minister's decision to prohibit construction activities in area of Hindmarsh Island—Aboriginal Heritage—Whether statutory requirements as to notice fulfilled—Meaning of 'specified area'—Whether Minister had properly considered representations—Aboriginal and Torres Strait Islander Heritage Protection Act 1984 (Cth).

Bedford and Billings JJ.[1]

Colonial administrative law and due recognition of Aboriginal cultural and spiritual values: is reconciliation possible?

[1] Sometimes different worldviews and cultural values collide and the courts are called on to resolve disputes arising from that clash of cultures. Ngarrindjeri life and culture came from the Murrundi River, as it flows to meet the saltwater. The Ngarrindjeri Nation believe Murrundi is a living body, formed during the Creation, and the Traditional Owners are part of its existence. The fresh water that flows through Murrundi is the lifeblood of the Nation. This is a different history that people may be unaware of, as most Australians are more familiar with and comprehend the colonial version of the 'Murray River' and its importance to trade and commerce.

[2] Concerned members of the Ngarrindjeri Nation have sought a ministerial declaration to prevent construction of a bridge at Goolwa in South Australia, utilising the means made available to them by the dominant culture's federal legislature and through the dominant legal system's heritage protection legislation and institutions (including this Court). As such, the Ngarrindjeri are reliant 'upon the benevolence of the dominant culture for the enjoyment and enforcement of the rights that they [non-Aboriginals] have defined as fundamental'.[2]

[3] The Chapman family (who, in 1977, acquired proprietary interests in Kumarangk, also called 'Hindmarsh Island') have, via judicial review

proceedings, challenged the legality of a ministerial determination to make a 25-year, protective declaration over significant Aboriginal areas located adjacent to the bridge approaches and sites on Kumarangk. The Chapmans have also challenged the legality of the independent report on which the determination was based.

[4] The trial judge, O'Loughlin J, determined that the declaratory decision-making process pursuant to s 10 of the *Aboriginal and Torres Strait Islander Heritage Protection Act 1984* ('*HPA*') was procedurally unfair and ultra vires.[3] His Honour determined that the public notification and reporting process was defective because it did not adequately particularise the location of the area of heritage significance. Nor did the notice provide a reasonable indication of the apprehended injury or desecration and nature of the threat to the area. Consequently, the notice failed to reasonably inform the public about the subject of the heritage protection application, thereby denying interested people an effective opportunity to make representations. Furthermore, O'Loughlin J determined that the Minister for Aboriginal Affairs ('Minister') had failed to discharge his personal statutory duty to actively 'consider', to the requisite degree, representations relating to spiritual and cultural beliefs of Aboriginal women. These are appeals against the orders made by His Honour.

[5] This case concerns executive-government determinations about ancient Aboriginal sites and their importance to Aboriginal people, the fairness of administrative justice processes, and the nature and extent of ministerial powers. By implication, the case raises profound questions about the ability of the colonial legal system—its administrative law requirements and values—to comprehend and respect the traditions, customs, and beliefs of the Ngarrindjeri Nation, and to adapt appropriately.

Historical context

[6] The Ngarrindjeri are among many discrete Aboriginal communities who traditionally inhabited the areas (known alternatively as 'Echuca' or 'Millewa') around Murrundi. Historical accounts of the Ngarrindjeri—of their early contact with Europeans and the Ngarrindjeri's response to invasion—record that they owned a great triangle of land, some of it rich and fertile, all of it beautiful and near substantial stretches of water.[4]

[7] In settler history, the British Parliament passed the *South Australia Act 1834* (UK) ('*Founding Act*') without consultation with the local Aboriginals. The *Founding Act* contained no reference to the Ngarrindjeri or other Aboriginal communities. No attempt was made by the British to notify the Aboriginals that the land was no longer theirs to occupy and enjoy, nor that their ancient legal systems no longer applied.[5] The *Founding Act* sanctioned colonisation triggering the dispossession of the Aboriginal tribes—whose land was anything but 'waste and unoccupied' as the Act's Preamble proclaimed—rendering them alien in their own land.

[8] The terms of the *Founding Act* imperilled Aboriginal people's interests. Seemingly, certain British Government officials were concerned with ensuring that Aboriginals would not be dispossessed from lands that they were occupying.[6] Accordingly, a proviso to Letters Patent of 19 February 1836 stipulated that Aboriginal land rights in the Province of South Australia were to be respected. This stipulation did not explicitly afford constitutional protection for those Aboriginals occupying or possessing any right of property in the land. The professed preservation of proprietary rights to land within the Letters Patent was incompatible with s 6 of the *Founding Act*, which declared all lands of the Province (with minor exceptions) to be public lands open to purchase by British subjects.

[9] The British Government informed the first colonists, arriving in South Australia from 1836 onwards, that there was land for lease or sale, and in accordance with those laws, the colonists paid for property and acquired tracts of Ngarrindjeri land. By 1840, Kumarangk had been leased to Europeans for agricultural and pastoral purposes. By 1860, the Select Committee of the Legislative Council upon the Aborigines (SA) admitted that those Aboriginals that had survived the occupation had lost almost everything and gained practically nothing by their contact with Europeans.[7] Some Ngarrindjeri remained on Kumarangk until 1910 when they were forcibly moved onto a mission at Raukkan (previously, 'Port McLeay'). The dominant legal system regulated their segregated lives on the Mission. The *Aborigines Act 1911* (SA) sustained the extensive powers of the chief protector to restrict or coerce movement and institutionalise children. The dislocation from traditional landscapes and family break-up impacted the traditional knowledge retained and its transmission to others.[8]

[10] Worrorra elder Albert Barunga has stated: 'The Aboriginal, he gets hurt. Strangers dig around his land without his knowing. Nobody even bothers to tell him. People just walk in and spoil everything. The Aboriginal is deeply hurt, but can do nothing'.[9] Similarly, Black CJ reflected on Europeans' negligence of Aboriginal heritage in *Tickner v Bropho*,[10] observing that 'the significance of areas and objects of profound cultural and spiritual significance to Aboriginals was simply not appreciated' and even when there was such an appreciation, the interests of the settlers prevailed 'without any proper or informed consideration of the interests of Aboriginals'.[11]

The human rights and interests affected

[11] The legal questions before this Court have far-reaching consequences for the distinctive rights of the Ngarrindjeri People. Also implicated are the rights and interests of others; including other Aboriginal peoples (who may have different ancestral traditions), governmental agencies, developers, and private property owners.

[12] Although the rights of Indigenous peoples are not explicitly enshrined in international law yet,[12] principles addressing the status and rights of Indigenous peoples are emerging and supply a useful frame of reference. The United Nations Commission on Human Rights stated it is important to acknowledge, comprehend, and respect the land, cultural and religious rights of Indigenous peoples:

> Indigenous peoples have a natural and inalienable right to keep the territories they possess and to claim the land of which they have been deprived. In other words, they have *the right to the natural cultural heritage* contained in the territory [our emphasis].[13]

[13] The preservation of human cultural heritage is a public duty that is, as French J has explained,

> recognised at international law by the Convention for the Protection of the World Cultural and Natural Heritage to which Australia is a party. The cultural heritage of any country extends to the language, traditions, customs, stories and religions of its peoples past and present.[14]

[14] Australia's ratification of the *World Cultural and Heritage Convention*—in force since 1975—has significance for domestic law. As the High Court of Australia has established, so far as the language of a statute permits, legislation must be interpreted so that it conforms, rather than conflicts, with Australia's international obligations.[15]

Comparative perspectives

[15] Australia does not exist in a vacuum. Therefore, it is useful to survey legal recognition and protection of Indigenous peoples' rights and interests in comparative cognate jurisdictions, so that we are cognizant of jurisprudential developments elsewhere. A review of the jurisprudence (although not specifically confined to cultural heritage protection) reveals four guiding concepts applicable in litigation respecting Indigenous peoples:

(i) The historical position of Indigenous peoples should not be ignored, and colonial legacies should be acknowledged;[16]
(ii) The appropriateness of using and respecting Indigenous knowledge in proceedings;[17]
(iii) The appropriateness of using non-legal sources;[18] and
(iv) The importance of giving expression to the views of Indigenous scholars and Elders.[19] Opportunities to give judicial notice to these voices should be actively sought out, so that their distinctive perspectives are given full consideration.

[16] In this particular context, inspired by the ideas and principles emerging in international law and comparative law, equipped with an appreciation of

the history and impacts of colonisation in South Australia, and with a critical awareness of the deeply spiritual and foundational relationship between Indigenous peoples and their land, this Court must approach its supervisory function of declaring and enforcing the law.

The purpose and structure of the *Heritage Protection Act 1984* (Cth)

[17] The then Minister for Aboriginal Affairs, giving the second reading speech, stated that the legislative policy is to safeguard what remains of Aboriginal cultural heritage and remedy social injustice and disadvantage.[20] The Minister stressed the statute's socio-historical context. Citing the *Tasmanian Dams* case, he quoted Murphy J who stated that since European settlement, Aboriginal people of Australia 'have been the subject of unprovoked aggression, conquest, pillage, rape, brutalisation, attempted genocide and systematic and unsystematic destruction of their culture'.[21]

[18] The mischief addressed by the *HPA* arose out of the perceived inadequacy or non-enforcement of State heritage protection laws.[22] The *HPA* is, primarily, directed to the preservation and protection of areas and objects in Australia and Australian waters that are of particular historical, cultural, or spiritual significance to Aboriginals.[23] The legislative intention, reflected in s 4, identifies the two main purposes of the Act as 'the preservation and protection from injury or desecration of...areas and objects that are of particular significance to Aboriginals in accordance with Aboriginal tradition'.[24]

[19] In *Tickner v Bropho*, French J stated that the *HPA* was enacted 'to preserve what remains of a beautiful and intricate culture and mythology. Its protection is a matter of public interest. There will, however, be occasions on which that objective will conflict with other public interests'.[25] Indeed, a secondary social goal of the *HPA* is the promotion of participation by interested community members that may wish to object to a heritage application.

[20] The legislative objectives, subject matter and wider context are factors that inform construction of procedural justice provisions.[26] The particular scheme of the *HPA* provides for a deliberative decision-making process;[27] it is not an adversarial, quasi-judicial process in which potential objectors 'test' or 'rebut' the veracity of Aboriginal traditions and beliefs.[28] Aboriginal perspectives on matters of significance and tradition assume crucial, if not decisive, importance in the scheme.[29]

[21] The mandatory language of s 10 indicates that an essential, preliminary stage involves public consultation via a statutory notice and a general invitation to 'interested persons' to furnish written representations in connection with the making of a report about the heritage application to a nominated Reporter.[30]

[22] The Reporter collates and assesses material, including any representations, and then issues a report to the Minister. The matters to be dealt with in the

report are listed in s 10(4) which makes several references to 'the area' that is of particular significance to Aboriginals, that is under threat and which should be protected.

[23] The final step in the deliberative process requires 'consideration' of the report and any representations attached to it. This is integral to the valid exercise of the declaratory power. The task of weighing up the matters canvassed in the report is given to the Minister, and whether a declaration should be made is a personal, non-delegable, discretionary determination of a policy or political character.[31] Strikingly, the Minister could accept that the area is significant to Aboriginals and threatened with injury or desecration, and still decline to make a declaration in relation to a 'specified area'.

[24] A ministerial declaration is apt to affect people's rights and interests in a direct and immediate way. Parliament has squarely addressed 'fair hearing' rights and supplied the public with prior notice and an opportunity to make written representations. The legislature has not made detailed procedural provision for a 'hearing' before the initial stage of deliberations, nor after the Reporter has completed their statutory task.[32] Therefore, we are cautious about grafting additional procedural requirements onto the statutory scheme in circumstances where such implied conditions may frustrate the social justice goals.

[25] We have had the advantage of reading, in draft, the reasons given by Black CJ, Burchett J, and Kiefel J who have, effectively, affirmed the primary judge's finding that the public notice was defective because it was too vague. In their Honours' view, the notice did not facilitate wider community understanding and meaningful participation in the reporting process due to the absence of a reasonable description of the focus of the application.

[26] Additionally, Burchett and Kiefel JJ separately reasoned that stating the purpose of the application requires publication of the reason for the application—articulating the anticipated injury or desecration (including the activities constituting the threat *and* the Aboriginal traditions and beliefs affected) that a declaration will prevent.

The validity of the public notice given under s 10(3)(a): was the public notice sufficient?

[27] Sub-sections 10(3)–(4) guide the notice, consultative, and reporting processes. Section 10(3)(a) stipulates that a notice must be published in the *Gazette* and in a local newspaper (if any) stating the purpose of the heritage application and the matters to be dealt with in the report.[33]

[28] Inadequate notice—in time or substance—prevents interested people from being able to make meaningful representations and is unfair. Equally, in this statutory context, reading in broad disclosure requirements relating to the 'purpose' of a heritage application may well frustrate the primary protective purposes of the *HPA*,[34] as well as being incompatible with Australia's international treaty obligations.

[29] The *HPA's* notice provisions are ambiguous about the degree of disclosure required in the public advertisements regarding the 'purpose of the application'. Constructional choices are open to this Court and our approach is to interpret the rules so as to avoid inconvenience or injustice to persons,[35] especially the Ngarrindjeri applicants.

[30] The *HPA's* mandatory notice requirements are imprecise. By contrast, town-planning legislation typically contains specific notice provisions which serve to confirm their importance in that regulatory context.[36] In both planning systems and heritage contexts, public notice requirements function to permit interested community members to comment on the beneficial or detrimental effects of proposed action by officialdom. This promotes informed, intelligible, and rational administrative decision making. Unlike planning systems,[37] we do not consider that the 'integrity' of the heritage protection scheme hinges on a high degree of particularity in public notices. At least two reasons support this view.

[31] First, because the administrative procedures service the public interest that inheres in the *HPA's* two protective objectives in s 4. In our opinion, it follows that the public interest in heritage protection requires public notice requirements to be interpreted narrowly—in order to respect and preserve confidential Aboriginal traditions and beliefs—even at the cost of perceived unfairness to the wider public.[38] A narrow construction of due process is warranted so as to preserve secret and sacred information: specifically, confidentiality about areas and/or activities of particular significance to Ngarrindjeri women, and/or the identities of applicants.[39] Otherwise, we believe the *HPA* will lose contact with the social conditions and needs that it exists to serve.[40]

[32] Second, because the legislative goal of community participation in heritage decision making appears, to us, to be a subordinate social goal compared to s 4. Undoubtedly, there may be far-reaching, potentially prejudicial, consequences of a declaration for the wider community. But the purpose of community participation in the deliberative process is illuminated by s 10(4)(e) which provides that the Reporter deal with 'the effects the making of a declaration may have on the proprietary or pecuniary interests of persons other than the Aboriginal or Aboriginals' seeking heritage protection. This specific provision expresses the main value of public participation in this context. The public's opportunity to be heard permits the Reporter to be informed about potential detriment to the interests of others.

Does the reporter's duty to give reasonable notice to the wider community involve specific or general revelation of the area's location in the public notice?

[33] Section 10(1) speaks to preservation or protection of a 'specified area'. The ordinary meaning of the term 'specified' indicates clarity, not generality.

Conversely, the bill's second reading speech evidences that the word 'area' was employed to permit flexibility in recognising what space Aboriginals believe to be significant, but was not intended to result in huge areas being closed off.[41]

[34] There are two cogent reasons for construing statutory notice requirements in a way that promotes a reasonable degree of certainty about the *location* of significant and threatened areas. First, it will permit interested persons to comment, meaningfully, on potential detriment to their proprietary or pecuniary interests and so contribute to an informed evaluation and ministerial decision. Second, the protection afforded by the *HPA* ultimately does involve public identification of the areas being protected. Otherwise, the public could inadvertently breach the law and incur serious penalties under the Act.

[35] There are strong countervailing considerations in this context that militate against identifying sacred sites with precision.[42] Aboriginal applicants may be adversely affected by a notice requirement that demands particular identification and publication of an area sought to be protected because this might lead to further injury or desecration of the area or violation of traditional beliefs. Furthermore, the publicity attending an application for heritage protection may result in reluctance among Aboriginal people to initiate such applications. There is also a potential welfare risk: namely, the possibility that if there is public disclosure of discrete areas of particular significance, Aboriginal applicants may come into conflict with other Aboriginals wishing to maintain strict privacy around sacred sites.[43]

[36] These are weighty considerations, but we agree with the trial judge and other members of this Court that heritage protection involves *reasonably* precise identification of the area's location. Indeed, the emergency (s 9) declaration made by the Minister on 12 May 1994 that preceded the s 10 declaration was in fact sufficiently clear about the relevant area: the bridge site and immediate approaches to it.[44]

[37] Therefore, in this aspect, the ordinary meaning of the statutory terms is adopted. Potentially, this requirement may disrupt an Aboriginal community's interest in keeping information about the location of sacred sites closely guarded. This appears to be an unfortunate consequence of seeking the protection this legislation offers.

Does revealing the purpose of the application entail disclosing the nature of the activities constituting the threat of injury or desecration and *the reasons why such activities are regarded as constituting injury or desecration to an area of significance?*

[38] In our opinion, a valid public notice must reveal the nature of the activities (e.g. earthworks) constituting the perceived threat of injury or desecration to a specified area, but we find it unnecessary to insist upon the statement

of purpose revealing anything about the traditions and beliefs affected by those activities. As the Chief Justice has stated in his separate judgment, this Court must be 'particularly mindful of the policy of the Act with respect to preservation, and the danger of offending traditions of Aboriginal people by disclosing beliefs of a particular character to the world at large'.[45] We agree.

[39] Parliament was cognisant of the importance of the retention of sacred knowledge to Aboriginal people when it enacted social legislation for heritage protection. It is well known that Aboriginal law insists on certain subjects being kept secret. Section 27 of the *HPA* goes some way towards recognising this aspect of Aboriginal law and preserving secrecy by giving to the Court power to conduct proceedings *in camera* where the Court is satisfied that it is desirable to do so, in the interests of justice and Aboriginal tradition. Surrounding statutory provisions, such as s 27, supply another relevant contextual factor when determining the nature and extent of public disclosure requirements.

[40] Respecting the rights and beliefs of Aboriginal people means reading provisions down and favouring non-disclosure of confidential traditions and beliefs. To paraphrase Woodward J in *ASSPA v Re Maurice; Re Warumungu*,[46] the outrage in an Aboriginal community caused by a forced public disclosure of information about a sacred site outweighs the importance, in this decision-making context, of explaining why it was sacred.[47] This approach extends to cover both Aboriginal guardians of the information and other persons to whom they had extended their confidence.

[41] The non-identification of the Aboriginal tradition or belief that might suffer injury or desecration might appear to constrain the public's capacity to make effective comments about those matters, as other learned judges in this Court have suggested. Conversely, we harbour serious doubts that ordinary members of the public could express their opinions about Aboriginal beliefs and traditions in an informed way. It is doubtful whether members of the public, excluding certain Ngarrindjeri and perhaps other neighbouring Aboriginal groups, would have the knowledge to make meaningful submissions about whether an area was, or was not, of 'particular significance' *to Aboriginals* in accordance with their tradition. Likewise, how would the public really know about and comprehend matters pertaining to 'the nature and extent of the threat of injury to or desecration of, the area'?

[42] It appears to us that, logically, only Aboriginal people can furnish meaningful submissions on the 'particular significance' of land or water—be that historical, spiritual, and/or cultural significance—and the nature and extent of the threat to (inter alia) dreaming tracks, campsites, or burial places. Essentially, these are matters for particular Aboriginal people, as Justice Brennan identified in the *Tasmanian Dams* case, in respect of a similar expression in s 8(3) of the *World Heritage Properties Conservation Act 1983* (Cth).[48]

[43] We do not comprehend that the purpose of community consultation is to permit ordinary members of the public to respond to or challenge the veracity of claims about the significance of an area to an Aboriginal society or group. That is not a right expressly given to the public under the *HPA*, and nor should it be implied because it artificially creates an adversarial scheme that may frustrate statutory objectives. The public notification and comment scheme enables the public to present material about, relevantly, the effects a declaration may have on their proprietary rights or pecuniary interests. The structure of the *HPA* requires the Reporter to assess that input as part of their independent evaluation of the heritage claim. Then it is for the Minister to weigh up opinions and resolve competing arguments before making the final and operative decision.

[44] Our approach to the content of procedures required by law does not deny a role for others, including anthropologists or archaeologists, in the deliberative process.[49] The structure of the *HPA* is such that the Reporter's account will, inevitably it seems, be informed by the opinions of non-Indigenous professionals. Even so, those qualified opinions must draw on the views, understanding, and lived experience of certain Aboriginal people regarding the 'particular significance of an area', 'the nature and extent of the threat of injury or desecration to the area', and 'extent of the area' that warrants protection. We recognise that reliance upon non-Indigenous people's knowledge to inform assessments about a heritage protection claim—as the *HPA* appears to anticipate—will be difficult for some Aboriginal custodians of the land to fathom.

[45] In short, disclosure of the physical *activities* threatening the area is sufficient to afford the wider community prior substantive notice about the purpose of an application. In conjunction with revealing the area affected with reasonable precision, that constitutes adequate disclosure. We strongly disagree with Burchett J who, in his reasons, intimates that without full revelation of the basis of the heritage claim, the administrative procedure smacks of the Inquisition.[50]

Does revealing the purpose of the application warrant disclosing the identity (or identities) of the applicant(s)?

[46] If the disclosure of the claimants' identities is tied to the necessity for disclosure of Aboriginal tradition or beliefs (as O'Loughlin J reasoned it was), logically, it follows from our reasoning stated above that there is no requirement to state the identity of an applicant for heritage protection. Our view coheres with that of Black CJ, whose reasons state that

> it is stretching the meaning of 'purpose' to conclude that a requirement to state the purpose of the application involves a requirement to state by whom the application is made, particularly when there is no statutory requirement for the applicant to have any greater connection with the

area sought to be protected other than to be, or to act on behalf of, an Aboriginal person or a group of Aboriginal people.[51]

Did the Minister lawfully 'consider' the representations received by the Reporter?

[47] Section 10(1)(c) of the *HPA* provides that the Minister must 'consider' the report and any representations attached to it before making a valid declaration. There is probative material evidencing that the Minister 'considered' the report by Professor Saunders.[52] Accordingly, the critical factual and legal issue for our determination is whether the Minister properly 'considered' the confidential representations marked 'women's business'.

[48] The issue arises for determination as the Minister did not read the representations pertaining to the cultural and spiritual beliefs of Ngarrindjeri women, and yet his amended statement of reasons reveal it was central to his decision. Instead, the Minister was informed by the Reporter's interpretation and assessment of them, and his aide subsequently confirmed the content of the restricted material. He adopted this course of action due to 'the depth and conviction with which the Aboriginal women of the region hold and maintain their spiritual and cultural beliefs for the area'.[53] Specifically, the women's business contained sacred information that was traditionally confined to certain Ngarrindjeri women and could not be disclosed to men.

[49] We agree with O'Loughlin J, who decided that 'considering the representations must involve a balanced mixture of staff assistance and personal involvement'.[54] Where we differ from the learned trial judge is on the question of what the appropriate mixture is. Relying upon dictionary meanings, O'Loughlin J found that the statutory obligation to 'consider' the report and representations demanded substantial personal involvement, requiring the Minister to read the content of the envelopes himself. Other members of this Court agree with that analysis. We do not consider that s 10(1)(c) should be read so strictly in this particular context.

[50] In making our assessment, we pay close attention to the *HPA's* statutory purpose to respect Aboriginal traditions. This is fitting given the confidential and gendered nature of representations from certain Ngarrindjeri women reflecting their traditional cultural beliefs. The statutory objectives frame and inform our conclusion that the male Minister, evidently relying on the informed assessment of facts, issues, and contentions by the female Reporter, and with the assistance of a female ministerial aide, achieved the appropriate, balanced mixture in this case. This administrative arrangement was made out of respect for the Ngarrindjeri beliefs and sensitivity to their traditions. Our broader, less formal construction of s 10(1)(c) causes no injustice or inconvenience to the Ngarrindjeri women and is consistent with the principal statutory objectives and international law as outlined earlier in our reasons.

[51] O'Loughlin J recognised that 'a busy Minister of the Crown is entitled to receive assistance from his staff...But that entitlement does not, of course, permit him to delegate his decision-making power'.[55] Certainly, the Minister could not lawfully delegate his statutory duty under s 10. This is attributable to the magnitude of the declaratory decision for the Ngarrindjeri applicants and the wider public. This reason supports the view that only the Minister can exercise the power personally. Additionally, s 31(1) of the *HPA* expressly permits formal delegation of the Minister's powers except for those contained in s 10 (amongst others). We observe that the Minister was not delegating or abrogating his power. He was trusting the nominated Reporter's assessment of the issues and representations (as he surely must do under the legislated scheme). He then held discussions with his ministerial aide, thereby taking note of the 'women's business'.

[52] O'Loughlin J concluded that 'the extent and description' of the Minister's discussion with his aide were 'vague and nebulous'.[56] Notwithstanding this conclusion, the wider regulatory context and the timelines the *HPA* imposed form part of the assessment of the adequacy of the 'consideration'. The ministerial office was sent a copy of the Saunders report on 7 July 1994 and statutory timelines dictated that Mr Tickner was required to make a decision about issuing a permanent declaration by 10 July 1994.

[53] The gender division of sacred information and knowledge is generally accepted as a feature of pre- and post-colonisation Aboriginal societies. There is some information and knowledge that can only be held by one gender and not the other. Even within that one gender, there can be some individuals who hold knowledge and others who do not. This explanation has been relayed by Ngarrindjeri females, was recorded by a female anthropologist and documented by a female Reporter, and a female aide then briefed the Minister. Given this situation, we accept that the Minister has properly taken into account and considered the confidential material consistently with both the *HPA* and in recognition of Aboriginal law.

[54] By accepting and respecting the traditions of certain Ngarrindjeri women, the Minister pursued a just course of administrative action. It is to be preferred over other possible viable arrangements, such as the Minister recusing himself and requesting the Prime Minister appoint an acting Minister, who was female, to read the sacred women's business and make a decision about the declaration. The latter approach could introduce delays and additional complexity to the (time-sensitive) declaratory decision-making process, which are neither necessary (not being prescribed in the *HPA*) nor desirable.

Conclusions

[55] The Minister lawfully 'considered' the Ngarrindjeri women's representations. The public notice was not, however, authorised by the Act because the

location of the significant area was not identified clearly enough. As such the appeal is dismissed on that basis.

[56] In light of the significant public interest in matters raised by this case and the finding of compliance with the *HPA* requirements of ministerial consideration, we exercise the Court's discretion and order that each party to the proceedings bear their own costs, rather than the losing party paying the winner's legal costs.

[57] Finally, we acknowledge the challenges of reconciling Aboriginal philosophies and traditions with other competing perspectives and property interests founded on colonisation. In this case, we have attempted to demonstrate that, although difficult, if legislative terms permit and the special context and purpose of cultural heritage is given due credence, it is possible to achieve a modicum of reconciliation via purposive statutory interpretation and the flexible application of administrative law principles.

Notes

1 Narelle Bedford and Peter Billings.
2 Larissa Behrendt, 'No One Can Own the Land' (1994) 1(1) *Australian Journal of Human Rights* 43, 47.
3 *Chapman v Tickner* (1995) 55 FCR 316, 365–70.
4 Graham Jenkin, *Conquest of the Ngarrindjeri* (Rigby, 1979) 11.
5 Ibid., 51.
6 *Milirrpum v Nabalco* (1979) 17 FLR 141, 281 (Blackburn J).
7 Select Committee of the Legislative Council, Parliament of South Australia, *Report of the Select Committee of the Legislative Council upon the Aborigines* (Report No 165, 16 October 1860) 1.
8 Ronald Berndt and Catherine Berndt with John Stanton, *A World that Was: The Yaraldi of the Murray River and Lakes* (Melbourne University Press, 1993) 297.
9 Albert Barunga, 'Sacred Sites and Their Protection' in Robert Edwards (ed), *The Preservation of Australia's Aboriginal Heritage* (Australian Institute of Aboriginal Studies, 1975) 76.
10 (1993) 40 FCR 183.
11 Ibid., 193.
12 We note the draft *Declaration on the Rights of Indigenous Peoples* (UN Doc E/CN.4/Sub.2/1994/2/Add.1 (1994), especially art 12 (cultural preservation and protection) and art 13 (spiritual and religious freedom). Also, Indigenous peoples' cultural and religious rights fall within *International Covenant on Civil and Political Rights* art 27.
13 Commission on Human Rights, *Study of the Problem of Discrimination against Indigenous Populations—Final Report Submitted by the Special Rapporteur, Mr Jose R Martinez Cobo*, E/CN.4/Sub.2/1983/21/Add.8 (30 September 1983) [198]. And further at [236], '[S]acred land or land of historical or spiritual significance for Indigenous peoples must in all cases be...protected from intrusions of all kinds'.
14 *Tickner v Bropho* (1993) 40 FCR 183, 211 (French J).
15 *Polites v The Commonwealth* (1945) 70 CLR 60, 68–9 (Latham CJ); *Minister for Immigration and Ethnic Affairs v Teoh* (1995 183 CLR 273, 287–28 (Mason CJ and Deane J).
16 See e.g. *New Zealand Maori Council v Attorney-General* [1987] 1 NZLR 641, 655–6; *R v Calder* [1973] SCR 313.
17 See e.g. *R v Calder* [1973] SCR 313, 317; *Guerin v R* [1984] 2 SCR 335, 375, 382; *R v Sparrow* [1990] 1 SCR 1075; *New Zealand Maori Council v Attorney-General* [1987] 1 NZLR 641, 673.

18 See *R v Calder* [1973] SCR 313, 318, 328, citing Wilson Duff, *The Indian History of British Columbia* (The Royal British Columbia Museum, 1964). See also *New Zealand Maori Council v Attorney-General* [1987] 1 NZLR 641, 655 where the Court had regard to 'historical works, historical and legal theses and other writings' in addition to usual legal sources and submissions.
19 See *R v Sparrow* [1990] 1 SCR 1075, 1112, citing Leroy Little Bear, 'A Concept of Native Title' (1982) 5 *Canadian Legal Aid Bulletin* 99. *Sparrow* was the first time the Canadian Supreme Court cited a First Nations academic.
20 Commonwealth, *Parliamentary Debates*, House of Representatives, 9 May 1984, 2133 (Clyde Holding).
21 Ibid., citing *Commonwealth v Tasmania* (1983) 158 CLR 1, 180 (Murphy J).
22 *Tickner v Bropho* (1993) 40 FCR 183, 221 (French J).
23 Commonwealth, *Parliamentary Debates*, House of Representatives, 16 April 1986, 2420 (Clyde Holding).
24 Injury or desecration is to be understood broadly in accordance with Aboriginal tradition and not in a more limited 'western' sense. See also *HPA* s 3, which defines 'significant Aboriginal area'.
25 *Tickner v Bropho* (1993) 40 FCR 183, 223 (French J).
26 *Kioa v West* (1985) 159 CLR 550, 584–5 (Mason J).
27 *Chapman v Tickner* (1995) 55 FCR 316, 331–4.
28 Cf. *State of Western Australia v Minister for Aboriginal and Torres Strait Islander Affairs* (1995) 37 ALD 633 (Carr J) for an expansive view of the procedures implied in relation to s 10.
29 *Aboriginal and Torres Strait Islander Heritage Protection Act 1984* (Cth) s 10(1)(a)–(b) ('*HPA*'). A significant Aboriginal area is defined in s 3 as 'an area of particular significance to Aboriginals in accordance with Aboriginal tradition'.
30 Ibid., s 10(1)(c).
31 *Tickner v Bropho* (1993) 40 FCR 183, 224 (French J).
32 *South Australia v O'Shea* (1987) 163 CLR 378, 389 (Mason CJ), 402–3 (Wilson and Toohey JJ), 409–10, 412 (Brennan J).
33 *HPA* s 10(3)(a)(i). The seven matters to be dealt with are identified in s 10(4).
34 *Caltex Oil (Australia) Pty Ltd v Best* (1990) 170 CLR 516, 525 (Mason CJ, Gaudron and McHugh JJ).
35 See *Cooper Brookes (Wollongong) Pty Ltd v Federal Commissioner of Taxation* (1980) 147 CLR 297, 305 (Gibbs CJ).
36 *Scurr v Brisbane City Council* (1973) 133 CLR 242, 252 (Stephen J).
37 *Curac v Shoalhaven City Council* (1993) 81 LGERA 124, 128 (Stein J).
38 See, eg, *Church of Scientology v Woodward* (1982) 154 CLR 25, 76 (Brennan J), in the context of the secret work of a national security and intelligence agency.
39 At common law, modifications of ordinary disclosure principles of procedural fairness are well recognised as acceptable by the courts where there is a risk to the public interest, including damage to national security or the welfare of children.
40 The courts have acknowledged that non-disclosure of culturally sensitive Aboriginal information is an aspect of the law of public interest immunity: see *ASSPA v Maurice; Re Warumungu* (1986) 10 FCR 104; *Western Australia v Minister for Aboriginal and Torres Strait Islander Affairs* (1995) 54 FCR 144.
41 Commonwealth, *Parliamentary Debates*, House of Representatives, 9 May 1984, 2133 (Clyde Holding).
42 As acknowledged in *ASSPA v Maurice; Re Warumungu Land Claim* (1986) 10 FCR 104, 114 (Woodward J).
43 Relatedly, see *ASSPA v Maurice; Re Warumungu Land Claim* (1986) 10 FCR 104, 110 (Bowen CJ).
44 *Chapman v Tickner* (1995) 55 FCR 316, 348–9.
45 *Tickner v Chapman* (1995) 57 FCR 451, 461 (Black CJ).

46 (1986) 10 FCR 104. In this case, public interest immunity was recognised as covering secret and sacred Aboriginal information and beliefs.
47 Ibid., 114.
48 *Commonwealth v Tasmania* (1983) 57 ALJR 450, 539.
49 The provision of expert evidence is not unproblematic; for instance, 'authoritative' accounts of Aboriginal tradition may be quite dated, be based on a small number of informants, and/or ignore the voices of women and children.
50 *Tickner v Chapman* (1995) 57 FCR 451, 479.
51 Ibid., 461.
52 *Chapman v Tickner* (1995) 55 FCR 316, 367.
53 Ibid., 370 (O'Loughlin J).
54 Ibid., 369.
55 Ibid., 370, citing *Minister for Aboriginal Affairs v Peko-Wallsend* (1986) 162 CLR 24, 30 (Gibbs CJ), 65 (Brennan J).
56 *Chapman v Tickner* (1995) 55 FCR 316, 370.

6

MEMBERS OF THE YORTA YORTA ABORIGINAL COMMUNITY v VICTORIA (2002) 214 CLR 422

Commentary: *Members of the Yorta Yorta Aboriginal Community v Victoria* (2002) 214 CLR 422

Simon Young

Social, political, and legal context

The 1992 decision in *Mabo v Queensland (No 2)*[1] ('*Mabo*') was unarguably a major turning point in Australia's legal and cultural maturation. A majority of the High Court belatedly revisited the old orthodoxy that the Crown's title was 'absolute' and the underlying fiction that Australia was 'practically unoccupied' at the time of British assertion of sovereignty. Native title was held to be capable of surviving as a burden upon the Crown's acquired 'radical title'. Accordingly, beyond certain lands that had been the subject of specific dealings, the Meriam people of the Torres Strait were 'entitled as against the whole world to possession, occupation, use and enjoyment of the lands of the Murray Islands'.[2]

Yet there would be uncertainty in the application of these principles to mainland Australia—the product of subtle differences within and between the majority judgments, the uncertain scope of key terms underpinning the new principles, and the uniqueness of the facts in *Mabo*. Most importantly for present purposes, and critical to the progress of Australia's legal renaissance, questions soon emerged about the position of communities more heavily impacted by colonisation. How would the succeeding cases and laws acknowledge the pervasive impact of Western laws and priorities in many parts of Australia? And how would they conceptualise the adaptation, resilience, and proud survival of many communities? These were questions that would profoundly test the Western understanding of Aboriginal identity and connection, and the depth of Australia's new reckoning with its silenced history. This new judgment on the *Yorta Yorta*[3] appeal seeks to restart the post-*Mabo* handling of these questions, re-centre the First Peoples' voice in the measurement of First Peoples' survival, and walk back the legal thinking that has led us away from *Mabo*'s spark of essential truth.

In the leading *Mabo* judgment, Brennan J had emphasised that native title is sourced in and owes its content to 'traditional laws acknowledged' and 'traditional customs observed'—and the need for a community's substantial maintenance of 'traditional connection' by continued acknowledgement and observance.[4] A full reading of the case reveals that the key terms were often used with deliberate flexibility and qualification, and the detailed analysis and findings in the case appear not to support a strict interpretation of these principles. Moreover, the heavy emphasis on 'traditional laws and customs' can, to a degree, be explained by the precedential context (most notably the 'absence of law' theory of pre-existing Aboriginal and Torres Strait Islander occupation) and indeed the factual context (an initial focus on *inter se* rights within the Meriam community). Yet without this fuller reading and broader context, Brennan J's words could present a narrowing door for claimant communities more impacted by colonisation. And it was the bare passages that were preserved in key provisions of the *Native Title Act 1993* (Cth)—most importantly s 223.

Legal commentators of the time highlighted quite early the risks attending a restrictive approach to the *Mabo* principles.[5] However, the succeeding years saw some habitually selective referencing of *Mabo* and a pattern of litigation that in various ways encouraged quite specific explication of community laws and customs and their survival in fact—for example, to resist Crown assertions of past *legal* extinguishment (at least in part). Moreover, the focus in this era on northern communities perhaps masked the grievous implications of a strict approach for many communities in the south. In all of this context, the more restrictive thinking on requisite 'continuity' did appear to gain some ascendancy.[6]

The *Yorta Yorta* decision

Judicial attention turned directly to these issues in the *Yorta Yorta* litigation, which concerned a claim over land and waters in the early-settled and intensively used Murray River area. The new judgment recounts the history of the litigation. Critically, the trial judge concluded that whatever the contemporary practices of the community, before the end of the 19th century, the claimants' ancestors had ceased to occupy their traditional lands in accordance with their traditional laws and customs. Indeed, the 'tide of history' had 'washed away' any real acknowledgement of traditional laws and real observance of their traditional customs.[7] A Full Federal Court majority noted possible errors in the detail of the approach taken at trial but considered them immaterial given their view that the trial findings did require a rejection of the claim on continuity grounds.[8]

In the critical High Court judgment of Gleeson CJ, Gummow J, and Hayne J, there was a notable focus on the 'intersection' of the traditional system and the common law system—at the point of British assertion of sovereignty.[9] Their

Honours emphasised that the traditional system could not validly create rights, duties, or interests after that point—and hence only ones with origins in prior law and custom could be recognised.[10] More critically, drawing upon s 223, their Honours emphasised that the 'normative system' supporting the rights and interests (and only pre-sovereignty normative rules were to be considered 'traditional'[11]) must have had a 'continuous existence and vitality' for those rights and interests to have survived.[12] It was accordingly considered that the original 'society' must have had continuous survival.[13] Their Honours indicated that 'some' change and adaptation in traditional law and custom or 'some' interruption in the enjoyment or exercise of rights and interests would 'not necessarily be fatal'. However, there appeared to be relatively little scope (or guidance) offered for accommodating the stark realities of many community histories.[14]

Ultimately, their Honours rejected the appeal on the basis of the trial findings as to discontinuity of observance of traditional laws and custom, and discontinuity of traditional 'society'.[15]

How was the decision received?

Much debate emerged around the reasoning in *Yorta Yorta*—particularly as regards the difficulty of both annulling and requiring ongoing 'vitality' in the Aboriginal 'system', and the possible adoption of a quite constricted notion of 'society'. More broadly, commentators have criticised this approach for its denial of past transformations of landscapes and economies,[16] its evidential complexity,[17] its potentially intrusive and divisive differentiation of communities and re-dispossession of those most impacted by past oppression,[18] and more broadly, its dismantling of the promise (and relevance) of the whole native title doctrine.[19] Some of these criticisms have been amplified in proposals for deliberate law reform. Former Chief Justice French suggested some reversal of the relevant onus of proof,[20] and others have argued for clarification (or even removal) of the word 'traditional' in the statute.[21] The Australian Law Reform Commission recommended statutory reform to acknowledge the adaptive nature of traditional laws and customs and mitigate the onerous inquiries drawn from *Yorta Yorta*.[22] Yet political action has come indirectly and at state level—most notably (and partly in response to *Yorta Yorta*) in the *Traditional Owner Settlement Act 2010* (Vic) which offers something of a supported alternative path for communities and turns continuity inquiries more towards contemporary connections.[23]

In the courts, there have been periodic signs of broader thinking on continuity requirements. Prominently, in Black CJ's dissent in the first *Yorta Yorta* appeal, his Honour emphasised that it was wrong to see 'traditional' as a concept concerned with what is 'dead, frozen or otherwise incapable of change'.[24] Gaudron and Kirby JJ (in their own High Court dissent) pressed for a more flexible concept of 'society' and less insistence on close comparison of contemporary and pre-settlement laws and customs. Their Honours suggested that laws and customs qualified as 'traditional' if they had their 'origins' in the past and differences constituted 'adaptations, alterations, modifications or extensions made in accordance with the shared values or the customs and practices of the people who acknowledge and observe those laws and customs'.[25] After the High Court decision in *Yorta Yorta*, lower courts proceeded in both directions. Some embraced the stricter thinking,[26] but others continued the ad hoc search for flexibility within the bounds of the *Yorta Yorta* framework.[27]

Significant advances are now underway in the Australian approach to native title 'content', driven particularly by the decision in *Akiba v Commonwealth.*[28] Yet there appears to be no significant movement in the continuity principles, beyond ad hoc work at the boundaries,[29] signalling more heavy work for communities struggling to meet the *Yorta Yorta* standard.[30] Moreover, the recent critical compensation decision in *Northern Territory v Griffiths*,[31] with its focus upon the strength and purity of cultural and spiritual connection (in the consideration of non-economic loss),[32] perhaps risks some further discounting (in line with the *Yorta Yorta* heritage) of the strength of First Peoples' *contemporary* connections with land.

The new judgment

This new judgment seeks to retrieve the First Peoples' perspective—too often lost in the complexity of arduous continuity inquiries. It seeks to demonstrate that the most confounding elements of the Australian native title doctrine can be recast into a clearer and more illuminating inquiry and that the doctrine can thereby have a more principled and enduring relevance. The judgment's ultimate focus is on the survival of the Yorta Yorta peoples' custodial ethic. What more can logically and justly be asked of a people pressed into crisis for generations by the dispossession of pastoralism and policy? The challenge for the court is thus reframed as one of recognising adaptation and resilience—rather than measuring cultural erosion.

Notes

1 (1992) 175 CLR 1 ('*Mabo*').
2 Ibid., 76 (Brennan J); 217 (Order of the Court).
3 *Members of the Yorta Yorta Aboriginal Community v Victoria* (2002) 214 CLR 422 ('*Yorta Yorta*').
4 *Mabo* (1992) 175 CLR 1, 57–60, 70 (Brennan J).
5 See e.g. works by Noel Pearson, Tony McAvoy, Richard H Bartlett, Hal Wootten, Gary D Myers, Luke McNamara and Scott Grattan, Jeremy Webber, Kent McNeil, and Lisa Strelein.
6 See e.g. *Western Australia v Commonwealth* (1995) 183 CLR 373, 452 (Mason CJ, Brennan, Deane, Toohey, Gaudron, and McHugh JJ) (quoted by Brennan CJ in *Wik Peoples v Queensland* (1996) 187 CLR 1, 92); *Commonwealth v Yarmirr* (2001) 208 CLR 1, 46–52 [37]–[50] (Gleeson CJ, Gaudron, Gummow, and Hayne JJ).
7 *Members of the Yorta Yorta Aboriginal Community v Victoria* [1998] FCA 1606, [122]–[125], [129] (Olney J).

8 *Members of the Yorta Yorta Aboriginal Community v Victoria* (2001) 110 FCR 244, 291–92 [187]–[191] (Branson and Katz JJ).
9 *Yorta Yorta* (2002) 214 CLR 422, 439–40 [31].
10 Ibid., 441–4 [37]–[44].
11 Ibid., 444 [46].
12 Ibid., 444–7 [47]–[55], 456 [87].
13 Ibid., 445–7 [49]–[55], 456–7 [87]–[89].
14 See ibid., 454–7 [78]–[89].
15 Ibid., [95]–[96]. See also 468 [135] (McHugh J).
16 See e.g. Marcia Langton, 'The Aboriginal Balancing Act' (2013) (115) *Australian Geographic* 39.
17 See e.g. Paul Finn, 'A Judge's Reflections on Native Title' in Sean Brennan et al. (eds), *Native Title from Mabo to Akiba: A Vehicle for Change and Empowerment?* (Federation Press, 2015) 23, 26–7.
18 See e.g. Richard Bartlett, 'An Obsession with Traditional Laws and Customs Creates Difficulty Establishing Native Title Claims in the South: *Yorta Yorta*' (2003) 31(1) *University of Western Australia Law Review* 35.
19 See further Simon Young, *The Trouble with Tradition: Native Title and Cultural Change* (Federation Press, 2008).
20 See Robert French, 'Lifting the Burden of Native Title: Some Modest Proposals for Improvement' (Speech, Federal Court Native Title User Group, 9 July 2008).
21 See e.g. Noel Pearson, *Up from the Mission: Selected Writings* (Black Ink Books, 2009) 75.
22 Australian Law Reform Commission, *Connection to Country: Review of the Native Title Act 1993 (Cth)* (Report No 126, April 2015), recommendations 5-1, 5-2, 5-3, 5-4.
23 Relevant here also, but beyond the scope of this discussion, are the broader progress towards treaty negotiations (including in Victoria) and the Noongar native title settlement in the south of Western Australia.
24 *Members of the Yorta Yorta Aboriginal Community v Victoria* (2001) 110 FCR 244, 256 [35].
25 *Yorta Yorta* (2002) 214 CLR 422, 464 [114]–[119].
26 See e.g. *Daniel v Western Australia* [2003] FCA 666; *Risk v Northern Territory* [2006] FCA 404; *Risk v Northern Territory* (2007) 240 ALR 75.
27 See e.g. *De Rose v South Australia* (2003) 133 FCR 325; *De Rose v South Australia [No 2]* (2005) 145 FCR 290; *Bennell v Western Australia* (2006) 153 FCR 120. But see *Bodney v Bennell* (2008) 167 FCR 84.
28 (2013) 250 CLR 209 (recognition of a subsisting broad resource use right).
29 See e.g. *Croft on behalf of Barngarla Native Title Claim Group v South Australia* (2015) 325 ALR 213; *Narrier v Western Australia* [2016] FCA 1519; *Ashwin on behalf of Wutha People v Western Australia [No 4]* (2019) 369 ALR 1.
30 See e.g. *CG (dec'd) on behalf of the Badimia People v Western Australia* [2015] FCA 204; *Sandy on behalf of Yugara People v Queensland* (2017) 254 FCR 107; *Starkey on behalf of Kokatha People v South Australia* (2018) 261 FCR 183.
31 *Northern Territory v Griffiths (dec'd) on behalf of Ngaliwurru and Nungali Peoples* (2019) 364 ALR 208.
32 See e.g. ibid., 238 [98], 257 [166], 269–70 [217] (Kiefel CJ, Bell, Keane, Nettle, and Gordon JJ). Cf. 256–7 [163], 268 [230] (Kiefel CJ, Bell, Keane, Nettle, and Gordon JJ).

MEMBERS OF THE YORTA YORTA ABORIGINAL COMMUNITY .... APPELLANT;

AND

VICTORIA .... RESPONDENT;

(2002) 214 CLR 422

Native title—Continuity of laws and customs—Custodial responsibilities to country—Inherent sovereignty as peoples.

Burns J.[1]

Introduction

[1] According to First Peoples' protocols, it is incumbent on me to introduce myself and my cultural affiliations. I am a Gomeroi-Kamilaroi woman. My family connections are to Bingara on the Gwydir River in north-west New South Wales. My great-grandmother was a member of the stolen generations—her removal from Country meant that we were denied the opportunity of learning language and culture. However, as the following discussion of First Peoples' philosophical worldviews explains, this does not necessarily mean that our connection to Country is 'lost'.

[2] It is also incumbent on me to state that under First Peoples' laws, I have no authority whatsoever to sit in judgment of another First Peoples group. This is a fundamental recognition of the diversity and inherent sovereignty of First Peoples. The questions before this court, however, go to the relationship between the Yorta Yorta peoples and the agencies of the Australian nation-state. They come before the court rather belatedly, and regrettably in the absence of any formal treaty between the Yorta Yorta peoples and the British colonial government (or its successors). This case, however, presents an opportunity to set the relationship between the Yorta Yorta peoples and Australian governments on a new footing, one based on equality and mutual respect. Acknowledging the inherent sovereignty of First Peoples must be the starting point for re-setting this relationship and for consideration of the issues in this case.

The application

[3] The Yorta Yorta peoples have brought a claim under the *Native Title Act 1993* (Cth) ('*NTA*') for recognition of native title over their ancestral lands.

The claimant group is represented by eight applicants: Ella Anselmi, Wayne Atkinson, Geraldine Briggs, Kenneth Briggs, Elizabeth Hoffman, Desmond Morgan, Colin Walker, and Margaret Wirrpunda. Broadly speaking, the claim encompasses all 'public lands' within an oval-shaped area of some 5,000 square kilometres which straddles what is now known as the border between Victoria and New South Wales. The details of the claim are set out in the judgment.[2] While the state boundaries were immaterial to the Yorta Yorta peoples pre-1788, they are significant in this case because they determine the different colonial statutory regimes that the court must apply in this case and the consequences of such regimes for the continuing enjoyment of native rights and interests. Within the scheme of the *NTA*, the various statutory regimes and the rights and interests they grant to other parties may have the effect of 'extinguishing' the Yorta Yorta peoples' native title.

[4] The Yorta Yorta peoples' native title claim was made on the basis that their current beliefs and practices were an expression of their 'traditional' laws and customs in an 'adapted form'. In short, these beliefs and practices go to the exercise of the Yorta Yorta peoples' custodial responsibilities to Country.[3] The Yorta Yorta peoples also argued that since colonisation of their lands in the 1840s, they have made numerous attempts to assert their custodial responsibilities towards Country, which is evidence of the continuation of their laws and customs.[4]

[5] The Yorta Yorta peoples' native title claim was vigorously opposed. The main respondents, New South Wales and Victoria, both denied the existence of the Yorta Yorta peoples' native title.[5] There were over 500 non-claimant parties to the proceedings, most of which also denied the existence of native title.[6] The respondents primarily asserted that their interests were likely to be adversely affected by a positive determination of native title.[7]

[6] In my view, the Yorta Yorta peoples have proven their native title claim. This is because the Yorta Yorta peoples' present observance of their laws and customs is an incident of their inherent sovereignty as *peoples*. The Yorta Yorta peoples' present acknowledgement and observance of their laws and customs also reflect their custodial responsibilities to care for Country. Despite the ravages of colonisation and the concerted efforts of colonial governments to disrupt the Yorta Yorta peoples' laws and culture, they have maintained their identity as *peoples* through their connection to their ancestral lands. In my opinion, these are the critical elements that must be proven in this case.

Findings of the trial judge

[7] The key finding of the trial judge, Olney J, was that by the end of the 19th century, the claimants' ancestors had:

> ceased to occupy their traditional lands in accordance with their traditional laws and customs. The tide of history has indeed washed away any

> real acknowledgement of their traditional laws and any real observance of their traditional customs.[8]

[8] Based on this finding, the trial judge concluded that the foundation of the Yorta Yorta peoples' claim had 'disappeared', and therefore any native title rights and interests they might have previously held had suffered a similar fate. The trial judge also found that once native title is 'lost', it is not capable of revival.[9] In making this assessment, the trial judge regarded the writing of an early settler, Edward Curr, who lived in Yorta Yorta country for ten years, as the most credible source of evidence of the 'traditional' laws and customs of the group.[10] This evidence was afforded considerable weight in comparison to the testimony of the Yorta Yorta peoples themselves, which was based on 'oral traditions passed down through *many generations extending over a period in excess of two hundred years*'.[11] In addition, the trial judge found that the Yorta Yorta peoples' petition to the Governor of New South Wales in 1881 provided 'positive evidence' of the discontinuation of their laws and customs.[12] The details of this petition and its interpretation by the courts will be discussed further below.

Appeals

[9] The fundamental questions raised in this appeal go to the interpretation of s 223 of the *NTA*, which defines native title as:

> the communal, group or individual rights and interests of Aboriginal peoples or Torres Strait Islanders in relation to land or waters, where: (a) the rights and interests are possessed under the traditional laws acknowledged, and the traditional customs observed, by the Aboriginal peoples or Torres Strait Islanders; and (b) the Aboriginal peoples or Torres Strait Islanders, by those laws and customs, have a connection with the land or waters; and (c) the rights and interests are recognised by the common law of Australia.

[10] The Yorta Yorta peoples appealed the decision of the trial judge.[13] The primary grounds for the appeal were that the trial judge adopted a 'frozen in time' approach to determining the existence of traditional laws and custom by requiring evidence of 'traditional' laws and customs as they existed at the point of first contact, and their continued acknowledgement and observance until the present time.[14] Further, it was argued that the trial judge had failed to give consideration to the capacity of 'traditional' laws and customs to adapt to changed circumstances.[15] In short, the appellants contended that the trial judge wrongly equated native title with the existence of a 'traditional society' or a 'traditional lifestyle'.[16]

[11] The appellants also argued that the trial judge had erred by ignoring historical evidence of the Yorta Yorta peoples' continuing connection with

Country and the evidence of living witnesses about the circumstances in which the Yorta Yorta peoples found themselves by the end of the 19th century.[17] While the majority in the Federal Court found that the trial judge had erred in his approach to issues of proof of 'traditional' laws and customs, they concurred with the trial judge's conclusion that the Yorta Yorta peoples' native title had been lost, through the 'abandonment' of their laws and customs, as established on the facts of the case.[18]

[12] The matter is now the subject of appeal before this court. The grounds for the appeal include, inter alia, that both the trial judge and the Full Court of the Federal Court took an overly restrictive approach to questions of proof, requiring the claimants to provide positive evidence of the continued observance of traditional laws and customs from the time of British colonisation to the present.[19] It was also argued that s 223(1) of the *NTA* directs attention to the rights and interests '*presently* possessed under traditional laws *presently* acknowledged and customs *presently* observed', and also to continuing connection by those laws and customs.[20] That appeal has been dismissed by the majority judges in this court. This dissenting judgment will set out the reasons for finding in favour of the Yorta Yorta peoples. Importantly, it centres an Indigenous knowledges approach and an understanding of First Peoples' legal philosophies to the questions for determination by this court. Given the protracted history leading to the belated recognition of native title in this country (and other issues which I will address in this judgment), the inclusion of First Peoples' knowledges and legal philosophies provides a welcome and necessary addition to the court's jurisprudence. Before doing so, I will make some brief observations about the role of the courts in deciding native title claims, and also some of the problems with the approach taken by the majority judges in this case.

The role of the courts

[13] This case is of great significance because it is the first time this court will interpret the requirements for proof of native title under the *NTA* as amended by the *Native Title Amendment Act 1998* (Cth).[21] It is also the first case to consider the potential for native title to be enjoyed in the areas most extensively affected by British colonisation, the south-eastern parts of what is now known as Australia. Therefore, the case is of great importance because it will set the scope for the potential for native title into the future, with significant consequences for the legal, political, cultural, social, and economic status of First Peoples in this country. The role of the courts in adjudicating cases of such import cannot be understated.

[14] The case of *Mabo v Queensland (No 2)*[22] ('*Mabo*') recognised a fundamental injustice. That the Australian nation-state came into being by virtue of a 'legal fiction',· the doctrine of terra nullius.[23] *Mabo* found that as a consequence of the application of terra nullius, First Peoples were denied their

rights and interests in land.[24] The belated recognition of First Peoples' native title was, however, subject to a limitation—it was said to be 'precluded if such recognition would fracture a skeletal principle of the Australian nation state'.[25] Precisely what was meant by the term 'skeletal principle' was not made entirely clear.

[15] While the High Court's decision in *Mabo* has been celebrated for ostensibly rejecting the doctrine of terra nullius, it shied away from any consideration of the legitimacy of the British assertion of sovereignty in Australia, declaring that such a matter was an 'act of state' that could not be challenged in the municipal courts.[26] This view has been strongly criticised, and for good reasons.[27] It is entirely contradictory for the court to reject terra nullius on one hand—to give belated recognition to First Peoples' native title—while on the other hand leaving terra nullius intact for all other purposes. There is a strange and irreconcilable incoherence[28] between the High Court's recognition of 'native title', based on First Peoples' laws and customs, and the denial of the inherent sovereignty of First Peoples, from which those laws and customs are derived.

[16] The opinion of the trial judge was that the *NTA* did not provide a warrant for the 'court to play the role of social engineer, righting the wrongs of the past centuries and dispensing justice according to contemporary notions of political correctness rather than according to law.'[29] This contention, however, is problematic for a number of reasons.

[17] As was observed by Merkel J in *Shaw v Wolf*,[30] a case where the Aboriginality of several persons was contested for the purpose of their eligibility to stand for election to the former Aboriginal and Torres Strait Islander Commission:

> it is unfortunate that the determination of a person's Aboriginal identity, a highly personal matter, has been left by a Parliament that is not representative of Aboriginal people to be determined by a Court which is also not representative of Aboriginal people. Whilst many would say that this is an inevitable incident of political and legal life in Australia, I do not accept that that must always be necessarily so. It is to be hoped that one day if questions such as those that have arisen in the present case are again required to be determined that that determination might be made by independently constituted bodies or tribunals which are representative of Aboriginal people.[31]

[18] The same caution must be exercised—*a fortiori*—with respect to claims brought under the *NTA* generally, and specifically to the case before the court. There is an inherent danger in colonial courts adjudicating matters pertaining to First Peoples' identity and rights by requiring proof of the existence of 'traditional' laws and customs to establish such rights. Such a process inevitably involves an exercise of judicial power to determine whether the rights arising under First Peoples' laws can be translated to a

form which is acceptable to the colonial legal system. As the passage of this case before the courts has shown, and as has been admitted by the majority judges in this court, such a process is 'fraught with evident difficulty'.[32] It invokes the now repugnant common law 'scale of organisation' test,[33] which was firmly rejected in *Mabo*.[34] But there is a much more compelling reason to reject this approach: the rights (and obligations) arising from First Peoples' laws are an incident of the inherent sovereignty of First Peoples. It is no longer acceptable to maintain that the current circumstances First Peoples find themselves in is 'an inevitable incident of political and legal life in Australia'. It must also be acknowledged that First Peoples' laws and customs with respect to Country (or in fact any other matters those laws address) are derived from the inherent sovereignty of First Peoples. To deny this fundamental truth would maintain the legal fiction of terra nullius, both in theory and substance. Acknowledging the inherent sovereignty of First Peoples as the starting point for interpreting the *NTA* can be achieved without 'fracturing a skeletal principle' of the Australian legal system.

The majority judgment

[19] In my view, the majority judgment produced an unnecessarily restrictive construction of native title which is completely unwarranted by the text of the *NTA*. The problem stems from what the majority judges regarded as a 'fundamental principle' which should inform the interpretation of the *NTA*—that after the British assertion of sovereignty, there could be 'no parallel law-making system'. This 'fundamental principle' infected all other aspects of the majority judgment. It informed the majority's view that the *NTA* requires proof of both the existence and the continuation of 'traditional' laws and customs *from the time of the British assertion of sovereignty to the present*. In effect, it introduces a *presumption of terra nullius*. Such an approach is repugnant to contemporary standards of justice and must be firmly rejected. This approach is also entirely contrary to First Peoples' concepts of law, as the following discussion of First Peoples' legal philosophies will show.

First Peoples' philosophies and laws

[20] First Nations and Peoples are diverse.[35] From First Peoples' perspectives, this land now known as Australia is a 'continent' and not a country.[36] This understanding reflects the diversity of First Peoples and the inter-national relationships between different First Peoples. It is an acknowledgement of the inherent sovereignty of each First Peoples group, and a philosophical worldview based on inclusivity and respect for difference, co-existence, and co-operation.[37] The diversity of First Peoples means that it is not possible to

articulate a 'universal' concept of First Peoples' law, or more correctly, laws. Indeed, to attempt to do so would be antithetical to First Peoples' respect for diversity and difference. For the purposes of the present case, however, it is helpful to identify some shared philosophical features of First Peoples' laws and worldviews, which will inform my judgment.

[21] First Peoples' laws are sourced from our creation ancestors, who travelled across the landscape, putting people on Country and giving us laws to live by. Being descended from the creation ancestors, First Peoples are born from Country. Our ancestral lines connect us to Country. Our embodiment is the physical manifestation of our connection to Country.[38] Our identification with Country and kin is the basis of our law and culture. This connection to Country has been described as an 'ontological relationship to land'.[39]

[22] First Peoples' worldviews emphasise the 'inter-connectedness' of all living things.[40] This inter-connectedness has also been expressed as 'relationality'[41] and 'relatedness'.[42] Relationality means First Peoples' identity is understood in the context of our relationships to our ancestral beings, kin, and Country.[43] From First Peoples' perspectives, relatedness is to 'know who you are, where you are from and how you are related'.[44] Relatedness also extends to other living entities, including animals, plants, waterways, climate, skies, and spirits.[45] First Peoples' 'relationality' is also underpinned by both 'connections with one's country and the spirit world'[46] and a belief that the land is a living entity.[47] Our spiritual connection to Country and kin provide the foundation for First Peoples' identity, culture, and law, which do not fit neatly into positivistic legal doctrinal categories.[48] This understanding has particular significance for the case at hand.

[23] First Peoples' relationality to land means that Country forms part of our kinship systems. While kinship may have been damaged by colonisation, the kinship system never changes because each individual and clan group is connected to Country through their creation ancestors.[49] Maintaining relationships with Country is so fundamental to First Peoples' ways of knowing and being that looking after Country is an imperative under First Peoples' laws.[50] The relationship with land is so central to First Peoples' ontologies and ways of being that 'the land is the law'.[51] The kinship relation between people and Country also instils a 'custodial ethic' towards land, which is fundamentally different from Western concepts of property ownership.[52] The depth of the kinship between people and Country is frequently expressed as 'belonging to Country'.[53]

[24] Relationality and relatedness are also reflected in the principle of reciprocity, which is central to First Peoples' understandings of law and sovereignty. Reciprocity is a major principle of Aboriginal law, and 'the highest level of reciprocity is to the land. We must care for the land (or place), because it cares for us and provides all of our needs'.[54] Reciprocity is also reflected in First Peoples' concepts of sovereignty, which are fundamentally different from the Euro-centred construction of the sovereign nation-state. First

Nations sovereignty is underpinned by the understanding that: '[o]ur obligations were to law and we were responsible for the maintenance of country for the benefit of future carers of law and country'.[55]

[25] Because First Peoples' law and relatedness to Country is grounded in our creation ancestors, it is described by Mary Graham as 'natural moral law' which, unlike Western positivist concepts of law, is not the product of human agency, nor can it be extinguished.[56] However, this concept of 'natural moral law' is not to be confused with the Western canon of 'natural law', which is derived from 'divine law' or the precepts of Christianity.[57] It is a distinction that recognises the enduring nature of First Nations' laws which are deeply embedded in Country: they are omnipresent and eternal.

[26] While Australian courts have attempted to grapple with these differences to a degree,[58] the outcome for First Peoples has generally been that our connections to Country are not equally valued or seen as commensurate with Western constructs of 'property rights'. As mentioned earlier, this case presents an opportunity to correct this misconception—which has led to gross injustices for First Peoples. The interpretation of the *NTA* through the lens of First Peoples' sovereign connections to Country is an important step towards bridging this gap.

Proof of native title

[27] As stated above, the primary issues on appeal go to the interpretation of s 223(1) of the *NTA*, which defines native title rights and interests. Interpretation of this provision must be informed by an understanding of First Peoples' legal philosophy and come from a First Peoples' sovereignty perspective.

Meaning of 'traditional' law and customs

[28] The ordinary meaning of the word 'traditional' is continuity with the past.[59] First Peoples' understanding of law as being birthed by the creation ancestors putting both people and law on Country gives rise to a different understanding of 'traditional' in this context. As human beings are the living embodiment of First Peoples' laws, the identification of people with a particular tract of Country is evidence itself that traditional law exists. What is important to establish proof of 'traditional' laws and customs is that a group of people continue to identify themselves by their relationship to a particular tract of Country. This 'belonging' to Country is evidence of 'tradition' in the sense of continuity with the past.

[29] In this case, the Yorta Yorta peoples have demonstrated that they are descended from human ancestors, Edward Walker and Kitty Atkinson/Cooper, who were descended from persons who inhabited part of the claim area in the early 1800s.[60] From this, it can be inferred that those same

ancestors were descended from people in occupation of that same country prior to 1788. The Yorta Yorta peoples have shown that they have maintained their identity as a people through their ongoing relationship with Country. Thus, the Yorta Yorta peoples have proven the existence of 'traditional' laws and customs as required by s 223.

Continuity of laws and customs

[30] The ongoing identification of a First Peoples with Country is also strong evidence of the continuity of laws and customs. There are also other factors that must also be taken into account from a First Peoples' perspective.

[31] There is no doubt that the dramatic changes wrought upon First Peoples as a result of colonial government policies of relocation and the active suppression of Aboriginal languages and cultures have had a significant impact on the modes and practices of laws and customs. What is important for the purpose of this inquiry is that the fundamental principles that underpin First Peoples' laws are still active and operative in the contemporary context. The 'custodial ethic' that is imperative to First Peoples' laws and customs provides a strong indicium of the continuity of law and customs.

[32] In this case, the Yorta Yorta peoples have demonstrated a long history of asserting custodial responsibilities for their ancestral lands. In evidence, it was shown that since colonisation, there were no less than 12 significant attempts by the Yorta Yorta peoples to assert their custodial responsibilities.[61] The evidence also demonstrated that the Yorta Yorta peoples continue to assert custodial responsibilities for Country today, particularly in relation to the protection of sacred sites, the conservation of food, timber, and natural resources, and the 'proper management' of land.[62]

[33] Before the Federal Court, much significance was accorded to a petition made by the Yorta Yorta peoples to the Governor of New South Wales in 1881, which was interpreted as positive evidence of the loss of traditional laws and customs. In my view, this petition has been completely misconstrued and the interpretation given to it by the court to date fails to appreciate the extreme oppression and deprivation that the Yorta Yorta peoples were living under at the time it was made. To put this petition into its proper context, it is necessary to map out the evidence of the Yorta Yorta peoples' experiences of colonisation and the profound changes to their material conditions and way of life in the period leading to the petition.

Yorta Yorta peoples' experiences of colonisation

[34] The first Europeans to enter the claim area were Hamilton Hume and William Hovell in 1824.[63] Major Thomas Mitchell closely followed in 1836, an encounter which included violent clashes with Aboriginal groups along the Murray River 'downstream from the claim area'.[64] Charles Sturt first

travelled in the vicinity of Yorta Yorta country in 1829. Upon returning to the claim area in 1838, Sturt observed that many Aboriginal people were infected with smallpox and that '[i]t must have committed dreadful havoc amongst them, since on this journey, I did not see hundreds to the thousands I saw on my former expedition'.[65] Between 1837 and 1839, tens of thousands of stock were brought into the area, and by 1840 most land along the Murray and Goulburn rivers had been occupied by pastoralists.[66] The trial judge observed that '[c]onflict occurred at numerous stations. In many cases large, organised groups of Aborigines were involved'.[67] Clearly, the Yorta Yorta peoples fiercely resisted the colonial invasion of their lands.[68] By the 1850s, however, the Aboriginal population had been 'drastically reduced' by disease and conflict, and it was recorded that 'physical resistance to settlement had ceased'.[69] By 1857, just 20 years after the start of the colonial occupation of Victoria, there were only 1,769 Aborigines left living in the whole of Victoria.[70]

[35] In 1858, a Select Committee was appointed to investigate the present condition of Aboriginal people and the 'best means of alleviating their absolute wants'.[71] Following this inquiry, a number of government-sponsored missions and reserves were established in Victoria; however, in Yorta Yorta country, only ration depots were created. Local squatters were appointed as 'guardians' of Aboriginal people, and children were removed from their families to be 'properly' educated and to dissociate them from 'traditional distractions'.[72] In 1865, Daniel and Edward Matthews took up Moira Station, an area of 800 acres. After discovering that part of the station had been traditionally used as a meeting place, 20 acres were set aside in 1874 to establish Maloga Mission.[73] By the 1880s, serious problems emerged at Maloga because Aboriginal people resented moves by Daniel Matthews to 'limit traditional ceremonial activities and the sanctions imposed such as loss of rations, if people failed to attend Christian services'.[74] He had also taken to 'physically beat children and young women if they committed offences of a moral or religious nature'.[75] Aboriginal men at Maloga also 'resented the intrusions on their freedom and demanded greater autonomy'.[76] These events coincided with proposals by the Victorian government to disperse 'half castes' from missions and stations which were enshrined in legislation in 1886.[77] Although the Aboriginal Protection Association installed a new manager, George Bellenger, in 1887, he also proved to be extremely unpopular.[78] In 1888, a number of huts and houses were moved from Maloga to a new reserve established at Cummeragunja, across the New South Wales border.[79]

[36] This brief history of the Yorta Yorta peoples' experiences of dispossession and oppression under British colonial rule provides an important context for interpreting the petition to the Governor of New South Wales in 1881. This petition has been cited by the trial judge as positive evidence of the Yorta Yorta peoples' loss of traditional laws and customs.[80] However, such an interpretation fails to appreciate the conditions Yorta Yorta peoples were

living under at the time it was made. The text of the petition is reproduced here:

> To His Excellency Lord Augustus Loftus, G.C.B., Governor of the colony of New South Wales—The humble petition of the undersigned Aboriginal natives, residents on the Murray River in the colony of New South Wales, members of the Moira and Ulupna tribes, respectfully showeth:
>
> 1. That all the land within our tribal boundaries has been taken possession of by the Government and white settlers; our hunting grounds are used for sheep pasturage and the game reduced and in many places exterminated, rendering our means of subsistence extremely precarious, and often reducing us and our wives and children to beggary.
> 2. We, the men of our several tribes, are desirous of honestly maintaining our young and infirm, who are in many cases the subjects of extreme want and semi-starvation, and we believe we could, in a few years support ourselves by our own industry, were a sufficient area of land granted to us to cultivate and raise stock.
> 3. We have been under training for some years and feel that our old mode of life is not in keeping with the instructions we have received and we are earnestly desirous of settling down to more orderly habits of industry, that we may form homes for our families. We more confidently ask this favour of a grant of land as our fellow natives in other colonies have proven capable of supporting themselves, where suitable land has been reserved for them.
>
> We hopefully appeal to your Excellency, as we recognise you, The Protector specially appointed by Her Gracious Majesty the Queen 'to promote religion and education among the Aboriginal natives of the colony', and to protect us in our persons and in the free enjoyment of our possessions, and to take such measures as may be necessary for our advancement in civilization.

[37] The trial judge's assessment of this petition was that it expressed a desire to change from the 'old mode of life' in favour of 'settling down to more orderly habits of industry'.[81] Although it was acknowledged that Edward Matthews most likely played a part in composing the petition, it was concluded that the extent of his influence on the document was unknown.[82] But the conditions at Maloga at the time and the language deployed suggest that Matthews' influence over the petitioners was strong. Other aspects of the evidence also provide important context for interpreting the petition. The petition documents how the totality of Yorta Yorta country had been occupied by the government and white settlers, that their traditional food sources were severely depleted or exterminated. It also highlights their 'extreme want and semi-starvation' and a genuine desire to be able to provide for

their families. These statements must also be understood in light of the circumstances at Maloga mission at the time—where Matthews was limiting traditional ceremonial activities and withholding rations from people who challenged his authority. Not surprisingly, Aboriginal men resented the curtailment of their autonomy and independence. There is no doubt that the petitioners were living under circumstances of extreme oppression and coercive control. By reading the petition with these factors in mind, it can be better understood as an assertion of the Yorta Yorta peoples' inherent sovereignty, a plea to have greater control over their own affairs and to regain a foothold in their country which had been unjustly usurped from them. What is most remarkable is the Yorta Yorta peoples' resilience and steadfast determination to maintain their authority in Country in the face of almost complete colonial domination.

[38] The Yorta Yorta peoples have demonstrated a long history of asserting custodial authority over their ancestral lands. As earlier observed, the trial judge noted that the evidence showed no less than 12 significant attempts by the Yorta Yorta peoples to regain some control over their Country.[83] The evidence also demonstrated that the Yorta Yorta peoples continue to uphold their custodial responsibilities for Country today, through their advocacy to ensure the protection of sacred sites, the conservation of food resources, and the 'proper management' of land. Clearly, the evidence of Yorta Yorta peoples' sustained and ongoing endeavours to exercise their custodial obligations to Country is proof of the continuing acknowledgement and observance of their laws and customs. As Black CJ in the dissenting judgment of the Federal Court said, '[t]he law and custom at the heart of the application was that the claimants are the owners according to Aboriginal tradition…They had maintained their connection with the land: *they were, and remained, the indigenous people of the claimed land and waters*'.[84]

Connection to Country

[39] The findings in relation to continuity of the Yorta Yorta peoples' laws and customs equally apply to the issue of connection to Country. However, for the sake of completion, this element will now be addressed. First Peoples' laws are sourced from the creation ancestors, who put people on Country and gave them laws to live by. First Peoples' relatedness to Country and the laws flowing from that relationship reflect a custodial ethic towards Country. The continuing and ongoing exercise of custodial responsibilities flowing from the laws and customs of the group provides strong evidence of connection to Country. In this case, the Yorta Yorta peoples have demonstrated their relatedness to Country through their ongoing assertion of custodial responsibilities to look after Country. Therefore, the Yorta Yorta peoples have demonstrated their connection to Country under their laws and customs.

Conclusion on proof of native title

[40] The evidence in this case has demonstrated that the Yorta Yorta peoples, having descended from the creation ancestors and by following the laws and customs given to them, have maintained their relatedness and connection to Country. I must stress that what is crucial here is that the Yorta Yorta community have survived *as peoples*. Most importantly, the Yorta Yorta peoples' law and customs are incidents of their inherent sovereignty as *peoples*. Despite the ravages of colonisation and concerted efforts to undermine their law, culture, and way of life, the Yorta Yorta peoples have shown extraordinary persistence, strength, determination, and resilience. They have maintained their relatedness to Country against the odds. And they have consistently and persistently asserted their custodial responsibilities towards Country. Although these efforts have been mostly met with bureaucratic ignorance and indifference, over the past 200 years they have continued to assert their custodial responsibilities for Country at every available opportunity. I find that the Yorta Yorta peoples have proven their native title over their ancestral lands and waters. Yorta Yorta Country needs its people, and the Yorta Yorta peoples have always been there for Country.

Notes

1 Marcelle Burns. This research has been supported by an Australian Government Research Training Program Scholarship.
2 *Members of the Yorta Yorta Aboriginal Community v Victoria* (2002) 214 CLR 422, 423–4, ('*Yorta Yorta HCA*').
3 *Members of the Yorta Yorta Aboriginal Community v Victoria* [1998] FCA 1606, [122]–[125] ('*Yorta Yorta FCA*').
4 Ibid., [122]–[125].
5 Ibid., [18].
6 Ibid., [7].
7 Ibid., [18].
8 Ibid., [129].
9 Ibid., [129].
10 Ibid., [105]. See Edward M Curr, *Recollections of Squatting in Victoria, Then Called the Port Phillip District (From 1841–1851)* (George Robertson, 1883); Edward M Curr, *The Australian Race: Its Origins, Language, Customs, Place of Landing in Australia and the Routes by Which It Spread Itself Over that Continent* (John Farnes, 1886).
11 *Yorta Yorta FCA*, [106] (emphasis added).
12 Ibid., [119].
13 See *Members of the Yorta Yorta Aboriginal Community v Victoria* (2001) 110 FCR 244 ('*Yorta Yorta FCAFC*').
14 Ibid., 264, [64]–[66].
15 Ibid., 249, [11].
16 Ibid.
17 Ibid.
18 Ibid., 283, [145]; 286–287, [164] (Branson and Katz JJ); 271, [91] (Black CJ, dissenting).
19 *Yorta Yorta HCA*, 438–439, [26]–[28].

20 Ibid., 438–439, [28].
21 Ibid., 431, [4].
22 *Mabo v Queensland (No 2)* (1992) 175 CLR 1 ('*Mabo*').
23 Ibid., 42.
24 Ibid.
25 Ibid., 43.
26 Ibid., 31.
27 Michael Mansell, 'The Court Gives an Inch but Takes Another Mile' (1992) 2(57) *Aboriginal Law Bulletin* 4, 4–5; Irene Watson, 'Indigenous Peoples' Law-Ways: Survival against the Colonial State' (1997) 8 *Australian Feminist Law Journal* 39, 48.
28 Kimberlee Crenshaw, 'Race, Reform and Retrenchment: Transformation and Legitimation in Anti-Discrimination Law' (1998) in Michael DA Freeman (ed), *Lloyd's Introduction to Jurisprudence* (Sweet & Maxwell, 7th ed, 2001) 1346, 1360. Crenshaw speaks of the incoherence of legal doctrines which purport to recognise equality yet which fail to effect equality in real terms.
29 *Yorta Yorta FCA*, [17].
30 *Shaw v Wolf* (1998) 83 FCR 113.
31 Ibid., 137.
32 *Yorta Yorta HCA*, 447, [55].
33 *In Re Southern Rhodesia* [1919] AC 211, 233–4; *Milirrpum v Nabalco Pty Ltd* (1971) 17 FLR 141.
34 *Mabo* (1992) 175 CLR 1, 40.
35 Irene Watson, 'Settled and Unsettled Spaces: Are We Free to Roam?' in Aileen Moreton-Robinson (ed), *Sovereign Subjects: Indigenous Sovereignty Matters* (Allen and Unwin, 2007), 20–1.
36 Ambellin Kwaymullina, 'Aboriginal Nations, the Australian Nation-State and Indigenous International Legal Traditions' in Irene Watson (ed), *Indigenous Peoples as Subjects of International Law* (Routledge, 2018), 5.
37 Watson (n 35).
38 Aileen Moreton-Robinson, 'The Possessive Logic of Patriarchal White Sovereignty: The High Court and the Yorta Yorta Decision' (2004) 3(2) *Borderlands e-Journal*, [24].
39 Aileen Moreton-Robinson, 'I Still Call Australia Home: Indigenous Belonging and Place in a White Postcolonizing Society' in Sara Ahmed et al. (eds), *Uprootings/Regroundings: Questions of Home and Migration* (Berg Press, 2003), 33 ('I Still Call Australia Home').
40 Irene Watson, 'Kaldowinyeri-Munaintya: In the Beginning' (2000) 4(1) *Flinders Journal of Law Reform* 3, 6.
41 Moreton-Robinson, 'I Still Call Australia Home' (n 39) 34.
42 Karin Martin, *Please Knock before You Enter: Aboriginal Regulation of Outsiders and the Implications for Researchers* (Post Pressed, 2008) 66; Karin Martin and Booran Mirraboopa, 'Ways of Knowing, Being and Doing: A Theoretical Framework and Methods for Indigenous and Indigenist Research' (2003) 27(76) *Journal of Australian Studies* 203, 205.
43 Martin (n 42) 76; Mary Graham, 'Some Thoughts about the Philosophical Underpinnings of Aboriginal Worldviews' (2008) 45 *Australian Humanities Review* 181, 182–3.
44 Martin (n 42) 69–71.
45 Martin and Mirraboopa (n 42) 207.
46 Moreton-Robinson, 'I Still Call Australia Home' (n 39) 34.
47 Central Land Council, *The Land is Always Alive* (Australian Print Group, 1994) 4.
48 See also Marcelle Burns, *Challenging the Assumptions of Positivism: An Analysis of the Concept of Society in Sampi on behalf of the Bardi and Jawi People v Western Australia [2010] and Bodney v Bennell [2008]* (Native Title Research Unit Issues Paper No 7, May 2011) 2–6; Marcelle Burns and Jennifer Nielsen, 'Dealing with the "Wicked" Problem of

Race and the Law: A Critical Journey for Students (and Academics)' (2018) 28(2) *Legal Education Review* 1, 18.
49 Graham (n 43) 182–3.
50 Martin and Mirraboopa (n 42) 211.
51 Graham (n 43) 181–3.
52 Ibid.
53 Watson (n 40).
54 Penny Tripcony, 'The Native Title Mediation Process in Relation to Quandamooka: An Overview' in R Ganter (ed), *Stradbroke Island: Facilitating Change Public Seminar held by the Queensland Studies Centre with Quandamooka Land Council* (Griffith University, 1997) 61, cited in Martin (n 42) 78.
55 Irene Watson, 'Aboriginal Laws and the Sovereignty of Terra Nullius' (2002) 1(2) *Borderlands e-Journal* 49.
56 Graham (n 43) 190–1.
57 See e.g. Hugo Grotius, *On the Law of War and Peace*, tr Francis W Kelsey (Bobbs-Merrill, 1925), who regarded natural law as the precepts of divine or Christian law, as dictated by 'right' reason: xl–xli.
58 *Milirrpum v Nabalco Pty Ltd* (1971) 17 FLR 141; *Western Australia v Ward* [2002] 213 CLR 1.
59 *Yorta Yorta HCA*, 459, [101] (Gaudron and Kirby JJ).
60 *Yorta Yorta FCA*, [104].
61 Ibid., [119].
62 Ibid., [112]–[113].
63 Ibid., [27].
64 Ibid., [28].
65 Ibid., [31].
66 Ibid., [34].
67 Ibid., [34].
68 See also Aboriginal Community Elders Service, *Aboriginal Elders' Voices: Stories of the 'Tide of History': Victorian Indigenous Elders Life Stories & Oral Histories* (Language Australia Limited, 2003) 167–71.
69 *Yorta Yorta FCA*, [35].
70 Ibid., [36].
71 Ibid., [36].
72 Ibid.
73 Ibid., [36]–[37].
74 Ibid., [40].
75 Ibid.
76 Ibid.
77 Ibid., [39].
78 Ibid., [41].
79 Ibid., [40].
80 Ibid., [121].
81 Ibid., [120].
82 Ibid., [121].
83 Ibid., [61].
84 *Yorta Yorta FCAFC*, 269, [83] (emphasis added).

7

AKIBA ON BEHALF OF THE TORRES STRAIT REGIONAL SEA CLAIMS GROUP v COMMONWEALTH [2013] HCA 33

Commentary: *Akiba on behalf of the Torres Strait Regional Seas Claim Group v Commonwealth* [2013] HCA 33

Alison Whittaker

Australian legal history is replete with opportunities, all missed, to address its existential dread. This is a dramatic way to open a commentary. I hope it sets the scene for Marshall's own dramatic rethink of another relatively recent missed turning point—*Akiba v Commonwealth*.

Akiba on behalf of the Torres Strait Regional Seas Claim Group v Commonwealth [2013] HCA 33, which Marshall reimagines here, is a significant case.

The mob, in this case, were 13 distinct but interrelated Torres Strait Islander communities. They sought non-exclusive native title rights over portions of the sea for approximately 44,000 square kilometres. The Torres Strait Regional Seas Claim Group asserted two broad kinds of rights important for Marshall's new judgment—fishing rights to those waters and reciprocal rights to access and use those waters. The High Court in 2013 came to understand the fishing rights as encompassing commercial fishing rights and to understand that they had not been extinguished by fisheries legislation. On this claim, the Torres Strait Regional Seas Claim Group were successful.

Reciprocal rights, unfortunately, did not enjoy the endorsement of the High Court. Reciprocal rights are those held by a network of relationships under the law of an Indigenous nation or community, in this case, a group of obligations among neighbouring Torres Strait Islander mobs to share relational access to particular places and things, like waters and sea life.

The High Court concluded that reciprocal rights were not a native title right that Australian law understood—especially under s 223 of the *Native Title Act 1993* (Cth), the cornerstone of the native title legislative and regulatory regime which defines possible rights in relation to water and land. That section of the *Native Title Act* provides that native title rights can only be held 'in relation to land or waters'. Because the rights, the High Court said, were personal in nature and reliant upon particular status and relationships in the community to be conferred, they were not a right 'in relation to land or waters'. Therefore, they were not a native title right cognisable to Australian settler law—as it then stood and probably still stands when you read this.

Of course, my messy summation is not a complete way to cover the logic of the decision, but it gives you enough to know what is necessary for understanding newly-minted (just for this project, for now) Chief Justice Virginia Marshall's decision, which follows this little commentary. The judgment, coming from the helm of a quite different High Court, invites us to think in a more complicated, and certainly less mercenary, way about the native title regime altogether. It challenges settler law's compartmentalising of Country across multiple axes (owned, related, continuous, discontinuous, land, sea, extinguished, regulated).

Marshall CJ remarks, at the core of her renewed decision:

> The Western classification of a body of rules, values, and traditions as 'law' has caused divisions of opinions for positivist lawyers and anthropologists in adopting the definitions of law from Indigenous tradition. This impacts the interpretation of Indigenous laws. The systems of Indigenous customary laws include customs which may appear to observers as rules of etiquette or beliefs, rather than Western-style legal rules and procedures.

Marshall CJ also reveals to us some of the very foundational epistemic tensions in Australian settler law trying to understand or comprehend social systems under its own terms. In part, the application is of a white anthropological lens, clumsily or callously constructed in its trusted sources from the early frontier of amateurs and eugenicists. It is also a failing of the settler Australian legal system to consider itself anthropologically—its distinctions between substance and procedure, land and sea, property holder and property.

Marshall CJ demonstrates a failure of Australian legal systems to adequately consider, even on a most simple level, the idea that First Nations are comparative jurisdictions and subject to their own logics, as one would consider a comparative domestic jurisdiction overseas. This critical Indigenous scholar, and others in this project, might say that this approach, tacitly recognising not only a limited idea of First Nations title but a complex epistemological system of law and legality, is incommensurate with the existence of an Australian colony itself and that might be why it hasn't yet happened. But, moving with the assumption of commensurability, Marshall presents an enticing alternate reality that helps us envision what is possible even with the limited tools presented to us.

With the vision of First Nations law as its own comparative and sovereign legal system, as Marshall CJ presents it (I think rightly), also comes the knowledge that procedure, as well as hierarchies and disciplinary fields of lawmaking, property, crime, claim, amends, precedent, and authority, may well be distinct from the legal ontology of settler Australia's lawmaking tradition. While this might be outside of what a settler legal system could understand, the original decision by the High Court in *Akiba v Commonwealth* did not acknowledge its limitations in understanding.

It stands as an important point that the Torres Strait Regional Seas Claim Group led by Akiba was not claiming anything exclusive about their water rights. This has been out of grasp for sea claimants since *Commonwealth v Yarmirr*,[1] at which point the claimant group in this case amended their claim to exclusivity. These are the kind of seemingly ancillary, but strategically significant, compromises that many Indigenous civil claimants make to shoehorn possible claims into settler law.

This is a preference for Australian settler legal systems—to see and consider anthropological views of First Nations laws in limited instances (as evidence/questions of fact/historical contexts/matters of cultural safety, rather than of law) and is more or less the extent of the concessions granted by courts. One such concession is the *Treaty between Australia and the Independent State of Papua New Guinea Concerning Sovereignty and Maritime Boundaries in the Area between the Two Countries, Including the Area Known as the Torres Strait*—a treaty not between First Nations of the Torres Strait or Papua New Guinea, but between states who stake authoritative claims on 'allowing' defined traditional practices. As Marshall CJ herself says in the judgment:

> [it] involves concepts which have been unintentionally and erroneously reinterpreted and reconstructed as normative Indigenous practices.

In Marshall's construction, this slippage is fundamental to the decision—she prods at settler legal conceptions of claimable rights over Country in *Akiba* which go to Western concepts of property in itself. What if reciprocal rights were capable of being understood as a way of relating to Country through its peoples, a way that conferred a cognisable responsibility and right that is as directly related to 'land and waters' as a more formally cognisable native title claim?

It is a question Marshall frames as a distinct claim further to the High Court decision, rather than supplanting it.

> Does the common law interpretation of reciprocal rights as 'inferior rights' unfairly impact upon Torres Strait Islander peoples and their extended families in the exercise of their laws, customs, and practice?

Of course, the short answer is 'yes'. The failure of Western legal systems to treat procedure, rights, relationships, rules, Country, and obligations as enmeshed together in other legal systems creates the construction of 'inferior rights' that rely on all of these for their construction—not just in establishing that they exist, but in forming the substance of the right itself. This allows, as noted in Marshall's judgment, for the Federal Court and High Court to construct reciprocal rights to Country as 'subordinate' rights of other kinds of native title. Marshall rejects and reimagines this:

> Indigenous rights and interests can exist anywhere within the web, and not in chronological or linear form. In essence, the nexus with all things within the Indigenous environment (traditional laws and customs) are innately joined together in a web of relationships. The web of relationships exists within all aspects of property...
>
> The framing of 'ancestral occupation based rights and reciprocal rights', the latter characterised as 'inferior', is structurally flawed.
>
> *(citations omitted)*

Marshall CJ's judgment opens up the possibility for recognition of reciprocal rights within the existing structure of settler law—'in relation to land or waters' in s 223 of the *Native Title Act*, which, she argues, is capable of carrying the relationships of reciprocal rights of customary marine tenure in the Torres Strait. The refusal of the High Court originally to see this was not an easy doctrinal choice, but it was an indolent epistemological one. Any recognition of water rights or land rights must also include reciprocal rights or be unrecognisable to First Nations who claim native title. Recognition of reciprocal rights is not just an accommodation of cultural concepts of property into the native title regime, but it is also recognition that for the mob, these questions are first and foremost relational.

Note

1 (2001) 208 CLR 1.

Leo Akiba on behalf of the Torres Strait Regional Sea Claim Group..Appellant

AND

Commonwealth .... Respondent

[2013] HCA 33

Native title—Sea Country—Reciprocal rights—Torres Strait Islander peoples—Traditional customs.

Acknowledgment of Country

Ngangadha garraygu bilagalanggu, yandu garraybu bilagalangbu ngangagirri nginyalgir

Warning: Aboriginal and Torres Strait Islander peoples are warned that the following content includes photos of, references to, and/or comments from people who have passed away.

Marshall CJ.[1]

Background

[1] Finn J, a Judge of the Federal Court of Australia, delivered reasons for judgment on 2 July 2010 in an application made on behalf of 13 Torres Strait Island communities for a determination of native title over the (sovereign) waters.[2] This determination defined 'group rights' which comprised the native title held by each of the communities, severally and collectively. The native title rights and interests asserted included the right to access resources and to take for any purpose resources in the native title areas.

[2] The right to access resources is a non-exclusive right, and it is exercised in a variety of ways, including by taking fish for commercial or trading purposes, though it does not confer any right to control the conduct of others.[3] It is a right that is exercised in accordance with the native title holder's traditional laws and customs, subject to the laws of Queensland and the Commonwealth of Australia and the common law.[4]

[3] The Full Court of the Federal Court, by majority, on 14 March 2012, allowed an appeal against the decision of Finn J.[5] The majority held that successive fisheries legislation enacted by colonial and Queensland legislatures and by the Commonwealth Parliament had extinguished any right to take

fish and other aquatic life for commercial purposes. The Full Court varied Order 5(b) of the determination by adding the words:

> This right does not, extend to taking fish and other aquatic life for sale or trade.

[4] The Full Court dismissed a cross-appeal by the appellant against a finding by Finn J that reciprocity-based rights and interests existing between the members of the Torres Strait Island communities did not constitute native title rights and interests within the meaning of s 223 of the *Native Title Act 1993* (Cth) ('*NTA*').

[5] This Court granted the appellant special leave to appeal the decision of the Full Court. The appeal should be allowed in relation to the reciprocal rights issue.

Question to consider

[6] There is one question that arises for this Court: does the common law interpretation of reciprocal rights as 'inferior rights' unfairly impact upon Torres Strait Islander peoples and their extended families in the exercise of their laws, customs, and practice?

Introduction

[7] From the perspective of Leo Akiba (Boigu) and George Mye (Erub), members of the Torres Strait Regional Seas Claim Group ('the Claim Group'), this matter is about recognition of rights and obligations to their sea Country, which, the Claim Group contend, they have held since 'time immemorial'.[6] With over 120 islands in the Torres Strait, many of them small, both trade and fishing are at the epicentre of their community identity.[7] Islands which are embedded with water relationships are comprised of 'rich layers of law dimensions that dwarf the narrow descriptors of Australian water policy'.[8] The principle of reciprocity exercised by Torres Strait Islander peoples promotes equality, with the assurance that each member will observe this ancient traditional custom.[9]

[8] The majority of the High Court in *Mabo v Queensland (No 2)* (1992) 175 CLR 1 ('*Mabo (No 2)*') declared that, 'the Meriam Peoples are entitled as against the whole world to possession, occupation, use and enjoyment of the [lands of Mer]'—setting the legal precedent for land.[10] The Claim Group is recognised by the Court as a 'single society'[11] that claims native title rights and interests in the waters of the Torres Strait.[12] Those rights and interests are exercised by the Claim Group in accordance with one normative system of laws and customs.[13] The Court acknowledges the problematic issues which continue to arise in the lack of clarification of 'society',[14] noting

that the Court's conceptualisation of society does not always align with the communal and individual identity that Indigenous peoples recognised at sovereignty.

Conceptualising Indigeneity

[9] A veritable flaw exists when European descriptions of human beings are explained in binary terms—such as Black/White, Traditional/Western, Islander/Mainstream,[15] or Indigenous law/Australian law. Moynihan J recognised the difficulties in evaluating witness evidence and considerations as to whether the *Mabo* plaintiffs were members of the Murray Island (Mer) society in the Torres Strait—that is, evaluating evidence 'from the perception of one culture from the perspective of another'.[16] Moynihan J explained that making the determination 'from his perspective'[17] meant that this 'led to different conclusions'[18] and 'the potential for misunderstandings'.[19] The European value system is promulgated as the standard to measure and reconstruct Indigenous ontologies and Indigenous epistemologies. This is problematic.

[10] Conceptualising Indigenous laws, traditions, and customs within the framework of native title, itself a creature of Australian law, involves proprietary concepts which have been unintentionally and erroneously reinterpreted and reconstructed as normative Indigenous practices.[20] Such inquiries invariably over-complicate, misunderstand, and misrepresent the taxonomy of Indigenous property systems.

[11] The European classification for organising, classifying, and storing knowledge inevitably leads to theorising the meanings of how to value Indigeneity—in terms of contemporary colonialism.[21] An Indigenous ontological perspective, however, is valuable because it highlights the depth and complexity of the relationships held by Indigenous peoples with their land and waters[22]—insights which can build an understanding to bridge the gap between non-Indigenous and Indigenous peoples.[23]

[12] Knowledge is not what some possess and others do not because it is a resourceful capacity of being that creates the context and texture of life.[24]

[13] 'At the age of seven my mother and her sister were sent away to a Catholic Convent School on Thursday Island. Mother learnt to read, write and received an education to Year 4 (primary school). She learnt to boil nuns' habits in the (old-style) copper. Scrub, starch, iron, mend clothes, prepare food, wait on priests at tables, garden and milk goats. Without any formal training, by the time she was a teenager'.[25] The colonial institutions concluded that 'You have to educate coloured people to make the sacrifice to have their children adopted and so give them the chance to enjoy the privileges of the white community'.[26] In the 1960s, governments saw no value in keeping a Torres Strait Islander workforce when the marine economy collapsed—only then were they freed to leave.[27]

[14] The impact of European visitors, governments, and secular institutions on the Torres Strait Islander society imposed draconian measures to regulate and control Islander society in order to exploit resources. The Eurocentric compliance mechanisms of social control sought to deconstruct, revalue, and reorder every facet of their lives, based upon race.[28]

[15] History teaches that there are many dangers in enacting special laws that target people of a particular race and disadvantage their rights to liberty, property, and other entitlements by reference to that criterion.[29] British settlers (and others) who came into contact with the Indigenous peoples of Australia observed a people exercising their own well-developed structures, traditions, laws, and customs.[30]

[16] The significance of the interface of European society and the history of Torres Strait Islander peoples is akin to the history of mainland Aboriginal society in Australia. 'The heritage of an Indigenous people is not merely a collection of objects, stories and ceremonies, but a complete knowledge system with its own concepts of epistemology, philosophy, and scientific and logical validity'.[31]

[17] However, from the earliest point of contact with British society, Indigenous peoples and Indigenous women in particular were, and remain, 'virtually invisible in archival sources'.[32] This is in spite of Indigenous women's important contributions to the maintenance of oral traditions, laws, customs, and practices from 'mothers to daughters and grandmothers and aunties'.[33]

[18] The evidence heard by the primary judge in *Akiba v Queensland (No 2)* [2010] FCA 643 and by the Full Court in *Commonwealth v Akiba* [2012] FCAFC 25 will now be considered. In particular, I will consider evidence given by the Torres Strait Islander peoples on the issue of 'reciprocity rights' which establish a social and territorial system in the Torres Strait.

The anthropological gaze

[19] From the early British settlement/invasion of Indigenous territories, now Australia, countless documents recorded the minutiae of Indigenous lives, anatomy, artefacts, and religious and cultural practices.[34] Through a Western lens, and based on the study of anthropology and ethnography,[35] these settlers/invaders embarked upon making observations and drawing assumptions about Indigenous peoples. Often reliant on the written word of these observers, others would later theorise about Indigenous human society.

[20] The Western classification of a body of rules, values, and traditions as 'law' has caused divisions of opinions for positivist lawyers and anthropologists in adopting the definitions of law from Indigenous tradition.[36] This impacts the interpretation of Indigenous laws. The systems of Indigenous customary laws include customs which may appear to observers as rules of etiquette or beliefs, rather than Western-style legal rules and procedures.[37]

[21] In terms of intellectually organising Western knowledge, it is ordered as a discipline, which in turn is partitioned, where individuals are separated and space is compartmentalised.[38] Parties rely on anthropological reports as evidence to make a native title determination application under the *NTA*. The preparation of these reports, as a rule, is undertaken through non-Indigenous disciplines and by non-Indigenous researchers and professionals. Much of the 'evidence' relies on the work of amateur ethnographers and 18th- and 19th-century unannounced[39] expeditions.

[22] Five of six reports from Alfred Cort Haddon, a British marine zoologist who led the 1898 Cambridge Anthropological Expedition to the Torres Straits,[40] are in evidence.[41] The modus operandi of the Cambridge Expedition was 'to salvage a reconstructed picture of the disappearing primitive cultures while the native informants[42] were alive'[43]—'a window on a reconstructable and pristine pre-colonial past'.[44] Concerns are raised about considering Haddon's reports and others of this ilk where the probative value of such reports is outweighed by being[45] unfairly prejudicial[46] or misleading and confusing[47] to the appellant. The primary judge noted that the reports ordered for the conference of anthropological experts produced 86 very different propositions[48]—reports declared and signed by the experts. It is the case that experts of varying degrees are at odds with their professional colleagues.

The breadth of traditional laws and customs

[23] The Torres Strait Islander peoples do not accept the artificial distinction between the aquatic and the terrestrial.[49] They say this is antithetical to their law. The sea is a 'watery extension of estates on land'.[50] Notions that the common law ends at the low-water mark,[51] or that Indigenous peoples' use of the territorial seas may be calculated in nautical limits,[52] are also antithetical to Torres Strait Islander peoples' law. The Torres Strait Islander peoples seek recognition of native title rights and interests in the seas that belong to them[53]—and have for thousands of years, as the evidence before the Court shows.

[24] The reciprocal traditional law relationships between the Torres Strait Islander peoples (Badu, Boigu, Poruma, Erub, Dauan, Kubin, St Pauls, Mabuiag, Mer, Saibai, Ugar, Warraber, Iama, and Masig) and the peoples of Papua New Guinea were recognised in the *Treaty between Australia and the Independent State of Papua New Guinea Concerning Sovereignty and Maritime Boundaries in the Area between the Two Countries, Including the Area Known as the Torres Strait.*[54] This Treaty recognises 'the importance of protecting the traditional way of life and livelihood of Australians who are Torres Strait Islanders and Papua New Guineans who live in the coastal area of Papua New Guinea in, and adjacent to, the Torres Strait'.[55] However, Torres Strait Islander peoples were not a party to the agreement[56]—it was between the nation-states of Australia and Papua New Guinea.

[25] The Treaty, among other things, recognises that the 'traditional inhabitants'[57] of the Torres Strait Islands 'shall continue free movement and the performance of lawful traditional activities'[58] and 'enjoy traditional customary rights of access to and usage of areas of land, seabed, seas, estuaries and coastal tidal areas'.[59] Furthermore, 'traditional inhabitants who wish to enter the other country for a temporary stay for the performance of traditional activities are not subject to immigration, customs, health and quarantine requirements and procedures as citizens of that Party who are not traditional inhabitants'.[60] The definitions in the Treaty in regards to activities include barter and market trade,[61] traditional fishing,[62] and the maintenance of traditional customary associations[63] with Papua New Guinea and its peoples.

[26] The evidence shows that 'long-standing and deep trading relationships exist between Torres Strait Islanders and coastal Papua New Guinea peoples', namely by 'intermarriage, fishing in the Torres Strait waters and island connections'.[64] If by way of conceptualising a larger society[65] which may extend into coastal Papua New Guinea, then on that basis, laws and customs may be shared.[66]

Defining laws and customs: reciprocity

[27] The primary judge accepted that the 'Torres Strait Islander society has a body of laws and customs founded on the principle of reciprocity and exchange' and that 'this principle is dominant and pervasive in relationships'.[67] His Honour stated, 'I am satisfied there have been, and are, laws and customs which regulate rights and obligations between persons in certain "reciprocal relationships" creating a network of inter-island relationships'.[68] I concur with the learned primary judge that the principle of reciprocity exists, and furthermore, that reciprocity flows from the rights and interests of the Torres Strait Islander peoples in the lands and waters.

[28] A finding by the primary judge that reciprocal rights were 'subordinate or inferior rights' is not correct.[69] The reciprocal rights pervasive in these relationships flow from the traditions, laws, and customs of the landholder and the landholder's delegates. Further, these reciprocal rights are not discretionary in nature and all parties are bound by mutual obligation mandated by traditional laws and customs.

[29] The Claim Group contended that the primary judge 'fell into error by concluding that reciprocal rights were not native title rights and by failing to accommodate them'.[70] I respectfully disagree with the primary judge and conclude that reciprocal rights *are* native title rights.

[30] What impact does the conceptualisation of reciprocity rights as 'inferior' have on Torres Strait Islander men, women, their families, and extended relationships in exercising their laws, customs, and practices?

[31] The Torres Strait Islander society comprises a body of laws, customs, and practices, of which reciprocal relationships and the principle of reciprocity are indivisible. There are no strands nor cords.

[32] Indigenous norms (in Australia) are the basis for defining and interpreting Indigenous water rights and interests.[71] If we use a web of rights and interests concept to explore Indigenous values and beliefs, it is easier to understand Indigenous relationships to the water[72]—and to sea Country in the Torres Strait. Indigenous rights and interests can exist anywhere within the web, and not in chronological or linear form.

[33] In essence, the nexus with all things within the Indigenous environment (traditional laws and customs) are innately joined together in a web of relationships.[73] The web of relationships exists within all aspects of property.[74]

[34] The mis-conceptualising of traditional laws and customs has its roots in Western theorising on how to reconstruct Indigenous framing to configure Indigenous property concepts through Western property concepts—including by adopting metaphors such as the bundle of rights[75] concept. The framing of 'ancestral occupation based rights and reciprocal rights',[76] the latter characterised as 'inferior', is structurally flawed.

Indigenous property rights in the sea

[35] The primary judge identified that the statutory structure of s. 223(1) of the *NTA* did not accord with notions of 'property'[77] because reciprocal rights cannot be defined as 'real property'.[78] This is a narrow interpretation and only focussed on the words 'in relation to land and waters'. The meaning of s 223 should be read in its entirety—it was designed as a statutory housing of the common-law native title and in the expectation that the courts would amplify that title.[79]

[36] Section 223 defines common law native title interests:

> (1) The expression native title or native title rights and interests means the communal, group, or individual rights and interests of Aboriginal peoples or Torres Strait Islanders *in relation to* land or waters, where:
> > (a) The rights and interests are possessed under the traditional laws acknowledged, and the traditional customs observed, by the Aboriginal peoples or Torres Strait Islanders; and
> > (b) The Aboriginal peoples or Torres Strait Islanders, by those laws and customs, have a connection with the land or waters; and
> > (c) The rights and interests are recognised by the common law of Australia. (emphasis added)

[37] Thomas Grey asserted that property is a 'bundle of rights equally malleable, divisible, disaggregable and functional'.[80] The bundle of rights theory/metaphor has been applied in native title, seeking to demonstrate that Indigenous traditions, customs, and laws can be, 'neatly compartmentalised into unconnected strands of cultural and legal rights'.[81] The bundle of rights theory fails to grasp the concepts of the 'interconnection between things and human relationships in property'.[82]

[38] The primary judge characterises ancestral-based rights within the customary marine tenure model put forward by the Claim Group, which is described as 'a body of laws and customs founded on "principles" which "give rise to rights and obligations"; through status based[83] relationships held by each person or group'.[84] This characterisation raised similar issues in *Western Australia v Ward*[85] where the nature or character of rights was referred to as 'the bundle of rights' and explained as divisible. Such judicial metaphors are flawed—and disconnected from Indigenous concepts of the body of laws, customs, and practices.[86]

[39] The body of Torres Strait Islander laws and customs and the property rights to the sea Country are interconnected by a web of relationships which consist of communal occupation-based rights *and* reciprocal rights. Reciprocal rights may be either group or individual rights. These webs of property relationships are regulated within a property paradigm[87] where ancestral occupation rights are mandatory and enforceable and reciprocal rights require mutual obligation and certainty.

[40] Both types of rights have ramifications for breaches, non-compliance, and termination of legal relationships, for instance, the severing of the relationship. From this perspective, the Indigenous rule of law over water rights 'lies within an Indigenous concept where Indigenous laws determine that water is inseparable from the land'.[88] So it is that the body of laws, customs, and practice is not divisible or malleable—there are no strands or cords.

Consideration

[41] Interpreting the meaning of ancestral rights to the marine estate is an ongoing challenge for the common law to move beyond the English language used and interpreted in the legal system. Resolving this linguistic impasse requires a more nuanced approach to evaluating Indigenous marine estates.[89]

[42] Indigenous law is central to how communal and individual rights are exercised, who has the authority to speak for land and sea Country, and how those rights and interests are characterised among the many layers of communal and personal relationships.

[43] The impact upon women, children, and their extended families who are bound to this body of laws, customs, and practices of the Torres Strait is contained in their sworn affidavits[90] and the evidence tested in cross-examination. The voices of Torres Strait Islander women are explained (but not always heard)[91] through 'laws and customs relating to inter-island marriage, affinal relationships, hereditary friendships and tebud, permission and ailin pasin'.[92] These relationships are also described by various and regular fishing trips on sea Country in order to sustain commercial livelihoods, property relationships, and boundaries of shared country and ownership. Mr Billy's mother's family fishing business was presented in evidence to illustrate some of these issues.[93] Both marriage and affinal relationships were the subjects

of 'considerable historical and Torres Strait Islander evidence' before the Federal Court.[94]

[44] The Torres Strait has had 22 determinations in relation to land above the high water mark since *Mabo (No 2)*.[95] The issue raised by this Court was: if reciprocal rights were accepted as co-existing legal rights in the Torres Strait marine estate, to exist among ownership rights and rights to the shared marine estate, could the Court recognise such rights? The answer is in the affirmative.

[45] Irrespective of the 'practical inconsistencies that would arise in native title'[96] from such recognition, the basis for recognition is the laws, customs, and practices of the Torres Strait Islander peoples, which are evident in the complexity of their marine estate.[97]

[46] In a finding of fact, the primary judge 'did not accept that the conceptualisation of reciprocity rights was included in the words, "in relation to" the land and the waters in s. 223(1) of the *Native Title Act 1993* (Cth)'. Further, His Honour did not accept that reciprocity rights could be included in s 223(1) 'for the purposes of the *Native Title Act 1993* (Cth)'.[98] His Honour did allude to the Commonwealth's position that reform would be difficult in accommodating the concept of reciprocity rights,[99] but possible. Their Honours, on the same issue, concluded that 'practical inconsistencies would arise',[100] and left the question open. I find that the assertion of reciprocal rights by the Torres Strait Islanders Claim Group can be accommodated in native title.

[47] Brennan J in the High Court in *Mabo (No 2)* stated:

> The common law does not necessarily conform to international law, but international law is a legitimate and important influence on the development of the common law, especially when international law declares the existence of universal human rights. A common law doctrine founded on unjust discrimination in the enjoyment of civil and political rights demands reconsideration. It is contrary both to international standards and to the fundamental values of our common law to entrench a discriminatory rule.[101]

[48] This Court acknowledges that the *United Nations Declaration on the Rights of Indigenous Peoples*, to which Australia has subscribed, recognises the rights of Indigenous peoples to promote, develop, and maintain 'juridical systems or customs' and their distinctive customs, spirituality, traditions, procedures, and practices in Article 34. It also states in Article 46(2) that nothing in the exercise of rights under the Declaration undermines these 'human rights and fundamental freedoms'.[102]

[49] I conclude that the intention of the legislature stated in the Preamble of the *NTA* is to 'rectify the consequences of past injustices' and 'to ensure that Aboriginal Peoples and Torres Strait Islander peoples receive the full

recognition and status within the Australian nation to which history, their prior rights and interests, and their rich and diverse culture, fully entitle them to aspire'. The intention of the legislature was to 'provide a fair way to deal with land in the future (which includes the waters) based on contemporary notions of justice'. A compelling contemporary system of justice is inclusive of the international standards influential to the development of the common law and native title. It supports the recognition that the reciprocal rights of the Torres Strait Islander peoples exist as an integral and indivisible part of the whole, where the fabric of the Torres Strait Islander peoples is intricately woven into native title.

Notes

1 Virginia Marshall.
2 *Akiba v Queensland (No 3)* (2010) 204 FCR 1.
3 Determination, Order 7.
4 Determination, Order 8.
5 *The Commonwealth v Akiba* (2012) 204 FCR 260.
6 Australian Law Reform Commission, *Recognition of Aboriginal Customary Laws* (Report No 31, 12 June 1986) 50. Note the concept of 'time immemorial' is a doctrine of the common law where a custom has existed and has been exercised both continuously and peaceably.
7 Bryan Keon-Cohen, *A Mabo Memoir: Islan Kustom to Native Title* (Zemvic Press, 2013) 16–7.
8 Virginia Marshall, *Overturning Aqua Nullius: Securing Aboriginal Water Rights* (Aboriginal Studies Press, 2017) 51, citing Nicolas Peterson and Bruce Rigsby (eds) *Customary Marine Tenure in Australia* (1998) 48(2) *Oceania Monograph University of Sydney*.
9 Elizabeth Osborne, *Throwing Off the Cloak: Reclaiming Self-Reliance in Torres Strait* (Aboriginal Studies Press, rev ed, 2020) 7.
10 Marshall (n 8) [76]. Subject to inconsistent grants of interests and extinguishment by the Queensland Government and subject to Commonwealth laws.
11 *Mabo v Queensland (No 2)* (1992) 175 CLR 1, 61 ('*Mabo (No 2)*').
12 *Akiba v Queensland (No 3)* (2010) 204 FCR 1, [9].
13 Ibid., 55 [159].
14 Australian Law Reform Commission, *Connection to Country: Review of the Native Title Act 1993* (Cth) (Final Report No 126, 4 June 2015) 126. Cited in this report were recommendations highlighted by the former Finn J in Paul Finn, '*Mabo* into the Future: Native Title Jurisprudence' (2012) 8 *Indigenous Law Bulletin* 5, 6.
15 Martin Nakata, *Disciplining the Savages: Savaging the Disciplines* (Aboriginal Studies Press, 2007) 200.
16 Keon-Cohen (n 7) 370. See *Mabo v Queensland* [1990] QSC 409.
17 Ibid.
18 Ibid.
19 Ibid.
20 Marshall (n 8) 75.
21 Linda Tuhiwai Smith, *Decolonizing Methodologies: Research and Indigenous Peoples* (Zed, 2006) 60.
22 See Peter Drahos, *Intellectual Property, Indigenous People and Their Knowledge* (Cambridge University Press, 2014) 42.
23 Government of South Australia, *Murray-Darling Basin Royal Commission Report* (Report, 29 January 2019) 470.

24 Marie Battiste, 'Indigenous Knowledge and Pedagogy in First Nations Education: A Literature Review with Recommendations' (National Working Group on Education and the Minister of Indian and Northern Affairs Canada, Ottowa Ontario Canada, 2002) 15.
25 Nakata (n 15) 4.
26 Human Rights and Equal Opportunity Commission, *Bringing Them Home: Report of the National Inquiry into the Separation of Aboriginal and Torres Strait Islander Children from Their Families* (1997) 71, citing Cornelius O'Leary, Director of Native Affairs (1942 to 1963), speaking at a Superintendents' Conference in October 1960, quoted by Rosalind Kidd, 'Regulating Bodies: Administration and Aborigines in Queensland: 1840–1988 (PhD Thesis, Griffith University, 1994) 83.
27 Human Rights and Equal Opportunity Commission (n 26) 78.
28 See also Osborne (n 9) ch 1 'The Early Years'.
29 *Wurridjal v Commonwealth* [2009] HCA 2, 393 [210].
30 Australian Law Reform Commission (n 6) [37].
31 James (Sakej) Youngblood Henderson, Marjorie L Benson and Isobel M Findlay, *Aboriginal Tenure in the Constitution of Canada* (Carswell, 2000) 7, citing Erica-Irene Daes, the Special Rapporteur, UN Sub-Commission on Prevention of Discrimination and Protection of Minorities, Commission on Human Rights, United Nations Economic and Social Council, *Protection of the Heritage of Indigenous People: Preliminary Report of the Special Rapporteur*, UN ESC, 1994, UN Doc.E/CN.4/Sub.2/1994/31, [8].
32 Christine Choo, *Mission Girls: Aboriginal Women on Catholic Missions in the Kimberley, Western Australia, 1900–1950* (University of Western Australia Press, 2004) 9.
33 Ibid., 1.
34 Marshall (n 8) 26.
35 Ibid., 27.
36 Australian Law Reform Commission (n 6) 76.
37 Ibid.
38 Tuhiwai Smith (n 21) 68. See also Linda Tuhiwai Smith, *Decolonizing Methodologies: Research and Indigenous Peoples* (Otago University Press, 2nd ed, 2012).
39 The expeditions of Europeans and the British to Indigenous territories such as the Torres Strait.
40 The Cambridge Anthropological Expedition included the following members: CS Meyers, WHR Rivers, SH Ray, William McDougal, and CG Seligman. The Cambridge Expedition reports were edited and published by Haddon in six volumes from 1901 to 1935.
41 *Akiba v Queensland (No 2)* [2010] FCA 643, [107].
42 Nakata (n 15) 103 states that, 'Haddon engaged middle-aged men as informants to collect the knowledge from the old men of the community'.
43 Ibid., 39 [107], [109]: Professor Scott in giving evidence on the Cambridge Anthropological Expedition to the Torres Strait Reports; volume 2 of the reports was not tendered in evidence.
44 Ibid.
45 Ibid., 45 [126].
46 *Evidence Act 1995* (Cth) s 135(a).
47 Ibid., s 135(b).
48 *Akiba v Queensland (No 3)* (2010) 204 FCR 1, 46 [129].
49 Osborne (n 9) 110, citing Gary D Myers, Malcolm O'Dell, Guy Wright, and Simone C Muller, 'A Sea Change in Land Rights Law: The Extension of Native Title to Australia's Offshore Areas' (Native Title Research Unit, Australian Institute of Aboriginal and Torres Strait Islander Studies, 1996) 3.
50 Ibid.
51 Ibid. See *Regina v Keyn* 1876 2 Law Reports (Exchequer Division) 63 (1876): the technical issue in this criminal law matter where a foreign vessel collided into a

British vessel two and a half nautical miles off the coast of Dover, which resulted in the death of a passenger on the British vessel, was whether the German officer in command could be charged with manslaughter.

52 Osbourne (n 9). See *Commonwealth v Yarmirr* (2002) 208 CLR 1: the majority of the High Court (Gleeson CJ, Gaudron, Gummow, and Hayne JJ) held that native title rights did exist offshore and such rights are non-exclusive (resulting from the international right of free passage, the common law public right to navigate and fish) and to free access of the sea and seabed in accordance with traditional laws and customs for limited purposes. Prior to the determination the Commonwealth's position was that native title did not exist offshore. See also *Western Australia v Ward* (2002) 213 CLR 1, confirming that the seas are non-exclusive areas under native title.

53 Osborne (n 9) 115.

54 *Treaty between Australia and the Independent State of Papua New Guinea Concerning Sovereignty and Maritime Boundaries in the Area between the Two Countries, Including the Area Known as the Torres Strait*, signed 18 December 1978, ATS 4 (entered into force 15 February 1985) ('*Treaty between Australia and Papua New Guinea*').

55 Ibid.

56 Osbourne (n 9) 118, citing Heron Loban 'Reflection on a Treaty by a Torres Strait Islander Lawyer' (2002) 5(21) *Indigenous Law Bulletin* 1.

57 *Treaty between Australia and Papua New Guinea*, art 1(m).

58 Ibid., art 11.1.

59 Ibid., art 12.

60 Ibid., art 16.3(a).

61 Ibid., art 1(k)(iv).

62 Ibid., art 1(l).

63 Ibid., art 1(l)(iii).

64 *Akiba v Queensland (No 2)* [2010] FCA 643, [998].

65 Ibid., [999].

66 Ibid.

67 Ibid., [505].

68 Ibid., [71].

69 *Commonwealth v Akiba* [2012] FCAFC 25, 11 [28].

70 Ibid., 11 [29].

71 Marshall (n 8) 105.

72 Ibid.

73 Ibid. See Craig Anthony Tony Arnold, 'The Reconstruction of Property: Property as a Web of Interests' (2002) 26 *Harvard Environmental Law Review* 281.

74 Virginia Marshall (n 8) 107, citing Arnold (n 73) 282, 296.

75 See *Western Australia v Ward* (2002) 213 CLR 1.

76 *Commonwealth v Akiba* [2012] FCAFC 25, 34 [115]. The Torres Strait Islands Sea Claim Group set out 'their argument on reciprocity based rights using the Claim Group's customary marine tenure model: where two types of rights exist, the first type is ancestral occupation based rights and the second is reciprocal rights'.

77 Ibid., 34 [119].

78 Ibid.

79 P G McHugh, *Aboriginal Title: The Modern Jurisprudence of Tribal Land Rights* (Oxford University Press, 2011) 124.

80 Thomas C Grey, 'The Disintegration of Property' (1980) 22 *NOMOS* 69, cited in Marshall (n 8) 107.

81 Marshall (n 8) 107.

82 Ibid., 108, citing Arnold (n 73).

83 *Commonwealth v Akiba* [2012] FCAFC 25, 34 [115]–[118]. See also 35 [120]: status-based reciprocal relationships include affinal and tebud.

84 Ibid., 34–5 [115]–[121].

85 (2002) 213 CLR 1.

86 *Commonwealth v Akiba* [2012] FCAFC 25, 167 [538]. The primary judge questions why the applicant has not 'sought sufficiently to unbundle the rights possessed under the laws and customs of the Torres Strait Islanders'.
87 Marshall (n 8) 108, citing Arnold (n 73) 283.
88 Virginia Marshall, 'Overturning *Aqua Nullius*: Pathways to National Law Reform' in Ron Levy et al. (eds), *New Directions for Law in Australia: Essays in Contemporary Law Reform* (ANU Press, 2017) 226, citing Virginia Marshall, 'The Progress of Aboriginal Water Rights and Interests in the Murray-Darling Basin in NSW: An Essential Element of Culture' (2015) 30(6/7) *Australian Environment Review* 158. See also Virginia Marshall, *A Web of Aboriginal Water Rights: Examining the Competing Aboriginal Claim for Water Property Rights and Interests in Australia* (PhD Thesis, Macquarie University, 2014).
89 Marshall (n 8) 82.
90 *Akiba v Queensland (No 2)* (2010) 204 FCR 1, 36 [96]–[97].
91 The Federal Court decisions and the decision of this Court in relation to the Torres Strait Islander Claim Group could have included the voices of Torres Strait Islander women, their roles for sea country, and their participation in communal life; however, the focus was on patrilineal rights and interests.
92 *Akiba v Queensland (No 2)* (2010) 204 FCR 1, 146–7 [463], [469].
93 Ibid., 184 [592].
94 Ibid., 70 [215].
95 Ibid., 37 [133].
96 Ibid.
97 See *Tackamore v Clarke* [2011] NZCA 587: the Supreme Court heard on appeal from the Court of Appeal decision in relation to the requirements for recognition of Maori custom *tikanga* by the New Zealand common law. See also *Tackamore v Clarke* [2012] NZSC 116.
98 *Akiba v Queensland (No 2)* [2010] FCA 643.
99 Ibid., 159 [508]–[510].
100 Ibid., 37 [133].
101 *Mabo (No 2)* (1992) 175 CLR 1, 13 [42].
102 See Kirsty Gover, 'Treaties and the UN Declaration on the Rights of Indigenous Peoples: The Significance of Article 37' in *UNDRIP Implementation Comparative Approaches, Indigenous Voices from CANZUS* (Centre for International Governance Innovation Canada, 10 March 2020) 77–85. See also Claire Charters, 'The UN Declaration on the Rights of Indigenous Peoples in New Zealand Courts: A Case for Cautious Optimism' in *UNDRIP Implementation Comparative Approaches, Indigenous Voices from CANZUS* (Centre for International Governance Innovation Canada, 10 March 2020) 43–54.

PART III
Racism and discrimination

8

KARTINYERI v COMMONWEALTH [1998] HCA 22

Commentary: *Kartinyeri v Commonwealth* [1998] HCA 22

Larissa Behrendt and Taryn Lee

This case speaks to the structural marginalisation of Aboriginal and Torres Strait Islander peoples—especially women—as part of the colonial project in Australia. It also speaks to the continuing attacks, sanctioned by colonial laws and drawing upon a colonial archive, on Aboriginal culture and heritage.

Why revisit *Kartinyeri v Commonwealth*?

The *Hindmarsh Island Bridge* case was an opportunity to evolve the meaning of the race power in the Constitution. It was a chance to take the Constitution from a document which aimed to preserve the white Australia policy and marginalise Indigenous people within the Commonwealth to one which challenged racism and protected Indigenous rights. Sadly, this did not happen. It was a missed opportunity.

Narrow interpretation of the law

The majority of the court avoided the broader underlying issues and kept their decisions to narrow questions of law. Gaudron, Gummow, and Hayne JJ considered the question of the race power and concluded there was no requirement that it be used beneficially. Gummow and Hayne JJ considered the words 'deemed necessary' and determined that the power to enact a law includes the power to repeal it. Gaudron J held it was for Parliament to decide what was 'deemed necessary'. That is, if the Parliament deems it necessary to maintain race relations that are discriminatory and prioritise commercial interests over the cultural rights of Aboriginal and Torres Strait Islander peoples, the law will not interfere.

Brennan CJ and McHugh J limited their responses to the single issue of whether the *Hindmarsh Island Bridge Act 1997* (Cth) was valid. They concluded that if the power to pass the *Aboriginal and Torres Strait Islander Heritage Protection Act 1984* (Cth) existed, the 1997 Act merely amended it, so that it was a valid exercise of power. They met the question of whether the race power was confined to beneficial use with silence, but tacitly answered in the negative.

Kirby J, in dissent, concluded the race power had to be used beneficially. Justice Kirby's broader view was that because the Australian people effected change through section 128 of the *Australian Constitution* ('*Constitution*'), this needs to be taken into consideration when interpreting the race power post-1967. Unfortunately, at the time, this view was not adopted by the majority of the High Court. His judgment has provided some interpretative guidance and, for the purposes of this project, has been explored further.

Gummow and Hayne JJ argued that the 1967 referendum did not change the original meaning of the *Constitution* so that the race power can be used for the benefit or the detriment of Aboriginal and Torres Strait Islander peoples.

This is clearly a case where limiting the questions before the court to their most legalistic meaning denies consideration of the broader context. It also avoids larger, more important questions relating to Aboriginal and Torres Strait Islander peoples, thereby missing an opportunity to redress past wrongs and set a new pathway for the future.

Ignoring whether the race power has to be used beneficially cements a view that the three arms of government cannot be relied upon to act in a way that is beneficial to Aboriginal and Torres Strait Islander peoples. Past and current laws and policies repeat the same mistakes. The possibility that the race power would be used beneficially has never come to fruition: despite several opportunities, the High Court has never resolved that it cannot be used detrimentally.

Our approach and what we would do differently

> The coloniser's ability to frame disputes with the colonised within colonial law is a key process in perpetuating the norms of colonialism. This action involves removing disputes from Aboriginal peoples, communities and ways, and into an arena and discourse where the coloniser has a monopoly on the interpretation of Aboriginal peoples' experience. Colonial law provides the coloniser the ability to exclude and with the exclusive power to interpret.[1]

The race power needs to be interpreted to ensure there is no ambiguity as to its use in relation to Aboriginal and Torres Strait Islander peoples. Moreover, the Parliament's power to make laws in relation to Aboriginal and Torres Strait

Islander peoples should be confined to laws that can be characterised as beneficial. In determining whether a law is beneficial, the perspectives of Aboriginal and Torres Strait Islander peoples should be decisive.

A framework: the inclusion of women's voices

In approaching this case, it was important to move the voices of the Ngarrindjeri women from the margins of the legal process and place them in the centre. Accordingly, when considering the cultural rights raised in the case, the women's knowledge has been privileged as the most reliable authority on cultural matters.

In doing so, this project has challenged the legal norms which preference colonial structures that were inherited as a result of invasion and continue to be dominated by white men. Furthermore, we query whether any non-Ngarrindjeri anthropological expert can ever have sufficient expertise in the subject matter to qualify as an expert.

Our approach to legislative interpretation

Our approach to a reinterpretation of the race power is grounded in taking into account the intention of the 1967 referendum. When the Australian public voted for the change, it was clearly with the intention that the transfer of power from the states to the federal government was with a view that they would do a better job of protecting the rights and improving the lives of Aboriginal and Torres Strait Islander peoples.[2]

The High Court's majority approach to narrowly interpreting the race power, confined to the words in the text, gave no protection from actions by government that would undermine the rights of Indigenous people. As a result, the *Constitution* continued to be a vehicle to strip Aboriginal and Torres Strait Islander peoples of protections, rather than a modern document that reflected the emerging human rights frameworks that were developing internationally.

Since the *Hindmarsh Island Bridge* case, the Commonwealth has used the race power to enact detrimental laws for Aboriginal people, which have included the suspension of the *Racial Discrimination Act 1975* (Cth) ('*RDA*').[3] This failure to protect Aboriginal and Torres Strait Islander peoples from racial discrimination underlines how few human rights are protected in the *Constitution* and how this disproportionately impacts Indigenous people. This was most starkly illustrated in *Kruger v Commonwealth*[4] where the High Court considered wrongs done to children removed from their families under government policy. The plaintiffs argued that their rights to freedom of movement, equality before the law, due process, and freedom of religion had been violated.[5] The Court denied each claim on the basis that none of those rights are protected by the *Constitution*.[6]

Recognise a fiduciary obligation

We consider that the *Hindmarsh Island Bridge* case was an opportunity to consider the fiduciary obligation owed by the Crown to Aboriginal and Torres Strait Islander peoples due to their unique historical relationship.

In the comparative jurisdiction of Canada, it has been recognised that the Crown has a higher duty to its Indigenous peoples as a result of historical wrongs they have suffered. By way of analogy, a fiduciary duty owed by the Commonwealth would ensure that not only did it enact laws that were beneficial to Indigenous peoples, but it would also be subject to a higher standard for Aboriginal peoples in recognition of past wrongs and their ongoing impacts. Our interpretation of the race power is consistent with this jurisprudence.

The use of other principles of interpretation including international norms

At the time, the High Court's majority decision was a departure from international instruments ratified by Australia, specifically the *International Convention on the Elimination of All Forms of Racial Discrimination*.[7] As a result, international rights protections recognised as normative standards have not been applied as a framework for laws and policies that affect Aboriginal people. We contend that these standards should provide a benchmark for government actions and decision making and should have guided the approach in the *Hindmarsh Island Bridge* case, particularly in preventing the suspension of the *RDA*. If decided today, there would be an opportunity to incorporate the standards of the *United Nations Declaration on the Rights of Indigenous Peoples*. Of particular relevance are the protections and standards set around self-determination and consent.

The benefits of the approach that we argue for would have extended beyond the *Hindmarsh Island Bridge* case. If the case had been decided with the rights framework that we are suggesting, it may have provided some recourse for the subsequent overriding of Indigenous rights, particularly in relation to the Northern Territory Intervention.

This approach is not a departure from the legal norms and shows that a broader approach that considers established international human rights norms and the unique relationship between Aboriginal and Torres Strait Islander peoples and the Australian state can provide a pathway towards greater protections for the rights of Aboriginal and Torres Strait Islander peoples.

Notes

1 D'Arcy Vermette, 'Colonialism and the Suppression of Aboriginal Voice' (2009) 40(2) *Ottawa Law Review* 225, 227–65.
2 See e.g. a poster for the 1967 Referendum, *State Library of New South Wales*.
3 Such as the *Northern Territory National Emergency Response Act 2007* (Cth) and the Wik Amendments to the *Native Title Act 1993* (Cth) in 1998.

4 *Kruger v Commonwealth; Bray v Commonwealth* (1997) 190 CLR 1.
5 See *Australian Constitution* s 116.
6 See Lachlan Kennedy and Deborah Nance, 'The Stolen Generations Litigation: Kruger, Bray v Commonwealth' (1997) 4(6) *Indigenous Law Bulletin* 22.
7 *International Convention on the Elimination of All Forms of Racial Discrimination*, GA Res 2106(XX), (7 March 1966).

Kartinyeri .... Plaintiffs;

AND

The Commonwealth.. Defendant;

[1998] HCA 22

Constitutional law—Race power—Racial discrimination—Heritage protection—Indigenous women's business—International norms—Fiduciary duty.

[1] Behrendt and Lee JJ.[1] In her evidence received by this Court, Ngarrindjeri traditional owner Doreen Kartinyeri stated:

> Our beliefs are in our hearts. They're our grandmothers' stories. Those who are interfering are interfering with our grandmothers' lore. It amounts to being forced to break our law to prove to Europeans that our law still exists…it threatens our culture, not just one or two individuals. The stories belong to us and are part of Aboriginal women's stories in this country.[2]

[2] It is acknowledged by this Court that the Ngarrindjeri have been present on their land for over 65,000 years, and during that time they have had their own system of governance and laws. The stability of this self-government is evident in the way that the Ngarrindjeri, together with other Aboriginal and Torres Strait Islander nations across Australia, are the oldest living cultures in the world. They have a deep connection to their traditional Country that includes cultural, social, economic, and spiritual attachment. This relationship continues to this day and is more complex and multifaceted than Western notions of land ownership.

Background to the case

[3] This case concerns a parcel of land in Goolwa, South Australia, on Ngarrindjeri Ruwe and Yarluwar-Ruwe.[3] It is a site of special significance for the women of the community. We accept the evidence that the destruction of this sacred place would result in spiritual and emotional damage to the Ngarrindjeri community. We have not required the Ngarrindjeri women to disclose the sacred stories that relate to the place, but accept their

sworn evidence that they do exist in accordance with Ngarrindjeri traditional laws and customs, known as Yannarumi.[4]

[4] The matter before the Court arose from the granting of approval for a bridge to be built from Goolwa to Kumarangk ('Hindmarsh Island'). Binalong Pty Ltd ('Binalong') purchased land on Hindmarsh Island in 1977 with the view to building a 560-berth marina, residential development, conference centre, golf course, and associated buildings and infrastructure. An application was made by Binalong to increase the size of the original project, but the Planning Assessment Commission determined that the expansion would require a bridge to be built since the existing cable ferry would not be able to handle the increased traffic.

[5] It is unclear to the Court if there were any other alternatives explored between the parties that could address the issue of increased traffic while maintaining the preservation of areas of cultural significance to Ngarrindjeri peoples.

[6] Approval for the bridge was granted in 1989 but subject to an Environmental Impact Study ('EIS'). The EIS report was completed in two weeks but raised the need for an anthropological study. In January 1990, Binalong funded an anthropological study that found, based only on written records, that no cultural sites were identified in the area. But the report did caution that consultation with Indigenous groups would be required. It is important to note that 'written records' in this context would have been predominantly in the colonial archive and from a non-Indigenous, colonial point of view.

[7] In 1990, the State Minister for Environment and Planning wrote to Binalong granting permission for the bridge to be built subject to several provisos that included consultation with 'relevant Aboriginal representative bodies'.

[8] In 1994, a group of Ngarrindjeri women, to whom the site is of particular cultural importance, successfully applied under s 10 of the *Aboriginal and Torres Strait Islander Heritage Protection Act 1984* (Cth) ('*Heritage Act*') for a declaration to protect the area. In granting this application, the Minister for Aboriginal and Torres Strait Islander Affairs was satisfied, based upon a report provided by Professor Cheryl Saunders, that, amongst other things, the Ngarrindjeri women regarded the mouth of the Murray River, Hindmarsh and Mundoo Islands, and the surrounding waters as 'crucial for the reproduction of the Ngarrindjeri people and their continued existence'.[5]

[9] As is their cultural protocol, the Ngarrindjeri women, as custodians of secret women's business, did not disclose this information to Ngarrindjeri men or to other men. Significantly, this information was confidentially and sensitively referred to in the *Saunders Report* and accepted by the Minister on that basis.[6] Accordingly, the area was identified as a significant Aboriginal area and under threat of injury or desecration due to the construction of the bridge.

[10] As a result, the Keating government declared a 25-year moratorium on the building of the bridge. This was overturned by the Federal Court on a technicality.[7] In particular, O'Loughlin J held that the Minister erred by relying

on the issue of 'secret women's business' contained within the *Saunders Report* when he had not read the confidential and culturally sensitive information contained within the report on the basis that he was a man.

[11] Consequently, the Ngarrindjeri women made another application under the *Heritage Act* in 1995 and 1996.[8]

[12] In 1996, the newly elected Howard government intervened in the dispute between the Ngarrindjeri women and Binalong by passing the *Hindmarsh Island Bridge Act 1997* (Cth) ('*Bridge Act*'). The effect of this legislation was to suspend the application of the *Heritage Act* from the areas where the Hindmarsh Island bridge was to be constructed. It provided that the *Heritage Act* 'does not authorise the making of a declaration in relation to the preservation or protection of an area or object' with respect to the construction of a bridge and associated activities in the area prescribed as the 'Hindmarsh Island bridge area'.[9]

[13] In order to overcome the discriminatory nature of this legislation, the Commonwealth Parliament also suspended the *Racial Discrimination Act 1975* (Cth) ('*RDA*') from applying to the *Bridge Act.*

[14] As a result, the only two applicable pieces of legislation that protected the unique cultural rights of Aboriginal and Torres Strait Islander peoples in this matter were no longer relevant.

The veracity, perspective, and voice of Aboriginal and Torres Strait Islander women

[15] Both the EIS study and the 1990 Binalong-funded report acknowledged the need to obtain the Aboriginal perspective on the site.

[16] It is critically important to note that, even where anthropological evidence is offered, it needs to be looked at with deep scrutiny to ensure there is no bias or cultural misunderstandings that lead to erroneous conclusions. Anthropologists and colonial diarists have historically observed Aboriginal and Torres Strait Islander cultures through their European gaze. Of the many misinterpretations that resulted from this inherent unconscious bias, one was that it was assumed that Aboriginal and Torres Strait Islander cultures were patrilineal. It followed that women had no power and were treated as chattels. Their sites were often not recorded as these early recorders of Aboriginal and Torres Strait Islander cultures did not bother to ask about the customs, law, and spiritual life of women. However, it is now understood that Aboriginal and Torres Strait Islander women played and continue to play a significant cultural role in their societies. And, in more recent times, Aboriginal and Torres Strait Islander women themselves are addressing this historical wrong.[10] For example, Behrendt has highlighted that:

> Aboriginal women played an important role spiritually within Australian society. The rainbow serpent, the spirit of creation, was a female energy. Spiritual rites were inherited through the mother. The place of conception

and birth of a child were chosen by the mother, not the father. These places would have spiritual significance in a person's life.[11]

[17] In the context of the case before the Court, it is critical to acknowledge that Aboriginal and Torres Strait Islander women's voices, experiences, and cultures are not only missing from the historical archive but are also missing from many anthropological accounts.[12] The absence and marginalising of this voice is symptomatic of the broader societal exclusion of Aboriginal and Torres Strait Islander women that continues in contemporary society.[13]

[18] There is no substitute for the perspectives and accounts of Aboriginal and Torres Strait Islander women of their own culture in their own words. However, the Court acknowledges that Aboriginal and Torres Strait Islander women's voices have been affected by colonisation. That is, past laws and government policies have not welcomed Aboriginal and Torres Strait Islander women to share their stories outside of their communities, whether they are bound by cultural protocols or not.[14] This is illuminated by the lived experience as told by Doreen Kartinyeri:

> I was born in the mission in 1935 and I lived there until I was 10 then I was taken away by the Protector put in a home. I was expelled from school at 14 and so I returned to the mission and tried to learn all I could about my Aboriginal background. I was told of Kumarangk 'women's business' by my Auntie Rosie and my Auntie Laura who said that prior to the establishment of the mission in 1854 there was 'women's business' all around the Lower Murray and on Kumarangk. The women's stories told to me I kept to myself and just spoke to my daughter about it. It's very hard trying to live a European style of life and practice these things by yourself, you need to practice them as a community which is how they were done traditionally.[15]

[19] In this context, Aboriginal and Torres Strait Islander women's voices and experiences must be privileged. It is also acknowledged that there were disputes within the Ngarrindjeri community about the cultural sites. But it is the firm view of this Court that discussions about Ngarrindjeri culture should and must be decided by the Ngarrindjeri people using their own governance and dispute resolution methods. It is not the role of the colonial courts to determine cultural matters within Aboriginal and Torres Strait Islander nations unless asked by both parties to do so. This is not a case where such adjudication is required.

The legal issues arising

[20] The key legal question for this Court to decide in this case is about the validity of the *Bridge Act*. That is, does the Commonwealth have the power to make laws that are discriminatory towards Ngarrindjeri peoples?

[21] The Ngarrindjeri women have challenged the legality of the *Bridge Act* on the basis that it is said to be discriminatory. A large part of their argument rests on the assertion that when the Commonwealth was granted the power to make laws for Aboriginal and Torres Strait Islander people as a result of the 1967 referendum, it was with the assumption that the laws would be used beneficially.

[22] The contrary argument looks not to the intention of the constitutional amendment but to the actual text of s 51(xxvi) of the *Australian Constitution* ('*Constitution*') (otherwise known as the 'race power') after the 1967 referendum:

> The Parliament shall, subject to this Constitution, have power to make laws for the peace, order, and good government of the Commonwealth with respect to:
>
> ...
>
> (xxvi) the people of any race, ~~other than the aboriginal race in any State~~, for whom it is deemed necessary to make special laws.

[23] This argument asserts that, on the face of it, the race power is mute about whether the power should be used only beneficially and can just as equally be used detrimentally on a strict reading. In addition, the defendant argues that if the Commonwealth Parliament has the power to make a law—in this case, the *Heritage Act*—it has the power to effectively repeal it (as was done by the *Bridge Act*).

The 'race power'

[24] This case cannot be viewed outside of its historical and colonial context. That is, the impact of colonisation has resulted in the historical and continued power imbalance between Aboriginal and Torres Strait Islander peoples and the Crown. Realising this unique relationship, additional care must be given to ensure that meaningful engagement and consultation with Aboriginal and Torres Strait Islander peoples occurs when referring to unanswered legal matters carried out by the Crown.[16]

[25] It is not enough to dismiss the matter by characterising the situation as merely repealing an existing piece of legislation with the argument that if Parliament has the power to make a law, it has the power to rescind it.

[26] The law must fall within the power conferred under the Constitution and the court must be satisfied that the foundation for making the law exists in the first place. This is true of both enacting legislation and legislation that is designed to repeal or take away existing legislative rights.

[27] The *Constitution* as enacted in 1901 made several assumptions about Aboriginal and Torres Strait Islander peoples. The people involved in

drafting the *Constitution* were exclusively white men and Australia's foundational document is imbued with their prejudices.

[28] First, it was assumed at the time by a majority of people that Aboriginal and Torres Strait Islander peoples were a dying race in the face of superior races, and hence would eventually no longer be a burden on the state. These views were informed by Darwinism's process of 'survival of the fittest'. It was believed that Aboriginal and Torres Strait Islander peoples were inevitably doomed, and governments and missionaries were required to 'smooth the dying pillow'.[17]

[29] The second assumption was that this burden, as long as it did exist, was to be a matter for the states and not a matter for the Commonwealth government. This distribution of power is reflected in the original wording of s 51(xxiv) that excluded the race power from applying to Aboriginal and Torres Strait Islander peoples. As reflected by the government:

> We recognise that the effect of the treatment of aborigines on the reputation of Australia furnishes a powerful argument for a transference of control to the Commonwealth. But we think that on the whole the States are better equipped for controlling aborigines than the Commonwealth. The States control the police and the lands, and they to a large extent control the conditions of industry. We think that a Commonwealth authority would be at a disadvantage in dealing with the aborigines [sic], and that the States are better qualified to do so.[18]

[30] Finally, there was another important assumption that rights would not be protected within the *Constitution*. The framers of the *Constitution* debated whether to include rights in the *Constitution*, including the right to due process before the law and equality before the law, but decided against it. They wanted, firstly, to leave the protection of rights to the legislature rather than entrench them as they are in the Constitution of the United States of America. And, secondly, they wanted to allow for the enactment of laws that allowed for discrimination on the basis of race. This is evidenced by the fact that the first substantial legislation to go through the Australian Parliament was the *Immigration Restriction Act 1901* (Cth) which provided the basis for the White Australia Policy.[19]

[31] The background to the 1967 referendum is critical in understanding how to read the race power today. The drive to transfer power from the states to the Commonwealth government came from the belief held by a majority of Australians that the states had a dismal record in relation to the treatment of Aboriginal and Torres Strait Islander peoples, and the Commonwealth, if tasked with legislative responsibility for them, would do a better job of it.

[32] From the time of invasion, Aboriginal and Torres Strait Islander peoples' deprivation of political autonomy has been profound. In the early years of colonisation, Aboriginal and Torres Strait Islander peoples were reduced to

wards of the state and 'protection boards' exercised complete control and power over their lives.[20] The process of 'protection' resulted in extreme disadvantage for most Indigenous peoples.[21] It is this context of state control that fostered a growing community belief that uniform Commonwealth legislation could be beneficial for Aboriginal and Torres Strait Islander peoples. Prime Minister Holt said when introducing the *Constitution Alteration (Aboriginals) Bill 1967* (Cth):

> If the words 'other than the aboriginal race in any State' were deleted from the section 51(xxvi), the result would be that the Commonwealth Parliament would have vested in it a concurrent legislative power with respect to aboriginals as such, they being the people of a race, provided the Parliament deemed it necessary to make special laws for them. It is the view of the Government that the National Parliament should have this power. If the proposals relating to aboriginals are approved by the people, the *Government would regard it as desirable to hold discussions with the states to secure the widest measure of agreement with respect to aboriginal advancement.*[22]

[33] In supporting the bill, the Leader of the Opposition referred to the disadvantage suffered by Aboriginal and Torres Strait Islander peoples and the need for positive Commonwealth initiatives.[23] As a result, he acknowledged that some race-based discrimination was necessary but 'it should be favourable, not unfavourable'.[24] The Leader of the Opposition in the Senate went further in addressing the race power and stated that:

> The simple fact is that they are different from other persons and that they do need special laws. They themselves believe that they need special laws. In this proposed law there is no suggestion of any intended discrimination in respect of Aboriginals except a discrimination in their favour.[25]

[34] The bill passed through the House of Representatives and was approved by the Senate without a dissenting vote.[26] As Tom Calma reflects, 'the 1967 referendum was one of those times in Australia's history where every single one of us could hold our head up high—knowing that we were each doing our bit to make sure Indigenous people had a better future in this country'.[27]

[35] In the 1967 referendum, 90.77 per cent of Australians voted 'yes' for change. The 'Vote Yes for Aborigines' campaign leading up to the referendum built community expectations about the proposed reform leading to rights to improve the lives of Indigenous peoples. These expectations reflected a hope for a new era of equality. Examples of this newfound hope include the Freedom Rides led by Charlie Perkins, which brought together Aboriginal and non-Aboriginal people, who travelled into rural areas in New South Wales to expose race-based discrimination.[28]

[36] This case is the first to determine the scope of the race power since the 1967 referendum.

Addressing the ambiguity of the 'race power'

[37] The wording of s 51(xxvi) is ambiguous. While it does not mention the word 'beneficial', it also does not specifically mention the words 'Aboriginal or Torres Strait Islander people'. As George Williams states in relation to the 1967 referendum:

> Indigenous peoples were not granted any particular rights to land or otherwise. The change left the Constitution...devoid of any reference to Indigenous peoples. Discrimination was replaced with silence.[29]

It is the ambiguity of the section that allows the Court to look into other interpretive tools.

[38] In interpreting s 51(xxvi), we have been guided by three considerations. First, in the Court's view, the intention of the 1967 amendment was to provide the Commonwealth Parliament with the power to pass legislation that would be to the benefit of Aboriginal and Torres Strait Islander peoples, which is critical in interpreting the section.[30] Second, the Court adopts the principles and norms of international human rights law when interpreting the race power.[31] Finally, the Court accepts that it has a duty to ensure that racial discrimination is not perpetuated in the judicial system.

Intention

[39] As highlighted above, 90.77 per cent of Australians voted to change the race power with a view that it would better the position of Aboriginal and Torres Strait Islander peoples. The Court acknowledges the disappointment within the community about the lack of beneficial change for Indigenous peoples, which saw the establishment of the Aboriginal Tent Embassy in 1972. Reflecting on its establishment, Behrendt states:

> It was more than a mere act of political defiance born of frustration by the lack of change to people's lives as a result of the 1967 referendum. It was part of a political movement that had begun at the time a colony was first established in Sydney, shared a heart with freedom fighters like Pemulwuy, found momentum in the articulate and statesmanlike voices of William Cooper and Fred Maynard, and interacted with political movements such as those for sovereignty, citizenship rights, black power, feminism, decolonisation and post-colonialism.[32]

[40] It is clear that there was a community expectation that the Commonwealth, given its new power, would make laws for the benefit of Aboriginal people and herald a new era of equality. Ongoing Aboriginal activism is evidence that the intention expressed in 1967 has not been realised.

Principles of international law

[41] The ambiguity of the 'race power' allows for the use of other principles of interpretation, including international norms. We agree with the reasoning of Kirby J[33] that this Court must adopt an interpretation of a constitutional provision that conforms with the principles of universal and fundamental rights reflected in international instruments that Australia has ratified, rather than an interpretation that would involve a departure from such rights.[34] Importantly, these principles include those embodied in the *International Convention on the Elimination of All Forms of Racial Discrimination*.[35]

Duty for the judiciary not to be racist

[42] This Court accepts that whatever may have been the scope of the race power in 1901, it should no longer extend to laws that are detrimental to a group of people on the basis of their race.

[43] Furthermore, this Court interprets the race power to ensure that there is a duty to see that racism is not allowed to operate within the judicial system. In *Neal*,[36] Murphy J highlighted racial discrimination in the judicial system when he criticised the Queensland Court of Criminal Appeal, stating that it had 'a duty to see that racism is not allowed to operate within the judicial system' and therefore it 'should have disapproved of the unjudicial manner in which the magistrate dealt with sentence'.[37]

[44] The culmination of the intention of the 1967 referendum, the introduction into Australian common law of international human rights law, and the shifting legal landscape as a result of the recognition of Aboriginal and Torres Strait Islander peoples' laws and cultures in the *Mabo* case,[38] all support the proposition that the power given to the Commonwealth under s 51(xxvi) is to be used beneficially.

[45] What is beneficial is a subjective thing. There are historical examples of where a law has been deemed by government to be beneficial and it has had the opposite effect. 'Protection laws' that implemented race-based child removal policies and restricted freedom of movement and the right to work were deemed to be in the best interest of Indigenous people, but clearly were not. In interpreting whether a law is beneficial, consideration should be given to emerging international human rights norms such as those embodied in human rights instruments, particularly the right to self-determination.

[46] Further, in interpreting whether government action is beneficial, consideration also needs to be given to the historical relationship between Indigenous peoples and the Crown, which has led to the creation of fiduciary obligations. This requires the Crown to act to a higher standard when dealing with the rights of Aboriginal and Torres Strait Islander peoples.

Is the *Hindmarsh Island Bridge Act* 'beneficial'?

[47] Maz Ooft has stated:

> In the past, Indigenous peoples were living peacefully in their homelands, in harmony with nature. Then came 'civilization' which wanted to conquer, with a hunger for richness for only a few, the ambition of capital and power. They conquered the land, we lost our homes, our sacred sites, our agricultural areas, our hunting fields, our fishing waters. They called it development, we called it destruction. They said it would raise living standards, we said it brings humiliation. They earned money, we got poor. They founded big companies, we became cheap labour. They ruined the biodiversity, we lost our sources of traditional medicines. They spoke of equality, we saw discrimination. They said infrastructure, we saw invasion. They thought civilisation, we lost our culture, our language, our religion. They subjected us to their laws, we saw them claiming our land. They brought illnesses, weapons, drugs and alcohol, but not equal education and healthcare. It has been going on for more than 500 years. And it still goes on.[39]

[48] The loss of rights, whether common law or legislative, needs to be considered diligently, especially when the rights being taken away are those of the most marginalised and socio-economically disadvantaged within the community. The Court must accept that where the laws have been created to protect those who are most disadvantaged in the community, the Court must consider these rights equally—that they co-exist in the application of the law at a minimum.

[49] However, this Court also accepts that the Commonwealth owes a fiduciary duty to Aboriginal and Torres Strait Islander peoples. As a result, the Commonwealth has to hold itself to a higher standard when it comes to ensuring the protection of Aboriginal and Torres Strait Islander peoples' enjoyment of rights in relation to land, water, sky, and culture.

[50] Too often, Aboriginal and Torres Strait Islander peoples' cultural rights become secondary to other property rights despite the existence of laws to protect their unique cultural rights.

[51] The *Bridge Act* has been designed to deprive the Ngarrindjeri people exclusively of their cultural rights, in favour of the development of a bridge. Therefore, the legislation is not beneficial to the Ngarrindjeri peoples.

[52] There cannot be a clearer indication of a law being racially discriminatory against a particular group of people if its passage also requires a suspension of protections against racial discrimination. The need to suspend the *RDA* in order to protect the intention of the *Bridge Act* is clear evidence of the detriment inherent in the legislation.

[53] In addition to the inherent race-based discrimination, the *Bridge Act* continues to silence the Ngarrindjeri women in the tide of colonial historical record keeping.

Commonwealth's fiduciary duty to Aboriginal peoples

[54] Finally, it is appropriate that the Court consider the Commonwealth's fiduciary obligation to Aboriginal people when asking if the legislation is beneficial. [40]

[55] Brian Slattery explains the obligation as it is understood in the Canadian context, which is analogous to the situation in Australia:

> The Crown has a general fiduciary duty toward native people to protect them in the enjoyment of their aboriginal rights and in particular in the possession and use of their lands. This general fiduciary duty has its origins in the Crown's historical commitment to protect native peoples from the inroads of British settlers, in return for a native undertaking to renounce the use of force to defend themselves and to accept instead the protection of the Crown as its subjects.[41]

[56] Behrendt further explains the fiduciary obligation:

> such a fiduciary obligation may derive from a power inherent in the government that, if exercised, would cause detriment to the specific group that is particularly vulnerable to the exercise of that power. It may be that the action involved would be analogous to commercial activities rather than be mere policy consideration.[42]

[57] In *Mabo v Queensland (No. 2)*[43] Toohey J found that the Crown owes a general fiduciary duty to Aboriginal and Torres Strait Islander people from the 'circumstances of the relationship'.

[58] In the current circumstances, this fiduciary obligation requires that the Commonwealth not deprive Doreen Kartinyeri and other traditional owners of rights under the *Heritage Act* to challenge a development on their lands, as the *Bridge Act* sought to do.

[59] Further evidence of the Commonwealth's failure to reach this standard is seen by the need to suspend the operation of the *RDA* from applying to this situation in order to enact the *Bridge Act.*

[60] As well as evidence of a breach of the international human rights standards under the *International Convention on the Elimination of All Forms of Racial Discrimination* that the Commonwealth Act sought to introduce into Australian law, it is a clear indication that if the *RDA* needs to be suspended in order for a particular action to be valid, that action is racist and therefore not beneficial.

[61] The fiduciary obligation also gives rise to a duty to consult.[44] This duty requires the Crown to consult in good faith to obtain Aboriginal and Torres Strait Islander peoples' free and informed consent prior to the Crown making decisions that affect them, consistent with human rights norms.

Orders

[34] The *Hindmarsh Island Bridge Act 1997* (Cth) is invalid. The Ngarrindjeri women are entitled to use the mechanisms under s 10 of the *Aboriginal and Torres Strait Islander Heritage Protection Act 1984* (Cth) to protect their lands and waters.

Notes

1 Larissa Behrendt and Taryn Lee. The authors would like to thank Professor Daryle Rigney and Tim Goodwin for their cultural advice and professional expertise in reviewing this paper. Their ongoing commitment to promoting and protecting Aboriginal and Torres Strait Islanders' rights, both as professionals and Aboriginal people, not only benefits this work but our ongoing assertion of Aboriginal leadership in this country.

2 Quoted in Paul McGeough, 'Unfinished Business' *Sydney Morning Herald* (Sydney, 27 May 1995) 27.

3 Ruwe and Yarluwar-Ruwe are the Ngarrindjeri terms for Country and sea-country. Njarrindjeri language and cultural expertise was shared with the authors by Njarrindjeri traditional owner, Professor Daryle Rigney. The authors acknowledge and thank Professor Rigney for his leadership and expertise in providing Njarrindjeri language and culture for the purposes of this paper. The authors also acknowledge the Ngarrindjeri people's traditional and ongoing connection with their laws and customs.

4 Yannarumi is a Ngarrindjeri term which translates as 'acting lawfully as ruwe/country'.

5 In accordance with the *Aboriginal and Torres Strait Islander Heritage Protection Act 1984* (Cth) s 10 ('Heritage Act'), Professor Cheryl Saunders provided a report to the Minister for Aboriginal and Torres Strait Islander Affairs on 9 July 1994: ibid., 28.

6 Professor Saunders did not provide detailed accounts of the Ngarrindjeri 'women's business' but provided a confidential attachment to the report which included information by anthropologist Dr Deane Fergie. Professor Saunders stated that: '*This attachment is confidential and should be read by women only.* Even without it, however, it is in my view open to the Minister to conclude that the area has particular significance for Aboriginal people within the meaning of the Act' (ibid., 35).

7 *Chapman v Tickner* (1995) 55 FCR 316.

8 See *Tickner v Chapman* (1995) 57 FCR 451; *Wilson v Minister for Aboriginal and Torres Strait Islander Affairs* (1996) 186 CLR 1.

9 *Hindmarsh Island Bridge Act 1997* (Cth) s 4(1) ('*Bridge Act*').

10 Aileen Moreton-Robinson, *Talkin' Up to the White Woman: Aboriginal Women and Feminism* (University of Queensland Press, 2000); Irene Watson, *Aboriginal Peoples, Colonialism and International Law: Raw Law* (Routledge, 2015).

11 Larissa Behrendt, 'Aboriginal Women and the White Lies of the Feminist Movement: Implications for Aboriginal Women in Rights Discourse' (1993) 1 *Australian Feminist Law Journal* 27, 31.

12 See e.g. the extensive works of Professor Fay Gale. Her PhD thesis, 'A Study of Assimilation: Part Aborigines in South Australia' (The University of Adelaide, 1960), explored the lives of Aboriginal women who had been taken from their mothers as children. See also her collection of work: 'Gale, (Gwendoline) Fay (1932–2008) Papers 1936–1979', *The University of Adelaide* (18 July 2017) <https://www.adelaide.edu.au/library/special/mss/gayle_f/?textonly=1>.

13 See e.g. Gina Rushton, 'This is What it is Like to be an Indigenous Woman Online' *BuzzFeed News* (12 February 2018) <https://www.buzzfeed.com/ginarushton/heres-what-indigenous-women-have-to-put-up-with-online>.

14 See e.g. Aboriginal women's stories about their lived experience of survival: Margaret Tucker, *If Everyone Cared* (U Smith, 1977); Glenyse Ward, *Wandering Girl* (Magabala Books, 1987); Sally Morgan, *My Place* (Fremantle Arts Centre Press, 1987); Ruby Langford, *Don't Take Your Love to Town* (Penguin, 1988); Rita Huggins and Jackie Huggins, *Aunty Rita* (Aboriginal Studies Press, 1994); Alice Nannup, *When the Pelican Laughed* (Fremantle Arts Centre Press, 1995); Doris Pilkington Garimara, *Follow the Rabbit Proof Fence* (University of Queensland Press, 1996); Rosalie Fraser, *Shadow Child: A Memoir of the Stolen Generation* (Hale & Iremonger, 1998); Doreen Kartinyeri, *Doreen Kartinyeri: My Ngarrindjeri Calling* (Aboriginal Studies Press, 2009); Anita Heiss, *Am I Black Enough for You?* (University of Hawai'i Press, 2012).

15 Interview with Doreen Kartinyeri (Tom Morton, ABC Radio National, 17 September 1995).

16 See for example, in Canada a duty to consult with Aboriginal people is established in common law: *Guerin v. The Queen* (1984) 2 SCR 335, 390; *Sparrow v. The Queen* (1990) 1 SCR 1075.

17 National Inquiry into the Separation of Aboriginal and Torres Strait Islander Children from their Families, *Bringing Them Home: The Report of the National Inquiry into the Separation of Aboriginal and Torres Strait Islander Children from Their Families* (1997) 28.

18 Royal Commission on the Constitution of the Commonwealth (Australia), *Report of the Royal Commission on the Constitution* (1929) 270.

19 Larissa Behrendt, *Achieving Social Justice: Indigenous Rights and Australia's Future* (Federation Press, 2004).

20 Victoria provides an example. In the late 1880s, the Board for the Protection of Aborigines was established under the *Aboriginal Protection Act 1869* (Vic). Later, similar legislation was passed in other colonies: New South Wales (1883); Queensland (1897); Western Australia (1905); and South Australia (1911). The Northern Territory Aboriginals Ordinance made the Chief Protector the legal guardian of every Aboriginal and 'half-caste' person under 18 years old. Boards were progressively empowered to remove Indigenous children from their families under the legislation.

21 *Overcoming Indigenous Disadvantage: Key Indicators 2016* (Report, 17 November 2016).

22 Commonwealth, *Parliamentary Debates*, House of Representatives, 1 March 1967, 263 (Harold Holt, Prime Minister) (emphasis added).

23 Commonwealth, *Parliamentary Debates*, House of Representatives, 1 March 1967, 276.

24 Ibid., 281.

25 Commonwealth, *Parliamentary Debates*, Senate, 8 March 1967, 359 (Lionel Murphy).

26 Commonwealth, *Parliamentary Debates*, House of Representatives, 1 March 1967, 287; Commonwealth, *Parliamentary Debates*, Senate, 8 March 1967, 372.

27 Tom Calma, 'The '67 Referendum: Where to Now?' (2007) 11 (SE) *Australian Indigenous Law Review* 2.

28 See the Koori History Website, *Timeline of Significant Moments in the Indigenous Struggle in South East Australia*, 1965, <http://www.kooriweb.org/foley/timeline/histimeline.html>.

29 George Williams, 'The Races Power and the 1967 Referendum' (2007) 11 *Australian Indigenous Law Review* 9.

30 There have been members of this Court who have expressed a view that the race power, since the 1967 referendum, is for the benefit of Aboriginal and Torres Strait Islander peoples and not to their detriment. See e.g. Murphy J in *Koowarta v Bjelke-Petersen* (1982) 153 CLR 168, 242; *Commonwealth v Tasmania* (1983) 158 CLR 1, 180; Gaudron J in *Chu Khen Lim v Minister for Immigration* (1992) 176 CLR 1, 56.

31 See *Charter of the United Nations* arts 1(3), 55(c), 56; *Universal Declaration of Human Rights* art 2; *International Convention on the Elimination of All Forms of Racial Discrimination*, GA Res 2106(XX), (7 March 1966) arts 1(1), 1(4), 2, 6; *International Covenant on Civil and Political Rights*, GA Res 2200A(XXI), (16 December 1966) art 2(1); *International Covenant on Economic, Social and Cultural Rights*, GA Res2200A(XXI), (16 December

1966) art 2(2); *Declaration on Race and Racial Prejudice*, (27 November 1978) art 9(1). Australia signed the *International Convention on the Elimination of All Forms of Racial Discrimination* on 13 December 1966 and ratified the Convention on 30 September 1975, enacting the *Racial Discrimination Act 1975* (Cth) ('*RDA*').

32 See Gary Foley, Andrew Schaap and Edwina Howell, *The Aboriginal Tent Embassy: Sovereignty, Black Power, Land Rights and the State* (Routledge, 1st ed, 2014).
33 *Kartinyeri v Commonwealth* [1998] HCA 22, 22.
34 *Newcrest Mining v Commonwealth* (1997) 71 ALJR 1346, 1423.
35 *International Convention on the Elimination of All Forms of Racial Discrimination*, GA Res 2106(XX), (7 March 1966).
36 *Neal v The Queen* (1982) 149 CLR 305.
37 Ibid., 316–7.
38 *Mabo v Queensland (No 2)* (1992) 175 CLR 1 ('*Mabo*').
39 Statement of Maz Ooft, *Organization of Indigenous Peoples in Suriname*, UN Doc E/CN.4/Sub.2/1995/24 [54].
40 *Guerin v The Queen* [1984] 2 S.C.R. 338; *R v Van Der Peet* [1996] 2 S.C.R. 507; *R v Gladstone* [1997] 2 S.C.R. 723; *Delgamuukw v British Columbia* [1997] 3 S.C.R. 1010, [186].
41 Brian Slattery, 'Understanding Aboriginal Rights' (1987) 66 *Canadian Bar Review* 727.
42 Larissa Behrendt, 'Lacking in Good Faith: Australia, Fiduciary Duties, and the Lonely Place of Indigenous Rights' in Law Commission of Canada and Association of Iroquois and Allied Indians (ed), *In Whom We Trust: A Forum on Fiduciary Relationships* (Law Commission of Canada, 2002) 247–68.
43 *Mabo* (1992) 175 CLR 1.
44 *R v Van Der Peet* [1996] 2 S.C.R. 507.

9

COMMISSIONER OF CORRECTIVE SERVICES v ALDRIDGE (NO 2) [2002] NSWADTAP 6

Commentary: *Commissioner of Corrective Services v Aldridge (No 2)* [2002] NSWADTAP 6

Debbie Bargallie and Jennifer Nielsen

Aldridge v Commissioner of Corrective Services[1] was a complaint heard by the New South Wales Administrative Decisions Tribunal ('ADT') of discrimination in employment on the grounds of race and disability, and of victimisation under the *Anti-Discrimination Act 1977* (NSW). Mr Richard Aldridge was a senior manager of the Department's Aboriginal Resources Unit ('ARU') who was leading work to implement the recommendations of the Royal Commission into Aboriginal Deaths in Custody ('RCIADIC'). He complained about his treatment by the Assistant Commissioner, Mr Ronald George Woodham, including that Mr Woodham removed Mr Aldridge from his position. At first instance, the ADT upheld his complaint of direct race discrimination, finding he was removed from his position because he asserted his standpoint as an Aboriginal man. However, the Department successfully appealed this decision in the Administrative Decision Tribunal Appeal Panel ('Appeal Panel').[2]

Richard Aldridge's case remains one of the few workplace racial discrimination cases litigated by an Indigenous person in Australia, and like most, it was unsuccessful. To legal and other commentators, the lack of success is notorious as complaints of race discrimination are extremely difficult to prove.[3] This is a consequence of deficiencies in how anti-discrimination laws are defined and interpreted,[4] and the lack of public racial literacy—that is, knowledge of what racism is, what racism is not, and how race works.[5] Mr Aldridge's case exemplifies Indigenous employees' experiences of racism in the public service, which do not emerge in isolation but reflect historical institutional policies, practices, and hierarchical racial power relations.[6]

We chose to rewrite the judgment in *Aldridge* because we are both situated knowers of corrective services and the criminal justice system. Separately, we have experienced the culture and operations of the prison system and been ethical witnesses to its institutional toxicity, especially to Indigenous Australian peoples as prisoners, families, and employees. Additionally, both of us have undertaken research that informs our understanding of this case. Bargallie is an Indigenous Australian critical race theorist. Her research focuses on the experiences by Indigenous employees of everyday and structural racism in workplaces such as the Australian Public Service, finding that racism is normalised in white institutions.[7] Nielsen is a white Australian researcher who also applies critical race and whiteness theory to critique normative standards in Australian law. Her research on discrimination laws found that they preserve and naturalise racial legacies that structure the workplace in favour of white people and white privilege. Consequently, Indigenous Australian peoples carry the cumulative weight of systemic *and* everyday race discrimination.[8]

We decided to hear an appeal by Mr Aldridge to the Supreme Court of NSW so that we could critique the Appeal Panel's reasoning. To write our judgment, it was imperative for us as critical race theorists to centre race in our examination. Critical race theory is largely untapped in Australian research[9]—particularly legal research—which is surprising given the significant amount of attention applied to Indigenous legal issues. We used critical race storytelling (a method to understand and interpret people's experiences with racism) and the Indigenous methodology of yarning[10] to exchange our knowledge and stories as Indigenous and non-Indigenous researchers and share the personal and academic context of our understanding of *Aldridge*'s case. This allowed us to identify common ground and differences in our perspectives and thus apply a deeper critique to interpreting and reframing the judgment.

As well as our own work, we also drew upon the work of key Indigenous Australian theorists. The work of Distinguished Professor Aileen Moreton-Robinson, a Goenpul woman of the Quandamooka nation, was particularly helpful.[11] Her 2007 paper, 'Witnessing the Workings of White Possession in the Workplace: Leesa's Testimony', significantly influenced our approach to rewriting *Aldridge*.[12] It tells the story of Leesa, an Indigenous nurse in Queensland Health. Moreton-Robinson found that Leesa had experienced different treatment from her non-Indigenous colleagues, including alienation and exclusion from training opportunities, and comments by her non-Indigenous colleagues that were 'consistent with racial stereotypes that position Indigenous peoples as inferior'.[13] Moreton-Robinson identified an 'obvious collaboration of testimonies' in the statements made by white nurses and 'institutional support' for them. Moreover, Indigenous peoples who raised issues of racism within the workforce were typically positioned as 'troublemakers' or represented as being 'too sensitive'.[14] Moreton-Robinson ultimately asks, 'Why do most white people believe that racism does not exist and most Indigenous peoples believe that it does?'[15] These findings prompted us to engage a deep critical analysis of the evidence and reasoning in the judgments by examining what was said and by whom, *and* what remained unspoken. Thus, our re-interpretation privileged Indigenous voices, thereby changing *whose* voices are central in the narrative, bringing vital attention to what *is* said and to what was *not* said in the original judgments.[16]

By centring race in our analysis, we could reinterpret the events in light of Mr Aldridge's knowledge and lived experience of racism—so that his experiences mattered. This necessarily brings attention to Mr Aldridge's experience as an *Aboriginal* employee: he was assertive of his Aboriginality, regularly requesting Mr Woodham to be accountable for the Department's approach to the RCIADIC's recommendations and to address the 'Aboriginal staffing shortages, lack of resources and inmate services'[17] required to implement those recommendations effectively. Mr Woodham appears to have construed Mr Aldridge as the problem to be fixed. This is evident from many facts in the case: Mr Woodham removed Mr Aldridge from the ARU, he did not follow ordinary departmental procedures that would have allowed Mr Aldridge to apply for a new and comparable position, and, ultimately, he removed Mr Aldridge from having *any* role working with Indigenous inmates and programmes. These events would have been dehumanising to Mr Aldridge—particularly as he was the most senior Aboriginal staff member in Corrective Services at that time. Mr Woodham's alienation and silencing of Mr Aldridge is better understood as putting Mr Aldridge in 'his place'.

Our reading of the evidence—unlike that of the Appeal Panel—confirms that it offers ample and probative proof that Mr Woodham treated Mr Aldridge less favourably than others. Our judgment also examines the totality of the evidence for proof that Mr Aldridge was treated less favourably *because* he was an Aboriginal person, that is, *because of his race*—an issue the Appeal Panel did not explore. We reinterpreted the events by putting them in context to bring the Department's dynamic of institutionalised racism to the foreground. The RCIADIC was an important part of this context, and a key deficiency of the original and appeal judgments was the failure to consider the significance of the RCIADIC to Mr Aldridge's work in the Department. The RCIADIC's findings and recommendations offer important and relevant historical insight into *Aldridge*'s case, as it found that the institutional culture, policies, and practices in corrective services had failed, and continue to fail, Indigenous Australian peoples. Moreover, it also found that the Department's institutional culture and practices were systemically infused by racism. This understanding is vital because racism is *normal* in a racist culture.[18]

Mr Aldridge was challenging a historically white hierarchy in a highly racialised environment. He raised concerns that corrective services had no real commitment to implementing the RCIADIC's recommendations. He complained when Mr Woodham failed to respond to his recommendations. In his role on the Aboriginal Justice Advisory Committee, he felt an expectation to say that 'the RCIADIC recommendations were being implemented when they were not'.[19] His Aboriginal knowledge and standpoint were, as the ADT had originally concluded, 'not welcome' through being inconsistent with the departmental hierarchy's preference for more celebratory accounts of its institutional life: symbolic responses, practices, and cultural events—reconciliation action plans and the like—rather than substantive, paradigm-shifting, and meaningful change. Mr Aldridge and his attempts to challenge this institutional culture were silenced and rendered inert, and he was painted as problematic and deviant within the Department.

We brought focus to this context by following the type of purposive and contextual analysis demonstrated in the earlier decision of *Slater v Brookton Farmers Co-operative Company Ltd*.[20] *Slater*'s case is a West Australian decision also involving a complaint of discrimination in employment by an Aboriginal person. It was one of the very first cases litigated by an Aboriginal person about race discrimination in employment—and remains one of the very few that has been successful.[21] That case is explained in some detail in our judgment (paras 31–34); its reasoning is applied to demonstrate how a contextual analysis allows a tribunal to discern from the totality of the evidence the presence and effect of race within the events examined in the case. Such reasoning gives sharp relief to the racist differentiations applied to Mr Aldridge—the accumulation of daily experiences of disrespect, humiliation, rejections, blocked opportunities, and hostilities—and to the cumulative impact upon him, as an Aboriginal employee, of everyday and structural racism. It also, as explained in our judgment (paras 40–42), allowed us to re-interpret the relevance of evidence given by Mr Aldridge's non-Indigenous colleagues and read it more accurately.

This reasoning also revealed the *cause* of Woodham's aggressive rejection of Mr Aldridge's standpoint as an Aboriginal man. Mr Aldridge was challenging the Department's dominant white culture; he was bringing Indigenous knowledge and perspectives to the fore on how to design and implement strategies to protect Aboriginal inmates within the corrective services system. That is, all of Mr Aldridge's actions were ways that he asserted his Indigeneity.[22] Mr Woodham persistently responded by applying racial differentiations to Mr Aldridge. Mr Woodham marginalised and alienated him, and sought to represent Mr Aldridge as deficient, 'the problem', and deviant within this institutional culture. At every turn, Mr Woodham excluded Mr Aldridge's attempts to work from his standpoint as an Aboriginal man. *Mr Aldridge's race—his Aboriginality—was the reason Woodham treated him as he did.*

We note, but could not explore in our judgment, that the ADT regarded Mr Woodham and the respondent's witnesses as highly unreliable. In particular, three of the respondent's witnesses—all Indigenous—may have been coerced because they were vulnerable to the power imbalance between them and Mr Woodham as the Assistant Commissioner at the time. It is notable because the Appeal Panel overlooked any problems with credibility, and even regarded the testimony of Mr Aldridge's white colleague, Mr Danni Mulvany (regarded as highly credible by the ADT), as offering mere opinion.

Despite Mr Woodham's aggressive behaviour and reputation, and what we interpret as his race discrimination against Mr Aldridge, he was elevated to the role of the Department's Commissioner—the same year that the Appeal Panel made its final decision. Perhaps this is not surprising as the Appeal Panel's judgments speak to the power of the common law to rewrite/re-narrate a story to uphold dominant interests and privilege white perspectives and power. This gives insight into the significant legal barriers that make it improbable that Indigenous Australian peoples could successfully prove complaints of the race discrimination they experience in white patriarchal institutions.

Indeed, Mr Aldridge, the complainant, became the complaint. For his audacity in making a complaint, he became the recipient of retaliation or racial backlash in forms of alienation, exclusion, over-surveillance of performance, criticism, and abuse. Bargallie's research concludes that Mr Aldridge's experience is not uncommon and that, like Mr Aldridge, Indigenous employees are often rendered disposable by being made redundant or being displaced.[23] It concerns us that Mr Aldridge's complaint of victimisation was not litigated, as there appears to be ample evidence to show that Mr Woodham wanted Mr Aldridge out of the role of working with Indigenous peoples after Mr Aldridge lodged his complaint. Due to space constraints, we could not cover this in our judgment but note its significance to Mr Aldridge's experience.

Mr Aldridge, in his evidence, made clear that his job was not just about the pay, status, and title attached to it but was about making a difference for Indigenous peoples within the system. By marginalising Mr Aldridge and removing him from the work that was most meaningful to him, Mr Woodham prevented Mr Aldridge from making a difference for his mob—Indigenous peoples while they were incarcerated by the justice system. This is significant as our reading suggests he was removed so that he could be silenced and not disrupt the operations of the Aboriginal Resources Unit/Indigenous Services Unit. Notably, it was an important consideration taken into account by the ADT at first instance, in ordering that he be restored to a position in the Department that involved 'direct contact with' Aboriginal peoples. That is, it recognised that Mr Aldridge's removal was dehumanising and the impact was much more than a loss of wages; the ADT's decision sought to remedy the loss and grief he suffered through being removed from working with and for his mob, his community.

To conclude, we acknowledge that our judgment sits within what Professor Irene Watson of the Tanganekald, Meintangk Boandik First Nations exposes as the problematic space of common law reasoning, an inherently violent colonial space that remains disrespectful to and ignorant of Indigenous knowledges, philosophies, and laws.[24] This critique raises important questions. How do we deploy reasoning guided by Indigenous knowledges, philosophies, or even perspectives within the context of colonial common law? As we found together through our yarns, there are many ways in which common law reasoning and Indigenous knowledges and philosophies are simply incommensurate. That is a dilemma of this project.[25] Can we critique white legalities to see if new legalities are possible? Is it possible to decolonise white Australian law? Is it possible to offer new ways of legal thinking within the colonial legal paradigm? These are the impossibilities that we are attempting to pursue.[26] We offer a judgment that reworks and redeploys common law reasoning through a critique of white legalities, attempting to make new legalities possible.

Notes

1 *Aldridge v Commissioner of Corrective Services* [1999] NSWADT 33.
2 Decided in two separate judgments: *Commissioner of Corrective Services v Aldridge* [2000] NSWADTAP 5 and *Commissioner of Corrective Services v Aldridge (No 2)* [2002] NSWADTAP 6.
3 See e.g. Beth Gaze, 'Problems of Proof in Equal Opportunity Cases' (1989) 63(8) *Law Institute Journal* 731; Margaret Thornton, 'Revisiting Race' in Racial Discrimination Commissioner, Parliament of Australia, *The Racial Discrimination Act—A Review* (Review Paper, December 1995).
4 Jennifer Nielsen, 'Whiteness and Anti-Discrimination Law—It's in the Design' (2008) 3(2) *ACRAWSA e-journal.*
5 Debbie Bargallie, *Unmasking the Racial Contract: Indigenous Voices on Racism in the Australian Public Service* (Aboriginal Studies Press, 2020).
6 Ibid.; Nicholas Biddle and Julie Lahn, *Understanding Aboriginal and Torres Strait Islander Employee Decisions to Exit the Australian Public Service* (CAEPR Working Paper 110/2016, June 2016).
7 Bargallie (n 5).
8 Jennifer Nielsen, '"There's Always an Easy Out": How "Innocence" and "Probability" Whitewash Race Discrimination' (2007) 3(1) *ACRAWSA e-journal.*
9 Bargallie (n 5); Marcelle Burns and Jennifer Nielsen, 'Dealing with the "Wicked" Problem of Race and the Law: A Critical Journey for Students (and Academics)' (2018) 28(2) *Legal Education Review* 1; Juliana McLaughlin and Susan Whatman, 'The Potential of Critical Race Theory in Decolonizing University Curricula' (2011) 31(4) *Asia Pacific Journal of Education* 365.
10 Dawn Bessarab and Bridget Ng'andu, 'Yarning about Yarning as a Legitimate Method in Indigenous Research' (2010) 3(1) *International Journal of Critical Indigenous Studies* 37.
11 See e.g. Aileen Moreton-Robinson, *The White Possessive: Property, Power, and Indigenous Sovereignty* (University of Minnesota Press, 2015).
12 Aileen Moreton-Robinson, 'Witnessing the Workings of White Possession in the Workplace: Leesa's Testimony' (2007) 26 *Australian Feminist Law Journal* 81.
13 Ibid., 91.
14 Ibid., 86.
15 Ibid., 84.
16 Bargallie (n 5).
17 *Commissioner of Corrective Services v Aldridge (No 2)* [2002] NSWADTAP 6, [32].
18 Bargallie (n 5).
19 *Aldridge v Commissioner of Corrective Services* [1999] NSWADT 33, [11].
20 *Slater v Brookton Farmers Co-operative Company Ltd* (1990) EOC 92–321.
21 See Jennifer Nielsen, 'Whiteness at Work' (2013) 26(3) *Australian Journal of Labour Law* 300.
22 Bargallie (n 5).
23 Bargallie (n 5).
24 See e.g. Irene Watson, 'Re-Centring First Nations Knowledge and Places in a Terra Nullius Space' (2014) 10(5) *AlterNative* 508.
25 Irene Watson, 'First Nations Stories, Grandmother's Law: Too Many Stories to Tell' in Heather Douglas et al. (eds), *The Australian Feminist Judgments Project: Writing and Re-writing Law* (Hart Publishing, 2014).
26 Irene Watson, 'Aboriginal Sovereignties', in Suvendrini Perera (ed), *Our Patch* (Network Books, 2007), 23, 26.

RICHARD ALDRIDGE .... APPELLANT;

AND

COMMISSIONER OF CORRECTIVE SERVICES .... RESPONDENT;

[2003] NSWSC 1170

Anti-Discrimination Act 1977 (NSW)—Racism—Race discrimination—Employment—Indigenous peoples—Less favourable treatment—Indigenous knowledges—Standpoint.

[1] NIELSEN AND BARGALLIE JJ.[1] On 15 April 1991, the Royal Commission into Aboriginal Deaths in Custody ('RCIADIC') completed its national investigation into the grossly disproportionate rate of incarceration of Aboriginal and Torres Strait Islander peoples. It investigated the cause of the deaths in custody of 88 men and 11 women between 1980 and 1989. The RCIADIC could not identify one 'common thread' to explain these deaths, but it did find that in every death, the person's 'Aboriginality played a significant and *in most cases dominant role* in their being in custody and dying in custody'.[2]

[2] The RCIADIC's vital purpose was to formulate recommendations to prevent such deaths in the future. Its reports offer significant commentary on the criminal justice system, including the corrections system and custodial institutions. It is profoundly relevant to the present case as its findings indicate a dynamic of institutionalised racism in the workplace and events to which this matter relates.

[3] The appellant, Richard Aldridge, is a Kamilaroi man,[3] who was a senior Aboriginal employee of the New South Wales Department of Corrective Services, a member of the Aboriginal Justice Advisory Committee, and Aboriginal Project and Policy Officer in the Aboriginal Resources Unit ('ARU'). That role involved advising the Department on implementing the RCIADIC's recommendations within the New South Wales custodial system. Mr Aldridge came to the role with relevant qualifications and significant experience gained through completion of a Corrective Services Welfare Officer Traineeship, a Diploma in Social Welfare, and as a welfare officer at Long Bay Correctional Centre. Imperative to the role was Mr Aldridge's Aboriginal standpoint and cultural knowledge. His standing was recognised by his appointment to the Aboriginal Justice Advisory Committee, a committee formed to advise government on the RCIADIC's recommendations.

[4] The respondent is the Department of Corrective Services and the Commissioner as its head. Mr Aldridge's complaint relates primarily to actions by one employee—Ronald George Woodham—who at the relevant time was the Department's Assistant Commissioner, but was appointed Commissioner in 2002. During the relevant period, 1995 to 1996, the rate of Indigenous deaths in custody in NSW remained disproportionately high, indicating that the Department needed to act urgently to abate this national disgrace.[4]

[5] Mr Aldridge was employed in a grade 7/8 position[5] within the Department. From February 1993 to November 1995, his role was to develop, set up, and work in the ARU (renamed the Indigenous Services Unit ['ISU'] in March 1996). Mr Woodham had Mr Aldridge removed from the ARU in February 1996, and despite the availability of a comparable position in the new ISU, Aldridge was not advised of or appointed to that role. Instead, the Department moved him to various positions, and ultimately to one that had no direct role with Indigenous peoples. Mr Aldridge based his complaint of race discrimination in employment on these events and other interactions with Mr Woodham. The Department denied that any of these actions occurred because of Aldridge's race, but instead occurred due to problems with his work performance within the ARU.

[6] In March 1996, Mr Aldridge lodged his complaint with the NSW Anti-Discrimination Board, alleging race and disability discrimination, and victimisation under the *Anti-Discrimination Act 1997* (NSW) ('*ADA*'). The board could not conciliate the complaint, and early in 1997, Aldridge commenced action in the Administrative Decisions Tribunal ('ADT'), which found his complaint of race discrimination had been proved in its 1999 decision ('ADT Decision').[6] The Department appealed to the Administrative Decisions Tribunal Appeal Panel ('Appeal Panel') which upheld the appeal in two separate judgments. The first judgment in 2000 ('AP Decision 1')[7] vacated the ADT's original decision and dismissed all but one incident that comprised Mr Aldridge's complaint ('the meeting of 23 August 1995'), remitting it for rehearing. The second judgment reheard and dismissed this complaint in 2002 ('AP Decision 2').[8] Prior to these hearings, Mr Aldridge withdrew his complaints of disability discrimination and victimisation.

[7] This Court granted Mr Aldridge leave to appeal against both Appeal Panel decisions. He appeals to this Court on questions of law under s 119 of the *Administrative Decisions Tribunal Act 1997* (NSW). Section 120 of that Act empowers this Court to 'hear and determine the appeal' and 'make such orders' considered appropriate, including (but not limited to) affirming or setting aside the Appeal Panel's decision, or remitting it 'to be heard and decided again'.

[8] The grounds of Mr Aldridge's appeal are as follows:

1. The Appeal Panel erred in law in failing to take a purposive approach to the interpretation and application of the *ADA*;

2. The Appeal Panel erred in law in failing to consider the totality of the evidence in determining if Mr Aldridge was treated less favourably when abused at the meeting of 23 August 1995; and
3. The Appeal Panel erred in law in failing to consider the totality of the evidence in determining if Mr Aldridge experienced other forms of less favourable treatment.

[9] Mr Aldridge submits that the Appeal Panel should have pursued a purposive interpretation of the *ADA* in accordance with s 33 of the *Interpretation Act 1987 No 15* (NSW). He also submits that the Appeal Panel failed to consider the inferences available on the totality of the evidence, which show that Mr Aldridge was treated less favourably as compared to non-Indigenous employees, on the ground of his race. This includes evidence that:

- Mr Woodham told Mr Aldridge to 'shut up and stop threatening' him when Aldridge raised the RCIADIC in a meeting on 10 July 1995;
- Mr Woodham abused Mr Aldridge at a meeting with his colleagues on 23 August 1995;
- Mr Aldridge was removed from his role in the ARU in November 1995;
- Mr Aldridge was removed from the ISU in February 1996;
- The Department failed to advise Mr Aldridge that ISU positions had been advertised in mid-1996; and
- The Department appointed Mr Aldridge to a role that did not involve working with Indigenous Australian peoples in July 1996.

The relevant law

[10] The relevant law is set out in ss 7 and 8 of the *ADA*. Section 7 defines race discrimination, while s 8 defines when race discrimination is unlawful within the employment relationship. Before s 8 applies, proof is required that s 7 has been breached.

[11] Mr Aldridge's complaint is that he experienced acts of direct discrimination on the ground of race as defined by s 7(1)(a) that, contrary to s 8(2), affected his employment by subjecting him to 'other detriment', tainting the 'terms or conditions' of his employment, and causing him to be denied opportunities and benefits associated with his employment. We concur with the Appeal Panel's view in AP Decision 1 that the Department could be directly liable for its employees' actions in line with s 53 ('Liability of principals and employers').[9] Relevantly, the former Commissioner Smethurst testified at first instance that he was aware of, but did not intervene to resolve the tension between, Mr Woodham and Mr Aldridge.

[12] Mr Aldridge's appeal puts in issue the Appeal Panel's approach to determining whether the acts complained of amounted to race discrimination under s 7, its approach in law to determining the evidence available to it, and whether the evidence was sufficiently probative to substantiate Mr Aldridge's claim.

The Appeal Panel's reasoning

[13] Section 7(1)(a) requires proof of two matters, namely that a complainant:

- (i) is treated less favourably than the perpetrator treats or would treat a person of a different race in the same circumstances or those 'which are not materially different' (less favourable treatment found by comparison);
- (ii) on the ground of the complainant's race (the causal nexus).

[14] It does not require proof of an intention to discriminate: if there is less favourable treatment because of race, the motives or suggested justifications for this are irrelevant.[10] Moreover, s 4A states that treatment may be discrimination even if done for two or more reasons. Thus, the Department's concerns about Mr Aldridge's work performance—even if credible—would not preclude a finding of race discrimination.

[15] At first instance, the ADT found that the Department discriminated against Mr Aldridge on the ground of race because it removed him:

> from his position [as leader of the ARU] because he made his views on matters known from an Aboriginal cultural standpoint which was not welcomed by the Department and specifically was not welcomed by Assistant Commissioner Woodham.[11]

[16] In AP Decision 1, the Appeal Panel vacated this decision because the ADT failed to state and apply s 7 correctly and did not 'pose and answer the questions of fact…needed to determine' and decide the case correctly.[12] The ADT had not explained the 'causation' element when stating the applicable law and, therefore, failed to make findings of fact (except one, discussed below) that could substantiate its decision that Mr Aldridge had proven his complaint. But the Appeal Panel upheld the ADT's finding of fact that Mr Woodham abused Mr Aldridge at the meeting of 23 August 1995. As this *could* amount to race discrimination as defined by s 7, the Appeal Panel decided to rehear this issue on its merits.

[17] In AP Decision 2, the Appeal Panel reheard and dismissed Mr Aldridge's complaint about the meeting of 23 August 1995.[13] It agreed that abusing an employee, 'even if it has no racial content, can constitute a "detriment" within the meaning of s 8(2)(c)' and can amount to race discrimination 'if the employee is treated less favourably than other employees in the same or similar circumstances'.[14] However, it observed that 'a reason or ground for that treatment' must be the employee's race, requiring a distinction between 'racially *based* abuse' and 'abuse' that occurs *because of* the complainant's race.[15] It concluded that the ADT asked the wrong question on this issue—the *correct* question was whether the abuse was 'directed at Mr Aldridge on the ground of his race' by considering 'whether Mr Woodham did abuse, or would have abused, non-Aboriginal persons in the same or similar circumstances':

> If Mr Woodham abused everyone, regardless of their race, the Tribunal would have been forced to conclude that while his employment practices may have fallen well short of the ideal, they did not constitute unlawful racial discrimination.[16]

[18] The Appeal Panel found that Mr Woodham abused two white employees at the meeting and did not directly abuse two Aboriginal employees, persuading it to conclude:

> [Mr] Woodham…abused Mr Aldridge, and…Mr Aldridge suffered detriment as a result of that abuse, [but] Mr Woodham did not treat Mr Aldridge less favourably than he treated non-Aboriginal people at the meeting. When Mr Mulvany was advocating for the rights of Aboriginal prisoners to receive family visits when in court or police cells, Mr Woodham became aggressive and said, 'Well, you're not even Aboriginal.'…Mr Woodham also told Ms Sutherland, a non-Aboriginal person, to 'shut-up'. While Mr Woodham was abusive and aggressive towards a number of people in the room, he allowed Mr Aldridge to speak. We are not persuaded that Mr Aldridge was singled out and treated differently from others at the meeting. [17]

[19] Put simply, as the Appeal Panel could not differentiate the abuse of the white employees from that of Mr Aldridge, it concluded that the abuse Mr Woodham directed at Mr Aldridge was not less favourable treatment as required by s 7(1)(a). Consequently, the Appeal Panel found it unnecessary to examine whether Mr Aldridge's race had a 'causally operative effect' upon his treatment by Mr Woodham.[18] It dismissed Mr Aldridge's complaint.

[20] We conclude that the errors of law asserted in Mr Aldridge's appeal are disclosed in the Appeal Panel's reasoning.

Errors in the Appeal Panel's judgments

[21] We agree with Mr Aldridge's submission that the Appeal Panel erred in law in its interpretative approach. It applied a too narrow interpretation of the legislative provisions that did not pursue the Act's purpose adequately. It also erred by ignoring the relevance and probative value of the evidence because it interpreted the events related to Mr Aldridge's complaint as occurring in a race-neutral environment and within a narrow temporal frame. However, the totality of the evidence points to a highly racialised work environment in which Mr Aldridge experienced the cumulative effect of continuous acts of racially based aggressions.

[22] Section 7(1)(a) requires proof that a respondent treated a complainant less favourably when compared to the treatment that has been or is likely to be

afforded to a person 'of a different race'. The Appeal Panel correctly drew the comparator as Mr Aldridge's white colleagues but did not apply the comparison correctly when it concluded that Mr Woodham did not treat Mr Aldridge less favourably because Mr Woodham also abused Mr Aldridge's white colleagues.

[23] Their conclusion is wrong because the Appeal Panel failed to discern several material differences in the circumstances between Mr Aldridge and his white colleagues. As it ignored the relevance and probative value of the totality of the evidence, the Appeal Panel also failed to consider the inferences available to it.

[24] Looking closely at Mr Mulvany's testimony (Mr Aldridge's white colleague in the ARU), he vividly recalled Mr Woodham

> storming into the building, sitting down at that table, pointing to [Aldridge] and saying, 'You can get fucked and if you don't like it, you can go somewhere else'. Looking at Ms Sutherland, telling her to shut up and just a tremendous amount of aggression towards the people in that room.[19]

Under cross-examination, Mr Mulvany testified that he believed that Mr Aldridge had been

> singled out [by Woodham]...because of his aboriginality [sic] and because of his position representing the other aboriginal [sic] people in that team, in that group. ...
>
> I think just there's such a power imbalance between the Assistant Commissioner...who has all these responsibilities and...privileges...and then to treat someone else who is not in the same position as him in such an appalling way in front of his peers it was just something that shocked me. That's why I remember it. I was literally shocked and disgusted by that behaviour.[20]

[25] Mr Mulvany disagreed when Counsel for the Department suggested that the fact that Ms Sutherland was told to 'shut up' meant that Mr Woodham's aggression at the meeting 'had nothing to do with the race of the persons who were participating but something to do with the policies and the attitudes of the people towards the work'.[21] Mr Mulvany disagreed because he had

> a different perception and a different way of seeing things because I worked in that group for a period of five months. I saw the way people within that group worked, I was a member of that team and...had participated in that group.[22]

[26] The ADT regarded Mr Mulvany as a reliable witness and preferred his evidence about this meeting to Mr Woodham's testimony (which it regarded as

'unreliable' and contradictory) and that of the respondent's other witnesses.[23] The ADT *did not*, as the Appeal Panel asserted,[24] simply adopt Mr Mulvany's opinion about the events as a fact but, instead, followed the inferences his evidence raised. The Appeal Panel failed to discern two of those in particular. First, Mr Woodham singled out Mr Aldridge—as an *Aboriginal* supervisor—by diminishing him in front of his team. Secondly, Mr Aldridge's white colleagues may have attracted similar treatment *because* they were supporting Mr Aldridge's position—that is, because of their *association* with him. This accords with the s 7(1) prohibition of treatment caused by 'the race of a relative or *associate* of the aggrieved person'.[25]

[27] Thus, the Appeal Panel failed to consider whether, in totality, the evidence demonstrated that Mr Aldridge was treated less favourably in the full material circumstances. The Appeal Panel also failed to consider whether the abuse directed at the white employees was part of an act of direct race discrimination against Mr Aldridge in that, as members of the ARU, they supported their Aboriginal team leader.

[28] Consequently, the Appeal Panel did not explore the causal nexus of these events as it had already reached the conclusion that they could *not* establish race discrimination because Mr Aldridge's white colleagues had experienced 'equally' abusive treatment. However, if the Appeal Panel had considered the events through a purposive analysis that placed them within the racial dynamics of this workplace, it may have reached a different conclusion.

The correct approach to interpretation—purposive and contextual

[29] Section 33 of the *Interpretation Act 1987 No 15* (NSW) states that to interpret any statutory provision a tribunal should prefer the construction that promotes 'the purpose or object underlying the Act' whether or not it 'is expressly stated'.

[30] The *ADA*'s purpose *is* not expressly stated but can be discerned from its Long Title, which describes it as an Act to render 'unlawful racial, sex and other types of discrimination in certain circumstances and to promote equality of opportunity between all persons'. Applying s 33, the accurate interpretation—and thus application—of the *ADA*'s provisions should be to promote its purpose of making acts of race (and other forms of) discrimination unlawful to secure Parliament's intent to promote equality of opportunity between all persons.

[31] As indicated by jurisprudence in other jurisdictions, the correct way to pursue a purposive approach to interpretation is by locating the events complained of in their context. In *Edmonton Journal v Alberta (Attorney General)*,[26] Madam Justice Wilson of the Supreme Court of Canada explains that this is important because:

> the contextual approach...recognizes that a particular right or freedom may have a different value depending on the context...The contextual approach attempts to bring into sharp relief the aspect of the right or freedom which is truly at stake in the case as well as the relevant aspects of any values in competition with it.[27]

[32] Significant guidance on applying this approach is illustrated in the Western Australian Equal Opportunity Commission's reasoning in *Slater v Brookton Farmers Co-Operative*.[28] This case also demonstrates how a contextual interpretation permits a tribunal to pursue appropriate inferences from the evidence. In particular, context can reveal that events and explanations, which initially seem racially neutral, instead are infused with systemically racist antipathies and practices.

[33] Mrs Slater, an Aboriginal woman living in the small town of Brookton, complained of direct race discrimination by the Co-Operative's bakery when it rejected her job application. The evidence showed that her interview with the Co-Operative's manager 'fell far short of even the most rudimentary standard for any reasonable job interview'—the manager had been 'peremptory to the point of rudeness' and treated her as if 'she almost did not exist'.[29] The tribunal found direct evidence that 'overt' racial bias influenced consideration of Mrs Slater's application by the Co-Operative's board, which had discussed it in terms that referred to her being an Aboriginal person. This persuaded the tribunal that the board's decision *was* because of her race, making the Co-Operative liable.[30] However, the tribunal could not find overt or direct evidence that the *manager's* behaviour was also because of Mrs Slater's race. Significantly, though, it continued to explore the evidence to test this issue.

[34] It did so because the sub-par treatment of Mrs Slater indicated that '[o]bviously something was wrong'. Consequently, the tribunal asked whether the manager's behaviour was 'best explained in relation to the institutional (structural) relations between the Aboriginal and non-Aboriginal people in Brookton, as a microcosm of wider Australian relationships'.[31] Viewed in totality, the witnesses' testimony provided significant evidence about race relations in Brookton, indicating a distance in the town's 'social/cultural relations between Aboriginal and non-Aboriginal people'.[32] It also showed that the Co-Operative had consistently failed to employ Aboriginal peoples (apart from several juniors on a temporary basis) though they made up 40 per cent of the town's population. The tribunal concluded that these matters were 'anchored in institutional racism',[33] leading it to understand that race discrimination was *not* an unusual event in Brookton.

[35] Analysing the 'evidence as a whole' and in context, the tribunal concluded that the reason it did not employ Mrs Slater, 'an Aboriginal senior', was 'likely to lie with the hiring practices of the Co-op'.[34] Upon examining these practices, and in particular, how Mrs Slater experienced them, the tribunal concluded that the manager 'just did not see her as she did not cross

his horizons as a serious contender for the job (reflecting the social/cultural distance referred to above)'. Thus, it was

> satisfied on the balance of probabilities that the non-selection of the complainant was a decision made by [the manager] and the board advertently on the dominant ground (though not necessarily the only ground) of her Aboriginality and that she was in that way treated less favourably than a non-Aboriginal applicant would have been treated in similar circumstances.[35]

[36] Two features of this reasoning are very important. First, the tribunal examined the discrete event complained of—Mrs Slater's experience with the Co-Operative's recruitment process—within its broader temporal frame, namely the history of the Co-Operative's practice in (not) employing Aboriginal peoples. Secondly, it accepted that race discrimination was a normal and systemic practice within the town of Brookton. Putting the specific events in this context, the tribunal could conclude by inference that the town's institutionalised racism against Aboriginal peoples informed the manager's rude and peremptory treatment of Mrs Slater during her interview (albeit unconsciously). Therefore, it was satisfied that Mrs Slater's treatment was causally connected to her race as required to prove her complaint.

[37] Importantly, this approach aligns with the evidential standard applied to such complaints. Recently, in *Dutt v Central Coast Area Health Service; Central Coast Area Health Service v Dutt*,[36] the Appeal Panel stated that a tribunal must only find discrimination if it is convinced 'on the balance of probabilities' by evidence that is 'logically probative and relevant to the issues before' it.[37] That is correct. It also said that to avoid an error of law,[38] tribunals must always apply Dixon J's considerations in *Briginshaw v Briginshaw* to assess the relevance and probative value of evidence—the 'seriousness of an allegation made, the inherent unlikelihood of an occurrence of a given description, or the gravity of the consequences flowing from a particular finding'.[39] That is not correct. The applicable law—which commenced after Mr Aldridge's complaint—is s 142(2) *Evidence Act 1995* (NSW) which requires tribunals to assess evidence in light of its importance in proceedings and the 'gravity of the matters alleged'. The approach applied to the evidence in *Slater* meets these requirements.

Reasons and decision

[38] The less favourable quality of treatment in discrimination cases is often obvious. At other times, that quality is only found by examining seemingly neutral events and material circumstances within their racial context. The existence of a racial dynamic by itself does not prove an individual act of less favourable treatment. However, to evaluate the quality and the

cause of the details of a complaint, a prudent tribunal must examine them in the context of the racial dynamic, to consider how racism may have influenced the culture, policies, and practices of the workplace. Otherwise, it may fail to detect the systemic, subtle, and sometimes casual habits of racism, which would undermine the *ADA* because these invidious and injurious behaviours are within the scope of its prohibition on race discrimination. The Act's purpose will not be achieved if these 'subtle' behaviours are not detected, named, and remedied.

[39] Section 144(1)(b) of the *Evidence Act 1995* (NSW) permits tribunals to take judicial notice of common knowledge, including that contained in documents whose authority 'cannot reasonably be questioned'. The RCIADIC's Reports are such documents and, as already stated, obviously relevant to the events in this complaint. The RCIADIC's findings and recommendations were integral to Mr Aldridge's former role within the Department and propelled his efforts to lead organisational change to stop Indigenous men and women from dying in NSW custodial institutions.

[40] The RCIADIC's observations give insight into the Department of Corrective Services' institutional dynamics. For example, it explains that a comment by one NSW prison superintendent—that no Aboriginal inmate had ever come to him 'with a complaint about problems with racism'—fails to appreciate that aggrieved Aboriginal prisoners are unlikely to complain to non-Aboriginal prison authorities, as the power differential puts them at risk of retaliatory action.[40] Commissioner Wootten also observed that this comment failed 'to distinguish between acts or expressions of racial prejudice and the racism embedded in institutional practices'.[41] Like the town of Brookton in *Slater*'s case, the RCIADIC's observations offer the Appeal Panel relevant and reliable evidence about the context of this case. Read in totality, the RCIADIC's insights show that the Department of Corrective Services was *not* a race-neutral environment, as racism and race discrimination were a normal part of its everyday operations and institutional practices.

[41] Examining the events in Mr Aldridge's case in this context foregrounds the racial dynamic of the Department of Corrective Services' work environment—it would not be surprising to detect racist attitudes and antipathies in this workplace. This is the context within which Mr Aldridge and Mr Woodham engaged and related to one another. Mr Aldridge was an Aboriginal leader working to challenge and transform a prison culture not attuned to the 'racism embedded in [its] everyday institutional practices'. In a setting where race discrimination was normal/everyday, it is highly doubtful that the dominant white hierarchy welcomed Mr Aldridge's challenge.

[42] Read in this context, the evidence reveals a more nuanced set of circumstances that become material and relevant to the events under consideration, and two in particular. First, Mr Aldridge was undertaking his role in materially different circumstances to those of his white colleagues. As the ARU's senior Aboriginal leader, he was responsible for applying Aboriginal

knowledge and perspective to critique and transform the Department's organisational practice. Mr Aldridge had challenged Mr Woodham on several occasions before the meeting of 23 August 1995. At that meeting, Mr Woodham abused Mr Aldridge as an *Aboriginal* team leader—bringing Mr Aldridge's leadership capacities and skills into the spotlight and trying to diminish him in front of his team. Mr Aldridge's white co-workers supported his leadership and his initiatives.

[43] Secondly, this context offers a proper basis to explore the inferences available in the evidence to explain the relational dynamic between Mr Woodham and Mr Aldridge. As Mr Mulvany observed, there was a clear power differential between Mr Woodham and Mr Aldridge. At the meeting of 23 August 1995, Mr Woodham singled Mr Aldridge out *because* Mr Aldridge was an Aboriginal leader challenging Mr Woodham in front of a group of Mr Woodham's subordinates. Mr Woodham subsequently took steps to remove Mr Aldridge from his position but did not act against any other staff. Read as a whole, Mr Woodham's antipathy towards Mr Aldridge was not discrete or isolated but was persistent.

[44] The reasoning in *Slater* provides a method to reveal the cause of Mr Woodham's antipathy towards Mr Aldridge and his recommendations by interpreting his antipathy in the context of the racial dynamics evident in this workplace. It is evident that Mr Woodham clearly did not appreciate Mr Aldridge's challenges to his authority and 'right way' of managing the Department; this is made evident by Mr Aldridge's evidence that in conversation with Mr Woodham, Mr Woodham made statements such as, 'don't threaten me' and 'You can get fucked and if you don't like it, you can go somewhere else'.[42] Mr Woodham's authority and knowledge of the 'right way' to manage the Department is not racially benign—it is sourced in the power and privilege he holds as a white man and executive manager in the Department. Mr Aldridge's testimony about the statements made to him by Mr Woodham suggests that Mr Woodham felt threatened by Mr Aldridge and his recommendation that significant change was needed in the Department's practices. Read, then, in the context of the Department's institutionalised habits of race discrimination (subtle or otherwise), the best explanation for this, Mr Woodham's persistent antipathy, is that he regarded Aboriginal leadership—Mr Aldridge and his Aboriginal ways of knowing, being, and doing—as having no valid place in the Department.

[45] Thus, these events *are* causally connected to Mr Aldridge being an Aboriginal person.[43] On the balance of probabilities, the totality of the evidence supports the inference that Mr Woodham's antipathy towards Aldridge was because he was an Aboriginal leader, that is, because of his race.

[46] For these reasons, we conclude that the Appeal Panel erred in law. It failed to apply a purposive approach when interpreting and applying the *ADA*. It failed to test the available evidence in the context of the Department's institutionalised racial dynamic to determine if it established, including by

inference, that the treatment afforded to Mr Aldridge by Mr Woodham was less favourable than the treatment that was or would be afforded to his white colleagues in the materially same circumstances. Thus, it should have examined whether the treatment was causally connected to Mr Aldridge being an Aboriginal person, that is, his race.

[47] We allow Mr Aldridge's appeal. He has waited far too long for a just outcome to his claim; we restore the ADT's decision dated 25 May 1999.

Orders

[48] We make these orders:

1. The appeal is allowed;
2. Set aside the decisions of the Appeal Panel made on 18 April 2000 and on 25 March 2002;
3. The ADT's judgment dated 25 May 1999 is reinstated; and
4. Costs are reserved and listed for hearing on a date to be fixed.

Notes

1 Jennifer Nielsen and Debbie Bargallie.
2 *Royal Commission into Aboriginal Deaths in Custody* ('*RCIADIC*') (National Report, 15 April 1991) vol 1, [1.1.1] (emphasis added).
3 The Kamilaroi are the First Peoples of an area in the northwest of New South Wales.
4 Vicki Dalton, *Australian Deaths in Custody and Custody-Related Police Operations, 1995–96* (Australian Institute of Criminology, 1996).
5 New South Wales public service positions range from Grade 1–8, Grade 9/10, Grade 11/12SEB 1–3.
6 *Aldridge v Commissioner of Corrective Services* [1999] NSWADT 33 ('ADT Decision').
7 *Commissioner of Corrective Services v Aldridge* [2000] NSWADTAP 5 ('AP Decision 1').
8 *Commissioner of Corrective Services v Aldridge (No. 2)* [2002] NSWADTAP 6 ('AP Decision 2').
9 AP Decision 2 [2002] NSWADTAP 6, [29].
10 *Haines v Leves* (1987) 8 NSWLR 442, 471.
11 ADT Decision [1999] NSWADT 33, [7], [55].
12 AP Decision 1 [2000] NSWADTAP 5, [34].
13 AP Decision 2 [2002] NSWADTAP 6, [44].
14 Ibid., [37].
15 Ibid.
16 Ibid., [7].
17 Ibid., [42].
18 Ibid., [44].
19 ADT Decision [1999] NSWADT 33, [32].
20 Ibid.
21 Ibid.
22 Ibid.
23 Ibid., [40], [26].
24 AP Decision 2 [2002] NSWADTAP 6, [43].
25 Emphasis added. See e.g. *Dowie v Northey & Anor* [2000] VCAT 823.
26 *Edmonton Journal v Alberta (Attorney General)* [1989] 2 SCR 1326.

27 Ibid., 1355.
28 *Slater v Brookton Farmers Co-Operative* (1990) EOC 92–321, 78, 187.
29 Ibid., 78, 181 and 78, 186.
30 Ibid., 78, 188.
31 Ibid., 78, 186.
32 Ibid.
33 Ibid., 78, 186.
34 Ibid., 78, 184–78, 188.
35 Ibid., 78, 188.
36 *Dutt v Central Coast Area Health Service; Central Coast Area Health Service v Dutt* [2003] NSWADTAP 3.
37 Ibid., [20], [12].
38 Ibid., [28].
39 *Briginshaw v Briginshaw* (1938) 60 CLR 336, 361.
40 *RCIADIC* (National Report, 15 April 1991) vol 3, [25.6.3].
41 *RCIADIC* (Regional Report of Inquiry in New South Wales, Victoria & Tasmania, 30 March 1991) ch 7, 74.
42 ADT Decision [1999] NSWADT 33, [14] and see [40]–[47].
43 'Race' includes a characteristic that 'appertains generally' to Aboriginal peoples; *Anti-Discrimination Act 1997* (NSW) s 7(2).

10

EATOCK v BOLT [2011] FCA 1103

Commentary: *Eatock v Bolt* [2011] FCA 1103

Simon Rice

Introduction

Alison Whittaker's 'judgment' is a poet's perspective on the task of 'bringing Indigenous voices into judicial decision making'. In writing about *Eatock v Bolt*, Alison gives an Indigenous perspective on, if not judicial decision making generally, on judicial decision making in a racial vilification case, and perhaps on racial vilification laws. Alison explains her approach in a note to her response.

The case was brought by Ms Pat Eatock,[1] and for reasons that I give below, I will refer to it as 'Ms Eatock's case'. My brief as a commentator is to place Ms Eatock's case in its context: to explain it, to say something about the issues it raised and how it was received, and to comment on the contribution that Alison's response makes.

The claim

It suffices to set out Adrienne Stone's footnoted, summary background to Ms Eatock's case:

> an action was brought against Andrew Bolt and The Herald and Weekly Times Pty Ltd ['HWT']...concerning a series of articles published in print and online by Melbourne newspaper the *Herald Sun* during 2009. The articles targeted prominent light-skinned Aboriginal people and criticised

their decision to identify as Aboriginal, given their mixed heritage. The tone of the articles was highly critical, sarcastic and insulting.

Pat Eatock, one of the people criticised in the articles, was the applicant in this action. Eight other people who were also featured in the articles gave evidence during the course of the hearing, though they were not formally parties to the proceedings. [2]

The law and procedure

Section 18C of the *Racial Discrimination Act 1975* (Cth) ('*RDA*') makes it unlawful to 'do an act otherwise than in private' if the act is 'reasonably likely, in all the circumstances, to offend, insult, humiliate or intimidate another person or a group of people', *and* the act is 'done because of the race, colour or national or ethnic origin of the other person or of some or all of the people in the group'.[3]

Section 18D sets out wide exceptions to this prohibition, leaving a lot of room for conduct that would otherwise be vilification. In summary, conduct is excepted if it is done 'reasonably and in good faith' and (1) for an artistic work, (2) for a genuine academic, artistic, scientific, or public interest purpose, (3) in a fair and accurate report of a matter of public interest, or (4) in a fair comment on a matter of public interest when expressing a genuinely held belief.[4]

Section 18C is not a criminal law. Rather, conduct is complained of by a victim and investigated by the Australian Human Rights Commission. If a conciliated resolution is not achieved then the complainant has the option of commencing conventional court proceedings in a federal jurisdiction, seeking to prove the vilification to a 'balance of probabilities' standard of proof. If the complainant is successful they will get some form of compensatory remedy (such as damages, an apology, or an undertaking), and if they lose they face an adverse costs order.

In summary, Ms Eatock complained to the Federal Court about race-based conduct that was reasonably likely, in all the circumstances, to offend, insult, humiliate, or intimidate.

A group claim

Ms Eatock made her application to the court as a 'group' claim, which the court dealt with as two groups. One was a broad group of 'Aboriginal persons of mixed descent who have a fairer, rather than darker skin, and who identify as Aboriginal persons in accordance with the popular meaning of those words'.[5] The other group comprised nine people—herself and eight others[6]—who were a sub-group of the broad group and shared the common feature of having been specifically identified in the conduct complained of.[7]

Ms Eatock complained that conduct was reasonably likely, in all the circumstances, to offend, insult, humiliate, or intimidate another person *or a group of people* and that the conduct was done because of the race, colour, or national or ethnic origin of her *or of some or all of the people in the group*.[8] Effectively, Ms Eatock was not saying '*I* was vilified'; she was saying '*many people* were vilified, and nine were in particular, of whom I am one'.[9] When Ms Eatock won her case, it was, formally, a win for a very large number of Aboriginal people.[10]

The courage of the nine people in Pat Eatock's group has to be acknowledged. Making and pursuing a complaint under the *RDA* (or any Australian anti-discrimination law) is a costly, gruelling and risky undertaking. It requires a victim to take on a perpetrator—in this case, a very powerful one—in a public forum, at personal cost and financial risk. Ms Cindy Prior's experience is illustrative: undoubtedly the subject of racially vilifying conduct, Ms Prior lost her case under s 18C,[11] faced bankruptcy over an adverse legal costs order, and was the target of online abuse from neo-Nazis and white supremacists.[12]

Not defamation

Ms Eatock's claim was a claim of vilification, even though the same conduct could have been complained of as defamation. These are two quite different ways of characterising the conduct. One of the nine members of Ms Eatock's group, Anita Heiss, explains it well:

> The defamation laws are largely based on the 'harm' done to the reputation of individuals, and this was not just about my reputation. While I needed to clear my professional name, I was more concerned about the greater ramifications for my own community at large and the damage and confusion Bolt's article had caused when it came to other so-called 'fair-skinned Aboriginal people' and their roles in our community. The RDA had the power to challenge those aspects of Bolt's article…I wanted the publication of under-researched, race-based misinformation to end.[13]

The next step in giving the context to the decision would be to go to the decision itself. But before I do, I address a question of identity and identification.

Naming the perpetrator

There is a growing practice of denying to a perpetrator of harm recognition of their identity. The argument is that when conduct causes harm, and the perpetrator stands to gain 'celebrity status, fame, and free advertising'[14] from that conduct, there is a case for denying recognition of the perpetrator.

There is also a case for naming the perpetrator, but the efficacy of shaming relies on the perpetrator caring about the values against which their conduct has been impugned. There is a risk that naming them will reinforce their views and attract like thinkers to their cause. In Ms Eatock's case, the perpetrator is 'a powerful adversary, and unlikely to be persuaded to change his behaviour'.[15] He is engaged in a continuing battle over Aboriginal identity.[16] He is able to exercise his right to free expression to a far greater extent than can almost anyone in Australia. His behaviour suggests that he cannot be shamed, so it seems to me that naming him risks promoting him. His identity is in the reported decision of the court, but I need not consistently remind you of it. Rather, I reverse the practice by which shorthand for the case is simply 'his' case; it is Ms Eatock's case.[17]

The decision

Kath Gelber and Luke McNamara summarise the decision, handed down in September 2011:[18]

> Bromberg J in the Federal Court...concluded that Bolt's public comments fell within the category of unlawful conduct defined by [section 18C of the *RDA*]. Bromberg J rejected the argument that the articles fell within the exemption in the legislation for conduct that was done reasonably and in good faith in the pursuit of making fair comment [section 18D(c)(ii)]. This was because 'they contained erroneous facts, distortions of the truth and inflammatory and provocative language'. As a remedy, he ordered that [the publisher] publish in the *Herald Sun* (print and online), and adjacent to Bolt's columns, a 'corrective notice' summarising the Court's findings. Bromberg J expressly noted that this injunction did not prevent [the publisher] from 'continuing to publish the Newspaper Articles on the *Herald Sun* website for historical or archival purposes' provided that they were accompanied by the corrective notice. The [perpetrator and publisher] were ordered to pay [Ms Eatock's] costs.

Ms Eatock won, for herself and the groups she represented. Justice Bromberg decided that 'at least some [fair-skinned Aboriginal people] were reasonably likely to have been offended, insulted, humiliated or intimidated',[19] and decided the same for the nine named people, except that they were unlikely to have been intimidated.[20] Stone points out that the perpetrator and publisher 'have not been required to apologise, to pay damages, or—crucially—to remove the material from the internet. The sum total in effect of the measure imposed on them is that the articles are *labelled* as having infringed the *RDA*'.[21]

The 'aftermath'

There is no data on how racial vilification complaints made under s 18C are resolved.[22] As is the case for discrimination matters generally, a small proportion of vilification complaints go on to an open court hearing after a mandatory conciliation process. Most of those few are unsuccessful for a range of reasons, from lacking merit to failing technical requirements. Ms Eatock's success was notable not only because it is among a minority of successful Aboriginal vilification cases,[23] but also because it was a success against a perpetrator and publisher with significant public profiles in Australia. Perhaps that explains the extraordinary backlash that followed. This backlash—more prosaically, 'the aftermath'[24]—is a necessary context for any revisiting of the decision.

Other high-profile journalists and national publishers have been found liable under s 18C,[25] and under state anti-vilification laws, but none has then pursued a sustained assault on those laws. Rather, the publisher in each case pursued vindication through conventional appeal processes, often successfully.[26]

The publisher in Ms Eatock's case stated that it did not intend to appeal:[27]

> we have decided against [an appeal]. Instead, it is our view that Section 18 of the *Racial Discrimination Act* overly detracts from free speech and should be revisited by the legislature. We will continue to engage in community debate and discussion to ensure free speech is protected.

The stated intention to 'continue to engage in community debate' belies the partisan aggression with which a particular view of the decision was pursued. On the day of the decision, outside court, the perpetrator reportedly said, 'This is a terrible day for free speech in this country'.[28] In Gelber and McNamara's view, the publisher

> decided to pursue its ongoing grievances by its own means, not in the courtroom (where the grounds of appeal would have to make specific and accurate reference to alleged errors in Justice Bromberg's reasoning). [They] had much greater freedom to frame the terms of the debate outside the courtroom and on the pages and websites of the *Herald Sun* and *The Australian*. They framed the main issues in a way that inaccurately characterised the decision and its effects, and positioned [the perpetrator] as the victim whose rights were violated instead of as the violator of the rights of others.[29]

Some measure of the backlash

The effect of the publisher's 'community debate and discussion' about s 18C was to 'morph [Ms Eatock's case]...into a new narrative untethered from the details of the legislation, facts, findings, reasoning and orders'.[30] A victory over vilifying conduct was turned into an assault on anti-vilification legislation, 'almost exclusively framed within a free speech context'.[31]

To illustrate the conduct of the publishers, I conducted simple searches for the term '18C' together with the word 'freedom' in the Factiva database. I searched the online and paper editions of (1) News Ltd titles: *The Australian*, *The Daily Telegraph*, the *Herald Sun*, and *news.com.au*; (2) the *Australian Broadcasting Corporation News*; and (3) Fairfax titles: *The Age*, *The Sydney Morning Herald*, *The Canberra Times*, and *The Australian Financial Review*.

In almost 12 years from 2000 to the decision on 28 September 2011, those news outlets together used the term '18C' together with the word 'freedom' just 21 times. In the 15 months from 28 September 2011 to the end of 2012, there were 38 occurrences, perhaps unremarkable in reporting Ms Eatock's case. But s 18C then took on a life of its own, as Figure 10.1 shows. In every year, the News Ltd occurrences were more than half the total, and in the peak years of 2016 and 2017, the News Ltd outlets' use of the term '18C' with the word 'freedom' was around 80 per cent of all occurrences.

The marked rise in 2014 was when the Coalition federal government proposed and then abandoned amending s 18C,[32] and in 2015 the Charlie Hebdo hostage attack in Paris 'gave Australian conservatives a new opportunity'[33] to promote amendments to s 18C. Occurrences rose sharply in 2016 when the Government referred to the Parliamentary Joint Committee on Human Rights a question in terms that echoed the stated aims of the campaign that the publisher had announced five years before: 'whether the operation of Part IIA of the *Racial Discrimination Act 1975* (Cth) (including section 18C and 18D) impose [sic] unreasonable restrictions

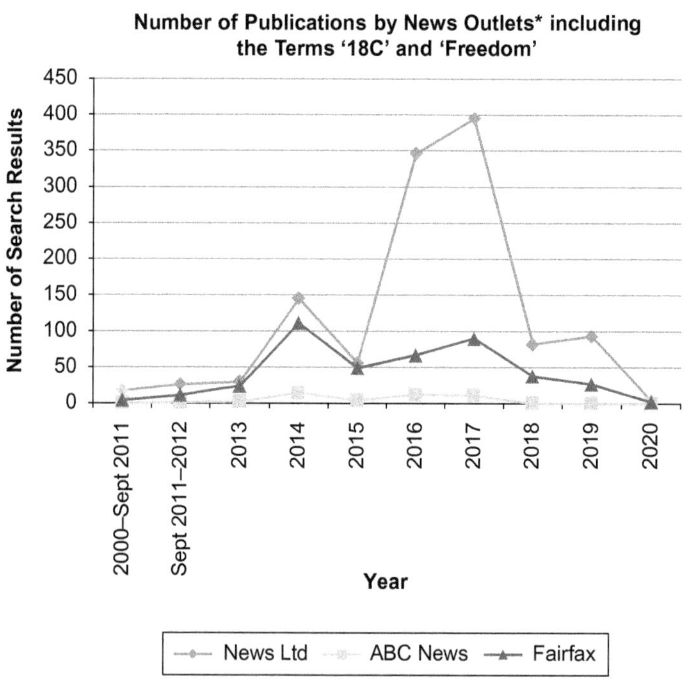

FIGURE 10.1 Number of publications by news outlets including the terms '18C' and 'freedom'. Note: includes online and print versions of (1) News Ltd titles: *The Australian, The Daily Telegraph*, the *Herald Sun*, and news.com.au; (2) the *Australian Broadcasting Corporation News*; and (3) Fairfax titles: *The Age, The Sydney Morning Herald, The Canberra Times*, and *The Australian Financial Review*

on freedom of speech'.[34] Occurrences peaked in 2017 when the Committee reported, making no recommendations for amendment or repeal.[35]

Evan Smith tells a similar story for mentions of s 18C in the federal parliament:[36] almost none between its enactment and Ms Eatock's case, and then an explosion from 2013–2017. Smith illustrates his research in Figure 10.2.

These graphs illustrate 'an aggressive campaign to reconstruct what the decision stood for, a 'counter-narrative [that] achieved powerful political traction'.[37] That counter-narrative had two strands to it. One 'questioned the legitimacy of Australia's hate speech laws; and strengthened a libertarian conception of free speech'.[38] It was a story that called for 're-asserting the importance of freedom of expression in Australia',[39] one where '[c]onservative, classical liberal, and libertarian commentators called for either a substantial amendment or a complete repeal of s. 18C'.[40]

The other counter-narrative was more insidious; it 'encouraged scepticism about the authenticity of fair-skinned Indigenous people and affirmed the validity of judgment by non-Indigenous people about the legitimacy of Indigenous identity according to skin colour'.[41] In this way, the backlash to Ms Eatock's case did for the public what Alison Whittaker has elsewhere said is being done in law: 'fundamentally shap[ing] Aboriginality in such a way that returns Aboriginality to its blood-quantum guise'.[42]

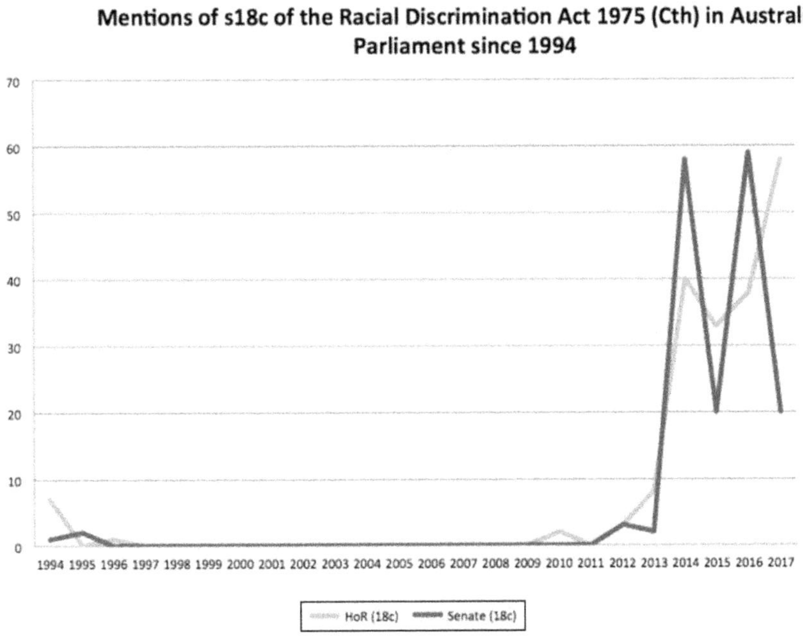

FIGURE 10.2 Mentions of s 18C of the *Racial Discrimination Act 1975* (Cth) in Australian Parliament since 1994

Alison's response

Ms Eatock's case is about 'lousy journalism'[43] that was so bad that it caused harm and was unlawful. But in the years since, a counter-narrative has deliberately and determinedly retold Ms Eatock's case as a story where a high-profile journalist perpetrator is the victim, and Aboriginal victims are effaced.

I read Alison's response to Ms Eatock's case as a judgment on the original judgment, a comment on the subsequent rewriting of the Federal Court's decision. Alison's response suggests to me that the aspirations for s 18C—that it would 'provide a safety net for racial harmony in Australia'[44]—are mere words on a page, to be played with as a trigram generator might, preserving the words but stripping away their intended meaning. The effacement of the victims of vilification in Ms Eatock's case is recognised in the effacement of the decision itself. This is, as I say, only my reading of Alison's response to Ms Eatock's case. I cannot go any further; her poem is there for anyone to read and appreciate, perhaps in the context I have set out.

I am finishing this piece at a time when the Black Lives Matter movement demands an end to the structural racism of the state. There is never a good time for a white man to 'comment' on the work of a black woman, but this must be one of the least auspicious. I am acutely conscious of my white race and male privilege,[45] but there is little I can do about it in this role other than to acknowledge it and withdraw. The stage is Alison's.

Notes

1 Ms Eatock died in 2015.
2 Adrienne Stone, 'The Ironic Aftermath of *Eatock v Bolt*' (2015) 38(3) *Melbourne University Law Review* 926, 928 (citations omitted).
3 See generally Neil Rees, Simon Rice, and Dominique Allen, *Australian Anti-Discrimination and Equal Opportunity Law* (The Federation Press, 3rd ed, 2018) 690–716.
4 Ibid., 716–30.
5 *Eatock v Bolt* [2011] FCA 1103, [280].
6 Mr Graham Atkinson, Dr Wayne Atkinson, Professor Larissa Behrendt, Mr Geoff Clark, Ms Bindi Cole, Ms Leeanne Enoch, Ms Anita Heiss, and Mr Mark McMillan.
7 *Eatock v Bolt* [2011] FCA 1103, [301].
8 Ibid., [246].
9 Ibid., [269]–[272].
10 For a critical evaluation of racial discrimination legislation and group identity, see David Rolph, 'Racial Discrimination Laws as a Means of Protecting Collective Reputation and Identity' in Matthew Rimmer (ed), *Indigenous Intellectual Property: A Handbook of Contemporary Research* (Edward Elgar, 2015).
11 *Prior v Queensland University of Technology (No.2)* [2016] FCCA 2853; *Prior v Wood* [2017] FCA 193.
12 Josh Robertson, 'Rape Threats and Racist Hate Followed Discrimination Case but Police Not Investigating' *ABC News* (online, 30 March 2019) <https://www.abc.net.au/news/2019-03-30/cindy-prior-rape-threats-and-hate-mail-followed-court-case/10954822>.

13 Anita Heiss, *Am I Black Enough for You?* (Bantam Press, 2012) 168–9, cited in Katherine Gelber and Luke McNamara, 'Freedom of Speech and Racial Vilification in Australia: "The Bolt Case" in Public Discourse' (2013) 48(4) *Australian Journal of Political Science* 470, 473–4 ('Freedom of Speech').
14 Adam Lankford and Eric Madfis, 'Media Coverage of Mass Killers: Content, Consequences, and Solutions' (2018) 62(2) *American Behavioral Scientist* 151, 158.
15 Gelber and McNamara, 'Freedom of Speech' (n 13) 474.
16 See e.g. Andrew Bolt, 'Bruce Pascoe Speaks! But Still Won't Prove He's Aboriginal' *The Herald Sun* (online, 14 May 2020) <https://www.heraldsun.com.au/blogs/andrew-bolt 14 May 2020>.
17 See e.g. Gareth Griffith, *Racial Vilification Laws: The Bolt Case from a State Perspective* (e-brief 14/2011, October 2011); Bibhu Aggarwal, 'The Bolt Case: Silencing Speech or Promoting Tolerance?' in Helen Sykes (ed), *More or Less: Democracy and New Media* (Future Leaders, 2012) 238–57; Gelber and McNamara (n 13); Jim Jose, 'Re-imagining the Global Colour Line: The Bolt Case and the Politics of Whiteness' (2020) 66(1) *Australian Journal of Politics and History* 94.
18 Gelber and McNamara, 'Freedom of Speech' (n 13) 471 (citations omitted).
19 *Eatock v Bolt* [2011] FCA 1103, [298].
20 Ibid., [302].
21 Stone (n 2) 939 (emphasis in original).
22 Ninety-seven complaints were made in 2018–2019: Australian Human Rights Commission, *2018–19 Complaint Statistics*, Tables 25, 26 and 27.
23 See *McMahon v Bowman* [2000] FMCA 3; *Wanjurri v Southern Cross Broadcasting (Aus) Ltd* [2001] HREOCA 2; *McGlade v Lightfoot* [2002] FCA 1457; *Campbell v Kirstenfeldt* [2008] FMCA 1356; *Dunne v Noonan* [2009] FMCA 362; *Clarke v Nationwide News Pty Ltd trading as The Sunday Times* [2012] FCA 307; *Barnes v Northern Territory Police & Anor* [2013] FCCA 30.
24 Stone (n 2); Gelber and McNamara, 'Freedom of Speech' (n 13).
25 See e.g. *Wanjurri v Southern Cross Broadcasting (Aus) Ltd* [2001] HREOCA 2; *Clarke v Nationwide News Pty Ltd trading as The Sunday Times* [2012] FCA 307.
26 *Attorney-General v 2UE Sydney Pty Ltd* (2006) FLR 62; *Jones v Trad* [2013] NSWCA 389.
27 'No Appeal in Andrew Bolt Case', *Herald Sun* (online, 20 October 2011).
28 Karl Quinn, 'True Colours', *The Age* (online, 29 September 2011).
29 Gelber and McNamara, 'Freedom of Speech' (n 13) 474.
30 Ibid., 481.
31 Jose (n 17) 95.
32 See e.g. Jillian Rudge, 'Australians' "Right" to Be Bigoted: Protecting Minorities' Rights from the Tyranny of the Majority' (2016) 41 *Brooklyn Journal of International Law* 825, 825–9.
33 Ibid., 829.
34 'Terms of Reference', *Parliament of Australia* (2020) <https://www.aph.gov.au/Parliamentary_Business/Committees/Joint/Human_Rights_inquiries/FreedomspeechAustralia/Terms_of_Reference>.
35 Parliamentary Joint Committee on Human Rights, Parliament of Australia, *Inquiry into the Operation of Part IIA of the Racial Discrimination Act 1975 (Cth) and Related Procedures under the Australian Human Rights Commission Act 1986 (Cth)* (Report, 28 February 2017).
36 Evan Smith, 'Parliament's Current Obsession with s18c' 22 March, 2017, <https://hatfulofhistory.wordpress.com/2017/03/22/parliaments-current-obsession-with-s18c/>.
37 Katharine Gelber and Luke McNamara, 'The Effects of Civil Hate Speech Laws: Lessons from Australia' (2015) 49(3) *Law & Society Review* 631, 655 ('Civil Hate Speech Laws').
38 Ibid.

39 Augusto Zimmermann and Lorraine Finlay, 'A Forgotten Freedom: Protecting Freedom of Speech in an Age of Political Correctness' (2014) 14 *Macquarie Law Journal* 185, 204.
40 Chris Berg and Sinclair Davidson, 'Section 18C, Human Rights, and Media Reform: An Institutional Analysis of the 2011–13 Australian Free Speech Debate' (2016) 23(1) *Agenda: A Journal of Policy Analysis and Reform* 5, 11.
41 Gelber and McNamara, 'Civil Hate Speech Laws' (n 37) 655.
42 Alison Whittaker, 'White Law, Blak Arbiters, Grey Legal Subjects: Deep Colonisation's Role and Impact in Defining Aboriginality at Law' (2017) 20 *Australian Indigenous Law Review* 4, 19.
43 David Marr, 'In Black and White, Andrew Bolt Trifled with the Facts' *The Sydney Morning Herald*, September 29, 2011.
44 Commonwealth, *Parliamentary Debates*, House of Representatives, 15 November 1994, 3336 (Michael Lavarch, Attorney-General).
45 Peggy McIntosh, 'White Privilege and Male Privilege: A Personal Account of Coming to See Correspondences through Work in Women's Studies' in Susan Maxine Shaw and Janet Lee (eds), *Women's Voices, Feminist Visions: Classic and Contemporary Readings* (McGraw-Hill, 2007) 91–8; see also Matthew Etchells et al., 'White Male Privilege: An Intersectional Deconstruction' (2017) 4(2) *Journal of Ethnic and Cultural Studies* 13; Bob Pease, 'Decentring White Men: Critical Reflections on Masculinity and White Studies' in Aileen Moreton-Robinson (ed), *Whitening Race: Essays in Social and Cultural Criticism* (Aboriginal Studies Press, 2004) 119–30; Greta Bird, 'The White Subject as Liberal Subject' (2008) 4(2) *Australian Critical Race and Whiteness Studies Association* 10.

EATOCK .... APPLICANT;

AND

BOLT .... RESPONDENT;

[2011] FCA 1103

Racial Discrimination Act 1975 (Cth)—Racial discrimination—Newspaper articles—Aboriginal peoples—Offensive, insulting, humiliating, or intimidating conduct—Conduct due to race, colour, or national or ethnic origin—Exemptions—Corrective notice.

Alison Whittaker.

Three-word phrases from the Federal Court decision, handed down by Bromberg J, ranked by the frequency in which they appeared.

an Aboriginal person

the newspaper articles

as an Aboriginal

Mr Bolt and

in relation to

Bolt and HWT

by Mr Bolt

freedom of expression

identify as Aboriginal

section 18C 1

group of people

to identify as

of public interest

by reference to

which I have

that Mr Bolt

the public interest

18c 1 a

in good faith

the first article

to be Aboriginal

reasonably likely to

of the RDA

likely to be

the *Herald Sun*

matter of public

a number of
each of the

to have been

or ethnic origin
conveyed by the

in my view

reference to the
by the articles

a group of
because of the
in the public

I have found
on the basis

people in the
reasonably and in

the Aboriginal community
and in good
is to be
of the people

i accept that
of section 18C

the people in

of the articles
of the individuals

race colour or

in the newspaper
by the newspaper
of Mr Bolt
of the newspaper
relation to the
in the context
and communal recognition
of part iia

as Aboriginal persons
the context of
entitled to regard
18c 1 b
one of the
the imputations conveyed
of the person
likely to have
members of the
by s 18d
is entitled to
the subject of
a matter of
the fact that
by reason of

in the trend
of Aboriginal descent

the purposes of
the second article
of freedom of
of the group

part of the
by Ms Eatock

communal recognition as
the basis of
national or ethnic
that it is

the purpose of
Aboriginal person and

to be a
be regarded as

Mr Bolt was
said to be
of the race

the three part
was reasonably likely

section 18C conduct
ethnic origin of
her Aboriginal identity
by section 18C
Mr Bolt to

for the purposes
and good faith
and insulted by

purpose in the
the articles or
member of the
s 18d c
of expression is

there is a
likely to offend
were reasonably likely
the imputations which
that the conduct

the conventional understanding
the section 18C
or parts thereof
the ordinary reasonable
in Bropho at
recognition as an
for Aboriginal people
in the manner

extent to which
identified as Aboriginal
have been offended

articles or parts
genuine purpose in
the terms of
Aboriginal she has
seems to me
freedom of speech
the race colour
is said to
done reasonably and

that the articles
the protection of
identify as an
to Aboriginal people

the extent to
his or her
of a person
as well as
to which i
in the articles
and in the
or national or
as a result
three part test

conventional understanding of
to s 18d
that he was
Mr McMillan was
identification and communal

Mr Bolt as
Aboriginal person she
a fair comment
self identification and
i have no
to which the
in section 18C
18d c ii
in which the
the question of
it is the—

A note by Alison Whittaker

I could not have anticipated how difficult it was to write for this project. Assuming the role of decision maker, accepting that in actions like the one undertaken in *Eatock v Bolt* I'd be tightly bound by statute and procedure that I'd critiqued, was not easy. I could rationalise it as a hypothetical exercise, but it felt like a betrayal to follow through. It's easy to reveal the structural racism of settler law—it's very hard to imagine a way out of it that doesn't replicate that structure.

I chose *Eatock v Bolt* for the project. The field I usually work in, inquests, seemed too high-stakes. Directly toying with inquiries on Indigenous peoples' lives and deaths seemed so directly mired in ethical and relational obligations, impossible for me to re-litigate without consequence.

In hindsight, something like *Eatock v Bolt* is only marginally less intimate and caught up in obligation. I know many of the applicants. I myself remember being a first-year law student in 2011 when the judgment was handed down.

I realised pretty quickly that the difference between critiquing how a decision is made and then making that decision yourself is one of responsibility. It means, at least for me in this instance, a sense of unwanted complicity. I couldn't make a decision in which I didn't feel like I was doing some violence to an (imperfect) victory for the complainants which was hard-fought, precious, and rare. I couldn't do it even if I thought parts of it were problematic, a word that seems so obvious and empty when you try to build a judgment around it.

There's a lesson in there about how Aboriginal and Torres Strait Islander peoples approach settler law, I think. The lesson is that settler law's remedies come with rhetoric and reasoning that we sometimes reject. The lesson is also that the rare instances when those systems work for us make a small, imperfect and material impact on our world as First Nations and peoples that can't be understated. The lesson is also that to become a decision maker in settler law, or to ask for decisions to be made in these forums, is itself a socio-legal choice and a strategic one in the colony. Placing an Indigenous judge in the position of decision maker does little to change the structure of that law or this reality.

From workshops throughout this project, it's clear that other Indigenous legal thinkers in this book face a similar dilemma, and have approached it in their own way—through scholarly analysis on Indigenous refusal, or through the hypothetical establishment of new forums. There are also those who have their own construction of these strategic choices, which I respect and learn from.

You might be wondering about the poem. It's a reflex, and I accept that it's a cowardice that I indulged. Unwilling to do any work of passing judgment myself, I ran the *Eatock v Bolt* decision through a trigram generator to produce a list of the most-common three-word phrases used in Bromberg J's decision, ranked by their frequency.

The result is this poem, roughly organised into three vertical groupings—the first, a focus on Bolt's actions and the subject of the proceedings in his claims; the second, the procedural detritus of the decision; and the third, the preoccupation with the Indigenous subjects who brought the action. Even in working strategically to seek a remedy and make whiteness and racism visible, the applicants became the unrelenting subjects of inquiry.

I leave it, as a relatively hands-off adaptation of Bromberg J's judgment, to your interpretation.

PART IV

Family and identity

11

DEMPSEY v RIGG [1914] ST R QD 245

Commentary: *Dempsey v Rigg* [1914] St R Qd 245

Trudie Broderick

The Protection Acts

In 1897 the Queensland Parliament enacted the *Aboriginals Protection and Restriction of the Sale of Opium Act* (*'Aboriginals Protection Act'*).[1] Its purpose was made clear in the Preamble—it was 'an Act to make provision for the better Protection and Care of the Aboriginal and Half-Caste Inhabitants of the Colony'. Under the guise of benevolence,[2] the draconian measures granted the Chief Protector of Aboriginals[3] broad powers to control every aspect of the lives of First Nations people.

Benevolent it was not. Removal from traditional homelands,[4] forced confinement onto reserves and missions,[5] the power to determine housing and employment conditions,[6] as well as complete control over wages were all powers granted under the legislation. Aboriginal people did not have the right to vote,[7] and their children became wards of the state by virtue of being Aboriginal. The Chief Protector acted as their guardian and routinely removed them from the care of their parents, placing them in dormitories or adopting them into non-Aboriginal families. The vulnerability of Aboriginal children to removal was exacerbated by the broad power of the Governor in Council to make regulations concerning the 'care, custody, and education of the children of aboriginals'.[8]

The *Aboriginals Protection Act* was also responsible for the creation of two separate classes of Aboriginal people. In one class, Aboriginal inhabitants of Queensland were entirely subject to the controlling measures imposed by the legislation. This class included all persons deemed to be 'half-caste' or 'the off-spring of an aboriginal mother and other than an aboriginal father'.[9]

In theory, the second class were granted the same legal rights as other Queenslanders. Aboriginal people who applied for and were granted a certificate of exemption fell into this category, along with the offspring of Aboriginal fathers and non-Aboriginal mothers.[10] Important to *Dempsey v Rigg*,[11] this class also included Aboriginal people who married non-Aboriginal people.[12]

Dempsey v Rigg is centred around the employment of Eliza Woree. Eliza, an Aboriginal woman and inhabitant of Queensland, automatically fell under the 'protection' of the *Aboriginals Protection Act*. In 1913, Joe Andrews sought and was granted permission from the Protector of Aborigines to marry Eliza. According to law, when Joe and Eliza married, she took on his last name and became his.[13] During the same year, Eliza secured work carrying out domestic duties in the home of Isaac Rigg.[14] In accordance with the *Aboriginals Protection Act*, an application had to be made by the employer of an Aboriginal person to the Protector of Aborigines prior to the employment taking place.[15]

Discovering that Rigg had employed Eliza without the appropriate permit, Constable Peter Dempsey charged Rigg with the offence of unlawfully employing an Aboriginal under s 14 of the *Aboriginals Protection Act*.[16] Police Magistrate Grant dismissed the complaint on the ground that Eliza, now married, was no longer subject to the provisions of the Act, and this entitled Rigg to employ her without the permission of the Protector of Aborigines. However, Police Magistrate Grant also made application for a special case, requesting that another court consider the question of whether Eliza remained subject to the provisions of the *Aboriginals Protection Act*. The matter was referred to Jameson J of the Northern Supreme Court who made the determination that permission must be granted, and a failure to do so was an offence under the Act.[17]

Dissatisfied with the decision, Rigg appealed to the Full Court arguing that Eliza was no longer under the 'protection' of the *Aboriginals Protection Act* and indeed, she had lost her Australian nationality when she married Joe, who was described as a Malay and a 'native of Batavia'.[18] Cooper CJ disagreed, concluding that 'her personal status as an [A]boriginal'[19] person had not changed with marriage.

Bound to give the law its 'natural and ordinary' meaning, His Honour chided that:

> [c]ertainly it seems rather hard that, a white man who has married an aboriginal woman is not permitted to take her to live with him if he were employed by some other employer and lived in the house of his employer; but, under s. 14, if he were employed on the premises of his employer, he could not have her living with him on those premises.[20]

Real, Chubb, and Lukin JJ concurred.[21] The appeal was dismissed.[22]

Aboriginal women and the law

This case occurred 12 years after a newly formed Commonwealth Parliament passed its first law on federal voting. The *Commonwealth Franchise Act 1902* (Cth) granted all men and women the right to vote in and stand for both state and federal elections. That is, unless you were a First Nations person in Australia. The law was clear that '[n]o aboriginal native of Australia shall be entitled to have *his* [emphasis added] name placed on an Electoral Roll unless so entitled under section forty-one of the Constitution'.[23]

The same legislation that enfranchised white women in Australia is the same legislation that further stripped First Nations people, specifically First Nations women, of access to political processes. During the late 1800s, non-Aboriginal women began to find success in the push for the right to vote. Believing that this would enable them to gain inclusion and grasp a right that had previously eluded them,[24] they sought to influence decision making and change working conditions, improve property rights, and gain a level of political citizenship already afforded to their white male counterparts.

Dempsey v Rigg highlights the importance of recognising the voices of Indigenous women in Australian law throughout history. Aboriginal women were impacted by the imposition of draconian laws in ways that white women never were.

The case also highlights something else, something that goes beyond the determinations and conclusions of judges, magistrates, and constables, far beyond decisions over who had the legal right to Eliza's life, body, and presence in society. Despite never having been asked who she was and what she wanted, Eliza existed outside of these determinations. Eliza left a legacy and a story of resistance.

Justice Nicole Watson's re-examination and scrutiny of the judgment tells a different story. The narrative now hinges upon the decision-making power of the First Nations Court of Australia, and Her Honour seeks to hear and understand the life of Eliza as she experienced it.

Notes

1 *Aboriginals Protection and Restriction of the Sale of Opium Act 1897* (Qld) ('*Aboriginals Protection Act*'). Subsequent amendments to the *Aboriginals Protection Act* occurred in 1899, 1901, 1928, and 1934. It was eventually replaced by the *Aboriginals Preservation and Protection Act 1939* (Qld). See also *Aborigines' and Torres Strait Islanders' Affairs Act 1965* (Qld) and *Aborigines Act 1971* (Qld).

2 See Queensland, *Parliamentary Debates*, Legislative Assembly, 15 November 1897 (The Honourable Horace Tozer, Home Secretary); see especially Human Rights and Equal Opportunity Commission, *Bringing Them Home: Report of the National Inquiry into the Separation of Aboriginal and Torres Strait Islander Children from Their Families* (1997) ('*Bringing Them Home Report*').

3 *Aboriginals Protection Act 1897* (Qld) s 6.

4 Ibid., s 9.

5 Ibid.

6 See e.g. ibid., s 9.

7 See *Elections Act 1885* (Qld) s 6; *Elections Act Amendment Act 1905* (Qld); *Elections Act 1915* (Qld). Indigenous people determined to be 'half caste' could not be excluded from voting.

8 *Aboriginals Protection Act 1897* (Qld) ss 31(6)–(8); Human Rights and Equal Opportunity Commission, *Bringing Them Home Report* (n 2); AIATSIS, 'Aboriginal Natives Shall Not be Counted' (18 May 2020) <https://aiatsis.gov.au/exhibitions/aboriginal-natives-shall-not-be-counted>.

9 *Aboriginals Protection Act* s 3.

10 Ibid. See discussion by Loretta de Plevitz, 'Working for the Man: Wages Lost to Queensland Workers "Under the Act"' (1996) 3(81) *Aboriginal Law Bulletin* 4.

11 [1914] St R Qd 245.

12 *Aboriginals Protection Act* s 10.

13 *Dempsey v Rigg* [1914] St R Qd 245.

14 Ibid.

15 *Aboriginals Protection Act* s 15.

16 Ibid., s 14 provides that '[a]ny person found guilty of an offence under this Act…shall be liable, on conviction, to a penalty not exceeding fifty pounds, or to imprisonment not exceeding six months'.

17 *Dempsey v Rigg* [1914] St R Qd 245, 246.

18 Ibid., 245.

19 Ibid., 248.

20 Ibid.

21 Ibid.

22 Debates about the identity and citizenship of Aboriginal and Torres Strait Islander people continue. See *Love v Commonwealth; Thoms v Commonwealth* [2020] HCA 3.

23 *Commonwealth Franchise Act 1902* (Cth) s 4. The exclusion extended to all non-whites who did not already have the right to vote in state elections. During this period, the states had the right to determine definitions of Aboriginality. These same definitions were used to exclude Indigenous people from the political process. For a contemporary consideration of the right of Indigenous people to vote in federal elections see Dani Larkin and Jonathan Crowe, *Roach v Electoral Commissioner* (2007) 233 CLR 162, in Chapter 14 of this collection.

24 Joy McCann and Marian Sawer, 'Australia: The Slow Road to Parliament' in Susan Franceschet, Mona Lena Krook and Netina Tan (eds), *The Palgrave Handbook of Women's Political Rights* (Palgrave McMillan, 2019) 483–502.

PETER DEMPSEY .... RESPONDENT;

AND

ISAAC RIGG .... APPELLANT;

[2055] FNCA 1

Criminal law—Employment of Aboriginal women—Marriage of Aboriginal woman to Malay man—Impact of the marriage on the application of the *Aboriginals Protection and Restriction of the Sale of Opium Act 1897* (Qld)—Indigenous women's lived experiences.

Watson J.[1]

[1] This is an application brought by the National Aboriginal and Torres Strait Islander Women Lawyers Association pursuant to s 25 of the *Treaty Between the Republic of Australia and the Confederation of Aboriginal and Torres Strait Islander Nations Act 2048* ('*Treaty Act*'). Section 25 compels the court to examine decisions that have diminished the enjoyment by Aboriginal and Torres Strait Islander people of their right to equality. The purpose of s 25 was explained by Foley CJ in *Re Walker*:

> The court's function under s 25 is but one aspect of the journey towards national maturity that began with the historic negotiations that preceded the enactment of the *Treaty Act*. Section 25 requires the court to construct the narratives of those Aboriginal and Torres Strait Islander people whose names appear in the judgments of Australian superior courts, but whose voices are absent. It is through this process that the court restores dignity to those who were dehumanised by the racism that has imbued all of Australia's institutions, and in particular, the legal system.[2]

[2] In performing its function under s 25, the court is constrained by neither the rules of evidence nor doctrine. Ultimately, its decisions will have no effect upon the rights and interests of those whose narratives have been pieced together. Nonetheless, the court's role under s 25 is vital to one of the objects of the *Treaty Act*, namely, the creation of a dialogue on 'truth-telling'.[3]

[3] Through imagining the stories of those who languished on the margins of Australian society, this court exhumes confronting truths about the nexus

between law, racism, and settler-colonialism. But it also casts a light on the indomitable resilience of Aboriginal and Torres Strait Islander people. By honouring the courage of those who survived the myriad blows of settler colonialism, this court is contributing to the development of a new and inclusive national story.

[4] The Applicant has asked the court to cast its lens over the decision of the Supreme Court of Queensland in *Dempsey v Rigg*.[4] The case arose from the prosecution of Isaac Rigg for the archaic offence of unlawfully employing an Aboriginal. However, the application relates to neither Isaac Rigg, nor the police officer who charged him, Constable Peter Dempsey. Rather, it concerns the Aboriginal woman who was unlawfully employed by Rigg, Eliza Woree.

The decision

[5] What the *Northern Herald* described as a 'most peculiar case'[5] began on 9 December 1913 in the home of Isaac Rigg, in the Cairns suburb of White Rock. Constable Dempsey would later tell the Cairns Summons Court that he had seen Eliza Woree in Rigg's home that afternoon.[6] She was ironing clothes. Rigg and Dempsey then had a conversation, during which it emerged that Rigg was employing Eliza in the absence of official sanction.

[6] Section 15 of the *Aboriginals Protection and Restriction of the Sale of Opium Act 1897* (Qld) (*'Aboriginals Protection Act'*) obliged any person who was 'desirous' of employing an 'aboriginal or female half-caste'[7] to seek the approval of a protector, and to enter into an employment agreement. As Rigg had not sought the permission of a protector to employ Eliza, he was charged with committing an offence under s 14 of the Act.[8] Section 14 provided:

> Any person who, except under the provisions of any Act or Regulations thereunder in force in Queensland, employs an aboriginal or a female half-caste otherwise than in accordance with the provisions of this Act or the Regulations, or suffers or permits an aboriginal or a female half-caste to be in or upon any house or premises in his occupation or under his control, shall be guilty of an offence against this Act, and shall be liable, on conviction, to a penalty not exceeding fifty pounds and not less than ten pounds, or to imprisonment for any term not exceeding six months.

[7] Three months earlier, Eliza had married Joe Andrews, a Malay and a 'native of Batavia',[9] now known as Java. Rigg argued that as a result of the marriage, Eliza Woree ceased to exist, and therefore, she was no longer an 'Aboriginal' within the meaning of the Act.[10] Rigg's defence was explicable by the common law doctrine of coverture. Under this doctrine, marriage resulted in the wife losing her own legal existence. Both parties were reduced to 'one person and that person [was] the husband'.[11]

[8] Coverture found resonance in the international phenomenon of marital denaturalisation. Upon marrying a foreigner, a married woman was stripped of her own nationality and gained that of her husband.[12] As Joe was a 'Malay', Eliza had apparently lost her Australian nationality. It followed that she could no longer be an 'Aboriginal' for the purposes of the *Aboriginals Protection Acts 1897–1901* (Qld).

[9] The prosecutor, Sergeant Hawkes, countered that upon entering the marriage Eliza became exempt from only s 9, which contained the Minister's power to remove Aboriginal people to and between reserves.[13]

[10] The Police Magistrate, Mr Grant, considered that the marriage was a 'perfect farce' if Joe did not gain 'control' over Eliza.[14] He dismissed the complaint and stated a special case under s 226 of the *Justices Act 1886* (Qld), a procedure in which a legal question is sent to another court for its determination. The question of law submitted to the Northern Supreme Court was:

> whether Eliza Woree, an aboriginal, having been married to Joe Andrews, a Malay, according to law, and with the consent of the Chief Protector of Aboriginals, was still subject to the provisions of *The Aboriginals Protection and Restriction of the Sale of Opium Acts,* 1897 to 1901.[15]

[11] Jameson J answered the question in the affirmative and remitted the matter back to the Police Magistrate.[16]

[12] Rigg appealed to the Full Court of the Supreme Court of Queensland. Once again, he argued that Eliza had lost her Australian nationality upon marrying Joe Andrews.[17] This change of status placed her outside of the *Aboriginals Protection Act.* Furthermore, the marriage itself had resulted in Eliza passing from the 'protection of the State under the Aboriginals Acts to the protection of her husband under the general law'.[18] The respondent submitted that Rigg had confused race with nationality. The Act was concerned with only the former.[19] The Full Court agreed.

[13] The lead judgment of Cooper CJ is less than a single page. The essence of his judgment is captured in the following passage:

> I am of opinion that the marriage of this woman with a Malay did not alter her personal status as an aboriginal. The marriage did not make her anything different from an aboriginal. She still remained an aboriginal inhabitant of Queensland, and therefore the employment of her by the appellant was an offence, unless he had the permission of the Protector. The appellant had not that permission, and therefore he committed an offence.[20]

[14] Cooper CJ conceded that his decision had the potential to cause hardship for the white husbands of Aboriginal women in some circumstances.[21] In particular, s 14 was construed as preventing husbands who lived on the premises of their employers from cohabiting with their wives.[22] However, he was

bound to give the words of the Act their 'natural and ordinary meaning'.[23] His brother judges, Real, Chubb, and Lukin JJ, concurred.[24]

Review by the First Nations Court of Australia

[15] Of those involved in this case, it was Eliza who had the greatest stake in the outcome. Isaac Rigg suffered the slur of a conviction. In contrast, Eliza's future liberty now hinged upon the whims of those within Queensland's Aboriginal and Torres Strait Islander bureaucracy. Given that she had so much to lose, it is extraordinary that Eliza's voice was entirely absent from the brief judgments.

[16] One hundred and thirty-six years later, it is finally time for Eliza to be heard. By drawing upon archival records, newspaper articles, and historical accounts, the court will imagine her story. It is a tale of great tragedy and dehumanising subjugation. But it is also a testament to the resilience of Aboriginal women who survived the brutalities of invasion and created new lives in a world that treated them with callous indifference at best.

Eliza's childhood on the Northern Frontier

[17] The task of constructing Eliza's story begins with the marriage certificate, which records her place of birth as Woree, Cairns.[25] Such sparse details do not allow us to learn about Eliza's Country, kin, or the language that she and her loved ones spoke. The time of her birth is also unclear. According to correspondence from the Cairns Police, Eliza was born around 1883.[26] However, the marriage certificate[27] provides that she was a decade older. Irrespective of whether she was born in 1873 or 1883, Eliza came into the world during a time of great upheaval.

[18] In the absence of negotiation or consultation with Aboriginal people, the township of Cairns was founded in October 1876.[28] Within a year the first land sale had taken place, together with the opening of bank branches and the erection of buildings for the Native Police and the Police Magistrate.[29] Far from being passive victims of dispossession, Aboriginal people valiantly resisted, stoking a 'war of extermination'[30] that would extend into the 1880s.

[19] Aboriginal resistance was answered by tactics that included poisoning[31] and the deployment of the Native Police. Akin to the Special Forces,[32] the Native Police served the singular purpose of eradicating the Aboriginal presence from the land. The term 'dispersal' was a euphemism for the force's indiscriminate killing of Aboriginal people.[33] Today, dispersals carried out near Cairns still resound in place names such as Skull Pocket and Skeleton Creek.[34]

[20] Starving and enfeebled by war, the dispossessed had little choice but to create an existence on the outskirts of Queensland's burgeoning towns. Reynolds has captured the desolation that characterised the fringe camps:

> They were, almost universally, ragged clusters of wind-breaks made from bark, bags, kerosene tins and other cast off scraps of wood and metal. Locations were remarkably uniform: half a mile to a mile from town; out near the cemetery, the Chinese gardens, the rubbish dump or along the creek bed, over the river, down in the mangroves; usually out of earshot, out of sight and out of mind.[35]

[21] It is likely that Eliza sought refuge in one such settlement. Grieving the loss of Country and no longer able to hunt, those who lived in the camps struggled to survive.[36] The plight of the dispossessed aroused little compassion among the white townsfolk of Cairns. The *Cairns Post* reflected the sentiments of many when it condemned the 'stunted, degraded, deformed blacks' who had 'infested' the town.[37]

[22] At the same time, settlers were desirous of exploiting Aboriginal people as casual labourers, whose meagre compensation consisted of food, tobacco, and opium.[38] In homes in Cairns and throughout the state, Aboriginal people performed the roles of 'house-boy', 'nurse-girl', and 'firewood cutter' among others.[39] Informal curfews forbade Aboriginal people from being within town precincts after sunset. Those who breached the curfew were liable to suffer the 'whip or the boot'.[40]

[23] Children like Eliza were at risk of abduction by Native Police and settlers who sought to rear them as servants.[41] Aboriginal child workers were rarely paid and often forced to perform arduous tasks.[42] Female servants were particularly vulnerable to molestation by their employers, and pregnancies that resulted from such abuse were commonly explained by the 'animal passions' of the victims.[43] Such was the world that Eliza was born into; one characterised by violence, scarcity, and breathtaking inhumanity. In order to survive into adulthood, she would have possessed great fortitude.

Adulthood

[24] What little we know of Eliza's adulthood mostly concerns her marriage to Joe Andrews. For most individuals, the decision to marry is a deeply personal affair. However, for Aboriginal women such as Eliza, the ability to marry was circumscribed by legislation. Section 9 of the *Aboriginals Protection Act 1901* (Qld) provided:

> No marriage of a female aboriginal with any person other than an aboriginal shall be celebrated without the permission, in writing, of a Protector authorised by the Minister to give such permission. And the Protector who grants such permission shall forthwith transmit a copy of the same to the Minister.

[25] Although the desire to marry was presumably mutual, Joe was the sole applicant for permission to wed.[44] Joe and Eliza were subsequently interviewed

by police. Both were found to be of good character.[45] As a matter of practice, police officers were obliged to ascertain that such unions were consensual.[46] This practice notwithstanding, there is no mention in the police correspondence concerning Eliza's consent to the marriage. For all intents and purposes, her opinions and aspirations were irrelevant. On 16 July 1913, the Deputy Chief Protector of Aboriginals sent a permit for the marriage to the Protector of Aboriginals Cairns.[47] Eliza and Joe exchanged their vows in the District Registrar's Office, Cairns on 18 September.[48]

[26] At the time of the marriage, Eliza was employed as a housemaid by one Mrs Steele.[49] Domestic service was the most common form of employment for Aboriginal girls and women during the earlier part of the 20th century. Life as a domestic servant was challenging for all women, but Aboriginal servants were generally paid less and expected to perform more gruelling tasks than their white counterparts.[50] According to the Bidjara and Birri-Gubba Juru historian, Jackie Huggins, Aboriginal domestics often worked 15-hour days catering for the 'needs, values and lifestyle' of their employers.[51]

[27] In spite of toiling for long hours, it is unlikely that Eliza had access to all of her remuneration. Aboriginal workers who were subject to agreements regulated under the *Aboriginals Protection Act* remained under the supervision of protectors,[52] who determined the amount of a wage that was received by a worker as 'pocket money', and the amount that would be deposited into a trust account.[53] In the event that Eliza wished to make use of funds in her trust account, she would have to endure the humiliation of seeking the permission of a protector.

[28] Today, it is impossible to determine if the protector who supervised Eliza treated her with fairness. Likewise, we will never know if Mrs Steele was a benevolent employer. However, it can be inferred that Eliza wanted more than life as a married domestic servant had to offer because by 1921 she had achieved the remarkable feat of living independently of both her husband and the authorities.

Freedom in Malaytown

[29] Six years after the Supreme Court of Queensland determined that Eliza remained subject to the *Aboriginals Protection Acts 1897–1901* (Qld), she once again attracted the attention of the police. Estranged from Joe Andrews, Eliza had taken residence in an informal settlement called 'Malaytown'.[54] Built on the banks of Alligator Creek on the 'swampy side of town',[55] Malaytown was a haven for those who were not welcome to live among the white residents of Cairns.

[30] Malaytown first appeared in the Cairns press in 1904, due to an outbreak of bubonic plague.[56] The *Morning Post* described the settlement as a 'motley township' that was inhabited by 'Chinese, Japanese, Javanese, Malays and

Cinghalese'.[57] By the 1920s, Torres Strait Islander and Aboriginal families had also joined the community.[58]

[31] Eliza's life in Malaytown would have involved a degree of hardship. Dwellings were perched on stilts over rotting mangroves and malaria was 'rife'.[59] There was only one tap for the entire community, and toilets were mere outhouses at the end of a jetty.[60] In spite of such conditions, former residents have described Malaytown as a welcoming and kind-hearted community.[61] Malaytown was also renowned for its Saturday evening dances where live music was played and alcohol flowed freely.[62]

[32] Those within Malaytown lived in relative autonomy. With the exception of a small number of individuals, most Aboriginal residents were able to manage their wages free of official control.[63] One can imagine that Eliza revelled in her independence. Perhaps for the first time, Eliza was making choices concerning her employment, how she spent her money, and the company that she kept. Tragically, her freedom would be short-lived.

[33] Eliza's fate was sealed by allegations contained in a letter to the Protector of Aboriginals from one Constable James of the Cairns Police District:

> I beg to report that [Eliza]…has for some considerable time past resided at Upper Kenny Street, Cairns. That portion of the Town is better known as Malaytown where a large number of Malays and others reside. I have received very reliable information from different sources that Eliza is carrying on as a Prostitute, and that she is visited regularly by Japanese, Malays, Aboriginals and others. Several complaints have been made to me of late regarding the conduct of this Gin. This Gin as far as I can ascertain is very much against signing on to an employae, and she certainly has a very great influence [over] other Aboriginals living in that locality.
>
> I would recommend that she be removed to Palm Island Mission Station.[64]

[34] Before dealing with the substance of Constable James' letter, it is important to draw attention to his description of Eliza as a 'Gin'. Together with 'black velvet' and 'lubra', 'gin' was part of a terminology that deprived Aboriginal women of their humanity.[65] Because they were represented as mere objects that were without feeling, generations of Aboriginal women were denied the protection of the law. The court acknowledges the pain and suffering associated with such language, the corrosive impacts of which continue to be felt by Aboriginal women in the present day.

[35] Just as Constable James' use of a notorious slur is revealing of his attitudes towards Aboriginal women, much can be inferred from the indignant tone of the letter. Indeed, one can almost imagine Constable James' fury as he struck the keys of his typewriter. His anger would have been fuelled, at least in part, by the double standards that were applied to liaisons between Aboriginal women and Asian men. Intercourse between white men and Aboriginal women was often justified as a 'necessary evil' on the frontier.[66]

In contrast, unions between Aboriginal women and Asian men were viewed with suspicion and invariably assumed to be immoral.[67]

[36] To make matters worse, Eliza had refused to sign on to an employment agreement, and become one of the thousands of disenfranchised Aboriginal workers throughout Queensland. Finally, she was exercising a 'very great influence' over other Aboriginal people. In other words, Eliza was intelligent, outspoken, and charismatic. An Aboriginal woman with such traits was anathema to the men within Queensland's Aboriginal and Torres Strait Islander bureaucracy.

[37] Less than a month after Constable James wrote his letter, the Home Secretary signed an order[68] for Eliza to be removed pursuant to s 9 of the *Aboriginals Protection Act 1897* (Qld). Section 9 provided:

> It shall be lawful for the Minister to cause every aboriginal within any District, not being an aboriginal excepted from the provisions of this section, to be removed to, and kept within the limits of, any reserve situated within such District, in such manner, and subject to such conditions, as may be prescribed. The Minister may, subject to the said conditions, cause any aboriginal to be removed from one reserve to another.

[38] The removals power was frequently used to extricate Aboriginal people who were unable to work, namely the elderly, the sick, and the disabled, from fringe camps and stations.[69] Deportation to a reserve was also a means of disciplining those who challenged the status quo. It was within this latter category that the order for Eliza's removal fell. According to the order, Eliza was to be taken to the state's most punitive reserve, Palm Island.[70] The ground for her removal was succinct—'prostitute'.[71]

[39] There would be no hearing during which Eliza would be afforded an opportunity to test Constable James' allegations. Not only was Eliza denied any semblance of a fair hearing, but she was also without a mechanism to appeal against the Home Secretary's order. On 16 November 1921, Eliza was arrested at the Cairns Watch House,[72] where she presumably spent the night. The following morning, she boarded the *S.S. Kuranda* for the voyage to Palm Island.[73]

Incarceration on Palm Island

[40] Just over 200 kilometres from Cairns, Palm Island is home to the Manbarra (traditional owners) and the Bwgcolman (historical residents).[74] Palm Island was selected by the Chief Protector of Aboriginals, J W Bleakley, to become a penitentiary for 'troublesome cases'.[75] For being an agitator, a 'communist', 'a larrikin', or a mere inconvenience, this was where Aboriginal people were sent.[76]

[41] For most of Eliza's incarceration, Palm Island was under the tyrannical rule of Superintendent Robert Henry Curry. During Curry's administration, inmates were controlled through curfews, Native Police patrols, and harsh reprisals for the slightest infractions.[77] Women who broke the rules were liable to suffer degrading punishments, such as having their heads shaved and being forced to wear hessian sack dresses.[78] Inmates were not only oppressed, but they were also vulnerable to poor health. Woefully inadequate rations led to malnutrition and a death rate that was almost double that of the state's.[79]

[42] In spite of his seeming omnipotence, Curry was not immune to scrutiny. In 1929, an inquiry was held into the allegation that Curry had used a whip resembling a cat-o-nine-tails to beat a female inmate 'senseless to the ground'.[80] Although the allegation was substantiated, Curry was merely cautioned.[81] His rule met an abrupt and violent end the following year.

[43] On the evening of 2 February 1930, Curry embarked on a rampage during which he murdered his two children, wounded the settlement doctor and his wife, and set several buildings alight.[82] As Curry's subordinates cowered in the bush with their families, it was up to the inmates to defend the settlement.[83] The siege would last for 16 hours before it was halted by an inmate, Peter Prior. Acting on the orders of officials, Prior shot and killed Curry.[84]

[44] One can only imagine the various hardships and indignities that Eliza suffered during her incarceration. In spite of everything that she endured, it seems that Eliza's spirit was not broken because in 1932 she agreed to marry a fellow inmate, Joe Salmon. The Chief Protector of Aboriginals granted permission for the marriage to proceed.[85] However, the wedding never took place due to some curious circumstances described by the Acting Superintendent, J A Cornell:

> as the day of the wedding approached, Eliza Andrews remembered that she had been married before and had a vague recollection that the marriage was performed in a Court House.[86]

[45] Had Eliza really forgotten that she remained married to Joe Andrews? Had she changed her mind about marrying Joe Salmon? We will never know the answers to those questions, and perhaps we never should, because those secrets belonged to Eliza alone. Three years later, this strong-willed Aboriginal woman died while still incarcerated on Palm Island.[87]

Conclusion

[46] Eliza Woree is one of the unsung heroines of our shared history. She endured in a time when the Native Police and settlers murdered Aboriginal people with impunity. She survived on the fringes of a society that was indifferent

to the dire circumstances of those whose lives had been torn apart by invasion. In pursuing the only real work available to Aboriginal women of her generation, Eliza would come under the service of Isaac Rigg. But for his failure to obtain a permit to employ her, we would now be denied the opportunity to learn about this courageous and resourceful woman.

[47] Eliza would go on to pursue a life that was unencumbered by either marriage or the heinous legislation that would deprive generations of Aboriginal people of the most elementary freedoms. Tragically, her independence was fleeting. As a punishment for her outspokenness and independence, Eliza was condemned to spend the final years of her life on Queensland's harshest reserve.

[48] Every person who becomes acquainted with Eliza will be enriched by her story, which has much to teach us about the beauty of perseverance in the face of devastation and unrelenting oppression. One hundred and fifteen years after her death, the court pays homage to Eliza Woree.

Notes

1 Nicole Watson.
2 *Re Walker* [2050] FNCA (1 February 2050).
3 *Treaty Between the Republic of Australia and the Confederation of Aboriginal and Torres Strait Islander Nations Act 2048* s 3(b) ('*Treaty Act*').
4 [1914] Qd St R 245.
5 'Employing an Aboriginal. The Lubra Who Was Married. What Control Has the Protector? Is the Wedding Ceremony a Farce', *Northern Herald* (Cairns, 26 December 1913) 26 <http://nla.gov.au/nla.news-article147173600> ('Employing an Aboriginal').
6 Ibid.
7 Section 3 defined 'half-caste' as any person 'being the offspring' of an Aboriginal mother and a non-Aboriginal father. The term 'half-caste' is evocative of the policies that gave rise to the Stolen Generations, and therefore, it is a source of great anguish for many Aboriginal and Torres Strait Islander people.
8 *Dempsey v Rigg* [1914] St R Qd 245.
9 Ibid.
10 'Employing an Aboriginal' (n 5).
11 Sir William Blackstone, cited by Alecia Simmonds, 'Courtship, Coverture and Marital Cruelty: Historicising Intimate Partner Violence in the Civil Courts' (2019) 45(1) *Australian Feminist Law Journal* 131, 139.
12 Helen Irving, *Citizenship, Alienage, and the Modern Constitutional State* (Cambridge University Press, 2016).
13 'Employing an Aboriginal' (n 5).
14 Ibid.
15 *Dempsey v Rigg* [1914] St R Qd 245, 246.
16 Ibid.
17 Ibid., 247.
18 Ibid.
19 Ibid.
20 Ibid., 248.
21 Ibid.
22 Ibid.
23 Ibid.

24 Ibid.
25 Queensland Marriage Certificate, Registration Number 1913/522 2055.
26 Letter from Constable Sticklen to the Inspector of Police Cairns, 28 June 1913, Queensland State Archives, Eliza and Joe Andrews—Marriages, 1913/1914, Item ID 336450.
27 Queensland Marriage Certificate, Registration Number 1913/522 2055.
28 Timothy Bottoms, *Cairns City of the South Pacific: A History 1770–1995* (Bunu Bunu Press, 2nd ed, 2016) 66.
29 Ibid., 73.
30 *The Queenslander*, cited by Matthew Daniel McCormack Richards, *Race around Cairns: Representations, Perceptions and Realities of Race in the Trinity Bay District 1876–1908* (PhD Thesis, James Cook University, 2010) 121.
31 Ibid., 122.
32 Jonathan Richards, *The Secret War* (University of Queensland Press, 2008) 8.
33 Ibid., 77.
34 Jonathan Richards, '"Many Were Killed from Falling Over Cliffs": The Naming of Mount Wheeler, Central Queensland' in Ian D Clark, Luise Hercus and Laura Kostanski (eds), *Indigenous and Minority Placenames: Australian and International Perspectives* (ANU Press, 2014) 148.
35 Henry Reynolds, 'Townspeople and Fringe-Dwellers' in Henry Reynolds (ed), *Race Relations in North Queensland* (History Department, James Cook University, 1978) 167.
36 Ibid., 170.
37 Richards (n 30) 123.
38 Bottoms (n 28) 151.
39 Henry Reynolds, *North of Capricorn: The Untold Story of the People of Australia's North* (Allen & Unwin, 2003) 32.
40 Ibid.
41 Richards (n 30) 153.
42 Shirleene Robinson, 'The Unregulated Employment of Aboriginal Children in Queensland, 1842–1902' (2002) 82 *Labour History* 1.
43 Richards (n 30) 165.
44 Letter from the Protector of Aboriginals to The Chief Protector of Aboriginals, 4 July 1913, Queensland State Archives, Crown Solicitor—Inwards Correspondence register, Other Departments miscellaneous, 1913–14, Item ID 302740.
45 Letter from Constable Sticklen to the Inspector of Police Cairns, 28 June 1913, Queensland State Archives, Crown Solicitor—Inwards Correspondence register, Other Departments miscellaneous, 1913–14, Item ID 302740.
46 Ann McGrath, *Illicit Love: Interracial Sex and Marriage in the United States of America and Australia* (University of Nebraska Press, 2015) 293.
47 Memo from the Deputy Chief Protector of Aboriginals to the Protector of Aboriginals Cairns, 16 July 1913, Queensland State Archives, Crown Solicitor—Inwards Correspondence register, Other Departments miscellaneous, 1913–14, Item ID 302740.
48 Queensland Marriage Certificate, Registration number 1913/522 2055.
49 Letter from the Protector of Aboriginals to The Chief Protector of Aboriginals, 4 July 1913, Queensland State Archives, Crown Solicitor—Inwards Correspondence register, Other Departments miscellaneous, 1913–14, Item ID 302740.
50 Joanne Scott and Raymond Evans, 'The Moulding of Menials: The Making of the Aboriginal Female Domestic Servant in Early Twentieth Century Queensland' (1996) 22(1) *Hecate* 139, 140.
51 Jackie Huggins, 'White Aprons, Black Hands: Aboriginal Women Domestic Servants in Queensland' (1995) 69 *Labour History* 188, 189.
52 *Aboriginals Protection and Restriction of the Sale of Opium Act 1897* (Qld) s 16 ('*Aboriginals Protection Act*').

53 Robert Castle and Jim Hagan, 'Regulation of Aboriginal Labour in Queensland: Protectors, Agreements and Trust Accounts 1897–1965' (1997) 72 *Labour History* 66, 68.
54 Letter from Constable James to the Protector of Aboriginals, 16 September 1921, Queensland State Archives, Eliza—Trust Accounts—Transfer and Miscellaneous, 1922/1010, Item ID 336727.
55 Regina Ganter, *Mixed Relations: Asian-Aboriginal Contact in North Australia* (University of Western Australia Press, 2006) 200.
56 'The Plague' *Morning Post* (Cairns, 15 March 1904) 5 <https://trove.nla.gov.au/newspaper/rendition/nla.news-article42957623.txt>.
57 Ibid.
58 Ganter (n 55).
59 Jeremy Hodes, 'Malaytown Talk Pt. 1' on Jeremy Hodes, *Queensland History: A Blog Devoted to Aspects of Queensland History that I Find Interesting* (8 March 2011) <queenslandhistory.blogspot.com/2011/03/malaytown-talk-pt-1.html>.
60 Jeremy Hodes, 'Malaytown Talk Pt. 2' on Jeremy Hodes, *Queensland History: A Blog Devoted to Aspects of Queensland History that I Find Interesting* (8 March 2011) <queenslandhistory.blogspot.com/2011/03/malaytown-talk-pt-2.html>.
61 'Malaytown' *Hindsight* (ABC Radio, 21 January 2007).
62 Ibid.
63 Ganter (n 55).
64 Letter from Constable James to the Protector of Aboriginals, 16 September 1921, Queensland State Archives, Eliza—Trust Accounts—Transfer and Miscellaneous, 1922/1010, Item ID 336727.
65 Hannah Robert, 'Disciplining the Female Aboriginal Body: Inter-racial Sex and the Pretence of Separation' (2001) 16(34) *Australian Feminist Studies* 69, 74.
66 Liz Conor, *Skin Deep: Settler Impressions of Aboriginal Women* (UWA Publishing, 2016) 288.
67 Regina Ganter, 'Living an Immoral Life: 'Coloured' Women and the Paternalistic State' (1998) 24(1) *Hecate* 13, 14
68 Order for Removal of Aboriginals, 9 October 1921, Queensland State Archives, Eliza—Trust Accounts—Transfer and Miscellaneous, 1922/1010, Item ID 336727.
69 Thom Blake, 'Deported...At the Sweet Will of the Government: The Removal of Aborigines to Reserves in Queensland 1897–1939' (1998) 22 *Aboriginal History* 51, 52–3.
70 Order for Removal of Aboriginals, 9 October 1921, Queensland State Archives, Eliza—Trust Accounts—Transfer and Miscellaneous, 1922/1010, Item ID 336727.
71 Ibid.
72 Letter from Actg. Sergt. H.S. Martin to Inspector Daley, Cairns, 19 November 1921, Queensland State Archives, Eliza—Trust Accounts—Transfer and Miscellaneous, 1922/1010, Item ID 336727.
73 Ibid.
74 Joanne Watson, 'A Century of Activism and Heartache: The Troubled History of Palm Island' (2018) 60 *Griffith Review* 220.
75 Ibid.
76 Ibid.
77 Ibid.
78 Ibid.
79 Toby Martin, '"Socialist Paradise" or "Inhospitable Island"? Visitor Responses to Palm Island in the 1920s and 1930s' (2014) 38 *Aboriginal History* 131, 134.
80 Joanne Watson, *Palm Island: Through a Long Lens* (Aboriginal Studies Press, 2010) 45.
81 Ibid., 46.
82 Ibid., 55–6.
83 Ibid., 60.
84 Ibid., 61.

85 Memorandum by the Chief Protector of Aboriginals, 8 November 1932, Queensland State Archives, Eliza Andrews and Joe Salmon—Marriages, 1932/8573, Item ID 336474.
86 Letter from the Acting Superintendent, E A Cornell to the Chief Protector of Aboriginals, 30 November 1932, Eliza Andrews and Joe Salmon—Marriages, 1932/8573, Queensland State Archives, Item ID 336474.
87 Eliza Andrews—Death Register, 1935, p. 55 Queensland State Archives, Item ID 302716.

12

SOUTH AUSTRALIA v LAMPARD-TREVORROW [2010] SASC 56

Commentary: *South Australia v Lampard-Trevorrow* [2010] SASC 56

False Imprisonment and a Public Vindication of Mr Trevorrow's Rights – Commentary on Kirsten Gray's Dissenting Judgment

Terri Libesman

Introduction

Bruce Trevorrow was removed from his family at 13 months old by stealth. He simply disappeared from hospital. His parents were given no explanation or opportunity to find out why.[1] When they tried to find him they experienced veiled threats with respect to removal of their other children.[2] State officials, pretending to have powers which they did not have, placed Bruce with a white family who had responded to a newspaper advertisement offering Aboriginal children for adoption.[3] This pernicious abuse of power is the stuff of nightmares. It is something which many living Indigenous peoples experienced and which suffuses their families and communities inter-generationally.[4] The ongoing lack of trust and failure by officials to Indigenous communities persists. These failings are highlighted by the Black Lives Matter movement.

Bruce Trevorrow was the first successful Stolen Generations litigant. Gray J's decision at first instance attracted much attention for this reason and because his analysis of both law and fact presented a shift, not a transformation, from previous Stolen Generations judgments.[5] When the Howard government rejected recommendations from the 'Stolen Generations' Inquiry with respect to an apology and reparations, members of the Stolen Generations placed their faith in the courts for vindication and redress.[6] The courts failed to provide justice for the litigants in *Kruger v Commonwealth*,[7] *Cubillo v Commonwealth*,[8] and *Williams v Minister of Aboriginal Land Rights Act and State of NSW (No 3)*,[9] with technical and narrow decisions. These decisions have been widely critiqued for their complicity in continuing harms and for the lost opportunity to provide a jurisprudence of regret.[10] The judiciary in these cases preferenced contemporaneous colonial documentary evidence over contextualised histories and the oral evidence of Indigenous witnesses.[11] The plaintiffs suffered immeasurable loss of family, culture, and identity in addition to brutal physical and sexual abuse, yet the courts provided no remedy for these harms.[12]

In contrast, Bruce successfully sued the State of South Australia for negligence, false imprisonment, misfeasance in public office, breach of fiduciary duties, and breach of procedural fairness. His success at first instance was related to colonial documentary evidence which was available to support his precise legal claims and the willingness of Justice Tom Gray to hear and give weight to Indigenous witnesses and expert socio-medical evidence.[13] The court was able to use the state's own records to prove that it had breached its own legislative scheme. The convergence of these factors is less likely to be available to other Stolen Generations litigants.

On appeal, Gray J's findings were upheld bar false imprisonment and breach of fiduciary duty.[14] Kirsten Gray provides a dissenting judgment with respect to false imprisonment. Whilst false imprisonment is a private tort, it holds public officials to account. The tort of misfeasance in public office, which is a public tort brought against officials for their abuse of power, was upheld in Bruce's case. However, it is notoriously difficult to prove and therefore unlikely to offer accountability to other Stolen Generations victims.[15]

The rule of law—with its core commitment to transparency and protection against the arbitrary exercise of power—is a foundational constitutional principle of the common law.[16] Most of us live secure lives without having to think about the rule of law or abuse of power by officials. When this does occur, we can expect redress. The intentional torts provide vindication for abuse of fundamental rights—often by state officials.[17] Kirsten Gray's dissenting judgment, which found that Bruce was falsely imprisoned, reveals the centrality of prejudiced attitudes and racist policy to his forced and unjustified removal.

This commentary makes three inter-related claims with respect to the Supreme Court's failure to uphold the trial judge's finding of false imprisonment and why Kirsten Gray's dissenting judgment is important. The first is with respect to the role of the intentional torts in vindicating rights to be free from unlawful interference by the executive and more generally to protect against the arbitrary exercise of power. The second is with respect to the significance of upholding these rights to protect common law constitutional values including the rule of law. The third is with respect to institutional and personal responsibility to reject racist behaviour. Related to this is the moral need to reflect upon and address latent sympathy for perpetrators, which mirrors and reinforces institutional bias.

A public vindication of rights

The intentional torts, including false imprisonment, provide for the vindication of rights and reparation. Vindication of rights through torts such as false imprisonment serves a hybrid private and public law purpose. They affirm values which are important not just to the particular litigant but to society. While the public significance of Stolen Generations litigation has been recognised by judicial officers,[18] their role in vindicating rights and adapting common law principles to address the circumstances before the court has not met this responsibility.

The tort of false imprisonment, whilst not often litigated, is usually brought against state officials to publicly hold them to account. It provides an important placeholder for and machinery with which to affirm foundational common law constitutional values. These include transparency and accountability of the executive to 'citizens and aliens'. Litigants such as Bruce afford the judiciary the opportunity to provide checks and balances with respect to the exercise of executive power, thereby affirming principles of responsible government and the rule of law.

Justice Tom Gray at first instance foregrounds these public aspects of false imprisonment with reference to frequently cited authorities:

> The tort addresses the unlawful restraint of personal liberty. Fullagar J described the 'mere interference with the plaintiff's person and liberty' as *prima facie* constituting 'a grave infringement of the most elementary and important of all common law rights'. In *Re Bolton; Ex parte Beane*, Deane J observed:
>
> The common law of Australian knows no *lettre de cachet* or executive warrant pursuant to which either citizen or alien can be deprived of his freedom by mere administrative decision or action. Any officer of the Commonwealth Executive who, without judicial warrant, purports to authorise or enforce the detention in custody of another person is acting lawfully only to the extent that his conduct is justified by clear statutory mandate.
>
> His Honour continued:
>
> It cannot be too strongly stressed that these basic matters are not the stuff of empty rhetoric. They are the very fabric of the freedom under the law which is the *prima facie* right of every citizen and alien in this land. They represent a bulwark against tyranny. Similarly, the House of Lords has described the tort of false imprisonment as one of the 'important constitutional safeguards of the liberty of the subject against the executive'.[19]

In this sense, litigants such as Bruce, as Kirsten Gray's judgment states at para 3, are not only bringing their case on behalf of themselves but also on behalf of other members of the Stolen Generations. Without affirmation of the 'place-holders' such as false imprisonment, the broader community—including other vulnerable groups—risks dilution or loss of these constitutional common law protections. Rights are hollow without a remedy for breach.

Julian Burnside, counsel for Bruce, observed that 'the Government of South Australia contested every point in the case. Nothing was too small to pass unchallenged'.[20] The State's 'concession' on appeal to refrain from challenging Bruce's compensation award smacks of blankets and rations. As Kirsten Gray's judgment notes at para 37, the state's appeal undermines the integrity of apologies and professed commitment to redress.[21] It also highlights the significance of the public vindicating function of false imprisonment—differentiated from its reparation function—and its moral and practical significance to contested colonial relationships. Here, as in other Stolen Generations litigation, we see the state and the courts complicit in using a narrow and technical argument to defeat not only the particular litigant's claim but the broader public acknowledgement of wrongs which offend common law rights. Kirsten Gray's judgment opines at paras 26 and 27:

> I do not accept that Mr Trevorrow was merely subject to 'no greater restraint' than 'many infants in his position'. We cannot compare the experiences of a young Mr Trevorrow to a non-Indigenous child who is not subject to the arm of the State through the actions of the APB. To do so is to compare apples with oranges.
>
> The restraint arose not from his infancy, his immaturity, or the duty of Mrs Davies to care for Bruce, but rather from the actions of the APB in the pursuit of a policy which only targeted Aboriginal children.

The removal of Bruce, and many other Indigenous children, was experienced as more akin to kidnapping, reflected in the descriptor 'Stolen' Generations, rather than lawful care by a foster parent or guardian. As the majority and Kirsten Gray's dissenting judgment notes, there was no false imprisonment case with facts directly applicable to Bruce's situation.[22] Applying common law principles to new fact situations is a staple common law method. The opportunity was open for the court to vindicate Bruce's rights yet, as Kirsten Gray's judgment states, they chose instead to apply ill-fitting analogies with thin justification.

While there has been a trend in limiting tort liability, in particular after the national Ipp review,[23] which resulted in reforms to the law of negligence nationally (such as the *Civil Liability Act 2002* (NSW), this contraction is challenged by a deeper and more enduring ethos of torts to protect those who are vulnerable.[24] It is particularly important to recognise and rectify past exclusions of Indigenous peoples from these protections, over contemporary and populist-fuelled trends which aim to limit tort liability. Reforms such as those after the Ipp review, to shift responsibility from those who caused harm to those who experienced harm, were fuelled by the media and insurance lobby.[25] The court's prioritising the containment of the limits of false imprisonment, with the contrived argument with respect to total restraint, serves to alienate and divide rather than express regret and remedy complicity in inequality. This further undermines the rule of law, as communities who fail to receive its protections lose faith in its veracity. While Bruce's situation did not fit neatly with existing categories of false imprisonment, the vindication of rights fits clearly with the purpose of this tort. Although the court recognised the significance of the litigation,[26] it failed to meet the challenge of justice through application of established principles to the facts.

The rule of law and equality

Widespread violations of rights, with the active toleration and participation of officials, needs to be addressed head-on. Law did not count for Aboriginal families such as Bruce's. Where law does not count this is a flouting of the rule of law which requires the strongest rejection and redress. Law failed Bruce and those who shared his experience twice. First with respect to the breaches by the APB and their officers, and second by the Court of Appeal in overturning the first instance finding that these individuals and institutions had falsely imprisoned Bruce.

The role of the common law in protecting 'constitutional' common law principles is more often assumed than expressed. However, the High Court has articulated the fundamental importance of courts providing remedies to those who have had their rights breached by executive and administrative bodies. Gaudron J states that the rule of law 'requires no less'.[27]

'Accountability' can be taken to refer to the need for the executive government and administrative bodies to comply with the law and, in particular, to observe relevant limitations on the exercise of their powers. Those exercising executive and administrative powers are as much subject to the law as are those who are or may be affected by the exercise of those powers. It follows that, within the limits of their jurisdiction and consistent with their obligation to act judicially, the courts should provide whatever remedies are available and appropriate to ensure that those possessed of executive and administrative powers exercise them only in accordance with the laws which govern their exercise. The rule of law requires no less.

The public has expectations that officials acting on behalf of the state fulfil their functions subject to the rule of law, that they act within the bounds of the law, and that the rights of plaintiffs such as Bruce are vindicated publicly. A foundational protection, which is enmeshed within the purpose of intentional torts—in particular, false imprisonment—is the protection against the arbitrary exercise of power. To retain or build faith in the rule of law it needs to hold individuals and institutions accountable for the power exercised over others. The failure, which Kirsten Gray's dissenting judgment addresses, is part of a long history of paradoxical colonial claims to equality before the law, and inclusion of

Aboriginal peoples within the protections of the common law, whilst in practice denying these legal rights.[28]

Rejection of racist values

We have an institutional and individual responsibility to reject racist behaviour and values. To do this requires a deep and ongoing commitment to reflect on our own attitudes and the standpoints of others, particularly those that are unfamiliar.[29] Within disputes, this requires attention to victim-blaming and sympathy for perpetrators.

While the common law claims to aspire to principles of equality and rejection of discrimination, these values sit incongruously with the Full Court overturning the judge at first instance's finding that Mrs Angas, the APB's agent, was prejudiced. The Full Court reversed the finding of prejudice with the anomalous '[w]e consider that the Judge's finding of prejudice cannot be supported, if by that he means that Mrs Angas was prejudiced against Joseph Trevorrow and Thora Karpany as individuals'.[30] Is prejudice not by definition applying general qualities without regard to the particular attributes of individuals? The finding of prejudice at first instance was qualified with the softener that 'she may well have been well-intentioned but unwittingly prejudiced'.[31] There seems, within these judgments, to be an anxiety to justify and minimise the moral culpability of the perpetrators of harm.

The Court of Appeal opined:

> No doubt the officers of the Department and of the APB, and others involved in the relevant events, thought that decisions they made and actions they took were in Bruce Trevorrow's best interests.[32]

Why was it necessary to speculate about and attribute good intentions to departments and people who implemented violent and racist policies? This attribution is in the face of findings that Mrs Angas was unsympathetic to Bruce's mother,[33] made unfounded presumptions about Bruce's parents' care for him being inadequate,[34] and misrepresented to Bruce's mother that Bruce was still recovering in hospital when he had been fostered to a white family, the Davies.[35] This judicial speculation is also in the context of the victim's evidence of the enduring harm which he experienced.

As Kirsten Gray's dissenting judgment notes at para 42, the Full Court's judgment may have been different had they experienced the wrongs:

> The majority suggest that it is 'artificial' to treat Mr Trevorrow's 'placement' with Mrs Davies as 'restraint'. One wonders how artificial these arguments would be if their children were suddenly the victims of such 'care' just because the State said so.[36]

There appears to be a desire to shield the perpetrators from shame or opprobrium, rather than focussing on the harm which their individual and institutional actions caused. To address these harms the focus should be on the impacts of Mrs Angas' actions as part of a systemic set of policies and attitudes which created a racist white world—a world which treated Bruce's, and other Indigenous peoples', legal and moral rights with utter disregard.

Conclusion

For the rule of law to be meaningful, when powers are abused the parties responsible must be held to account, and this is of particular importance when the abuse is systemic. Judicial institutions need to foster fidelity, through strengthening principles such as those found in torts such as false imprisonment, which support holding perpetrators to account. The rule of law is relational, and at the core of colonial-settler relations is a lack of fidelity. A necessary precondition to bringing fidelity to this relationship is an ethos of equality and inclusion in common law rights. The law needs to display fidelity to those whom it has overtly and indirectly excluded, to those to whom it has been complicit in prejudice and hypocrisy. The rule of law requires a reciprocal commitment between officials and citizens. The majority failed to deal with this unstated but writ large reason for the significance of Stolen Generations litigation in their narrow and unsatisfactory findings with respect to false imprisonment.

Community attitudes and actions also offer an avenue for public accountability-holding. Critical responses to the Stolen Generations litigation contribute to bringing officials and institutions, past and present, to account. Whilst courts play a special role, we must all hold public officials to account. Public advocacy and critical responses, such as Kirsten Gray's dissenting judgment and this book project, contribute to this commitment.

Notes

1 *South Australia v Lampard-Trevorrow* (2010) 106 SASR 331, 384 [246] ('*Lampard-Trevorrow*').
2 Ibid., [45].
3 Julian Burnside, 'The Stolen Generations' (20 June 2019) <https://www.julianburnside.com.au/the-stolen-generations/>.
4 Terri Libesman, *Decolonising Indigenous Child Welfare—Comparative Perspectives* (Routledge, 2014).
5 *Trevorrow v South Australia (No 5)* (2007) 98 SASR 136 ('*Trevorrow*').
6 Human Rights and Equal Opportunity Commission, *Bringing Them Home: Report of the National Inquiry into the Separation of Aboriginal and Torres Strait Islander Children from Their Families* (Report, 1997) ('*Bringing Them Home Report*').
7 (1997) 190 CLR 1.
8 (2001) 112 FCR 455 ('*Cubillo*').
9 (2000) Aust Torts Reports, 81–578.
10 See e.g. Antonio Buti, 'Kruger and Bray and the Common Law' (1998) 21(1) *University of New South Wales Law Journal* 232; Jennifer Clark, 'Cubillo v Commonwealth Case Note' (2001) 25(1) *Melbourne University Law Review* 218; Robert van Krieken, 'Is Assimilation Justiciable? Lorna Cubillo and Peter Gunner v Commonwealth' (2001) 23 *Sydney Law Review* 239; Chris Cunneen and Julia Grix, *The Limitations of Litigation*

in Stolen Generations Cases (Research Discussion Paper No 15, Australian Institute of Aboriginal and Torres Strait Islander Studies, 2004); Trish Luker, 'Intention and Iterability in *Cubillo v Commonwealth*' (2005) 28(84) *Journal of Australian Studies* 35; Ann Curthoys, Ann Genovese and Alexander Reilly, *Rights and Redemption: History, Law and Indigenous People* (University of New South Wales Press, 2008); Ann Genovese, 'Metaphor of Redemption, Myths of State: Historical Accountability in Luhrmann's Australia and Trevorrow v South Australia' (2011) 20 *Griffith Law Review* 67; Honni van Rijswick and Thalia Anthony, 'Can the Common Law Adjudicate Historical Suffering?' (2012) 36 *Melbourne University Law Review* 618.

11 Genovese (n 10); Curthoys et al. (n 10).

12 Cunneen and Grix (n 10).

13 Curthoys et al. (n 10).

14 *Lampard-Trevorrow* (2010) 106 SASR 331.

15 This is because the plaintiff has to prove malice or reckless indifference to the Briginshaw standard. This in practice means they have to prove beyond reasonable doubt the defendant's intention to carry out their public duty improperly. Unusually, in *Trevorrow* letters provided direct proof of the Aborigines Protection Board's ('APB') admission to acting illegally. A further hurdle is that courts do not usually apply vicarious liability to this tort. Again, unusually in this case, the Minister had a close relationship to and knowledge of the wrongs, including being a member of the APB.

16 *Australian Communist Party v Commonwealth* (1951) 83 CLR 1, 193.

17 Pam Stewart and Anita Stuhmcke, *Australian Principles of Tort Law* (The Federation Press, 4th ed, 2017).

18 *Cubillo* (2001) 112 FCR 455, [29]; *Trevorrow* (2007) 98 SASR 136, [431]; *Lampard-Trevorrow* (2010) 106 SASR 331, [426].

19 *Trevorrow* (2007) 98 SASR 136, [982].

20 Burnside (n 3).

21 *Lampard-Trevorrow* (2010) 106 SASR 331, [37].

22 Ibid., [30].

23 *Review of Law of Negligence Final Report* (Final Report, September 2002) ('*Ipp Report*').

24 Jane Stapelton, 'The Golden Thread at the Heart of Tort Law: Protection of the Vulnerable' (2003) 24 *Australian Bar Review* 135.

25 Margaret McMurdo, 'Dangerous Liaisons with the *Civil Liability Act 2003* (Qld)' (Speech, LexisNexis Professional Development Conference—Personal Injury in Queensland, 26 April 2006).

26 *Cubillo* (2001) 112 FCR 455, [29]; *Trevorrow* (2007) 98 SASR 136, [431]; *Lampard-Trevorrow* (2010) 106 SASR 331, [426].

27 *Corporation of the City of Enfield v Development Assessment Commission* (2000) 199 CLR 135.

28 Desmond Manderson, 'Not Yet: Aboriginal People and the Deferral of the Rule of Law' (2008) 29(30) *Arena Journal* 219.

29 Aileen Moreton-Robinson, *Whitening Race—Essays in Social and Cultural Criticism* (Aboriginal Studies Press, 2011).

30 *Lampard-Trevorrow* (2010) 106 SASR 331, 153.

31 *Trevorrow* (2007) 98 SASR 136, [144].

32 *Lampard-Trevorrow* (2010) 106 SASR 331, [13].

33 Ibid., [45].

34 Ibid., [29].

35 Ibid., [51].

36 Ibid., [42].

South Australia .... Appellant;

AND

Bruce Lampard-Trevorrow .... Respondent;

[2010] SASC 56

Torts—False imprisonment—Stolen Generations—Racist policies.

Gray J (dissenting).[1]

Introduction and acknowledgement

[1] I would like to begin by welcoming the representatives from the Ngarrindjeri Nation who are here today and who have welcomed us to their Country. We are on the beautiful land of Meningie, where the plaintiff in this case, Bruce Trevorrow, was born. As a stranger to these lands and as a fellow Aboriginal person, it is customary that I acknowledge that I walk on their Country and that I respect their laws whilst I do so. A failure to do this would subject me to their laws and its consequences. This is our way. This has always been our way as Indigenous peoples. We uphold and respect the rights of each other to exist against the world as mutual sovereigns of the Country to which our people have belonged for millennia.

[2] As a proud Muruwari and Yuwaalaraay woman, I pay my respects from my elders to the Ngarrindjeri, for their enduring survival and the resilience and pride which has marked and continues to mark their existence. I honour Uncle Bruce, who has recently passed, as well as his family, who are here today.

[3] Your resilience comes at a deep financial and personal cost, but I know that you are here, not only for yourselves and the person whom you loved, but for other Aboriginal people who may have been affected by similar wrongful removals at the hands of the state.

[4] It is fitting that the families have requested to have this matter be heard here, on the banks of the Coorong, not far from the Trevorrow family home all those years ago, where they have grown and fished and been nourished by the land which has sustained them since time immemorial.

[5] Conducting our proceedings on these lands provides the Court with an important opportunity to reckon with the life that was stolen from Mr

Trevorrow and his family. It is an opportunity to reflect on the way that non-Indigenous laws, which were motivated by misguided beliefs about what is better for Aboriginal people, can shatter those they were deemed to 'protect'.

Facts of the case

[6] Bruce Allan Trevorrow was born to parents Thora and Joseph on Kaurna Country in Adelaide in 1956. A proud Ngarrindjeri family, the Trevorrows lived a modest existence on the fringes at One Mile camp, just outside of Meningie. The Aborigines Protection Board ('APB') was in operation throughout the Trevorrows' time at One Mile, with Mr Trevorrow's brother, Tom, observing that from time to time he and his siblings, Hilda and George, would run and hide from the 'welfare'. Despite the presence of the APB in the region, the family remained together until the events that followed the hospitalisation of Mr Trevorrow in Adelaide Children's Hospital in 1957.

[7] On that fateful Christmas Day in 1957, Joseph sought assistance for Mr Trevorrow, who was unwell. Joseph's request to Sergeant Liebing for assistance in the form of an ambulance was not forthcoming, despite his insistence that the matter was urgent. Not having his own car meant that Joseph could not take Mr Trevorrow to the hospital. He managed to find help from neighbours, Mr and Mrs Evans, who drove a baby Bruce to the hospital. Little did Joseph know it was the last time that he would see his son.

[8] Mr Trevorrow was admitted to hospital with acute gastroenteritis. Following his admission, Mr Trevorrow recovered and was placed in the 'care' of Mrs Davies in early January 1958. This was the case despite there being no consent from Mr Trevorrow's parents, and the lack of licensing of Mrs Davies, who fostered Mr Trevorrow and continued to do so until he was returned to his mother nearly a decade later.

[9] Following his removal and subsequent placement with Mrs Davies, Mr Trevorrow suffered significant psychological, physical, and cultural harm which pervaded his existence.

[10] Whilst the facts of this case are unique, many children like Mr Trevorrow were removed unlawfully in South Australia, and under different assimilationist regimes across Australia. We know now that the experiences of those removed, who are called the 'Stolen Generations', directly affected between 20,000–25,000 people throughout the country and the effects can still be felt today.[2]

False imprisonment

[11] I disagree with the majority, Doyle CJ and Duggan and White JJ, who upheld the state's appeal and overturned Gray J's finding of false imprisonment. I

concur with their findings that the APB directly and unlawfully removed Mr Trevorrow from his family, that his lack of awareness of his removal was not material, and that he had no reasonable means of escape. However, I reject their finding that Mr Trevorrow was not under the total restraint of Mrs Davies whilst he was fostered in her care.[3]

[12] I disagree with the majority's finding that Mr Trevorrow's restraint arose only from his young age and the obligation of Mrs Davies to care for him. I do not accept that Mr Trevorrow had freedom of movement such as was available to other children. Mr Trevorrow was not like other children. In common with many Aboriginal children, Mr Trevorrow's removal from his family was based on policy and attitudes which often denigrated Aboriginal parents and culture. The majority have drawn ill-fitting comparisons between non-Aboriginal children in the lawful care of parents and guardians and Mr Trevorrow, whose circumstances are inseparable from his Aboriginality.

[13] The assessment of the majority fails to consider the entire context which brought Mr Trevorrow into the 'care' of Mrs Davies in the first place and the ongoing acts of the state in refusing to return him to his family.

[14] The majority are not treating like with like. The situation of an Aboriginal child in 1957 is not analogous to that of a non-Aboriginal child at the time. The 'care' provided by Mrs Davies was an extension of the original and ongoing total restraint of the state. I reject the argument that Mr Trevorrow somehow had the same freedom of movement appropriate to his age and stage of development and therefore his restraint was not total. Mr Trevorrow bore an additional burden of restraint that simply did not affect non-Indigenous children. The case law is clear that neither Mr Trevorrow's lack of knowledge nor physical inability to escape prevents making out a claim of false imprisonment.[4]

[15] The extent and nature of 'care' provided by the foster carers in this matter are immaterial to the overall restraint which commenced with the failure to return Mr Trevorrow from the hospital, and which continued for a decade with the ongoing failure to return him to his family. Whilst intention is not relevant to a finding of false imprisonment, the ongoing failure to return Mr Trevorrow to his family and the lack of care and support provided by the state when this finally did occur are relevant to the assessment of damages.

[16] Mr Trevorrow's total restraint was both ideological and physical. The state was ideologically opposed at the time to Aboriginal people raising their own children and sought to effect this ideology through policies of removal. Evidence from Mr Trevorrow's siblings in the trial attests to the ongoing presence of the 'welfare' in their lives, with Tom indicating that the 'welfare' would regularly conduct raids on the camps.[5]

[17] The state already assumed a degree of control over the lives of all Aboriginal people as their legal guardian at the time in South Australia. In Bruce's case,

this restraint was complete when the APB assumed physical custody of him. Mr Trevorrow was imprisoned without reasonable means of escape from the arms of the child removal policy of the day.

[18] The assimilationist ideas which underpinned welfare laws and policies were the basis for the actions of Mrs Angas of the APB in removing Mr Trevorrow from hospital and obstructing his family's numerous attempts to retrieve their child. However, it is important to note that these policies had changed by the time Mrs Angas separated Mr Trevorrow from his family. Mr Trevorrow's removal in spite of these changes demonstrates how such attitudes continued to be applied in practice, to devastating effect. Had the official policy been followed, Mr Trevorrow would never have been removed in these circumstances.

[19] The role of the Children's Hospital at the time must also be noted. Their records that Mr Trevorrow was 'obviously neglected' and suffering from 'malnutrition' were at odds with the comments made by Sergeant Liebing, who had observed him as well. The prejudice of the hospital staff, who had no information about and had never met Mr Trevorrow's family, yet recorded that they were off 'boozing', that the children were being nourished with alcohol and that Mr Trevorrow was 'one of [three] ¼ cast children', set the context for the actions of the APB which followed.[6]

[20] I concur with the findings of the trial judge with respect to false imprisonment. The state through the APB took Mr Trevorrow as a vulnerable infant and unlawfully placed him in the care of Mrs Davies, against the wishes of his family. They continued to support his placement with Mrs Davies whilst refusing his return to his parents. These actions constituted the initial and ongoing total restraint. This restraint caused Mr Trevorrow significant harm. What Mr Trevorrow lost in terms of his family, culture, and community—all of the things that make a person who they are—is irreplaceable.

[21] Mr Trevorrow was not the subject of a lawful 'care and protection' placement, and for this reason, I am not convinced by the state's invocation of his freedom within the care and protection system. Mrs Davies did not have ultimate control over whether Mr Trevorrow stayed in her care or was allowed to go home. The state retained this power in the form of the APB.

[22] Mr Trevorrow may have been in the care of Mrs Davies as a matter of fact, but he did not arrive at that destination through a process of law. Much evidence was presented to the trial judge which demonstrated this. I therefore concur with the reasoning of Gray J that:

> By placing the plaintiff with his foster family and refusing to return him to his parents for 10 years, the will of the plaintiff and his parents were overborne. Neither the plaintiff nor his parents consented to the removal. The plaintiff was imprisoned and the State and its emanations caused that imprisonment…The removal of the plaintiff that led to this imprisonment was unlawful. Therefore, the imprisonment was also unlawful.[7]

A gilded cage is still a cage

[23] For all intents and purposes, the care provided to Mr Trevorrow in those early years may have provided for some of his basic needs. However, it is the persistence of his removal from his family, not the apparent 'quality' of the care provided, which is in contention. Mr Trevorrow was held in this placement, unable to return home to his family, despite their desperate pleas. These were wilfully ignored, with the APB declaring that they had no intention of returning Mr Trevorrow to his family.[8] It is my conclusion, consistent with that of Gray J, that this constituted the false imprisonment of Mr Trevorrow.

[24] In reaching this conclusion, I draw on the findings of the trial judge at [991]–[992], as well as the comparable findings with respect to deprivation of liberty declared by Lady Hale in *P (by his litigation friend, the Official Solicitor) v Cheshire West and Chester Council & Anor* [2014] UKSC 19:

> If it would be a deprivation of my liberty to be obliged to live in a particular place, subject to constant monitoring and control, only allowed out with close supervision, and unable to move away without permission even if such an opportunity became available, then it must also be a deprivation of the liberty of a disabled person. The fact that my living arrangements are comfortable, and indeed make my life as enjoyable as it could possibly be, should make no difference. A gilded cage is still a cage.[9]

Ill-fitting comparisons

[25] I reject the well-meaning but nonetheless gratuitous analogy asserted by the majority that Mr Trevorrow's situation with his foster parents was somehow likened to an infant in a childcare centre.[10] For Aboriginal people, as I'm sure for others, and particularly Mr Trevorrow's family, this is offensive in the extreme.

[26] I do not accept that Mr Trevorrow was merely subject to 'no greater restraint' than 'many infants in his position'. We cannot compare the experiences of a young Mr Trevorrow to a non-Indigenous child who is not subject to the arm of the state through the actions of the APB. To do so is to compare apples with oranges.

[27] The restraint arose not from his infancy, his immaturity, or the duty of Mrs Davies to care for Bruce, but rather from the actions of the APB in the pursuit of a policy which only targeted Aboriginal children, to deprive them of their family. The trial judge found:

> that the South Australian Government, during the early to mid 20th century, engaged in the policy and practice of removing Aboriginal children from their families and communities with a view to absorbing the Aboriginal population into the remainder of the community.[11]

[28] The role of Mrs Davies, however well-meaning, was nevertheless a manifestation of the conditions and ultimately the restraint imposed by the state. Mr Trevorrow may have accompanied her and went wherever she allowed through the years, but ultimately, he was not able to go back to his family. It is worth considering whether, if Mrs Davies had not answered the advertisement looking for foster carers and refused to take Mr Trevorrow in those first days, the APB would have found some other non-Aboriginal person to care for him. Mrs Davies in this respect was merely a vessel carrying out a service to the state in furtherance of their 'benign' policy.

[29] The lack of directly relevant precedent has been highlighted in this case[12] and in its place, a number of references made to the situations of prisoners, child-care centres, and deportees. None of these assists the argument of the state in the present case, but rather, in my view, all offer various points of distinction.

[30] By refusing to identify the policies of child removal without consent as a form of false imprisonment, this court is being blind to the reality that faced a young Mr Trevorrow, his family, and his community. In doing so, it is complicit in the wrongs carried out by the state. Greater courage is needed to uphold the Trial Judge's finding at first instance and establish a more just precedent for other Aboriginal people who may have been removed by the state.

The voice of the community

[31] Alongside the evidence presented by Mr Trevorrow's family in this matter, I refer to the letter on behalf of a Ngarrindjeri Elder, which was submitted for the record in respect of the plaintiff.[13]

[32] The Elder submits that he has a rightful interest in this matter, given Mr Trevorrow's membership of the Ngarrindjeri peoples, and their place as the sovereign peoples over the land in the southern parts of the state, which span from Murray Bridge across to the Fleurieu Peninsular and then just south of Coorong near Kingston.[14] The letter is as follows:

> We, the Ngarrindjeri peoples, sovereign peoples…seek the reinstatement of the original judgment in this matter, to rightfully acknowledge the unlawful taking of Ngarrindjeri son, Bruce Trevorrow, from his parents Thora and Joe, from the Children's hospital in Adelaide following his discharge in 1958. We decry the actions of the State of South Australia in dismissing the deeds of their predecessors, which may prevent future cases being brought by Nunga people throughout the state.
>
> The actions of the State in bringing this case offend not only the memory of Bruce and his family that survive him, but also the pledges made by the State to not repeat mistakes of the past. Any such promises made either in furtherance of child welfare or other matters concerning Ngarrinderi peoples will be treated as false and hollow.

Bruce was denied the right to grow up on Country with his family, to speak his own language and to practise his culture with his peoples, we, the Ngarrindjeri. This matter has deeply affected all concerned, starting with Bruce and his family, and throughout the entire community.

The past is ever present

[33] Since the arrival of the British on our lands some 230 years ago, the Australian legal system has been inscribed with its own customs and values.

[34] The theory of eugenics has been imposed on our people, as it was in the lives of Mr Trevorrow and the Trevorrow family and countless other Aboriginal and Torres Strait Islander peoples through the separation of their children. This court acknowledges the current situation facing Aboriginal children and their over-representation within the child 'protection' system.

[35] The colonial legal system continues to impose its laws on Aboriginal peoples, including through removal and control over when and how Aboriginal parents get to see their children. The resemblance to past practice is evident in the letter from the Secretary of the APB to Constable Goldie dated 27 May 1959. This outlined Bruce's mother's wish to see him:

> As far as I am aware Mrs. Karpany has never requested that she actually see Bruce, but has demanded that the child be returned to her care. It would be possible for Mrs. Karpany to see Bruce in the presence of a Welfare Officer if suitable arrangements were made in advance. It would also be necessary for her to fully understand that the child will not be returned to her.[15]

[36] The state had an opportunity in this case to atone for the acts of its predecessors and leave the man it so damaged to live out the last of his years with his family, with the knowledge that the state had formally acknowledged its wrongdoing. Instead, the state, through these proceedings, offends the memory of the Plaintiff and the contrition it says it feels it honoured through the damages awarded to Mr Trevorrow.

[37] Counsel for the state pointed to the actions of their client in not seeking to retrieve these monies as evidence of honourable intent.

[38] On the contrary, in mounting this attack on the reasoning of Gray J in regards to his finding of false imprisonment, the state is not innocently seeking to correct the record, but rather manoeuvring to foreclose on legal responsibility for its past actions—actions which extend far beyond this matter and reach throughout the width and breadth of this state. This is the pernicious intent behind these proceedings.

[39] The path of the Plaintiff has been a particularly onerous one, which no financial compensation can make up for. That being said, unlike similar

matters involving members of the Stolen Generations, such as *Cubillo v Commonwealth [No 2]* (2000) 103 FCR 1 and *Williams v Minister, Aboriginal Land Rights Act 1983 and Anor* (1994) 35 NSWLR 497, the Plaintiff has succeeded where they have otherwise failed. Mr Trevorrow has jumped through the many hurdles required of him by the law, and particularly in regards to the evidence of the acts and omissions of the State of South Australia. These can be found in abundance in the various medical and administrative documents presented before Gray J.[16] This paper trail was of great benefit to the Plaintiff, a point emphasised by the trial judge, who made numerous findings based on that evidence.[17]

[40] However, in bringing this appeal, the state has sought to further burden those who come before the court in such matters. It is not enough that plaintiffs must prove wrongdoing at great cost and effort through the colonial historical record, which may be buried in state archives, destroyed, or inherently privileging colonial perceptions and experience; the state is seeking to make it even more difficult for ageing plaintiffs to seek redress for historical wrongs committed against them. For this, the state should be ashamed.

Addressing historical wrongs

[41] The majority suggests that it is 'artificial' to treat Mr Trevorrow's 'placement' with Mrs Davies as 'restraint'.[18] One wonders how artificial these arguments would be if their children were suddenly the victims of such 'care' just because the state said so.

[42] The law can see fit to call the application of false imprisonment 'artificial' in this case and yet it extends completely hypothetical comparisons to reality.

[43] What remedies, then, are available to those who have been wronged through policies of removal, as has happened in this case? It is not enough to say that the law has no remedy. The law, as an instrument of the state and the colonial powers at the time, had no trouble in creating a practice whereby Aboriginal children would be stripped from their cultural and familial ties. By their own advice from the Crown at the time, the state and its agents acted in a manner they knew was inconsistent and unlawful.

[44] The law should accordingly make room to provide redress for these past injustices perpetrated against Aboriginal and Torres Strait Islander peoples.

[45] I do not accept the position put by Counsel for the state that the application of the tort of false imprisonment in this instance amounts to an overreach of the law. On the contrary, I believe that it is the most relevant cause of action available to parties in situations involving the illegal and continued removal of their children by the state.

[46] A finding of false imprisonment holds the state accountable for their initial and ongoing acts that caused material harm to the plaintiff.

[47] By failing to draw a direct line between the behaviour of the state and false imprisonment, the Court is denying Aboriginal people acknowledgement of the truth that the law was complicit with the state in past acts of removal.

Orders

1. Appeal dismissed.
2. That representatives of the South Australian Government meet with the Trevorrow family and issue a formal apology for the actions of their predecessors in this case.

Notes

1 Kirsten Gray.
2 Australian Human Rights Commission, '2012 Face the Facts—Chapter 1' (2012) <https://humanrights.gov.au/our-work/2012-face-facts-chapter-1>.
3 *South Australia v Lampard-Trevorrow* (2010) 106 SASR 331, [307] ('*Lampard-Trevorrow*').
4 *Meering v Grahame-White Aviation Co* (1919) 122 LT 44; *Murray v Ministry of Defence* [1988] 1 WLR 692; *Herring v Boyle* (1834) 1 Cr M&R 377; *Lampard-Trevorrow* (2010) 106 SASR 331, [289].
5 *Trevorrow v South Australia (No 5)* (2007) 98 SASR 136, [300] ('*Trevorrow*').
6 *Lampard-Trevorrow* (2010) 106 SASR 331, [110].
7 *Trevorrow* (2007) 98 SASR 136, [991]–[992].
8 Ibid., [326].
9 *Lampard-Trevorrow* (2010) 106 SASR 331, [46].
10 Ibid., [298].
11 *Trevorrow* (2007) 98 SASR 136, [422].
12 *Lampard-Trevorrow* (2010) 106 SASR 331, [297].
13 This letter is a fictional account based on the broad views of Aboriginal child welfare advocates and peak bodies to the forcible removal of Aboriginal children from their families.
14 Mary-Anne Gale, 'Ngarringjeri', *Mobile Language Team* (2020) <https://mobilelanguageteam.com.au/languages/ngarrindjeri/>.
15 *Lampard-Trevorrow* (2010) 106 SASR 331, [42].
16 *Trevorrow* (2007) 98 SASR 136, [113]–[116].
17 Ibid., [826].
18 *Lampard-Trevorrow* (2010) 106 SASR 331, [307].

13

BACKFORD v BACKFORD [2017] FAMCAFC 1

Commentary: *Backford v Backford* [2017] FamCAFC 1

Keryn Ruska and Zoe Rathus

Introduction

This parenting case (*Backford*)[1] involves one Aboriginal mother, two fathers (one Indigenous and one not), and five children between the ages of six and 12 at the time of the trial in 2016. Our appeal judgment is written as a two-person joint judgment, imagining a sister judge, Bates J, who has written a separate judgment—the actual appellate judgment of the Full Court of the Family Court. We have also crafted different grounds of appeal for the mother than pleaded in the actual case. These two constructs enabled us to agree with Bates J regarding risk—a sad but inescapable central feature of this case. But we disagree with her in terms of the adequacy of consideration of the mother's Aboriginal culture and the right of her children to maintain their connection to that. We therefore allow some aspects of the mother's appeal, which leads to a different outcome and an order for a rehearing.

Close examination of this judgment reveals the issues and challenges for a Western legal system in recognising Aboriginal culture and identity as they exist in contemporary society. This is particularly so in urbanised communities, where Aboriginal and Torres Strait Islander families may be viewed as having no connection to 'traditional' culture, and therefore considered by external systems to have little or no culture at all. Although we accept that the trial judge had good reason to be concerned about risks for any children who live with the mother, we argue that better evidence about the mother's (and therefore the children's) Indigeneity could and should have been presented to the court, and this may well have changed how the overall family picture was perceived. We also argue that even the available evidence about Aboriginality was not interpreted in a culturally informed manner and this was also to the detriment of the mother.

Losing anonymity

Published family law judgments are anonymous, which we commend, but the result can be de-personalising of the parties—and places—and inconsistent practices are used. For example, in this judgment the two fathers are 'Mr Backford' and 'Mr Keys', the mother is 'the mother' (no name), her current partner is 'Mr E' (no name), and the children are all called by an initial—P, B, H, C, and G. Even the towns are rendered blank and characterless with letters. We have given names to all of the parties, the children, and some other key people. Where possible, we gave them a name starting with the first letter, or only letter, used in the judgment. For example, 'Mr Keyes' becomes 'Kevin' and 'B' becomes 'Belinda'. We have also given the three key towns names with Aboriginal meanings.[2] The case is obviously set in Country where there is a significant Aboriginal population and many towns are likely to have Aboriginal names. We have called T town 'Timbarra',[3] U town 'Ullamulla',[4] and Q town 'Quipolly'.[5]

We have included a diagram of the changing family constellations to assist in understanding the story being told.

Failure to properly consider Aboriginality

This case is the story of three interconnected households and the surrounding extended families and communities. Before the trial, the mother, who we have called Alison, was living with her current partner Eric and two of her daughters, Belinda and Carla. Belinda's father, Kevin, was living with Alison's other daughter Patricia, together with his current partner, Wendy, and their infant, Sonya. Carla's father, Barry, was living with his two sons from Alison, Henry and Gavin. A summary of the complex factual matrix is contained in our judgment. We have expressed the facts quite differently from both the trial judgment and the appeal. We deconstructed the facts presented across all of the available judgments and reconstructed the evidence in a manner more sensitive to culture and less surprised about, and critical of, some of Alison's decisions. This allowed a more nuanced narrative of the mother's life to emerge.

The mother is a proud member of the HH Nation.[6] That was part of her case. But our analysis reveals a strange contradiction between the stated attitude of a number of professionals involved in this case towards her Aboriginality and their ability to absorb that attitude into their actions and decision making. The judge, the mother's lawyers, and the family report writer (none of whom are Indigenous) all acknowledged and referred to the relevance of the mother's culture to the proceedings. Yet between them, they failed to facilitate its meaningful presence in the evidence or the ultimate decision.[7] They also failed to understand the extent to which evidence was in fact available. So, just what might these professionals be looking for to categorise as 'culture'? Is it ochre and digeridoos, or is it an appreciation of the experiences of colonisation—dislocation, poverty, and intergenerational trauma, but also resilience and strong family and community ties—that are deeply intrinsic to the shared experiences of Australia's Indigenous peoples?

We argue that, for the mother, her 'culture' involved both traits of traditional Indigenous ways of living and being and the shared experience of social chaos and separation from kin occasioned by colonisation. A revealing exchange between the trial judge and Alison portrays this dual identity perfectly. When asked about how she passed on culture to her children, she replied:

> By sitting them down with my grandfather. He tells a lot of stories of *what he went through with his mother as a stolen generation* as well and *what their culture is about.*

We also contend that the family law system provided vehicles for the relevant actors to obtain and consider material relevant to both these aspects of the mother's lived experience. Despite this, her Aboriginality was largely ignored in the final orders, which placed all five children with their respective fathers and provided for very limited visiting time with the mother, well away from her family and community.

The family law system and Aboriginal and Torres Strait Islander families

Our analysis of the history of recognition of Indigenous culture in family law parenting cases shows progressive change both legislatively and jurisprudentially. Since 1996 the *Family Law Act 1974* (Cth)[8] ('*FLA*') has included the recognition of Aboriginal and Torres Strait Islander culture as a factor in determining a child's best interests.[9] Parallel to this have been developments in case law that have explicitly noted the damaging consequences of colonisation and the importance of Aboriginal children understanding their place in a predominantly white culture. However, the trial judge only referenced some of the legislative provisions and no cases. The Full Court made reference to only one case[10] and excused the lack of specific reference to many sections of the *FLA* by the trial judge on the basis that her Honour was 'alive to the importance of the issue' of culture,[11] and the ultimate matter for determination was the best interests of the children.

In our judgment, we traverse all of the relevant sections and demonstrate how each deals with different elements of culture. They are a cumulative suite of sections rather than a menu to snack from. We also journey through the jurisprudence and note clear directions from the Full Court regarding the level of attention to be paid to both traditional culture and contemporary Black identity in all its multi-layered complexity.

In terms of the *FLA*, amendments in 2006 provided greater guidance on cultural issues. They explicitly recognise the right of an Aboriginal or Torres Strait Islander child to enjoy and maintain a connection with his or her culture.[12] They implemented the recommendations of the Family Law Council[13] (which endorsed the recommendations of the Family Law Pathways Advisory Group)[14] and would also likely have been influenced by the *Bringing Them Home* report.[15]

A review of research on Aboriginal child-rearing in Australia found that traditional child-rearing practices, although perhaps altered by colonialism and trauma, are still being widely practised and transmitted by Aboriginal people, and are often misinterpreted or misunderstood by mainstream professionals.[16] Mothers may be seen as less sensitive, vigilant, or attached to their child when assessments do not account for the differences in child-rearing practices. Of particular relevance to Alison's story is the extended family's role in child-rearing, differences in notions of attachment outside of the mainstream parent–child dyad, and the approach to child autonomy, which are common in many Indigenous cultures.[17]

In terms of jurisprudence, a seminal case regarding Aboriginal children occurred in 1995 just as the 1996 amendments were under consideration. *B v R and the Separate Representative*[18] ('*B v R*') involved an Aboriginal mother and a non-Indigenous father.[19] The Full Court held that evidence relevant to the case went 'well beyond any "right to know one's culture" assertion' and was required to understand 'the reality of Aboriginal experience' in Australia.[20] The court went on to say that in 'future cases' two types of material need to be 'explored': 'readily accessible public information of which it would be expected that a trial judge would inform himself or herself' as well as information from an 'appropriately qualified expert'.[21] Building on this case, and applying the subsequent changes to the *FLA*, jurisprudence started to emerge about the meaning of 'connection',[22] the breadth of family and kin relationships,[23] and the admissibility of evidence of Elders in relation to culture.[24]

Why the trial and appeal judgments fail to adequately deal with Aboriginality

Some of the cases where culture has been better accommodated involve families where a more orthodox view of culture is on display. In *Re CP*[25] and *Verran v Hort*[26] ('*Verran*') there are parties with Tiwi Islander heritage. The mother in *Verran* speaks Tiwi.[27] In *Davis v Spring* the mother is of the Western Arrernte peoples of central Australia and speaks Pitjantjara, Arrernte, and Luritja.[28] Expert evidence is garnered and its relevance is visible in the judgments. But in our case, culture seems invisible to the judge, even when presented to her.

While a narrative such as our case could apply to many Australian families, the facts of this case expose the 'reality of Aboriginal experience' (harking back to *B v R*). It is the reality of how the mother and her extended mob live their lives. As Goorie writer Melissa Lucashenko explained about the central family in her book *Too Much Lip*:[29] 'all they're doing is *living their lives* and completely Aboriginal. But they're *not performing* anything'.[30] According to *B v R*, these are the realities that the trial judge should have informed herself about.

The limited research which has investigated Indigenous people and the family law system shows that, despite the legislative and jurisprudential advances discussed, many Aboriginal and Torres Strait Islander people do not feel well understood. In Stephen Ralph's 2011 survey of Aboriginal and Torres Strait Islander litigants in the family law courts, the majority reported not believing that the cultural needs of the children had been properly considered by the court, and almost half did not believe the court had enough information about Indigenous cultural issues to be able to make a proper decision.[31] This suggests that the absence of information in *Backford* may not be unusual. Also, the vast majority believed that the Court did not display respect and understanding in response to their concerns about culture and its importance for Aboriginal and Torres Strait Islander children.[32] The family law practitioners surveyed held similar strong concerns about the courts' capacity to give due consideration to cultural issues.[33]

But in *Backford* it was not only the judge who had difficulty finding and understanding culture. The mother's lawyers never gathered the kind of specific evidence that would have built her case, such as affidavits from Elders and reports from cultural experts. It seems that they did not assist the mother to think about her cultural life and be ready to describe it to the judge. It may have been very difficult for Alison to give cogent instructions about her culture to her lawyers.[34] Likewise, how could Alison be expected to suddenly provide articulate testimony about her cultural and spiritual life and those of her children, when under cross-examination in family law proceedings?

Further, even though the family report writer was cognisant of the importance of culture, it is not clear how well this was dealt with in her report. Did she have the skills and knowledge to ask the right questions?[35] Research has also shown that Aboriginal clients often feel dissatisfied with family report writers and do not consider that they have a good understanding of Indigenous issues.[36] The 2012 report of the Family Law Council recommends the development of a cultural competency framework for the family law system at all levels, including family dispute resolution, family reports, and court processes.[37]

Contemporary Black culture

The complexity of contemporary Indigenous people and societies and the dynamic nature of cultural practices and identities are reflected not just in academic writing and government reports, but also continue to be expressed in popular culture. The Black Theatre in Redfern in the 1970s, Yirra Yaarkin Aboriginal Theatre Company in Western Australia, and Bangarra Dance Theatre, established in the 1980s, have all showcased this world. Television series such as *Redfern Now*[38] and the hilarious *Black Comedy*[39] provide all Australians

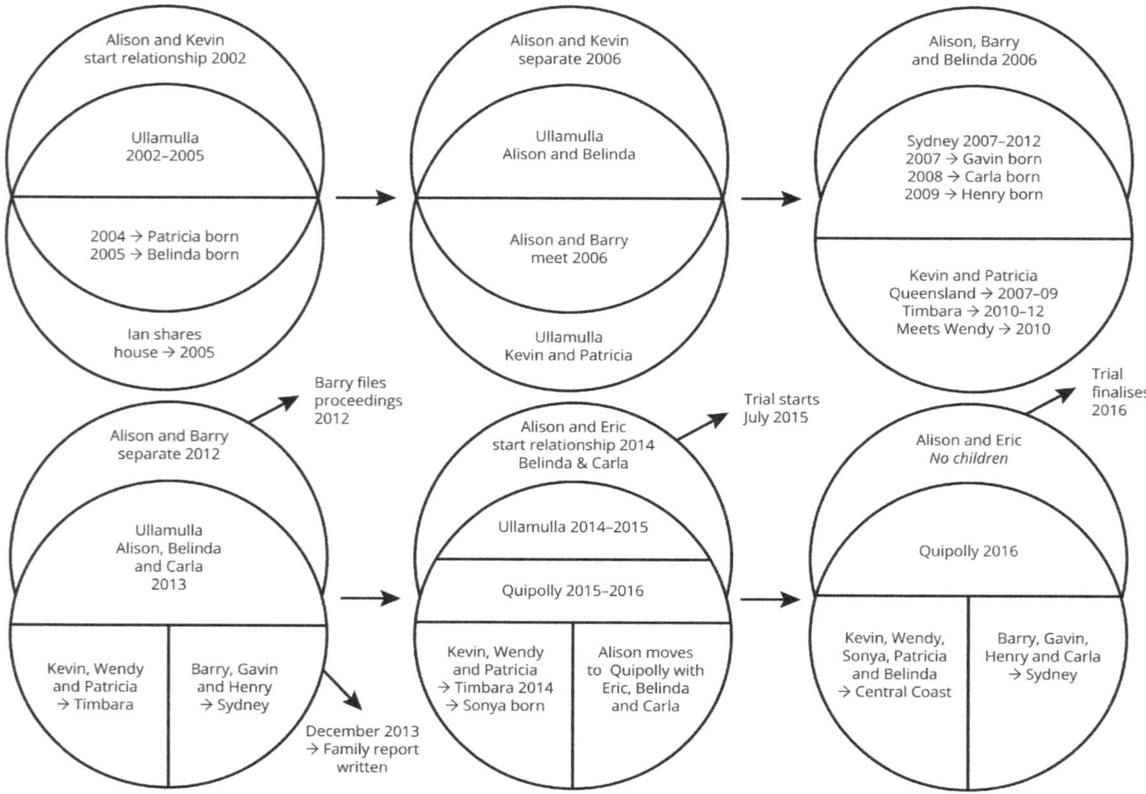

FIGURE 13.1 Family constellations over time and place.

with a glimpse into urban Indigenous life—with its bright talent, deep trauma, and abiding sense of humour.

Some contemporary Indigenous fiction beautifully expresses the multi-dimensional nature of pre and post-colonial 'culture' for 21st-century First Nations people. Alison and her life story could be dropped without a splash into Lucashenko's *Too Much Lip*,[40]—Alison's traditional cultural ties and ways of living and sharing, and her dislocation and displacement, simultaneously at play. But *Too Much Lip* also includes descriptions of the good times, the shared joys. These are totally absent from the narrative told in the judgment. This is what we say has been misunderstood in the *Backford* case. While looking for 'culture', all judges were missing the pervasive story about the shared experiences—traumatic and joyful—of Indigenous peoples in the 20th and 21st centuries.

Notes

1 Although we have rewritten the 2017 appeal, we had four other published judgments to draw from—three interim hearings in 2015 and 2016 and the trial in 2016: *Backford v Backford* [2015] FamCA 662, *Backford v Backford (No 2)* [2015] FamCA 678, *Backford v Backford* [2016] FamCA 106, and *Backford v Backford (No 2)* [2016] FamCA 206.

2 We chose names that started with the same initial letter from an old book of Aboriginal place names in New South Wales: WW Thorpe, *List of New South Wales Aboriginal Place Names and Their Meanings* (Australian Museum, 3rd ed, 1935).

3 Meaning 'grass tree'.

4 Meaning 'white gum trees'.

5 Meaning 'waterholes containing fish'.

6 We did not create a name for the mother's nation.

7 The independent children's lawyer does not seem to have played a very active role in this regard.

8 *Family Law Act 1975* (Cth) ('*FLA*').

9 *FLA* s 68F(2)(f) as amended by the *Family Law Reform Act 1995* (Cth).

10 *Donnell v Dovey* (2010) FLC 93–428. For a discussion about this case see Keryn Ruska and Zoe Rathus, 'The Place of Culture in Family Law Proceedings: Moving Beyond the Dominant Paradigm of the Nuclear Family' (2010) 7(20) *Indigenous Law Bulletin* 8.

11 *Backford v Backford* [2017] FamCAFC 1, 21.

12 See *FLA* ss 60B(2)(e), 60B(3), 60CC(3)(h), 60CC(6), 61F.

13 Family Law Council, *Recognition of Traditional Aboriginal and Torres Strait Islander Child-Rearing Practices—Response to Recommendation 22 Pathways Report: Out of the Maze* (Report, December 2004).

14 Family Law Pathways Advisory Group, *Out of the Maze—Pathways to the Future for Families Experiencing Separation* (Report, July 2001).

15 Human Rights and Equal Opportunity Commission, *Bringing Them Home: The Report of the National Inquiry into the Separation of Aboriginal and Torres Strait Islander Children from their Families* (1997).

16 Nicole Muir and Yvonne Bohr, 'Contemporary Practice of Traditional Aboriginal Child Rearing: A Review' (2019) 14(1) *First Peoples Child & Family Review* 153.

17 Ibid. See also Shaun Lohoar, Nick Butera, and Edita Kennedy, *Strengths of Australian Aboriginal Cultural Practices in Family Life and Child Rearing* (Child Family Community Australia Paper No 25, 2014); Gabrielle Lindstrom and Peter Choate, 'Nistawatsiman: Rethinking Assessment of Aboriginal Parents for Child Welfare Following the Truth and Reconciliation Commission' (2016) 11(2) *First Peoples Child and Family Review*

45; Soo See Yeo, 'Bonding and Attachment of Australian Aboriginal Children' (2003) 12(5) *Child Abuse Review* 292.
18 (1995) FLC 92–636 ('*B v R*').
19 Ibid.
20 Ibid., 82, 396.
21 Ibid., 82, 451.
22 See *Verran v Hort* [2009] FMCAFam 1 ('*Verran*'); *Sheldon v Weir* [2011] FamCAFC 212.
23 See e.g. *Donnell v Dovey* [2010] FLC 93–428.
24 See ibid.; *Verran* [2009] FMCAFam 1.
25 (1997) FLC 92–741.
26 *Verran* [2009] FMCAFam 1.
27 Ibid., 235.
28 *Davis v Spring* [2007] FamCA 1149, 1218.
29 Melissa Lucashenko, *Too Much Lip* (University of Queensland Press, 2018). Melissa Lucashenko won the 2019 Miles Franklin Award for this book.
30 Melissa Lucashenko in Conversation at Sydney Writers Festival, *Awaye!* (ABC Radio National, 11 May 2019) <https://www.abc.net.au/radionational/programs/awaye/11100752>.
31 Stephen Ralph, *Indigenous Australians & Family Law Litigation: Indigenous Perspectives on Access to Justice* (Research Report, October 2011) 31.
32 Ibid., 32.
33 Ibid., 35–8. See also Family Law Council, *Improving the Family Law System for Aboriginal and Torres Strait Islander Clients* (Report, February 2012) 52, which notes that a number of legal stakeholders raised concerns about insufficient attention being given to evidence about culture and a lack of understanding by judicial officers of the importance of culture in decision making about Aboriginal and Torres Strait Islander children. Similar feedback was received from Maori and Pacific Islander peoples and community organisations to New Zealand's Family Court Rewrite: *Te Korowai Ture a-Whanau: The Final Report of the Independent Panel Examining the 2014 Family Justice Reforms* (Final Report, May 2019), which highlighted the complexities that arise for legal systems in recognising culture and ways of being in a meaningful and inclusive way.
34 Diana Eades, 'Legal Recognition of Cultural Differences on Communication: The Case of Robyn Kina' (1996) 16(3) *Language & Communication* 215.
35 Ralph (n 31) 32, 37. In Ralph's survey, both Indigenous clients and legal practitioners were critical of family reports.
36 Ibid., 32, 52, 76; Keryn Ruska and Deborah Turner, 'Justice in Family Law: Through the Eyes of Aboriginal and Torres Strait Islander Women' (2009) 10(14) *Balayi: Culture, Law and Colonialism* 14.
37 Family Law Council (n 33) 98.
38 *Redfern Now* (Blackfella Films, 2012–2015), shown on Australian Broadcasting Corporation TV.
39 *Black Comedy* (Scarlett Pictures, 2014–2020), shown on Australian Broadcasting Corporation TV.
40 Melissa Lucashenko, *Too Much Lip* (University of Queensland Press, 2018).

Alison Backford .... Appellant;

AND

Barry Backford .... First Respondent;

AND

Kevin Keys .... Second Respondent;

[2017] FamCAFC 1

Family law—Children, infants, or minors—Parenting orders—Best interests of the child—Indigenous and non-Indigenous families—Cultural connection.

[1] Ruska and Rathus JJ.[1] This is an appeal by a First Nations mother, Alison, in a case where parenting orders for her five children were decided by Hannam J in the Family Court of Australia on 1 April 2016. The first respondent is Barry, the father of three of the children—Gavin, Carla, and Henry. The second respondent is Kevin, the father of Patricia and Belinda.

[2] When proceedings first commenced in 2012, Belinda and Carla lived with their mother, Patricia lived with her father, Kevin, and Gavin and Henry lived with their father, Barry. Some arrangements for the children to see the other parent and siblings were in place and we will turn to those in more detail later. When the trial commenced in July 2015 these were still the basic arrangements. By the time that judgment was delivered in April 2016, all five children were living with their respective fathers.

[3] In summary, the trial judge found that each parent's household presented some risk to the children. However, her Honour also found that each of the children would benefit from a meaningful relationship with both of their parents and should have an opportunity to develop stronger relationships with their siblings.

[4] The thrust of the orders made was as follows:

(i) That Patricia and Belinda live with their father, Kevin, and that he have sole parental responsibility for them;

(ii) That Gavin, Carla, and Henry live with their father, Barry, and that he have sole parental responsibility for them;

(iii) That the mother spend time with each of the two groups of siblings separately as agreed with their respective fathers or, failing agreement, every third weekend for three hours commencing at noon—on Saturday for Patricia and Belinda and on Sunday for Gavin, Carla, and Henry;

(iv) The mother is to collect the children from and return them to the respective father's residences;

(v) Orders were also made for other forms of communication.

(vi) The mother was restrained from allowing the children to come into contact with a family friend named Ian, and from leaving the children in the care of any other person when they are spending time with her.

Grounds of appeal

[5] The mother relies on five grounds of appeal. For the purposes of our judgment, we set out three:

(1) That the trial judge failed to have appropriate regard to the mother's Aboriginality;

(2) That the appellant was not afforded a fair trial because of the incompetence of her legal representatives as follows:[2]

(a) They failed to obtain appropriate expert evidence regarding the relevance of the mother's Aboriginality; and

(b) They failed to lead non-expert evidence regarding the mother's Aboriginality; and

(3) That the trial judge failed to order an updated family report despite material changes in the circumstances of the children between the date of the existing report and the trial.

We have not included her two grounds regarding the treatment of risks.

[6] We have had the advantage of reading the draft judgment of our sister, Bates J, which dealt with appeal grounds regarding risks. We reluctantly agree with her Honour's findings that the risks with the mother as currently known outweigh the benefits of the greater opportunity for connection to their culture that the children would enjoy if they were to live with or spend considerable time with her. On that basis, we agree that those grounds of the mother's appeal should be dismissed. However, we have interpreted the evidence about culture differently from our sister, and therefore disagree with her as to grounds 1 to 3 and uphold those grounds. Our reasons, findings, and orders are set out below.

Summary of case

[7] Alison is an Aboriginal woman of the HH Nation from north-west New South Wales. As a child, she lived in Ullamulla with her parents and six

sisters, of whom she is the oldest. Her grandparents and many other relatives lived there and in the surrounding towns.

[8] The second respondent father, Kevin, was at school with Alison. Kevin lived in Timbarra where the school was located, with his parents, grandparents, and other extended family. The towns are about 30 minutes' drive apart.

[9] Alison and Kevin were both born in 1985, and therefore, were 30 at the time of the trial. Their two children, Patricia and Belinda, were aged 12 and ten respectively at that time. The first respondent father, Barry, was born in 1972 and was 43 at trial. The three children he shares with Alison are Gavin, Carla, and Henry, who were eight, seven, and six respectively.

[10] All family law cases which reach the stage of a full trial involve complex family circumstances. However, this case is somewhat unusual in that the two men who are the fathers to the five children have been involved as parties to these proceedings from their commencement by the only non-Indigenous litigant, Barry, in December 2012.

[11] A number of the people whose interactions with Alison are relevant to this case were already known to her and part of her community in her early years. This includes the two men against whom the trial judge made findings of unacceptable risk to the children—Ian and Eric. Ian has lived on and off with Alison's family all of her life; with her parents when she was a child, with her when she was an adult, and later with various sisters. He was 44 when Alison was born and 74 at the time of the trial. Eric, who would become Alison's partner in 2014, was known to her when she was in high school.

[12] Alison and Kevin got together as a couple in 2002 when they were both 17. Their first child, Patricia, was born in 2004 when the parents were living in the mother's hometown, Ullamulla. In 2005 they shared a house there with Ian and their second child, Belinda, was born. By 2006 they had separated and, after some changes, Belinda stayed with Alison, who was still living with Ian, and Kevin took Patricia.

[13] Later in 2006, Alison met Barry online. He came to live with her, Belinda, and Ian in Ullamulla. Barry was 34 and the mother was 21. Over time Barry became a father figure to Belinda.

[14] In 2007, Alison, Barry, and Belinda moved to Sydney and Kevin moved to Queensland with Patricia. There was little or no contact between Kevin and Belinda and Alison and Patricia for a number of years after this.

[15] Later in 2007, Alison and Barry married and their first child, Gavin, was born.

[16] In January 2008, Ian indecently assaulted one of Alison's nieces in Ullamulla in a home where two of Alison's younger sisters and her grandfather were present. The assault was reported to police. Ian later pleaded guilty and he was sentenced to 12 months' imprisonment and placed on the Child Protection Register.

[17] Later in 2008, Alison and Barry's second child, Carla, was born.

[18] In 2009, Kevin moved back to Timbarra and his extended family with Patricia.

[19] In the same year, Henry was born to Alison and Barry. Alison was now 24 and had five children, four of whom lived with her and Barry.

[20] In 2010, Kevin met Wendy online and she moved to Timbarra to live with him. By this time Patricia was aged six years and started to call Wendy 'Mum'. Kevin was 25 and Wendy was 18. Both Kevin and Wendy are Aboriginal but neither actively identify as such.

[21] In 2012 there were a number of separations of the mother and Barry. At trial, Alison alleged that Barry was controlling and perpetrated family violence against her. Although we do not agree with the judge's dismissal of these allegations, we will not discuss that issue because her findings on that point do not affect our decision.

[22] Finally, the mother left Barry and went to Ullamulla, taking Belinda and Carla with her. She left Gavin and Henry with Barry in Sydney. By this time, Belinda and Carla were seven and four respectively and Gavin and Henry were five and three.

[23] She lived with her sister Jessica (whose daughter had been assaulted by Ian) for about 12 months. This was a time when Alison drank heavily and her sister's life was also chaotic. Belinda missed 104 days of school in 2013.

[24] Despite this, arrangements were made for all the children to see their non-resident parent. Alison re-established contact with Kevin and spent time with Patricia, and Kevin spent time with Belinda. Alison also spent time with Gavin and Henry in Sydney, and Barry spent time with Carla.

[25] At the end of 2012, Barry commenced parenting proceedings. Interim consent orders were made in February 2013 that the children each reside with the parent they were currently living with and spend time with their other parent.

[26] During that year, Alison moved to her paternal grandfather's home where her sister Marcia was also living with her boyfriend and their small child.

[27] A family report was prepared by Dr Ford in November 2013 and concerns were raised in respect of each household.

[28] In 2014, a number of unpleasant scenes occurred around Belinda, Carla, and Patricia involving abuse, violence, and excessive alcohol consumption in Alison's extended family.

[29] During this year Kevin and Wendy married and Sonya was born to them.

[30] In November 2014, Alison commenced a relationship with Eric. Eric is also Aboriginal. Eric had just been released on parole after serving a 12-year sentence for manslaughter. He also had other criminal convictions, including convictions for serious violence against a former partner.

[31] The evidence establishes that Alison had known Eric since she was at school. He is part of the extended family—brother to her sister Norma's husband Evan. The trial judge criticised the mother's decision to move to Quipolly to be with Eric. As Quipolly is 3.5 hours from Ullamulla, it was more difficult to arrange for the children to spend time with their non-residential parent.

Although we agree with Hannam J that the move occurred with haste and the mother should have advised the fathers, we do not find the relationship itself remarkable. Furthermore, the mother has a history of regular changes of residence, which is not uncommon among Aboriginal people.

[32] At Quipolly, Alison spent time with her two sisters who lived there—Yvonne and Norma. Ian continued to be a part of those sisters' lives despite his conviction for indecent assault of their niece.

[33] By December 2014, none of the parents made the children living with them available to the other parent.

[34] In 2015, the mother was charged with drink driving and driving with unrestrained child passengers and was disqualified from holding a licence.

[35] In May that year, Alison left the girls with Norma and Evan and an incident arose with Ian that has been fully described by Bates J in her judgment. Nothing eventuated from it.

[36] In about June 2015, all the children spent time with Alison, and Belinda spent time with Kevin and his household.

[37] The trial commenced on 20 July 2015 and details of Ian's and Eric's criminal histories emerged. As all the children and parents were in Sydney for the trial, her Honour suspended the existing orders and placed all five children with their respective fathers until the end of the trial, out of concern that the mother had no ability to protect them from the risk presented by Ian. At the end of the trial, and following the recommendations of the family report writer, the judge returned to the original orders on an interim basis and made orders restraining the mother from allowing the children to come into contact with Ian, Norma, and other named relatives.

[38] Submissions were made in September 2015 and the mother indicated that she would move to the Central Coast or Sydney to make it possible for all the children to spend time with both parents more easily. By then Kevin was living at the Central Coast and Barry was still in Sydney.

[39] In December, while the judgment was reserved, all the children spent time with Alison and then Belinda and Carla each spent time with their respective fathers. It was then discovered by each of the fathers that both girls had come into contact with Ian and some of the mother's sisters over the Christmas period. Barry applied to have the case re-opened and both fathers filed affidavits deposing to conversations with Patricia about contact with Ian while with her mother.

Appeal grounds 1 and 2

[40] The first two appeal grounds are:

(1) That the trial judge failed to have appropriate regard to the mother's Aboriginality;

(2) That the appellant was not afforded a fair trial because of the incompetence of her legal representatives as follows:

(a) They failed to obtain appropriate expert evidence regarding the relevance of the mother's Aboriginality; and
(b) They failed to lead non-expert evidence regarding the mother's Aboriginality.

[41] These grounds will be considered together because matters relevant to the trial judge's consideration of the mother's Aboriginality, and the presentation of this aspect of the mother's case by her lawyers, merge.

[42] Since 1996 the *FLA* has recognised the importance of connection to culture for Indigenous children, and now there are a number of sections directly relevant to this issue—ss 60B(2)(e), 60B(3), 60CC(3)(h), 60CC(6), and 61F, with definitions in s 4.

[43] Sections 60B(1) and (2) set out the objects and underlying principles of Part VII of the *FLA*. One of the principles articulated in s 60B(2)(e) is that children have a right to enjoy their culture (including the right to enjoy that culture with other people who share that culture). In considering the applicable law, the trial judge cited these objects and underlying principles but did not apply them to the evidence.

[44] Sub-section 60B(3) provides that Aboriginal and Torres Strait Islander children have the right to:

a) maintain a connection with that culture; and
b) have the support, opportunity and encouragement necessary:
   (i) to explore the full extent of that culture, consistent with the child's age and developmental level and the child's views; and
   (ii) to develop a positive appreciation of that culture.

[45] Her Honour made no reference to s 60B(3), although when considering Barry's parenting capacity, Hannam J noted the 'concerns' of Dr Ford 'about the capacity of [Barry] to facilitate the children staying connected with their cultural roots'.[3] Her Honour continued that, although Barry gave evidence 'that he thought it was very important for the children to maintain a connection with their Aboriginal culture', he also said that 'when the children lived with him and the mother as a family they never enjoyed any aspects of an aboriginal culture and the mother did not ever discuss with him the way in which the children could enjoy their aboriginal culture'.[4] It is of note that Barry 'denied denigrating Aboriginals and their culture'[5] under cross-examination because this assumes that the mother had instructed her lawyers that he did. The trial judge drew no conclusions from this evidence.[6]

[46] The trial judge then considered the primary considerations in s 60CC(2). She found that the children 'will be advantaged by having a meaningful relationship' with each of their parents, given the role each parent has played in their lives and the 'obvious bond[s]' which exist.[7] But she found that it was not in the children's best interests to live with the mother, given the unacceptable risk in the mother's household, implicitly applying s 60CC(2A).

[47] Her Honour then turned to the additional considerations in s 60CC(3). Although s 60CC(3)(h) is not explicitly referred to, we infer that the heading 'Aboriginal and Torres Strait Islander background and the children's right to enjoy their culture'[8] is intended to address this provision. Section 60CC(3)(h) provides a specific consideration in the determination of the best interests of an Aboriginal or Torres Strait Islander child as follows:

a) The child's right to enjoy his or her Aboriginal or Torres Strait Islander culture (including the right to enjoy that culture with other people who share that culture); and
b) The likely impact any proposed parenting order will have on that right.

[48] To understand how her Honour approached this section, it is necessary to trace her reasoning. She commenced by reflecting that Dr Ford had referred to '"cultural issues" a number of times'[9] and that a range of submissions had stressed the concern that the 'children would be denied the right to enjoy their culture' in their respective fathers' households.[10] To gain insight into the meaning of s 60CC(3)(h), her Honour properly turned to s 4 and cited the definition of 'Aboriginal or Torres Strait Islander culture'. In summary, s 4 states that 'culture' means the 'culture', including 'lifestyle and traditions' of the 'community or communities to which the child belongs'.

[49] This led her Honour to determine that:

> The mother did not adduce any evidence with respect to the culture of the Aboriginal community to which the children belong. There is also very little evidence of the lifestyle and traditions of this community.[11]

[50] Despite this, she acknowledged that 'the children would clearly have a greater likelihood of enjoying the culture of that community in her care than with their respective fathers'.[12] But this finding was not determinative, and Hannam J found that 'the issues relating to the enjoyment of Aboriginal culture are less weighty than matters concerning the protection of the children from harm and parental capacity'.[13]

[51] While we agree with the trial judge's findings in relation to risk, we disagree with her Honour on the question of culture. We find that considerable evidence was presented that demonstrated the role and significance of culture in the lives of Alison and the children. These differences are significant to how the orders in relation to the children's time with their mother should have been framed.

[52] The transcript shows support for the mother's position on appeal that evidence regarding her Aboriginality was not presented by her lawyers nor absorbed into the judgment. The exchange between the mother and the trial judge set out below was not included in her Honour's reasons:

Judge: So only you as a [HH Nation] person can make sure that a child has the advantages of a [HH Nation] culture?

Alison: Yes. That is correct. Yes.

Judge: And how have you done that to date? How have you given all of your children the advantages of their culture and their identity?

Alison: By sitting them down with my grandfather. He tells a lot of stories of what he went through with his mother as a stolen generation as well and what their culture is about.

Judge: So he educates them about those aspects of his culture?

Alison: Yes, yes.

Judge: Is that the *only way* in which you have your children take advantage of their Aboriginal culture?

Alison: Yes. Because my grandfather is the only elderly ... member left in the family.[14]

[53] The judge's follow-up question, with the words 'only way', may have shut down a fuller response from the mother. Perhaps if the judge had acknowledged the mother's connection to her family and country, and asked about that, a more fulsome reply may have occurred.

[54] Direct evidence of cultural practice and knowledge was also given by Eric. Under questioning from the judge, he testified that Carla and Belinda 'were aware of matters relevant to their heritage, including knowledge of their totem, food gathering practices and collecting significant rocks'.[15] This evidence is also not mentioned in the trial judgment.

[55] While it is clear from this exchange that the trial judge elicited relevant evidence from the mother and Eric as to the cultural practices of the mother and children, there is no reference to that evidence in her Honour's judgment when she addresses the issue of Aboriginal culture. It is a significant omission from the judgment in a case where the trial judge was concerned about the lack of evidence about culture.

[56] Section 60CC(6) adds greater detail to s 60CC(3)(h), providing that a child's right to enjoy his or her Aboriginal or Torres Strait Islander culture includes the right to:

a) Maintain a connection with that culture;
b) To have the support, opportunity and encouragement necessary:
   (i) To explore the full extent of that culture, consistent with the child's age and developmental level and the child's views; and
   (ii) To develop a positive appreciation for that culture.

[57] This section was also not referred to in the trial judgment. There was no consideration of how the children would maintain a connection with their culture or how they would be supported and encouraged to explore and develop an appreciation for their culture, despite submissions being made on the mother's behalf in relation to this issue. The mother was clearly concerned that the children's connection to their culture would not be supported. Consideration of the matters in s 60CC(6) is particularly important in matters such as this where the children will not be living with their Aboriginal mother.

[58] The case of *Lawson v Warren*[16] highlights the importance of connection to family for an Aboriginal or Torres Strait Islander child's sense of identity and belonging. The Court there said:

> As I understood [Mr W, expert] and the maternal great-grandmother's evidence, it is not about any specific aspect of culture, but rather for the child to have the opportunity to be around family in order to establish awareness, identity and belonging. Without this an indigenous child may feel confused and alienated. As they reach adolescence there may be an overwhelming sense of dislocation and confusion of identity. These matters are accepted.[17]

[59] Even though the trial judge had decided that the children should live with their respective fathers, the proper application of ss 60B(2)(e), 60B(3), and 60CC(3)(h) required a consideration of the cultural practices of the mother to determine what orders should be made regarding the children's time with her. The orders currently in place provide very limited contact with the mother, but also between siblings. Murphy J in *Nineth v Nineth [No 2]*[18] held that the relationship between Aboriginal siblings is particularly important because of their Aboriginality and the understood importance of family and kin.[19] Because the judge failed to appreciate the evidence that was available and found there was no evidence of culture, we find that there was no proper consideration of the children's right to maintain a connection to that culture under ss 60B(3), 60CC(3)(h), or 60CC(6).

[60] Section 61F was introduced in the *FLA* by the *Family Law Amendment (Shared Parental Responsibility) Act 2006* (Cth). The Full Court in *Donnell v Dovey*[20] provides guidance on its application:

> [183] It will be seen that s 61F, in the form ultimately enacted, applies to all cases involving an Aboriginal or Torres Strait Islander child. In proceedings under Part VII relating to such a child, the court *must* have regard to the child-rearing practices of the relevant Aboriginal or Torres Strait Islander culture. Failure to take account of that provision would, in our view, ordinarily amount to appealable error.[21]
>
> [184] Section 61F does not say that the outcome will be determined by application of the relevant kinship obligations and child-rearing practices, but the court must have regard to them. In our view, this can only be seen to be done if findings are made regarding those obligations/practices and adequate reasons are given to explain why a decision has been made that either follows or departs from them. We accept this can be done without the court making express reference to s 61F, but we consider it would be desirable that the section is at least mentioned, if not discussed.

[61] Although there is a discussion of the mother's relationship with her family, the trial judge does not mention s 61F. She noted the close relationship between the mother and her family, particularly her sisters, and quite rightly expressed concern about the ongoing relationships between at least two of

the mother's sisters and a cousin and Ian. While we agree with the trial judge's assessment of risk in relation to those family members, it is commonly known that there are broader family and kinship relationships in Aboriginal and Torres Strait Islander cultures and those should have been considered. That the trial judge did not do so may be in part due to the lack of evidence tendered on behalf of the mother. However as discussed above, additional evidence was adduced by her Honour's questioning of the mother and Eric but was not referred to in her judgment.

[62] In *B v R*[22] the Full Court concluded that in cases involving an Aboriginal child, evidence of particular cultural issues should consist of both 'readily accessible public information' that a trial judge would be expected to know and information that could be gathered and presented to the court by a suitably qualified expert.[23] Information about the broader family and kinship relationships of Aboriginal and Torres Strait Islander families is 'readily accessible public information' that could have informed her Honour's consideration on s 61F. We find that her Honour erred in not having appropriate regard to s 61F.

[63] We now turn to the question of whether the failure of the mother's legal representatives to obtain expert or non-expert evidence about the mother's Aboriginal culture denied her the opportunity of a fair trial. The trial judge was not assisted by the mother's lawyers, who failed to present cogent evidence regarding the mother's Aboriginality. Her Honour noted that the mother indicated that she wished to lead evidence about her culture and the trial 'languished for some time'[24] to allow her lawyers to gather this evidence. But the trial judge considered that no significant evidence regarding culture was provided.

[64] The mother's legal representatives were not limited to anthropological or peer-reviewed evidence. The Full Court has accepted that evidence related to Indigenous cultural practices need not be given by an anthropologist or other academic expert. Indeed, the best evidence may be that given by an Elder of the Indigenous community,[25] or 'such other person within the indigenous community who is accepted by the community as being able to speak with authority on its customs'.[26] Evidence from such a person from the mother's community would have assisted the court to understand not just the traditional culture of the mother's HH Nation but also the contemporary cultural practices of the mother. The former Indigenous Family Consultant and Indigenous Liaison Officer programmes of the Family Court were of invaluable assistance to judges in gathering, or assisting clients to present, such evidence to the Court in past years. It is lamentable that these programmes were discontinued.

Appeal Ground 3

[65] The third ground of appeal is:

(3) That the trial judge failed to order an updated family report despite material changes in the circumstances of the children between the date of the existing report and the trial.

[66] It is astounding to us that neither the trial judge nor any of the legal representatives sought an updated family report. It is not uncommon for a court to take note of a family report that is somewhat dated, but in this complex multi-party, mixed-race group of families, failing to have a contemporaneous family report at trial left huge gaps in the evidence about both culture and risk. Dr Ford had never even met the mother's new partner, Eric, because he was not on the scene in December 2015, and he was crucial to the assessment of both culture and risk. Further, she had not seen Kevin and Wendy with Sonya, nor observed how that blended family was functioning with the half-sisters who are about ten years apart in age.

[67] The orders we make will require a re-trial and it is quite likely that everything will have changed by the time this case returns to court or settles. More of the children will be able to express cogent views to a family report writer. There will be evidence of whether or not the mother has been able to implement the existing orders and see the children. Finally, the fathers' attitudes to the mother's ongoing relationships with the children will have been tested, as will their commitment to facilitating the children's connection to culture.

[68] Although we are cognisant of the costs and uncertainty that a re-trial will bring, we are somewhat buoyed by the unusual comments of our sister judge who said, at the conclusion of her judgment:

> While I do not wish to encourage further litigation, as presently advised I do not see anything in her Honour's reasons which would prevent the mother from making a further application for more time with the children if she was, for example, to relocate to the Central Coast or Sydney and able to persuade the court that Ian and Eric were no longer involved in her life.[27]

Orders

[69] We allow the mother's appeal in respect of grounds 1 to 3 and remit the matter for rehearing. We hope that, at any re-trial, there will be an updated family report regarding risk and appropriate evidence regarding the mother's cultural connections and lifestyle and the rights of her children to enjoy these essential elements of their identity.

Notes

1 Keryn Ruska and Zoe Rathus.
2 *Button v Lo Criccio* [2010] FamCAFC 87; *Badawi v Badawi* [2017] FamCAFC 129; *Leighton & Carey* [2010] FamCAFC 94.
3 *Backford v Backford (No 2)* [2016] FamCA 206, 227 [109].
4 Ibid.
5 Ibid.
6 Ibid.

7 Ibid., 41 [221].
8 Ibid., 56.
9 Ibid., 56 [298].
10 Ibid.
11 Ibid., 56 [300].
12 Ibid., 56 [302].
13 Ibid.
14 Transcript of Proceedings, *Backford v Backford (No 2)* (Family Court of Australia, 5703/2012, Hannam J, 20 July 2015) 341–2 (emphasis added).
15 Transcript of Proceedings, *Backford v Backford (No 2)* (Family Court of Australia, 5703/2012, Hannam J, 23 July 2015) 410–11.
16 [2011] FamCA 38.
17 Ibid., 72 [215].
18 [2010] FamCA 1144.
19 Ibid., [112].
20 *Donnell v Dovey* [2010] FLC 93–428.
21 The Full Court cited *Davis v Spring* [2007] FamCA 1149 as 'an illustration of a case in which s 61F was properly treated as an "integral" part of the decision making process'.
22 [1995] FLC 92–636.
23 Ibid., 82, 414.
24 Transcript of Proceedings, *Backford v Backford (No 2)* (Family Court of Australia, 5703/2012, Hannam J, 20 July 2015) 341–2.
25 *Hort v Verran* [2009] FamCAFC 214, [104]; *Donnell v Dovey* [2010] FLC 93–428.
26 *Donnell v Dovey* [2010] FLC 93–428.
27 We have inserted the names we have used in this judgment and changed 'we' to 'I'—otherwise this is the exact wording of the second-to-last paragraph of the rewritten judgment: *Backford v Backford* [2017] FamCAFC 1 [120].

PART V

Criminalisation and criminal neglect

14

ROACH v ELECTORAL COMMISSIONER (2007) 233 CLR 162

Commentary: *Roach v Electoral Commissioner* (2007) 233 CLR 162

Jonathan Crowe and Dani Larkin

Roach v Electoral Commissioner[1] ('*Roach*') is one of the most significant cases in recent Australian constitutional history. The plaintiff, Vickie Lee Roach, was an Aboriginal woman serving a six-year prison term. The case examined amendments to the *Commonwealth Electoral Act 1918* concerning the right of prisoners to vote in federal elections. The *Commonwealth Franchise Act 1902* had originally excluded federal and state prisoners serving sentences of one year or longer from the franchise. The *Commonwealth Electoral Act 1918* maintained this rule until 1983, when the disqualification was restricted to prisoners serving sentences of five years or longer. In 2004, the Act was amended to reduce the disqualifying sentence to three years. Then, in 2006, the legislation was further amended to make any prisoner serving a current sentence ineligible to vote.

A majority of the High Court (comprising Gleeson CJ, Gummow, Kirby, and Crennan JJ) upheld the 2004 amendment but struck down the 2006 change. Gleeson CJ recognised that 'the words of ss 7 and 24, because of changed historical circumstances including legislative history, have come to be a constitutional protection of the right to vote.'[2] However, the right is subject to exceptions. The disqualification of prisoners serving substantial sentences falls into this category. Gummow, Kirby, and Crennan JJ reached a similar result, using more cautious language. They did not speak explicitly of an implied constitutional right to vote[3] but nonetheless held that ss 7 and 24 rule out disproportionate restrictions on universal franchise.

The approach taken by the majority judges in *Roach* was reaffirmed in the 2010 case of *Rowe v Electoral Commissioner*[4] ('*Rowe*'). The case concerned the validity of amendments to the *Commonwealth Electoral Act 1918* that effectively prevented applications for inclusion or change of details on the Commonwealth electoral roll from being accepted after the day that writs were issued. Late applicants were therefore unable to vote, whether or not they were otherwise eligible. The previous arrangement, adopted in 1983, had allowed a seven-day grace period from the issuing of the writs to the closing of the rolls. The High Court ruled by a bare majority that the early closure of the rolls was unconstitutional. The majority, comprising French CJ, Gummow, Bell, and Crennan JJ, viewed the change as placing a disproportionate restriction on the franchise.

Roach and *Rowe* departed from the long-standing reluctance of the High Court to recognise any constitutional protection of the right to vote. The High Court rejected the notion of a constitutional guarantee of adult suffrage in *Attorney General* (Cth); *Ex rel McKinlay v Commonwealth*[5] ('*McKinlay*') and declined in *McGinty v Western Australia*[6] ('*McGinty*') to establish a guarantee of equal voting value. The express protection of the right to vote in s 41 of the *Constitution* was held in *R v Pearson; Ex parte Sipka*[7] to be a dead letter.[8] However, there were references throughout both these cases to the important position of representative democracy in the constitutional framework. McTiernan and Jacobs JJ took the view in *McKinlay* that 'the long established universal adult suffrage may now be recognised as a fact and as a result it is doubtful whether...anything less than this could now be described as choice by the people.'[9] In the same case, Murphy J reasoned that democratic elections necessarily required uniform adult suffrage.[10]

These sentiments were echoed by some of the judges in *McGinty*. Brennan CJ and Gummow J declined to uphold the principle of equal vote value, but they were nevertheless open to the possibility that Parliament cannot place new restrictions on adult franchise. Brennan CJ noted that the franchise has expanded in scope over time and thought that it was 'at least arguable that the qualifications of age, sex, race and property which limited the franchise in earlier times could not now be reimposed so as to deprive a citizen of the right to vote.'[11] Gummow J expressed a similar view, opining that what amounts to popular choice must be 'determined by reference to the particular stage which then has been reached in the evolution of representative government'.[12] Gaudron and Toohey JJ likewise opined that a system which denied universal adult franchise would not satisfy the requirement in ss 7 and 24 that representatives be 'chosen by the people'.[13]

The view of McTiernan and Jacobs JJ in *McKinlay* found further support in the judgment of Deane and Toohey JJ in *Nationwide News Pty Ltd v Wills*.[14] Their Honours adopted the position that representative government necessarily requires 'all citizens of the Commonwealth who are not under some special disability' to have equal voting rights.[15] This understanding of the democratic franchise as an evolving aspect of the constitutional framework was echoed by McHugh J in *Langer v Commonwealth*.[16] His Honour observed that the question '[w]hether or not a member has been "chosen by the people" depends on a judgment, based on the common understanding of the time, as to whether the people as a class have elected the member.'[17]

Nonetheless, it was not until *Roach* that a High Court majority clearly acknowledged the constitutional importance of a universal adult franchise and confirmed the need for a 'substantial reason' to justify a departure from universal suffrage.[18] The decision was therefore controversial. The dissenting judgments of Hayne and Heydon JJ in both *Roach* and *Rowe* criticised the majority judges for relying on unsupported constitutional implications.[19] Several prominent constitutional scholars, including Jeffrey Goldsworthy, Anne Twomey, and Nicholas Aroney, also criticised the cases for being insufficiently grounded in the original meaning and context of the Constitution.[20] Other commentators have defended the decisions, including one of the present authors.[21]

Our rewritten judgment endorses the view of the majority judges that the Constitution contains an implied, conditional guarantee of universal franchise. However, we contend that the majority, in upholding the 2004 Act and disenfranchising prisoners serving significant sentences, did not go far enough. In particular, the majority judges make only passing mention of the vastly disproportionate incarceration rates of Aboriginal and Torres Strait Islander people and the impact this has on their participation in the electoral system.[22] We draw attention to this important factor, discussing the social causes of Indigenous incarceration (including its impact on women), and use it to argue that any exclusion of prisoners from the franchise is disproportionate and therefore constitutionally invalid.

We also refer to Canadian constitutional jurisprudence, particularly the case of *Sauvé v Canada*.[23] This case is referenced by the High Court in *Roach*,[24] but we suggest it could have been utilised differently to draw out the disproportionate impact of the prisoner disqualification on Indigenous voting rights. Canada differs from Australia due to the role of the *Canadian Charter of Rights and Freedoms*. Nonetheless, the Supreme Court's nuanced discussion of the significance of Indigenous incarceration for electoral participation provides a model that Australian courts could follow in applying the implied rights jurisprudence in a more socially and historically contextualised manner, taking account of the ongoing impact of colonialism on Indigenous people today.

Notes

1 *Roach v Electoral Commissioner* (2007) 233 CLR 162 ('*Roach*').
2 Ibid., 174.
3 Ibid., 199–200.
4 *Rowe and Another v Electoral Commissioner* [2010] HCA 46 ('*Rowe*').
5 (1975) 135 CLR 1 ('*McKinlay*').
6 *McGinty and Others v Western Australia* (1996) 186 CLR 140 ('*McGinty*').
7 (1983) 152 CLR 254.
8 For criticism of this decision, see Jonathan Crowe and Peta Stephenson, 'An Express Constitutional Right to Vote? The Case for Reviving Section 41' (2014) 36 *Sydney Law Review* 205.
9 *McKinlay* (1975) 135 CLR 1, 36.
10 Ibid., 69.
11 *McGinty* (1996) 186 CLR 140, 166–7.
12 Ibid., 286–7.

13 Ibid., 201 (Toohey J), 221–2 (Gaudron J).
14 (1992) 177 CLR 1.
15 Ibid., 72.
16 (1996) 186 CLR 302.
17 Ibid., 343.
18 *Roach* (2007) 233 CLR 162, 174 (Brennan CJ), 199 (Gummow, Kirby and Crennan JJ).
19 *Roach* (2007) 233 CLR 162, [157]–[162] (Hayne J), [179] (Heydon J); *Rowe* (2010) 243 CLR 1, [194]–[205], [219]–[221] (Hayne J), [292]–[304] (Heydon J).
20 See e.g. Jeffrey Goldsworthy, 'Original Meanings and Contemporary Understandings in Constitutional Interpretation' in HP Lee and Peter Gerangelos (eds), *Constitutional Advancement in a Frozen Continent* (Federation Press, 2009) 267–8; Anne Twomey, '*Rowe v Electoral Commissioner*: Evolution or Creationism?' (2012) 13(2) *University of Queensland Law Journal* 181; Nicholas Aroney, 'Towards the "Best Explanation" of the Constitution: Text, Structure, History and Principle in *Roach v Electoral Commissioner*' (2011) 30(1) *University of Queensland Law Journal* 145; James Allan, 'The Three "Rs" of Recent Australian Judicial Activism: *Roach*, *Rowe* and (No)'Riginalism' (2012) 36(2) *Melbourne University Law Review* 743.
21 Jonathan Crowe, 'The Narrative Model of Constitutional Implications: A Defence of *Roach v Electoral Commissioner*' (2019) 42(1) *University of New South Wales Law Journal* 91. See also Graeme Orr and George Williams, 'The People's Choice: The Prisoner Franchise and the Constitutional Protection of Voting Rights in Australia' (2015) 8(2) *Election Law Journal* 123.
22 *Roach* (2007) 233 CLR 162, [36] (Gummow, Kirby and Crennan JJ), [173] (Hayne J). The judgment of Gleeson CJ recognises the disproportionate impact of the prisoner disqualification on vulnerable socio-economic groups but fails to specifically address the position of Indigenous Australians. See *Roach* (2007) 233 CLR 162, [22]–[23].
23 *Sauvé v Canada (Chief Electoral Officer)* [2002] 3 SCR 519.
24 *Roach* (2007) 233 CLR 162, [13]–[15], [18] (Gleeson CJ), [100] (Gummow, Kirby and Crennan JJ).

Vickie Lee Roach .... Plaintiff;

AND

Electoral Commissioner .... Defendants;

(2007) 233 CLR 162

Constitutional law—Legislative power—Universal franchise—Voting rights—Prisoners—Imprisonment—Aboriginal and Torres Strait Islander peoples.

[1] Larkin and Crowe JJ.[1] Vickie Lee Roach is an Aboriginal woman serving a six-year term of imprisonment at the Dame Phyllis Frost Centre in Deer Park, Victoria. She is enrolled to vote in the Federal Division of Kooyong in Victoria. Ms Roach grew up in Sydney's outer western suburbs. She was raised by a foster family, with whom she had a difficult relationship. She ran away from her foster family for the first time at age nine, and for the final time at age 13. After that, she was obliged to support herself and became involved with drugs and prostitution. It was around that time that she met her birth mother for the first time, and discovered she was Aboriginal. Her mother and Ms Roach both identify as members of the Stolen Generations.

[2] Ms Roach spent significant time in the juvenile justice system as a teenager and commenced her first prison sentence as an adult at the age of 17, after being convicted for self-administration of heroin. She served a six-month sentence, left prison for four months, then served another sentence for credit fraud. After that, she stayed out of prison for ten years. She married and had a son, but her partner was abusive and suffered from alcoholism, and the marriage eventually broke down. The dissolution of Ms Roach's marriage led to acrimonious and emotionally draining court proceedings where her ex-partner was named the residential parent for her son.

[3] Ms Roach formed another relationship, but that partner was also abusive. He almost killed her several times. She left the relationship, but he tracked her down. Ms Roach was arrested along with him after they robbed a convenience store in December 2002. She was driving the getaway car with police in pursuit when she struck a parked car at a traffic light. Ms Roach was sentenced to six years' imprisonment with a four-year non-parole period for recklessly causing injury. While in prison, she studied sociology, philosophy, and literature, and ultimately completed a master's degree in professional writing from Swinburne University. She is the plaintiff in this case.

[4] The *Australian Constitution* ('*Constitution*') was not the product of a legal and political culture, or of historical circumstances, that created expectations of enfranchisement and democratic representation for Indigenous peoples. It was, rather, the product of violent invasion, forced displacement, and colonial rule. That history is germane to this case. We concur with Gleeson CJ and Gummow, Kirby, and Crennan JJ that the *Australian Constitution* contains an implied, conditional guarantee of universal franchise, which cannot be abridged without a compelling reason. However, the majority judges' decision to uphold a ban on voting by prisoners serving significant sentences fails to take adequate account of its disproportionate impact on Indigenous voters.

The constitutional and legislative context

[5] Part VI (ss 81–92) of the *Commonwealth Electoral Act 1918* provides for the establishment and maintenance of a roll of electors for each electoral division. Part VII (ss 93–97) sets out the qualifications and disqualifications to enrol and vote. Section 93 provides that persons who have attained 18 years and are citizens are entitled to enrol and, if enrolled, to vote at Senate and House of Representatives elections. However, there are exceptions. One such exception, contained in s 93(8AA), concerns prisoners serving sentences under Commonwealth, state, or territory law. Between 2004 and 2006, this exclusion applied to prisoners serving sentences of three years or longer. However, it was amended in 2006 to apply to all prisoners without distinction.

[6] Gleeson CJ and Gummow, Kirby, and Crennan JJ hold that the 2006 law is invalid as a disproportionate restriction on the universal franchise. Hayne and Heydon JJ say this goes too far; they would uphold the 2006 Act. We say it does not go far enough; any ban on prisoners voting, provided they meet the usual criteria for enrolment, is constitutionally invalid. The present section explains the constitutional basis for the conditional guarantee of universal franchise. We agree with the majority judges that this guarantee is subject to reasonable and proportionate restrictions. However, we disagree that the 2004 Act is such a restriction. This is because it imposes a disproportionate burden on Indigenous Australians, who are particularly affected by the prisoner disqualification.

[7] Sections 7 and 24 of the *Constitution* provide that members of the Senate and House of Representatives must be 'directly chosen'. Those words are part of a broader constitutional scheme of representative government, as recognised by several members of this Court in *Nationwide News v Wills*[2] and *Australian Capital Television v Commonwealth*.[3] Sections 7 and 24 'further the institutions of representative and responsible government'; they should be given a purposive interpretation with this aim in mind.[4] These provisions do not exist in a vacuum; their meaning is influenced by surrounding social and

constitutional narratives, including narratives about the meaning of representative government. This meaning is not static, but evolves over time.

[8] McTiernan and Jacobs JJ said as long ago as 1975 that 'the long established universal adult suffrage may now be recognised as a fact.'[5] They meant that it is a social fact, but it is also a constitutional fact, for the *Constitution* is part of the social fabric. As Windeyer J famously and correctly observed, 'the enunciation by courts of constitutional principles based on the interpretation of a written constitution may vary and develop in response to changing circumstances'.[6] The so-called 'universal franchise' is, of course, not truly universal; even today, only 76% of the Indigenous population is enrolled to vote.[7] The expectation of universal franchise is, however, now well established as part of the normative framework of Australian representative government.

[9] There are some forms of disenfranchisement that would clearly be inconsistent with this normative expectation. These include, for example, disenfranchising voters who belong to a particular race, religion, gender, or political party. It was, indeed, the case at Federation that women could not vote in some state elections, and members of particular races (including not only Indigenous peoples but also people from Asia, Africa, or the Pacific Islands) were disenfranchised for significant parts of Australia's history.[8] However, the evolution of representative government is such that these forms of exclusion are no longer consistent with the terms and structure of the *Constitution*. They would not produce the kind of governmental system the *Constitution* requires.

[10] Those are easy cases. Others are more difficult. Representative government, like other legal concepts, creates both a 'core of settled meaning' and a 'penumbra of debatable cases'.[9] The disenfranchisement of prisoners is an issue on which the members of this Court disagree. Never in Australian history, prior to 2006, has that disqualification encompassed all prisoners without distinction. It is plausible that the Australian constitutional narrative does not recognise such a measure as consistent with the practice of representative government. On the other hand, Australian law has always disqualified at least some serious offenders. It is on this basis that the majority judges in this case find that the 2006 Act should be struck down, but the 2004 Act should be upheld.

[11] Legislative history is germane to constitutional reasoning since it shows the evolving boundaries of social conduct, but it is not the only factor this Court should consider in determining whether a restriction on the franchise is proportionate. Other aspects of history are also relevant. If a restriction on the franchise impacts disproportionately and unfairly on a segment of the population—particularly one that is already vulnerable and disadvantaged for other reasons—then this, too, should be taken into account. That is the case here, considering the disproportionate impact of restricting prisoners' voting rights on Australia's Indigenous population, as detailed further below.

Indigenous disenfranchisement

[12] Indigenous Australians have experienced significant political limitations placed upon their civil rights since colonisation.[10] They were politically excluded from the consultation and debates which led to the *Constitution*'s enactment.[11] As a result, the *Constitution* was created in a way that contradicted principles of equality and a true sense of representative democracy in excluding a portion of the nation's interests, namely those of Indigenous Australians, from consideration.[12] Those actions have led to the establishment of political institutions and electoral processes entrenched within the *Constitution* that have maintained the unequal political standing of Indigenous Australians by limiting their access to political engagement through voting.[13]

[13] Prior to Federation, for state elections, only Aborigines who held freehold title were allowed to vote in Queensland[14] and Western Australia.[15] However, New South Wales, South Australia, Tasmania, and Victoria did not exclude Aborigines from voting in their state elections, which meant they were also entitled to vote for the first federal parliament in 1901.[16] After Federation, the Indigenous franchise was limited again with the passing of the *Commonwealth Franchise Act 1902*. This legislation limited Indigenous Australians from enrolling and voting at Commonwealth elections through its explicit targeting of 'native people' of Australia and other countries.[17]

[14] The *Commonwealth Electoral Act 1918* was reformulated in 1949 to recognise Indigenous voting rights at federal elections, but only if they fell within s 41 of the *Constitution*.[18] Section 41 provides that 'no adult person' entitled to vote at state elections should be prevented from voting at federal elections 'by any law of the Commonwealth'.[19] Therefore, only Indigenous citizens who had the right to vote at the state or territory elections where they resided were able to enrol and to vote at Commonwealth elections. It was not until 1962 that the *Commonwealth Electoral Act 1918* was amended to give Indigenous Australians generally the right to vote. Indigenous Australians were also not subject to compulsory voting for Commonwealth elections until 1984.[20]

[15] The primary electoral disqualification that affects Indigenous voting in Commonwealth elections is the prisoner disqualification. The *Commonwealth Franchise Act 1902* had originally excluded federal and state prisoners serving sentences of one year or longer from the franchise. The *Commonwealth Electoral Act 1918* maintained this rule until 1983, when the disqualification was restricted to prisoners serving sentences of five years or longer. In 2004, the Act was amended to reduce the disqualifying sentence to three years. Then, in 2006, the legislation was further amended to make any prisoner serving a current sentence ineligible to vote. Prisoners will not appear on the certified list of voters for elections prepared by the Australian Electoral Commission if they fall within this disqualification provision.[21]

[16] The provision, on its face, appears neutral as to race. However, this does not take account of the statistical data that shows Aboriginal and Torres Strait Islanders are disproportionately incarcerated. Indigenous Australians comprise less than three per cent of Australia's population,[22] but 24 per cent of the national prison population. This figure, rather than reducing, continues to increase over time.[23] These rates of incarceration mean that Indigenous Australians are disproportionately affected by the prisoner disqualification.[24] This disadvantage, furthermore, occurs against a broader backdrop of vulnerability and dispossession, stemming from Australia's colonial history, which continues to affect Indigenous people today.

Indigenous pathways into incarceration

[17] Any discussion of Indigenous incarceration rates must include acknowledgement and understanding of continuing post-colonial dispossession and intergenerational trauma. Those experiences have been shown to cause significant levels of psychological and cultural disempowerment of Indigenous Australians, which can lead to frustrated, destructive, and anti-social behaviour towards authorities, agencies, and other people from the community.[25] The impact of European colonisation on Indigenous Australians was highlighted in the *National Report of the Royal Commission into Aboriginal Deaths In Custody*.[26] Limitations have historically been placed on the ability of Indigenous people to express their cultural identity and practice their cultural traditions.[27]

[18] Indigenous Australians across the country have also been subject to alarming rates of child removals. The Australian government targeted 'half-caste' Aboriginal children and removed them from their parents' care and into the care of the state without reason or justification to do so. Aboriginal children, like the plaintiff's mother, were placed in institutions and trained to grow up as good European labourers or domestic workers.[28] This is commonly referred to as the Stolen Generations. The *Bringing Them Home Report* of the National Inquiry into the Separation of Aboriginal and Torres Strait Islander Children from their Families identifies the severity of the trauma the Stolen Generations caused to parents, children, and future generations.[29]

[19] Indigenous children, like the plaintiff in this matter, suffered years of neglect as well as physical, emotional, mental, and sexual abuse whilst institutionalised.[30] Those who were taken as children during the Stolen Generations are more at risk from suffering mental health and substance abuse issues than the general population, due to the trauma and dislocation they experienced.[31] Those issues have also been the underlying cause of many Indigenous Australians who have suffered dispossession and displacement as part of the Stolen Generations entering into incarceration.

[20] In more contemporary times, often the pathway to incarceration begins for many Indigenous children with being placed in out-of-home care, which

further displaces those children from their culture, family, and friends.[32] Indigenous children occupy high rates of national child removal and their over-representation in out-of-home care continues to increase every year.[33] The *Health of Children in 'Out-of-Home' Care Report* produced by the Royal Australasian College of Physicians highlights that Indigenous children are 6.5 times more likely to enter out-of-home care compared to non-Indigenous children[34] and shows the health risks such placements can bring.

[21] Trauma from dispossession and the Stolen Generations becomes intergenerational by being passed down to younger generations through learned behaviours, economic hardship, and social disadvantage. Indigenous children hold a heavier health burden compared with the general population.[35] This includes social, emotional, mental health, and physical illness problems,[36] which place those children at higher risk of further adverse effects on their overall well-being coming into out-of-home care.

[22] The very first encounters Indigenous children have with authority are often negative. When a child is placed in out-of-home care, they can be moved to and from multiple schools, locations, and out-of-home care options throughout their lifetime.[37] Separating Indigenous children from their land and kin is a form of abuse in itself which can result in life-long harm and trauma.[38] The disruption those circumstances can bring to a child's life can lead to frustration with authority and the system and result in those children acting out in anti-social and criminal behaviour.[39]

[23] Statistically, Indigenous children are also more likely to enter into institutionalisation through early entry into a detention centre. From there, the likelihood that they proceed into adult incarceration increases.[40] Australian census data also evidences that Indigenous families usually have a different home structure compared to non-Indigenous families, including a higher rate of single-parent families.[41] Single-parent families are especially vulnerable to family separation and breakdown caused by incarceration of a parent, as well as other causes, such as ill health.

[24] These circumstances highlight a streamlined pathway into incarceration for Indigenous Australians, rendering them inherently more vulnerable than non-Indigenous people. Indigenous women, in particular, are severely over-represented among the prison population.[42] It is therefore relevant to take account of the special vulnerability and disadvantage Indigenous women face due to the intersectionality of race and gender identity.[43] Over 80 per cent of imprisoned Indigenous women are mothers.[44] These women are often not only sole carers to their own children but also kinship carers for other children from their community.[45]

[25] These extended caring roles place Indigenous women in financially vulnerable positions which can, under extreme cultural and parenting pressures, lead to criminal behaviour. The criminal acts may take the form of minor offences committed under circumstances of necessity (like repeated stealing offences to feed dependents or a financial inability to pay minor fines and

traffic offences). However, these offences, when repeated due to unchanging financial conditions and lack of support, can lead to incarceration. The historical barriers outlined above, which persist today, place Indigenous citizens (particularly women) at higher risks of being incarcerated and therefore excluded from voting at Commonwealth elections.

The Canadian approach

[26] Similar issues of Indigenous prisoner disenfranchisement were considered in Canada's landmark electoral law case of *Sauvé v Canada*.[46] This case provides a useful example of how a Commonwealth political system with a colonialist past has dealt with overcoming historically and democratically limiting electoral legislation that affected the participation of First Nations people. Like Indigenous Australians, First Nations of Canada were identified in *Sauvé* as experiencing higher levels of poverty, societal exclusion, institutionalisation, and racial discrimination than other Canadian citizens.

[27] The *Sauvé* litigation comprised two challenges to Canadian federal electoral legislation. In 1993, the defendant Richard Sauvé challenged a blanket ban against voting by prisoners in the Federal Court of Canada. The Federal Court declared the ban to conflict with the right to vote contained within the *Canadian Charter of Rights and Freedoms 1982*.[47] The Canadian Parliament responded by amending the law to limit the ban to prisoners serving sentences of two years or more.[48] The plaintiff successfully challenged those electoral law changes again in the Supreme Court in 2002.[49] The majority judges in the Supreme Court held that the justifications for disenfranchising prisoners relied upon by the Canadian Parliament were too vague. They lacked adequate consideration of principles of proportionality and did not consider important relevant extrinsic factors impacting on those individuals subject to disenfranchisement.[50]

[28] McLachlin CJ found that the social, economic, and historical conditions of First Nations people significantly led to their overrepresentation in Canadian prisons.[51] This, in turn, undermined the legitimacy of the disqualification. Her Honour also noted the disproportionate and arbitrary character of a ban on prisoners voting in elections based purely on the length of their sentences:

> Section 51(*e*) imposes blanket punishment on all penitentiary inmates regardless of the particular crimes they committed, the harm they caused, or the normative character of their conduct. It is not individually tailored to the particular offender's act. It does not, in short, meet the requirements of denunciatory, retributive punishment. It follows that it is not rationally connected to the goal of imposing legitimate punishment.[52]

[29] Accordingly, a ban of this kind was found to unjustifiably limit the right to vote conferred by the *Charter of Rights and Freedoms*.[53] *Sauvé* set a standard

for Canadian courts which requires them to uphold government legislation denying citizens the right to vote only where this can be 'demonstrably justified'.[54] Gleeson CJ suggests that this is a higher standard of review than that articulated by the joint reasons in this case. However, whether or not that is so, the distinction does not bear upon our conclusions here. Disqualifying prisoners from voting, given the disproportionate impact on Indigenous Australians, is clearly at odds with contemporary ideas of universal franchise, which (as we mentioned previously) do not admit of exclusions based on categories such as race.

[30] The Canadian Parliament is yet to repeal its electoral prisoner disqualifying legislation, but the invalidated provision is not applied. Prisoners in Canada are able to enrol and vote in both federal and provincial elections by way of special ballot.[55] This is done by Elections Canada appointing a staff member as an election liaison officer to govern the special ballot process within correctional institutions.[56] Those measures have increased voter registration in Canada of those incarcerated and, as a result, improved levels of First Nations voting due to their high incarceration rates.[57] Prisoners have been able to use their ballots to bring change to the correctional system of Canada.[58]

Conclusion and orders

[31] The blanket ban on voting by prisoners challenged in this case fails to take account of the distinct inequalities and experiences that exist between Indigenous and non-Indigenous Australians. However, the same point applies to the preceding provision applying to those serving sentences of three years or longer. Indeed, we find that any ban on prisoners voting would be contrary to s 24 for the reasons considered above. Removing the disqualification would have salutary consequences for prisoners' integration with the wider community. Denying a person an ongoing connection to society through the electoral process while incarcerated adds an additional layer of punishment. It is unnecessary for persons sentenced to imprisonment for a state offence to be further subject to Commonwealth legislation that adds an additional penalty to their sentence.

[32] Denying an incarcerated person voting rights also increases the difficulty of reforming social connections upon release. Exercise of voting and other civil rights ensures a person's basic links to society are maintained even while they are incarcerated. It provides those persons with a continued sense of civic responsibility and political inclusion to better enable them to reintegrate back into the community. This is particularly important for Indigenous Australians, given their low rates of electoral enrolment. It is crucial for incarcerated persons of Indigenous descent, who are still subject to the effects of colonisation, to vote and otherwise participate in political membership of the community if the cycle of incarceration and exclusion is not to continue.

[33] We therefore find that disqualifying prisoners from voting at Commonwealth elections is a disproportionate restriction on the democratic franchise enshrined in s 24 of the *Constitution*. We uphold the challenge to the validity of s 93(8AA) of the *Commonwealth Electoral Act 1918*. We further find that the previous legislation is also invalid. The plaintiff has raised points of important constitutional principle on behalf of a vulnerable segment of the community of which she is a member. It is appropriate for her to receive costs from the second defendant.

[34] The questions in the Amended Special Case should be answered as follows:

(1) Section 93(8AA) and s 208(2)(c) of the *Commonwealth Electoral Act 1918* are invalid.

(2), (3) Unnecessary to answer.

(3A) The provisions listed in the question are invalid.

(3B) The provisions listed in the question are invalid.

(3C) The provisions listed in the question are invalid.

(4) The second defendant.

(5) Unnecessary to answer, given the answer to Question 1.

Notes

1 Dani Larkin and Jonathan Crowe.
2 (1992) 177 CLR 1, 70–3 (Deane and Toohey JJ).
3 (1992) 177 CLR 106, 137 (Mason CJ), 209–10 (Gaudron J).
4 Ibid., 228 (McHugh J).
5 *Attorney General (Cth); Ex rel McKinlay v Commonwealth* (1975) 135 CLR 1, 36.
6 *Victoria v Commonwealth* (1971) 122 CLR 353, 396–7.
7 Australian Electoral Commission, *Indigenous Enrolment Rate* (11 October 2019) <https://www.aec.gov.au/Enrolling_to_vote/Enrolment_stats/performance/indigenous-enrolment-rate.htm>.
8 *Commonwealth Franchise Act 1902* s 4.
9 HLA Hart, 'Positivism and the Separation of Law and Morals' (1958) 71(4) *Harvard Law Review* 593, 607.
10 Tony Birch, 'The Last Refuge of the "Un-Australian"' (2001) 7(1) *University of Technology Sydney Review* 17, 17.
11 Michael Dodson, 'Citizenship in Australia: An Indigenous Perspective' (1997) 22(2) *Alternative Law Journal* 57, 58.
12 George Williams, 'Race and the Australian Constitution: From Federation to Reconciliation' (2000) 38(4) *Osgoode Hall Law Journal* 643, 649.
13 Owen Dixon, 'Two Constitutions Compared' in *Jesting Pilate and Other Papers and Addresses* (Law Book Co, 1965) 100, 102.
14 *Elections Act 1885* (Qld) s 6(1). This provision was amended in 1905 to deny even Aborigines holding freehold title the right to vote in Queensland elections.
15 *Constitution Amendment Act 1893* (WA) s 12.
16 Indigenous voters were, however, affected by other barriers to electoral participation, including for example the ban on voting when in receipt of charitable aid. See George Williams, *Human Rights under the Australian Constitution* (Oxford University Press, 1999) 96–103.
17 *Commonwealth Franchise Act 1902* s 4.

18 *Commonwealth Electoral Act 1949* s 3.
19 Jonathan Crowe and Peta Stephenson, 'An Express Constitutional Right to Vote? The Case for Reviving Section 41' (2014) 36 *Sydney Law Review* 205.
20 *Commonwealth Electoral Act 1949* s 42(5), as amended by *Commonwealth Electoral Legislation Amendment Act 1983* s 28(j).
21 *Commonwealth Electoral Act 1918* ss 208(2)(c), 221(3)(b).
22 Australian Bureau of Statistics, *Census: Aboriginal and Torres Strait Islander Population* (27 June 2017) <https://www.abs.gov.au/ausstats/abs@.nsf/MediaRealesesByCatalogue/02D50FAA9987D6B7CA25814800087E03>.
23 Australian Bureau of Statistics, *Prisoners in Australia* (5 December 2019) <https://www.abs.gov.au/ausstats/abs@.nsf/Lookup/by%20Subject/4517.0~2019~Main%20Features~Aboriginal%20and%20Torres%20Strait%20Islander%20prisoner%20characteristics%20~13>.
24 Compare Graeme Orr, 'Ballotless and Behind Bars: The Denial of the Franchise to Prisoners' (1998) 26(1) *Federal Law Review* 55, 75–80.
25 Roderic Broadhurst, 'Crime and Indigenous People' in Adam Graycar and Peter Grabosky (eds), *Cambridge Handbook of Australian Criminology* (Cambridge University Press, 2002) 256–80; Elliott Johnston, *National Report of the Royal Commission into Aboriginal Deaths in Custody* (Report, 15 April 1991) [1.4.3].
26 Johnston (n 25).
27 Ibid., [1.4.2].
28 Ibid., [1.4.3].
29 Human Rights and Equal Opportunity Commission, *Bringing Them Home Report* (Report, April 1997).
30 Ibid. See e.g. Confidential Submission 617, New South Wales, concerning a woman removed at eight years of age with her three sisters in the 1940s and placed in Cootamundra Girls' Home.
31 Johnston (n 25) [1.5]; Queensland Government, *Queensland Mental Health Policy Statement* (1996) 14.
32 Royal Australasian College of Physicians, *Health of Children in 'Out- of- Home' Care Report* (2006) 11.
33 Ibid.
34 Ibid.
35 Australian Bureau of Statistics, *The Health and Welfare of Australia's Aboriginal and Torres Strait Islander Peoples*, (Catalogue No 4704.0, 26 August 2005) [91].
36 Ibid.; Human Rights and Equal Opportunity Commission, *Report of the Aboriginal and Torres Strait Islander Social Justice Commissioner* (Report No 3/2005, 2005) [5].
37 Royal Australasian College of Physicians (n 32) 11.
38 Ibid., 13.
39 Human Rights and Equal Opportunity Commission (n 36) 4.
40 Ibid., 86.
41 Australian Bureau of Statistics, *Census of Population and Housing: Characteristics of Aboriginal and Torres Strait Islander Australians* (2016) <https://www.abs.gov.au/ausstats/abs@.nsf/mf/2076.0>.
42 Elizabeth Sullivan et al., 'Aboriginal Mothers in Prison in Australia: A Study of Social, Emotional and Physical Wellbeing' (2019) 43(3) *Australian and New Zealand Journal of Public Health* 241, 242. See also Rowena Lawrie, 'Speak Out Speak Strong: Rising Imprisonment Rates of Aboriginal Women' (2003) 5(24) *Indigenous Law Bulletin* 5.
43 Human Rights and Equal Opportunity Commission, *Report of the Aboriginal and Torres Strait Islander Social Justice Commissioner* (2002) 135–6.
44 Sullivan et al. (n 42) 242.
45 Lorana Bartels, 'Painting the Picture of Indigenous Women in Custody in Australia' (2012) 12(2) *Queensland University of Technology Law and Justice Journal* 1, 13.
46 *Sauvé v Canada (Chief Electoral Officer)* (2002) 3 SCR 519 ('*Sauvé*').

47 *Canadian Charter of Rights and Freedoms 1982* s 3.
48 *Canada Elections Act 2000* s 4(e).
49 *Sauvé* (2002) 3 SCR 519.
50 Ibid., 522.
51 Ibid., 555–556.
52 Ibid., 553.
53 *Canadian Charter of Rights and Freedoms 1982* s 3.
54 *Sauvé* (2002) 3 SCR 519, 557.
55 *Canada Elections Act 2000* Part 11 'Special Voting Rules', Div 5.
56 Ibid., ss 248(1), 251(1), 257.
57 Debra Parkes, 'Prisoner Voting Rights in Canada: Rejecting the Notion of Temporary Outcasts' in Christopher Mele and Teresa Miller (eds), *Civil Penalties, Social Consequences* (Psychology Press, 2005) 243–50.
58 Ibid., 250.

15

NONA AND AHMAT v BARNES [2012] QSC 35

Commentary: *Nona and Ahmat v Barnes* [2012] QSC 35

Heather Douglas and Heron Loban

Introduction

On 14 October 2005, a vessel called the *Malu Sara* disappeared in the Torres Strait. All five who were on board the vessel died. They were all Torres Strait Islander people.

The Torres Strait is located between the north-eastern tip of Australia and Papua New Guinea. The territory of Papua New Guinea and the Torres Strait Islands are very close together and, while the islands of the Torres Strait are recognised as Australian territory, some are within the waters of Papua New Guinea. The Torres Strait Treaty,[1] introduced in 1978, preserves the traditional rights of those who live in Papua New Guinea and the Torres Strait to travel in the region for trade and traditional activities.

The waters of the Torres Strait are known to be treacherous. The weather conditions change quickly and there are strong tides and many reefs. Despite this, there is significant travel in the region by local people and this is largely undertaken by boat. Since 1988, the Department of Immigration and Multicultural and Indigenous Affairs ('DIMIA')[2] has employed 'movement and monitoring officers' ('MMOs')[3] to conduct surveillance operations in the waters of the Torres Strait. Their role is to monitor the flow of inhabitants in the region and to report on movement to assist with managing issues such as introduced diseases and illegal activities including people, drugs, and firearm smuggling.

The *Malu Sara* was an Immigration Response Vessel ('IRV') owned and operated by DIMIA. Its skipper was Wilfred Baira, an MMO. The *Malu Sara* was travelling between Badu and Saibai Islands in the Torres Strait after a training workshop when it sank. Also on board were Ted Harry (another employee of DIMIA), Valerie Saub, Flora Enosa, and Flora's five-year-old daughter, Ethena. Only the body of Flora Enosa was found.

What went wrong?

Subsequent reports and inquiries identified numerous deficiencies in the management by DIMIA of the IRVs and in its training and support of MMOs.[4] Namely, DIMIA staff tasked to manage the procurement process of new IRVs were insufficiently trained and/or experienced, the tender evaluation process for the IRVs was inappropriate, the specifications outlined in the Request for Tender for the IRVs were inadequate, the vessels were not properly tested, contracts for the boat building were flawed, the design of the boats was defective, and the boats did not comply with appropriate standards and regulatory requirements.[5] In addition to the liability of the boat builder,[6] the coroner placed responsibility for key deficiencies squarely with Gary Chaston (DIMIA Regional Director). The coroner noted Chaston's overtly racist comments to local non-Islander business owners that 'the MMOs are two generations behind and would not be able to handle that type of equipment'[7] and 'quite a number of MMOs were not "technically minded"'.[8]

MMOs received minimal training on the new IRVs and, despite a report that the *Malu Sara* had taken on water two days before the tragedy, there was no proper investigation or response.[9] The skipper, Wilfred Baira, an experienced seaman, expressed concern about the weather conditions prior to departure and asked for a delay but was refused. The *Malu Sara* set off in concerning weather conditions with no risk assessment undertaken in preparation for the voyage. The boat was equipped only with a compass; it carried no charts or navigation equipment. The skipper lacked training in the use of the vessel's satellite phone. The vessel became lost in fog and called for help many times but the response of those tasked with responding was shocking.[10] As a result, the search for the *Malu Sara* began many hours later than it should have. Search and Rescue—Australian Maritime Safety Authority were initially not provided with clear information and took too long to recognise their responsibility for the search.[11]

Mr Chaston and Sergeant Flegg's contribution to the tragedy

While many individuals were identified by the coroner for their failures, only Mr Chaston and Sergeant Flegg were referred by the coroner for disciplinary action. Chaston was responsible for the occupational health and safety of the MMOs and Flegg was a police officer and the local search and rescue coordinator. Their role in the tragedy is outlined in the rewritten judgment.

The coroner referred Chaston to the relevant disciplinary body for possible breaches of the Australian Public Service code of conduct,[12] determining that

Chaston's conduct amounted to misconduct or that he acted incompetently in the discharge of his duties.[13]

Despite his responsibility for the badly managed search, it was Flegg who conducted the subsequent police investigation and provided a report on the sinking of the *Malu Sara*. The coroner noted the police report was 'flawed' and that it was inappropriate for Flegg to conduct the investigation given the central role he played in the search. Flegg was a material witness and had a conflict of interest.[14] The coroner observed that 'this conflict manifested alarmingly during the course of the [inquest] as he sought to disavow aspects of his report when it became apparent the evidence may have reflected on him badly'.[15]

The coroner is able to give information about police misconduct to a disciplinary body.[16] The coroner determined that Flegg's conduct amounted to misconduct or that he acted incompetently in the discharge of his duties and referred information to the relevant authority.[17] Later, the Queensland Police Service ('QPS') found Flegg failed to take appropriate and required action in carrying out his role in the search. In 2011, disciplinary action was taken. Flegg was demoted from Sergeant to Senior Constable for two years until 2013. The order was wholly suspended, however, for two years, on condition that he undertook specified courses.[18] This decision was appealed by the Crime and Misconduct Commission[19] but the QPS decision was ultimately confirmed.[20] In 2019, Flegg was a Senior Sergeant with the QPS working in far north Queensland.[21]

Criminal prosecution

Neither Chaston nor Flegg were ever charged with criminal offences in relation to their roles in the deaths. In Queensland, coroners cannot make a finding that someone has committed a criminal offence.[22] However, where a coroner reasonably suspects that a person has committed an offence, he or she must give the information to the Director of Public Prosecutions ('DPP').[23]

Wilfred Baira's siblings corresponded with the coroner after the inquest. This resulted in the coroner stating in a letter that he 'concluded there is no basis on which I should refer information obtained during my investigation' to the DPP. The siblings' lawyer requested reasons, which the coroner refused to provide. In *Nona and Ahmat v Barnes*,[24] the siblings applied to the Supreme Court seeking reasons for the coroner's decision not to refer information to the DPP. The Court dismissed the application on the basis that the decision of the coroner (not to give information to the DPP) was not a decision that could be judicially reviewed because it related to the administration of criminal justice.[25]

Nona and Ahmat v Barnes: through an Indigenous lens

The *Human Rights Act 2019* (Qld) recognises the cultural rights of Torres Strait Islander people.[26] We backdate the introduction of the *Human Rights Act* in 2019 to 2005 and re-imagine the decision of *Nona and Ahmat v Barnes*. We show how this decision could be written differently if Torres Strait Islander people's cultural rights are taken seriously.

It is possible for the coroner to refer information to the DPP and provide the reasons for the referral.[27] There is also no legislation that prevents the coroner from privately advising families of a reasonably held suspicion of criminal behaviour and of a referral to the DPP. In the rewritten judgment of *Nona and Ahmat v Barnes*, the Queensland Supreme Court finds that the decision not to refer information to the DPP was a reviewable decision and orders the coroner to provide reasons for the decision.

In the original judgment of the Supreme Court, there was no recognition of the effect of its decision and that of the coroner on the applicants, the other families of the deceased, and the broader Torres Strait Islander community. We address this point and reflect on this in our judgment. Finally, we also include translations of the orders in the Kala Lagau Ya language of Mabuiag; we thank Deenorah Yellub for her translation.

On the five-year anniversary of the loss of her brother, Ted Harry, and the *Malu Sara*, Abigail Harry said:

> It's hard for me still, and until today I look back and I think of the government departments involved and people who were responsible. Nothing's happened; there's still no justice and righteousness [sic]. I think there is a failure all round in everything. The government not taking up responsibility, the public prosecutor, you've got coroner Barnes, and everyone else is just sitting, and it's not finished; it's an unfinished business.[28]

Lily-Anne Ahmat (the second applicant), speaking in a documentary film series about the Torres Strait, explained:

> They haven't found the body. There's no body. So families [are] still walking around carrying that in their hearts. So there's no closure....Was it because of our race that they wouldn't help us? Or through arrogance? They just didn't care. Had no remorse, nothing.[29]

In an interview with the *Torres News* once all appeal mechanisms had been exhausted,[30] George Nona (the first applicant) expressed his feelings about the law:

> We don't feel like we are not [sic] living in Australia anymore, and that racism is definitely involved here...It makes us feel so small, the system has let us down.[31]

We honour them.

Notes

1 Recognised under *The Torres Strait Treaty (Miscellaneous Amendments) Act 1984* (Cth).

2 DIMIA changed its name on a number of occasions. It is currently known as the Department of Home Affairs.
3 MMOs are currently known as Border Monitoring Officers.
4 Australian Transport Safety Bureau, *Independent Investigation into the Loss of the Department of Immigration and Multicultural and Indigenous Affairs Vessel Malu Sara in Torres Strait, Queensland Australia* (Final Report, Marine Occurrence Investigation No 222, 15 October 2005) 1; *Inquest into the Loss of the* Malu Sara (Thursday Island Coroners Court, State Coroner Barnes, 12 February 2009) 4 ('Malu Sara *Inquest*').
5 Malu Sara *Inquest* (n 4) 44–6.
6 See *Comcare v Subsee Explorer Pty Ltd* [2011] FCA 837.
7 Malu Sara *Inquest* (n 4) 31.
8 Ibid.
9 Ibid., 52, 60.
10 Ibid., 71–2.
11 Ibid., 86–8.
12 *Coroners Act 2003* (Qld) s 48(3) ('*Coroners Act*').
13 Malu Sara *Inquest* (n 4) 96.
14 Ibid., 3.
15 Ibid.
16 *Coroners Act 2003* (Qld) s 48(3).
17 Malu Sara *Inquest* (n 4) 97.
18 *Flegg v Crime and Misconduct Commission* [2014] QCA 42, [1].
19 *Crime and Misconduct Commission v Flegg and Anor* [2012] QCAT 74; *Crime and Misconduct Commission v Flegg and Anor* [2013] QCATA 29; *Flegg v Crime and Misconduct Commission and Anor* [2013] QCA 376. The Crime and Misconduct Commission is now the Crime and Corruption Commission.
20 *Flegg v Crime and Misconduct Commission and Anor* [2013] QCA 376.
21 There is no more recent information available about Senior Sergeant Flegg.
22 *Coroners Act* s 45(5).
23 Ibid., s 48(3).
24 *Nona and Anor v Barnes* [2012] QSC 35. Subsequent appeals also failed: *Nona and Ahmat v Barnes* [2012] QCA 346; *Nona and Ahmat v Barnes and Ahamat* [2013] HCATrans 242 (11 October 2013).
25 *Judicial Review Act 1991* (Qld) s 31; sch 2, item 1.
26 *Human Rights Act 2019* (Qld) s 28.
27 See *Inquest into the Death of Andrew John Bornen* (Ipswich Coroners Court, State Coroner Barnes, 16 July 2010).
28 Stefan Armbruster, '*Malu Sara* "betrayal": Attorney-General Will Not Push for Any Prosecutions' *Torres News* (Thursday Island, 20 October 2010) 1.
29 'Episode 3' *Blue Water Empire* (Bunya Productions Pty Ltd, 2018).
30 *Nona and Anor v Barnes and Anor* [2013] HCATrans 242 (11 October 2013).
31 Mark Bousen and Aaron Smith, 'Family "devastated" by Flegg Finding: Rank Restored' *Torres News* (Thursday Island, 17 March 2014) 2.

George Nona .... First Applicant;

AND

Lily-Anne Ahmat .... Second Applicant;

AND

Michael Barnes .... Respondent;

[2012] QSC 35

Administrative law—Judicial review—Reviewable decisions and conduct—Human rights—Where the applicant challenges the respondent's 'decision' that there was no basis on which the Coroner should refer information obtained during his investigation to the DPP—Where the applicants sought reasons for this decision—Where the coroner's decision must be compatible with human rights.

Loban-Douglas J.[1]

[1] The coronial inquest at the heart of this application involved the loss of five people at sea in the Torres Strait.[2] All were Torres Strait Islander people. It was a tragic incident and, according to the State Coroner who published his report in February 2009, resulted in the avoidable loss of life. This tragedy continues to have a lasting impact on the families and communities of those lost and the wider Torres Strait Islander community. I take this opportunity to pay my respects to them. I recognise that Torres Strait Islanders are a patient and respectful people.

The applicants

[2] The applicants are the brother and sister of one of those lost at sea. Their brother, Mr Wilfred Baira, was the skipper of the *Malu Sara* vessel owned by the Department of Immigration and Multicultural and Indigenous Affairs

('DIMIA'). *Malu Sara* translates to 'the seagull flies out to sea—always searching for prey' in Kala Lagaw Ya (the language of the western islands of the Torres Strait).[3] Mr Wilfred Baira was a highly accomplished seaman.

The respondent

[3] The respondent is the coroner. The coroner does not actively defend these proceedings; the Attorney-General has intervened to do so pursuant to s 51 of the *Judicial Review Act 1991* (Qld) ('*JRA*').

The applicants' complaint

[4] The applicants' complaint is that the coroner refused to provide reasons for his decision that there was 'no basis' on which he should refer information obtained during his investigation into the deaths of five Torres Strait Islander people to the Director of Public Prosecutions ('DPP'). By these proceedings, they seek a statement of the respondent's reasons under *JRA* s 32. As part of their argument, the applicants claim that the provision of reasons is important so that they are in a position to know that their human rights were 'properly considered' pursuant to s 58 (read with s 9) of the *Human Rights Act 2005* (Qld) ('*HRA*') when the coroner made his decision. They also refer me to *HRA* s 31 and the right to a fair hearing in civil matters.

[5] In making my decision, the applicants have reminded me that *HRA* s 4(f) requires me to interpret statutory provisions, 'to the extent possible that is consistent with their purpose, in a way compatible with human rights'.[4] I accept that.[5]

The respondent's argument

[6] The respondent resists the application on two grounds. The first argument is that there is no statutory duty to provide a statement of reasons in this instance, pursuant to *JRA* s 33(2). This is because there was no relevant 'decision' to which Part 3 of the *JRA* applies. In particular, the Attorney-General argues, the decision in question was not 'a decision of an administrative character made…or required to be made, under an enactment'. The second and alternative argument is that this decision is excluded from the operation of the *JRA* because it is within the express exclusion in sch 2, item 1 of that Act, namely it is a decision 'relating to the administration of criminal justice'.

Timeline

[7] On 14 October 2005, the *Malu Sara*, a DIMIA vessel, left Saibai Island for Badu Island where it was based. It was skippered by Mr Baira. Also on board was a fellow immigration officer, Mr Ted Harry, and three passengers, Ms Flora Enosa, Miss Ethena Enosa, and Ms Valerie Saub. On 15 October 2005,

the *Malu Sara* was lost. The vessel was never recovered and only the body of Flora Enosa was found.

[8] A pre-inquest directions hearing was held at Brisbane on 15 February 2007. Hearings commenced at Thursday Island on 16 April 2007. The inquest findings were delivered by the State Coroner at Thursday Island on 12 February 2009. At this time, Mr Gary Chaston (DIMIA Regional Director) and Sergeant Warren Flegg (Search and Rescue Mission Co-ordinator) were both referred by the State Coroner for disciplinary action.

[9] With the passage of time, and having received no formal advice, the applicants ascertained that the State Coroner, Mr Barnes, had not referred any information to the Director of Public Prosecutions ('DPP') pursuant to s 48(2) of the *Coroners Act 2003* (Qld) ('*Coroners Act*'). This new information caused them to write to the Coroner through their solicitor seeking reasons for the decision. Mr Barnes replied to that correspondence in a letter dated 30 November 2010, which provided: 'As a result of giving careful consideration to my obligations under s 48(2) of the [Coroners] Act I have concluded there was no basis on which I should refer information obtained during my investigation into these deaths to the DPP'.

[10] Further correspondence between the applicants' solicitor and the State Coroner ensued, with the applicants seeking reasons for the decision that there was 'no basis' on which the coroner should refer information. Around 5 July 2011, the parties reached an impasse with the applicants continuing to seek reasons and the State Coroner holding firm in the belief he was not required to provide reasons.

Application of the Judicial Review Act 1991 (Qld)—the right to reasons

[11] For the purposes of judicial review, the word 'decision' takes its meaning from the definition of 'decision to which this Act applies' in s 4(a) of the *JRA*:

> a decision of an administrative character made, proposed to be made, or required to be made, under an enactment (whether or not in the exercise of a discretion).

This expression is comprised of three interconnected elements. First, there must be a 'decision'. Second, the decision must be of an 'administrative character'. Third, the decision must have been made, proposed or required to be made 'under an enactment'.[6]

A 'decision'

[12] Was the purported decision a reviewable 'decision' under the *JRA*? Pursuant to s 5(g) *JRA*, the making of a decision includes a reference to 'doing or refusing to do anything else'.

[13] The *Coroners Act* s 48(2) states:

> If, from information obtained while investigating a death, a coroner reasonably suspects a person has committed an offence, the coroner must give information to—
>
> (a) for an indictable offence—the director of public prosecutions.

[14] According to his letter to the applicants dated 30 November 2010, the coroner concluded there was 'no basis' on which he should refer information obtained during his investigation into these deaths to the DPP. That is, the coroner decided he did not reasonably suspect an indictable offence had been committed. It is this decision about whether or not a reasonable suspicion is held that informs the taking (or not taking) of action; that is, the giving of information to the DPP. The relevant decision then is the decision of whether the coroner 'reasonably suspects a person has committed an offence'.

[15] I find that the coroner's decision that there was 'no basis' on which he should refer information obtained during his investigation to the DPP was a decision about whether the coroner reasonably suspected a person had committed an offence pursuant to the *Coroners Act* s 48(2). This was a relevant decision for the purposes of *JRA* s 4.[7]

A decision of an 'administrative character'

[16] In order to be a reviewable decision under *JRA* s 4, the decision must be of an administrative character. The coroner's decision about whether he holds a reasonable suspicion falls short of making any determination of criminality. While the coroner must, if possible, make findings about the death(s), including how, when, and what caused the person(s) to die,[8] the coroner must not make a determination of guilt of an offence or of civil liability.[9] In construing a similar provision (*Coroners Act 1975* (SA) s 25(3)), her Honour Nyland J stated that 'criminal or civil liability can only be determined through the application of the relevant law to the facts, and it is only legal conclusions as to liability flowing from this process which are prohibited'.[10] In the second *Inquest into the Death of Mulrunji Domadgee*,[11] the Acting State Coroner emphasised 'that any decision to prosecute rests solely with other authorities'.[12]

[17] Furthermore, in the *Inquest into the Death of Andrew John Bornen*, the coroner determined that the test of 'reasonable suspicion' of an offence in *Coroners Act* s 48(2) fell well below any determination of guilt. Finding a decision about reasonable suspicion:

> is analogous to the test applied when a search warrant is sought [ie not issued]. In that context it has been held that a suspicion is a state of mind

> less certain than a belief and to be reasonable it must be based on some evidence, but not necessarily well founded or factually correct and be a suspicion that a reasonable person acting without passion or prejudice might hold. As a result, a relatively low level of certainty is needed to satisfy the test.[13]

[18] Courts have generally sought to avoid giving the phrase 'administrative character' a narrow or technical construction.[14] As the coroner identified in his findings in *Inquest into the loss of the* Malu Sara[15] ('Malu Sara *Inquest*'), the coronial office is an administrative one rather than a judicial one. The decision relating to whether a person holds a 'reasonable suspicion' under *Coroners Act* s 48(2) is an administrative decision.[16] An analogy may be made to magistrates presiding at a committal hearing who must determine whether to commit an alleged offender for trial in a higher court; in this context, the magistrate is performing an administrative function.[17] I find that the coroner's decision that there was 'no basis' on which he should refer information obtained during his investigation into the deaths to the DPP was a decision of an administrative character.

A decision made under an enactment

[19] In determining whether a decision is made under an enactment, the High Court[18] has identified *two* criteria: *(1)* the decision must be expressly or impliedly required or authorised by the enactment, and (2) the decision must in itself confer, alter, or otherwise affect legal rights or obligations.

The first criterion

[20] The first criterion is satisfied by *Coroners Act* s 48(2), which expressly states that where the coroner 'reasonably suspects a person has committed an offence' the coroner must give information to the DPP, where it is an indictable offence. This authorises the coroner to decide whether he or she holds a reasonable suspicion about the commission of an offence.

The second criterion

[21] The second criterion requires consideration of how the coroner's decision of whether he or she held a reasonable suspicion about the commission of an indictable offence confers, alters, or otherwise affects legal rights or obligations. In *Attorney-General (Cth) v Queensland*,[19] French J considered the requirement of effect on legal rights and obligations in the context of judicial review and stated that: 'nor is it necessary that the determination directly affect legal rights or obligations so long as it has some real or practical effect'.[20]

[22] In satisfying this second criterion, the applicants urge me to find their human rights were affected and engaged (pursuant to HRA s 28) when the coroner made his decision.[21]

Human Rights Act 2005 (Qld)

Interpretive provisions

[23] In considering the application of the *HRA* in this case, I note that the *HRA* recognises the special importance of the rights of Aboriginal and Torres Strait Islander people in its preamble:

> Although human rights belong to all individuals, human rights have a special importance for the Aboriginal peoples and Torres Strait Islander peoples of Queensland, as Australia's first people, with their distinctive and diverse spiritual, material and economic relationship with the lands, territories, waters, coastal seas and other resources with which they have a connection under Aboriginal tradition and Ailan Kastom. Of particular significance to Aboriginal peoples and Torres Strait Islander peoples of Queensland is the right to self-determination.

[24] Furthermore, I note that the *HRA* departs from other Acts in Australia in its strong and explicit recognition of the rights of Aboriginal and Torres Strait Islander people. Consequently, there can only be limited assistance drawn from cases decided on human rights in other Australian jurisdictions.

[25] *HRA* s 58(1) identifies that 'It is unlawful for a public entity…(b) in making a decision, to fail to give proper consideration to a human right relevant to the decision'.

[26] *HRA* s 9 defines 'public entity' for the purposes of the *HRA*; specifically, s 9(4) clarifies that a court or tribunal is not a public entity except when acting in an administrative capacity. As noted earlier, I have determined that the coroner acts in an administrative capacity. Thus, a coroner acting in an administrative capacity is a public entity for the purpose of the *HRA*.

The human rights held by the applicants and their community

[27] The *HRA* recognises and provides for the human rights of Aboriginal and Torres Strait Islander people and was directly drawn from Article 27 of the *International Covenant on Civil and Political Rights* ('ICCPR') and Articles 8, 25, 29, and 31 of the *United Nations Declaration on the Rights of Indigenous Peoples* ('UNDRIP'). Section 28(1) of the *HRA* identifies that Torres Strait Islander people hold 'distinct cultural rights' and these are laid out in s 28(2).

[28] The applicants seek reasons under the *JRA* in order to further their substantive claim that the coroner, in deciding that he had 'no basis' on which he

should refer information obtained during his investigation into the deaths to the DPP, failed to give proper consideration to the applicants and their community's right:

(a) To enjoy, maintain, control, protect, and develop their kinship ties (*HRA* s 28(2)(c)); and
(b) Not to be subjected to forced assimilation or destruction of their culture (*HRA* s 28(3)).

[29] The parties have provided me with a copy of the findings of the Coroner in relation to the Malu Sara *Inquest*.[22] I note the coroner's recognition of Torres Strait Islanders' knowledge of the sea in his report. The coroner also identifies that while interpreters were used in the hearings, the Torres Strait Islander witnesses had vastly different perceptions of the subjects being inquired into compared to that of the questioners. Nevertheless, he notes: 'no impartial observer could help but notice the painstaking efforts of many of the Torres Strait Islander witnesses to answer questions truthfully…I have given great weight to the evidence of the local Indigenous witnesses called at the inquest'.[23]

[30] The coroner's views about the Torres Strait Islander witnesses can be contrasted with his views about other witnesses, in particular, Mr Gary Chaston and Sergeant Warren Flegg. In his report, the coroner lays out the multitude of wilful, reckless, and seriously negligent actions of Chaston and Flegg.[24]

[31] It is clear that Mr Baira, the skipper of the *Malu Sara* and an expert seaman of the Torres Strait, assessed the weather conditions on that fateful day and requested not to sail on the basis that conditions were unsafe. Mr Chaston refused the request, later claiming, inconsistently with other witnesses, that conditions were calm on the relevant day.[25] The coroner observed that Mr Chaston had an 'authoritarian manner' and the coroner opined that Mr Baira may have seen 'no point' in approaching him further about delaying.[26] In any event, Mr Chaston, himself no seaman, made no enquiries of the skipper about safety, despite the weather becoming progressively worse, and ordered them to sail.[27]

[32] Later when the *Malu Sara* was reported to be clearly in trouble with water coming into the boat, the coroner described it as 'alarming' that Mr Chaston did not pass this information on to Mr Flegg who would be required to coordinate a rescue mission.

[33] The coroner noted that Sergeant Flegg had a 'cynical' attitude to the search that was 'coloured by his perception that people in the Torres Strait activate EPIRBs [distress signals] when they are inconvenienced rather than in peril'.[28] Flegg is reported to have remarked to an Australian Search and Rescue officer that the people on the *Malu Sara* were simply 'sick of being out there and wanted to get home'.[29] He also used the acronym EPIRB (emergency position-indicating radio beacon) to denote 'empty petrol I require boat'[30] in respect of Torres Strait Islanders. In considering Flegg's behaviour and evidence at the inquest proceedings, the coroner observed

that Flegg's notes were 'a fabrication' or 'wrongly recorded'[31] and were 'blatantly self-serving'.[32] Flegg's behaviour was identified by the coroner as inconsistent[33] and described as 'despicable'[34] and 'cynical'.[35] The coroner observed that Flegg 'knew he had failed to respond appropriately'.[36] As a result of Flegg's failings, the rescue mission was significantly delayed, possibly by up to four and a half hours.[37] Flegg's errors of judgment were described by the coroner as 'egregious'.[38]

[34] The coroner observed that 'the people lost when the Malu Sara sank didn't die because some unforeseeable, freak accident swept them away before anything could be done to save them. Rather they died because several people dismally failed to do their duty over many months…a totally avoidable disaster'.[39]

A failure to give proper consideration to the human rights of the applicants and their kin pursuant to the HRA

[35] What is required for a public entity to give proper consideration to human rights when making a decision? The Victorian case of *Bare v Independent Anti-Corruption Commission*[40] addressed this question, identifying that the proper approach to consideration has four elements:

(a) The decision maker must understand in general terms which of the rights of the person affected by the decision may be relevant;
(b) The decision maker must seriously turn his or her mind to the possible impact of the decision on a person's human rights and its implications for the affected person;
(c) The decision maker must identify the countervailing interests or obligations; and
(d) The decision maker must balance competing private and public interests as part of the exercise of justification.[41]

[36] The coroner's comments no doubt raised sound expectations among the applicants and other relatives and families of the deceased that the coroner would decide he had a reasonable suspicion that an indictable offence had been committed by Flegg or Chaston or both. There would seem to be ample evidence to raise a reasonable suspicion of negligent manslaughter in all the circumstances.[42] In light of the coroner's findings, the decision that he had 'no basis' on which he should refer information obtained during his investigation into the deaths to the DPP might, arguably, appear to be unreasonable (or perverse).[43] But that is not a question that is directly relevant to these proceedings, rather, this would be a matter for a court exercising its supervisory function in due course following the provision of reasons by the coroner.

[37] I have heard evidence that the decision of the coroner has created great sorrow, stress, and uncertainty for the applicants and their community. The community is already at breaking point and overwhelmed by trauma and

grief as a result of the loss of kin in the sinking of the *Malu Sara*. As the coroner identifies in his report, the inquest process can leave people feeling like they are accused of dishonesty or not believed and that they have not received justice.[44] I accept that the coroner's decision affects the applicants' and their community's rights to 'enjoy, maintain, control, protect and develop their kinship ties'[45] and, further, that it is conceivable that he failed to properly consider this human right in making his decision. The provision of written reasons will shed light on whether the cultural rights of the plaintiffs were duly considered in the course of the coroner's decision making and may (or may not) prompt a subsequent application for judicial review by the plaintiffs in this matter.

Is the decision exempt from the requirement to give reasons because it relates to the administration of criminal justice?

[38] The respondents make an alternative argument. They argue that the coroner's decision that there was 'no basis' on which he should refer information obtained during his investigation into the deaths to the DPP is excluded from the operation of the *JRA* because it is within the express exclusion in sch 2, item 1 of the *JRA*; namely, it is a decision 'relating to the administration of criminal justice'.

[39] Notably, sch 2, item 1 *JRA* states:

> Decisions relating to the administration of criminal justice, and, in particular—
>
> a) decisions in relation to the investigation or prosecution of persons for offences against the law of the State, the Commonwealth, another State, a Territory or a foreign country; and
>
> b) decisions in relation to the appointment of investigators or inspectors for the purposes of such investigations; and
>
> c) decisions in relation to the issue of search warrants under a law of the State; and
>
> d) decisions under a law of the State requiring—
>
> (i) the production of documents or things; or
>
> (ii) the giving of information; or
>
> (iii) the summoning of persons as witnesses.

[40] 'Administration of criminal justice' is not defined in either the *JRA* or the *Coroners Act*. The list of alternatives in *JRA* sch 2, item 1 relate clearly to specific things, all of which commence the process towards charging an offence. The coroner is specifically barred from going down that path.

[41] A decision about whether one has a reasonable suspicion is of a different character. The *ejusdem generis* rule of statutory construction identifies that general words should be confined to things of the same kind as those specified, although the legislator's intention remains important.[46] The

Explanatory Notes underpinning the introduction of the *Coroners Bill 2002* (Qld) emphasise that it is no longer the role of the coroner to commit an individual to trial.[47]

Order

[42] I acknowledge that an enduring attitude of colonial superiority pervaded and coloured the decision making and action with regards to the sinking of the *Malu Sara*, in particular, that of Chaston and Flegg. This much was identified in the coroner's findings considered earlier. Indeed, this attitude was exemplified by Mr Chaston's decision to ignore the marine expertise of his Torres Strait Islander charges and replace it with his own rudimentary knowledge of the sea. It had tragic consequences.

Ngath taima ngulaig gasaman kedha, kaipaipa kulai danalaig a Gabmarnau ia-wadhai matha mika.

Senub thonar koi poithainga dhadhal, iangu-kudu lumadhin palamun kukuil mabaignu. Parlai ukasar markai marbaig, Chaston a Flegg.

Palamun iangu-kudu kunia koi gabudharn, kedha maika na Gul (Malu Sara) si dudupaidhin malu ardha.

Inabi ia-dai iman moinu Coronau thusi nu.

Senu nui Chaston ubigi-asidhin a nungu kursai pagai-ginga Zenardh Kes au marbaig ka. Senu nubika lagalgan malu sesi-tamai tharnamun rangadhau lagaka.

Nuid Chaston nungu karawaeg ngulaig kadaka poidar. Wagel sipa kuth wati-nga.

[43] Given the special place of Aboriginal and Torres Strait Islander people in this state (as stated in the *HRA* preamble), it is particularly important that administrative decisions are transparent where they involve Aboriginal and Torres Strait Islander people. Public entities cannot hide behind arcane rules and technicalities to avoid transparency in decision making.

Inabi Lagau a Zenardh Kes au mabaigal, thana thanamun marap, laga a malu mina ia-wadhaik.

Kizi kedha bangal ithabi zapul a iangu-sakar-pudai koi-gethan gasamziw.

[44] Evidence of a coroner's compliance with the provisions of the *HRA* ought to be made available to parties who have a substantial interest. Such an approach is consistent with the *HRA* as an instrument of empowerment. The applicants in this matter are such interested parties. I can see no valid legal reason for the coroner in this matter to withhold his statement of reasons for his decision.

Nuid Coroner, nungu zagethal mina danthaiamidhin nai mabaiga-ka ngulaig palai-ka.

[45] I uphold the applicant's arguments. I am satisfied that the coroner did make a decision that he was not satisfied that the material warranted referral to the DPP; that is, that he did not have a reasonable suspicion that an offence

had been committed. Reasons for that decision should have been provided. I find that the decision was *not* a decision for which reasons need not be given under sch 2 of the *JRA*.

Ngath gima gasami ithabi mabaigau iadu-turai a iadu-tidai

Ngath iman koi balbalgi-za nungu Coronau iangu-kudul thusi nu, a nungu mulai-zinga, matha mina launga senubi zageth poiban DPP ka zapuka muika mina imaika.

Nungu sesi-thamaika kedha senubi zagethau mina kuik-aimaigina and mina-asigina.

[46] Pursuant to *JRA* s 38(2), I order that the respondent provide reasons to the applicants for his decision that there was 'no basis' on which the respondent should refer information obtained during his investigation into the deaths to the DPP. Reasons should be provided within 28 days.

Senubi thusi JRA s38(2), ngath kupai poiban kedha Coroner nidh ninu iangu-sakar-pudai a ngulaig poiban aiman, muinu inab thonarnu sar dhard zug goigil. Sipa muinu wadaigi-dagam zageth poidban DPP ka.

Notes

1 Heron Loban and Heather Douglas, translation of orders Deenorah Yellub.
2 *Inquest into the Loss of the* Malu Sara (Thursday Island Coroners Court, State Coroner Barnes, 12 February 2009) ('Malu Sara *Inquest*').
3 Ibid., 44.
4 See also *Human Rights Act 2005* (Qld) s 48(1) ('*HRA*').
5 *Bare v Independent Broad-Based Anti-Corruption Commission* (2015) 326 ALR 198, 257 [221] (Warren CJ), 273–5 [277]–[279] (Tate JA), 343–4 [534]–[535] (Santamaria JA).
6 *Griffith University v Tang* (2005) 221 CLR 99.
7 *ABT v Bond* (1990) 170 CLR 321, 337.
8 *Coroners Act 2003* (Qld) s 45(2) ('*Coroners Act*').
9 Ibid., s 45(5).
10 *Perre v Chivell* [2000] SASC 279, [57].
11 *Inquest into the Death of Mulrunji Domadgee* (Queensland Coroner's Court, Acting State Coroner Clements, 27 November 2006).
12 Ibid., 34.
13 *Inquest into the Death of Andrew John Bornen* (Ipswich Coroners Court, State Coroner Barnes, 16 July 2010).
14 *Hamblin v Duffy* (1981) 34 ALR 333.
15 Malu Sara *Inquest* (n 2) 11.
16 *Hytch v O'Connell* [2018] QSC 75, [64].
17 *Lamb v Moss & Ors* (1983) 49 ALR 533.
18 *Griffith University v Tang* (2005) 221 CLR 99, [89] (Gummow, Callinan and Heydon JJ).
19 (1990) 25 FCR 125.
20 Ibid., 142.
21 See *Certain Children by Their Litigation Guardian Sister Marie Brigid Arthur v Minister for Families and Children & Ors* [2016] VSC 796, [142].
22 Malu Sara *Inquest* (n 2).
23 Ibid., 11.
24 Ibid., 95–7.
25 Ibid., 62–3.

26 Ibid., 63.
27 Ibid.
28 Ibid., 69.
29 Ibid.
30 Ibid.
31 Ibid., 67.
32 Ibid.
33 Ibid., 66.
34 Ibid., 69.
35 Ibid., 70.
36 Ibid.
37 Ibid., 70, 75.
38 Ibid., 88.
39 Ibid., 98.
40 *Bare v Independent Anti-Corruption Commission* (2015) 48 VR 129.
41 Ibid., 217–24, 275–89, 617–26.
42 See *Australian Broadcasting Tribunal v Bond* (1990) 170 CLR 321, 359–60.
43 *Crime and Misconduct Commission v Swindells* [2009] QSC 409, [12].
44 Malu Sara *Inquest* (n 2) 11.
45 *HRA* s 28(2)(c).
46 Francis Bennion, *Statutory Interpretation* (LexisNexis Butterworths, 4th ed, 2002) 1064.
47 Explanatory Notes, Coroners Bill 2002 (Qld) 30.

16

BUGMY v THE QUEEN (2013) 302 ALR 192

Commentary: *Bugmy v The Queen* (2013) 302 ALR 192

Mary Spiers Williams

The relevance of colonialism and structural racism: 'Turning the gaze' in *Bugmy*

In 2013, the High Court of Australia allowed an appeal by Mr William Bugmy against a decision of the New South Wales Court of Criminal Appeal ('NSWCCA').[1] The NSWCCA had allowed a Crown appeal against his original sentence, holding that it was manifestly inadequate and resentenced him on that basis, increasing his term of imprisonment. Mr Bugmy injured terribly a prison guard who was acting in the execution of his duty. The NSWCCA emphasised the seriousness of Mr Bugmy's actions and the injuries he caused. It declared that 'with the passage of time, the extent to which social deprivation in a person's youth and background can be taken into account, must diminish',[2] thus apportioning little weight to the unhealed trauma arising from his tragic childhood of lateral violence and the state's neglectful wardship of him in his teenage years.

The High Court's decision on Mr Bugmy's appeal raises issues about the way in which judges make sense of colonisation and Indigenous peoples' experience of colonialism, and how colonialism affects judicial officers' application of sentencing principles, decisions about what material is relevant to sentencing, and how they interpret that material. The judgment invites examination of the way that sentencing courts conceive criminal responsibility and the purpose of sentencing—especially in the way that the idea of 'race' interferes with this.

The High Court dealt with some of these issues in ways that aligned with contemporary values—albeit narrowly understood—regarding identity,[3] substantive equality,[4] and the endorsement of anti-discrimination.[5] In key respects, however, the judgment was perplexing, notably the court's decision to recognise neither the impact of colonisation on not only the appellant, nor the reality of systemic discrimination against Indigenous peoples in Australia,[6] and the nexus of these to the criminalisation of Aboriginal people. The High Court narrowly determined what material is relevant to make sense of an offender's 'deprived background'. In doing so, it contributed to deficit discourse[7] regarding First Peoples, not least of which is the way that it declined to recognise the role of coloniser-settler society in creating the conditions of 'grave social difficulties'. This allows courts to represent 'Aboriginal identity' as if it is constituted by those 'grave social difficulties'[8] rather than recognising that these are an effect of the ongoing adversities of colonisation.

The *Bugmy* judgment raises questions about the insight of many judicial officers into the lived experiences of Aboriginal and Islander peoples. Almost all judicial officers in Australia are non-Indigenous. No statistics regarding the Indigenous status of judicial officers are readily available.[9] At the time the High Court judgment was delivered, I am aware of only four Indigenous judicial officers that were then sitting on the bench (only two others had previously been appointed but were no longer practising in 2013)—that is, 0.04 per cent of the judicial officers nationally.[10] This is significantly below parity of 2.5 per cent to 3 per cent (or approximately 30 judicial officers nationally).[11] One can infer from this that non-Indigenous judicial officers preside over and sentence almost all cases involving Indigenous people. This is troubling given that a significant proportion of the work of the criminal courts is built around the bodies of Indigenous people who typically have no agency within the system, only that of 'defendant'/'offender' to be processed or 'victim' who may occasionally be a 'witness'. The low representation of Indigenous peoples on the judiciary, the disproportionate representation of First Peoples in the criminal justice system—not as practitioners but as 'victims' and 'defendants'—and judicial precedents such as this that tolerate deficit accounts and perpetuate harmful stereotypes—together with the refusal to turn the judicial gaze onto the structural discrimination that First Peoples uniquely experience in society broadly—raise a legitimate apprehension of bias against First Peoples. In reviewing the judgment of the NSWCCA, the High Court missed the opportunity to enunciate the relevance of the impact of systemic discrimination—including the impact that systemic discrimination may have on individual judges sentencing an Aboriginal defendant—and to promote insight into First Peoples' lived experiences.

This imagined dissenting judgment goes beyond the constraints of what would be permissible in an Appellate judgment. The limitations on appeals prohibit straying beyond strictly patrolled limitations, such as grounds of appeal, the proviso, residual discretions, etc.—restrictions that interfere with the Courts' fundamental function to uphold the rule of law, that is, equality before the law and protection of the citizen against excesses of state power.[12] Ultimately, I had to concede that the straitjacket simply did not fit. Nevertheless, I have attempted to 'take law seriously'—especially coloniser-settler law's imaginary fairness and equality before the law. The Rule of Law is a great idea, and with respect to First Peoples in Australia, we really ought to try it.[13]

In writing this, I asked myself, 'What would Bob Bellear[14] have said?' Not because I have particular insight into his world view; I did not know him well. He was the only Aboriginal or Islander judge before whom I ever appeared, and I knew it. He struck me with his groundedness and strength, and his capacity to see through the workings of the system and speak truth back to it. I do not presume to speak as he did, but draw strength from his presence on the bench in the Wagga Wagga District Court in 1998, and that he represented the possibility of a judicial officer having another perspective.

Notes

1 *R v Bugmy* [2012] NSWCCA 223.
2 Ibid., [50].
3 The Plurality held that 'Aboriginal Australians Who Live in an Urban Environment Do Not Lose Their Aboriginal Identity'; *Bugmy v The Queen* (2013) 302 ALR 192, [41] ('*Bugmy*').
4 Ibid., [39], citing *Neal v The Queen* (1982) 149 CLR 305, 326 ('*Neal*').
5 Ibid., [36].
6 I use 'Aboriginal people' to refer to the First Peoples across the Australian continent, as distinct from Islander peoples of what is now called the Torres Strait. I refer to Indigenous peoples and First Peoples interchangeably. While I do not object to others using 'First Nations', I do not use it. Reasons for this include that not all First Peoples identify as 'First Nations' and I am concerned that use of this Western concept to define ourselves may cause epistemic damage. Mr Bugmy, the appellant, was referred to as 'a/Aboriginal' throughout the material and judgments.
7 Regarding deficit accounts broadly, see Lawrence Bamblett, 'Rags to Riches: Aboriginal Identity as Deficit' in Lawrence Bamblett, Fred Myers and Tim Rowse (eds), *The Difference Identity Makes: Indigenous Cultural Capital in Australian Cultural Fields* (Aboriginal Studies Press, 2019) 141.
8 For example, the remark by the Plurality in *Bugmy* (2013) 302 ALR 192, continues: 'and they, too, may be subject to the grave social difficulties discussed in *Fernando*', citing *R v Fernando* (1992) 76 A Crim R 58, 62–3. Criminalisation contributes to the representation of Indigenous identity as constituted by alcohol abuse and other anti-social behaviours: see e.g. Kate Seear, 'Sentencing Practices: On Assembling "Alcohol Effects" and the "Aboriginal Community" in Criminal Law' in *Law, Drugs and the Making of Addiction: Just Habits* (Routledge, 2019).
9 I found no information about this published by the various judicial organisations nor in the work of scholars who write about diversity on the bench: see e.g. Gabrielle Appleby et al., 'Contemporary Challenges Facing the Australian Judiciary: An Empirical Interruption' (2019) 42(2) *Melbourne University Law Review* 299. The latter, for example, refers broadly to 'diversity' but makes no reference to First Peoples by any of the usual terms.
10 Between 2013 and the time of writing this, I believe there have been a further six appointments nationally, five of whom are magistrates (or equivalent). There have only ever been two District Court judicial appointments.
11 The number of judges and magistrates in all jurisdictions in Australia in March 2019 was 1,084; Judicial Commission of New South Wales, 'Number of Judges and Magistrates in Australia, March 2019' (March 2019) <https://www.judcom.nsw.gov.au/number-of-judges-and-magistrates-in-australia-march-2018-2/>.

12 The Trial of Charles I (1649) discussed in, for example, Geoffrey Robertson, 'The Tyrannicide Brief' in Morten Bergsmo, et al. (ed), *Historical Origins of International Criminal Law: Volume 1, FICHL Publication Series No. 20 (2014)* (Torkel Opsahl, 2014).

13 Paraphrasing quote attributed to Mohandas Gandhi (various dates).

14 In 1996, Judge Bellear became the first Indigenous person to be appointed to a District Court in Australia. (The first judicial appointment was Magistrate Pat O'Shane.)

William Bugmy .... Appellant;

AND

The Queen .... Respondent;

(2013) 302 ALR 192

Criminal law—Sentencing principles—Consideration of unique circumstances of Aboriginal offenders—Colonialism—Systemic discrimination—Indigenous criminalisation—Transgenerational trauma—Standpoint—Deficit account of offender's life—Judicial bias.

Williams J.[1]

Background to this appeal

[1] This matter concerns an appeal against a decision of the New South Wales Court of Criminal Appeal (the intermediate court). The intermediate court allowed a Crown appeal against a sentencing decision of the New South Wales District Court[2] (the primary court), on the basis that it was manifestly inadequate.[3] The appellant had pleaded guilty to two offences of assaulting an officer—in this case, a prison officer—in the execution of his duty[4] and one offence of causing grievous bodily harm[5] to the prison officer. The primary court had ordered that the appellant be imprisoned for a total effective term of six years and three months with a non-parole period of four years and three months and that he be released on parole conditional that he attend full-time a residential rehabilitation facility until his treatment was completed. The intermediate court held that this sentence was manifestly inadequate and resentenced the appellant to a total effective term of seven years and nine months, with a non-parole period of five years and three months, and made no orders for parole conditions that the appellant undergo rehabilitation or any other treatment. The history of this matter—including the facts and some details from the primary court's sentencing reasons, the intermediate court's reasons, the appellant's submissions, and the respondent's reply—are set out in the judgment of the Plurality.[6] The appellant's synthesis of the facts are set out in the primary court's remarks on sentence ('ROS'):

> Briefly stated, the appellant was a 29 year old Aboriginal man from Wilcannia, who had been refused bail and remanded in the Broken Hill Correctional Centre at the time of the offences. The appellant had requested that gaol visiting hours be extended as visitors were not permitted entry after 1 pm, and his visitors might not arrive until after 1 pm. The victim, Officer Gould, said he would enquire of a senior officer whether the hours could be extended. The appellant then threatened Mr Gould, including saying: 'I'll split you open'. Mr Gould called for his superior officer, Mr Pitt, and the Emergency Team to attend. Mr Pitt arrived while the appellant was on the telephone to his partner and spoke to the appellant immediately afterwards. The appellant said to Mr Pitt 'You want a piece of me, I'll split you cunts'. He ran to a nearby pool table and took pool balls which he proceeded to throw at Corrections Officers. The appellant then threw two pool balls at Mr Gould through a gate, one of which struck Gould in the left eye. The incident continued until the appellant surrendered after negotiations (ROS [6]–[14]). Mr Gould suffered serious eye injury including retinal detachment, decompensated cornea, and eye socket fractures with a likelihood of full recovery of vision described by the treating doctor, Dr Males, as being very poor (ROS [15]–[18]).[7]

Allowing this appeal

[2] All members of this Court agree that the appellant must succeed, however, we are not *ad idem* in every respect. The Court agrees that the intermediate court failed to determine its residual discretion. The Plurality and Gageler J set out separate reasons. I prefer the reasons of Gageler J. The Court agrees that this matter be remitted to the intermediate court to consider its residual discretion and determine whether it ought to determine the Crown appeal. The majority held that the intermediate court should not have held that the trial judge erred in taking into account mental illness in moderating the 'weight to be given to general deterrence'; I agree. While I agree with the majority that the intermediate court erred in its determination regarding the trial judge's assessment of the gravamen of the offence and its proportionality to the disposition, I disagree in key respects as to how it erred.

[3] The intermediate court erred in that it did not apply the principle of individualised justice[8] to the appellant. The majority held that the 'effects of profound deprivation do not diminish over time and are to be given full weight in the determination of the appropriate sentence in every case'.[9] While this is correct, this determination is insufficient to correct the error of failing to apply the principle of individualised justice.

[4] The principle of individualised justice requires the court to take into account material pertinent to the unique circumstances of the appellant's life. Judicial officers cannot be expected to have insight into the circumstances of every

offender's life, and so ought to take into account contextual material that can help a court to make sense of those unique circumstances. In this case, the appellant provided the Court material establishing the existence of structural discrimination against First Peoples in Australia. Structural discrimination and overrepresentation of Indigenous peoples in the criminal justice system are so well established that they do not require proof, especially not by a defendant in an original sentencing hearing.[10] Given such material is so well established and well known, and particularly because so many Indigenous Australians come before our courts, judicial officers ought to be well acquainted with this information.[11]

[5] The intermediate court was aware that the appellant was Aboriginal and should have considered what effect structural discrimination—especially that which Aboriginal peoples have experienced and still do uniquely experience—had on the appellant. In the appellant's case, structural inequality and other forms of discrimination can help to make sense of the tragic trajectory of the appellant's life that led to the point where he committed this terrible offence. Not only the appellant but also many others in his life suffered the deleterious effects of structural inequality, and in his case, the material establishes that structural discrimination negatively affected his social, emotional, physical, and mental wellbeing that led to his socially destructive conduct. The intermediate court failed to give this its proper weight, and this gave rise to errors in applying principles of proportionality[12] and individualised justice. At the core of these errors is the intermediate court's misunderstanding about what the appellant's 'Aboriginality' signals.[13] At this point, it is necessary that I reflect upon and disclose my standpoint.

Standpoint

[6] I write this judgment as a descendant of First Peoples who has experience of the workings of the criminal justice system as a legal practitioner and advocate, and who has worked with other Aboriginal peoples in high and low population centres in central and south-eastern Australia. I was raised between sandstone country of the Sydney basin and the New South Wales central coast and lutruwina/Tasmania, very different places to Baarkanji country where the appellant was raised, but places that are, nevertheless, connected. My childhood experiences and education were different from those of the appellant. The appellant was seven when he left school. At the age of 12, I was finishing primary school; at that age, the appellant first went into foster care.[14] At the age that I finished my first year at an independent high school, he first 'came to the notice of the courts',[15] was detained in a juvenile justice centre, and then revolved between foster care and juvenile detention.[16] At the age when I was accepted to attend the oldest university in Australia, he was transferred from juvenile detention to an adult prison.[17] The appellant was 29 years old when in 2011, he committed the offence that

is the subject of this appeal; I was that age when I was completing my legal training. He is now 31 years old; at that age, I was working for a legal aid organisation in western New South Wales. I write this now at an age past that of the appellant's life expectancy of only 36.7 years;[18] I expect to live at least that many years more. While I have not had advantages of many others who sit on the bench and there were challenges in my childhood, these diminish compared to the adversities the appellant endured as a young man. It is my responsibility to endeavour to have insight into his experiences and to ensure that I am as well informed as possible about the experiences of the appellant and also of his kin, community, and Country.

[7] I recognise that law has been at the 'cutting edge' of European colonisation[19] of Indigenous peoples globally and that Australia is no exception. Criminalisation—with its attendant stigmatisation, state-sanctioned violence, and power to incapacitate and demoralise through separation of families and attempted severance from Country—is one of the law's sharpest edges. Indigenous Australians are not inherently criminal peoples[20]—no people are. The gross overrepresentation of one cohort should raise questions about those who criminalise, not just those who are criminalised, and about the effects of structural inequality and Indigenous discrimination. The criminal justice system and those of us who do its work are implicated in this. The judiciary is not solely responsible for the over-incarceration of Indigenous peoples—criminalisation is complex and there are multiple causes and factors, and multiple actors whose discretion affects this, not least being the offender—but judicial officers and courts play a role. The core role of a judicial officer is to extend the rule of law to all members of the community, including those who are descended from First Peoples. I recognise that colonial and post-federation Australian courts have not always done this, but I have a duty to ensure substantive equality before the law.

What a defendant's 'Aboriginality' signals

[8] The relevance of the appellant's Aboriginality in this case is neither 'race' nor 'ethnicity'. What is at issue is the appellant's *status* as a descendant of this country's First Peoples. In colonising this continent, coloniser-settlers have relied on various means to achieve the dispossession of First Peoples by severing connection from place, kin, and clan. This has included annihilation and other acts of physical violence (such as the forced removal from lands and the forced removal of children) and other less overtly violent forms of intervention and control (such as bureaucratic micro-management of lives). Racist discourse based on erroneous facts, 'science', and laws have legitimised reprehensible conduct by coloniser-settlers towards First Peoples. Since the British began colonising this place,[21] First Peoples have been transformed into a 'race' and even 'castes', fetishising skin pigmentation and appearance, and creating spurious categories that facilitate false typologies and negative

racial stereotyping, all the while erasing the connection to place. Obscuring Indigenous status and its attendant rights through racist ideology and discourse has been an effective means to delegitimise Indigenous claims to self-determination and sovereignty, and demoralise First Peoples while justifying subjugation, legitimising cruel policies and practices, and superordinating those colonising.

[9] The effects of this racism—systemic, unconscious, and otherwise—can be seen in the appellant's life story and, unhappily, in the way that his subjective features have been represented in this case. In this appeal, the issue of greatest concern is the intermediate court's decontextualised and selective account of the appellant's subjective features.

The deficit account of the appellant's life

[10] The intermediate court's account of the appellant's subjective features relies primarily on selected excerpts from the forensic psychiatrist's first report. The first paragraph excerpted reads:

> Mr Bugmy is a 29 year old man who was born into a large family. He said as a boy he was frequently in trouble and he told me that he had threatened teachers with knives. He said he had contact with the police and was placed in boys' homes and Juvenile Justice facilities. He witnessed domestic violence and said that his father had stabbed his mother.[22]

[11] The excerpt continues and relates the appellant's 'alcohol abuse and substance abuse' and 'head injuries'. The only information about the appellant's everyday life is that he was born into a 'large family', 'went downhill following the death of his mother six years ago', and that 'the history would suggest that he has had various serious problems for most of his life'. The balance of the intermediate court's account focuses on the appellant's contact with the criminal justice system,[23] his poor mental health, more detail on substance abuse, and notes that the appellant has never had the opportunity to attend rehabilitation.

[12] In relation to mental health, the intermediate court quoted from a supplementary report by the same forensic psychiatrist in which he concludes that the appellant 'suffered auditory hallucinations' and diagnosed that he has a 'schizophreniform illness', 'psychotic symptoms', and 'depressive disorder'.[24] No context is provided as to when or how these developed.

[13] In relation to contact with welfare and criminal justice agencies, there is a slim overview of the appellant as a child and then teenager revolving in and out of foster care and juvenile detention, who—when he turned 18 in 2000—was transferred from juvenile detention directly into an adult prison.[25] The intermediate court again quoted the forensic psychiatrist's first report to summarise his adult criminal history: 'From 26 June 2001 his offending had continued in an almost unbroken sequence until the

occurrence of these offences'. The report then provides a list of convictions without facts or other details similar to those committed as a child, and then continues, 'He received terms of imprisonment for those offences. He had spent much of the time between 26 June 2001 and the date of those offences in custody'.[26]

[14] The intermediate court noted the appellant's convictions for resisting police as a juvenile[27] and as an adult[28] and quoted the opinion of the forensic psychiatrist that the appellant had a 'disrespect of police' and that:

> [the appellant] has very negative attitudes towards authority figures, particularly Police and I suspect also prison officers. There may be some family 'cultural issues' which are also relevant to his negative views.[29]

[15] The intermediate court gave no details about these offences (such as facts) and omitted other context that the forensic psychiatrist had included in his report relevant to this.[30] Omitting context permitted an inference that the appellant's disrespect of police is irrational, unwarranted, and unsanctioned. In the context of the instant offence against the victim—a prison guard—the intermediate court appears to have relied upon the appellant's previous convictions for resisting police officers as sufficient justification for enlivening the purpose of incapacitation, punishment, and deterrence, and thus the subsequent resentencing to a harsher disposition. History, numerous government inquiries, and Royal Commissions demonstrate that since first contacts Aboriginal Peoples have had reason to be highly suspicious and indeed fearful of police.[31] These also show that police and others' discretionary choices tend to be harsher towards Aboriginal people despite less forceful, less intrusive, or de-escalating options being available.

[16] Problematic also is the intermediate court's apparent attribution of 'disrespect of police' to 'cultural issues'.[32] While there is more detail in the report of the forensic psychiatrist, the intermediate court did not include this. The intermediate court also elided the long history of coloniser–Indigenous conflict, colonial oppression, and systemic racism, and Aboriginal peoples' critique of and resistance to the exercise of police power against their communities. In quoting the report in this way, the intermediate court appears, somewhat bizarrely, to characterise 'disrespect of police' as a 'cultural practice' of First Peoples.

[17] The account of the appellant's background is a 'deficit' account.[33] The narrow selection of subjective material is the basis on which the intermediate court erroneously assessed the blameworthiness of the offender and thus misapplied the proportionality principle. Ignoring systemic, institutional, and social forces locates all responsibility in the appellant, who is constituted as wholly criminal, alcoholic, mentally ill, irrational, etc. This degrading reconstruction[34] of the appellant as 'criminal' here is inextricable from his identity and status as a descendant of First Peoples.[35] Eliding material that

would otherwise offer insight into the appellant's context and this offence impedes a sentencing court's ability to make meaningful sense of this terrible offence. As a result, the intermediate court's construction of responsibility in this case was crude and simplistic. The appellant—captured within this narrowly framed responsibility—is reconstituted as beyond rehabilitation and a legitimate subject for retributive punishment to be processed on the criminal justice 'conveyor belt',[36] treated as waste to be managed.[37] The primary court had ordered a parole condition regarding rehabilitation treatment, apparently the first time this had occurred; the intermediate court made no such order.

[18] There are sentencing principles that allow a sentencing court to mitigate the blameworthiness of an offender if it can rely on material demonstrating an offender's background of social disadvantage[38] where it has led a person into engaging in criminal conduct. Such material may also 'temper' the application of the principle of deterrence by 'considerations of compassion'[39] as it reduces the moral culpability of the offender. The appellant's representative presumably attempted to innervate these principles, but this strategy relies on representing the appellant through a deficit lens.[40] This allowed the intermediate court to reconstruct the appellant only in terms of substance abuse, violence, mental ill-health, etc.[41] While such material could be relied upon to temper punishment with mercy, it can also be relied upon to find that the appellant is dangerous,[42] legitimise responses that are more punitive, and justify lengthier incapacitation through imprisonment. In the appellant's case, the intermediate court did that—it relied on this material to find that a more punitive disposition was proportionate to the criminality. A key authority on which the intermediate court relied to do this was *Fernando*.[43]

Fernando

[19] Both parties in this matter relied on *Fernando* to advance propositions antithetical to each other. The appellant sought to rely on *Fernando* to advance the proposition that his moral culpability was lessened on the basis of his disadvantage understood in the broader dysfunctional social context, and asked this Court to extend this by formally recognising the unique circumstances of discrimination with which Aboriginal people—and thus Aboriginal offenders—contend. The respondent argued that *Fernando* stood for the proposition that no special principles nor methodology applied to Aboriginal defendants (or this appellant); this approach was adopted by the majority. Both approaches are epistemologically flawed, as is the case of *Fernando* itself.

[20] *Fernando* has come to have an influence that exceeds its authority as a judgment of a judge sitting alone and has been applied and interpreted in a way that does not reflect its problematic substance.[44] *Fernando* sets out fundamentally

incorrect approaches to sentencing methodology.[45] In that judgment are set out deficit generalisations about selective aspects of Aboriginal communities' lived experiences, and the primary court failed to contextualise its narrow account of social and economic exclusion, specifically First Peoples' adversities arising from colonisation and the structural discrimination that has arisen therefrom. This was despite the wealth of information pricking the collective national conscience at a period when Commonwealth inquiries raised awareness about recent state policies and practices that separated children from country, kin, and close family, and other underlying causes of Aboriginal deaths in custody that implicated the state.[46] *Fernando* did not express the perspectives and insight, for example, of the then Prime Minister in the 'Redfern Speech',[47] delivered the same year the *Fernando* judgment was delivered. *Fernando* could have been a timely—but was in fact a missed—opportunity for a sentencing court to acknowledge the role that we have played in legitimising overcriminalisation.

Recognising gaps in a deficit account

[21] When confronted with a deficit account of the appellant, the intermediate court ought to have reflected on material that can contextualise such an account and ensure that it had sufficient material to make sense of the whole person. The intermediate court's account of the appellant gives no sense of who the appellant is. That he is 'Aboriginal' only describes his status as indigenous to this place. The courts have been told that he is from Wilcannia—is he a man of the river?—is he Paakantji wiimpatya?[48] Or is he descended from another place—is he Koori, Murri, Yapa, Anangu...Noongar?[49] What is important to him? Where is his home? Who loves him and knows him? To whom is he connected? Such information should also be put before the court. For this, one requires insight into the appellant's context—what it means to have or to have lost those connections. An Aboriginal person close to the appellant's community—a report-writer, for example—would have been well-positioned to share such insight. The intermediate court should have inquired about this gap in the account of the appellant, and at least recognised the paucity of information on which the primary court was asked to sentence.

[22] Taking into account systemic discrimination goes beyond explaining the appellant's 'disadvantaged background'. The appellant's status as Aboriginal should have signalled to the intermediate court the need to reflect on the degree to which colonisation and structural discrimination affected or created the conditions for the appellant's disadvantaged background. This should have included consideration of the micro-aggressions of everyday racism,[50] 'casual racism',[51] or 'unconscious bias'[52] that the appellant may have experienced in Australian society, as well as the intergenerational impact of historical and contemporary state institutions' practices. The state took

control of the appellant's life at the age of 12 years. From then on, the discretionary decisions of police and welfare officers determined his pathway through foster homes and detention centres. The state took on the role of carer and protector of him in his developmental years; in this, it is clear that the state failed the appellant. Where deprivations experienced as a child are not addressed and an offender has not had an opportunity to heal, then the effects of a deprived background may exacerbate.

The significance of transgenerational trauma and the role of the state

[23] It is apparent that the appellant's traumatic childhood experiences arise from intergenerational trauma,[53] that is, they are the concatenation of multiple generations of 'disadvantaged backgrounds'. The use of the phrase 'disadvantaged background' is a highly inadequate way to describe the appellant's past. The material indicates that the appellant may have been a victim of lateral violence.[54] His life must be understood as part of a trajectory of historical practices before the appellant was born that continued into his life. This has a mitigatory effect on the blameworthiness of the offender and recognises the responsibility of the state to ameliorate the effects of historic practices. For this reason, purposes of restoration of balance [55]—a core aspect of the First laws—and reintegration arise in this case.

[24] A profoundly deprived background may be exacerbated by self-destructive conduct, poor judgment, social exclusion (which may also result in exposure to further victimology), and susceptibility to mental and emotional ill-health.[56] Institutionalisation—whether as a ward of the state, as a youth in detention, or as an adult imprisoned—can be symptomatic of, and compound, effects arising from a deprived background. There is a nexus between state intervention in the appellant's life on the basis of 'welfare' and his institutionalisation, substance abuse, poor mental health, emotional instability, resentment of authority, and criminalisation.[57]

[25] The appellant's blameworthiness is mitigated because of the impact of state institutions on his life. To expose the appellant to the prospect of further institutionalisation is harsh and disproportionate, does not ameliorate the ongoing and underlying issues that led to the appellant's criminal conduct, and may exacerbate it. Prior to the offence that is at the core of this appeal, the information before the court suggests that the only response to his antisocial behaviour as a child (who would ordinarily be presumed *doli incapax*), a teenager, and a young adult was juvenile homes or incarceration. It appears he had no opportunity to engage with community-based services nor undergo rehabilitation to heal from the traumas of his youth and those transmitted across generations. In this case, it is apparent that the purpose of protecting society has not been met by imprisoning the appellant repeatedly for offences prior to this incident; certainly, the victim in this offence

did not benefit from such protection. The tragic irony is that the appellant's incarceration at the time of this offence likely was exacerbating the unhealed traumas of his tragic background and contributed to the assault and grievous injury the victim suffered.

[26] New South Wales has been colonised longer and arguably more aggressively than other places. Many generations of Aboriginal peoples there have experienced social and economic exclusion as well as radical intervention in their personal autonomy that stymied control of their lives. The extinguishment of language (and along with it concepts and knowledge for which there are no English words); removal and attempted severance from Country, clan, and family; control and intervention into the micro-aspects of Indigenous people's lives by the state; denial of basic rights of social and economic participation (such as education and wages), health, and well-being; and being subjected to deficit discourse and other forms of racial stereotyping all contribute to social and economic deprivation of First Peoples as a cohort. The most powerful and deeply stigmatising form of deficit discourse—criminalisation—is part of this. All of these are structural effects of colonisation that have negatively affected and continue to affect all Indigenous peoples. These are so embedded in our society that those who work and live within its systems become fatalistic to this state of affairs to the extent that it seems to have become normalised. Normalisation and fatalism do not render this state of affairs just.

The impact of poor insight into structural discrimination on sentencing

[27] In failing to take into account this relevant material, the intermediate court erred in its synthesis of relevant material, misassessed the purposes of sentencing in the instant case, and misapplied principles. This resulted in finding—erroneously—that the trial judge had given undue weight to the appellant's deprived background. The appellant's deprived background—including his context and the impact of colonisation on his ancestors and himself—should have been given its full weight along with that of the terrible, unjustified, and irrational harm the appellant occasioned to the victim and the recognition of the victim's status as a prison officer.[58]

Ameliorating apprehension of judicial bias

[28] The intermediate court did not treat the appellant substantively equally. This gives rise to an apprehension of bias on the part of the intermediate court. The lack of insight into what the appellant's 'Aboriginality' signalled and how historical and contemporary experiences of First Peoples generally are relevant belies a lack of insight into the impact of colonisation on Australian society broadly, including our institutions such as the courts and individuals.

[29] When sentencing an Aboriginal offender, 'Aboriginality' is not a signal to intensify the gaze onto the offender[59]—thereby 'othering'[60] the offender—and then deriving conclusions about the offender based on generalisations about Aboriginal peoples or the state of affairs in Indigenous communities.[61] The tragic nature and untimeliness of Indigenous deaths in custody and grossly disproportionate rates of incarceration are relevant in this case, and indeed in all cases involving Indigenous people in this country. The statistics about rates and proportions of First Peoples demonstrate repeatedly and consistently the overselection of First Peoples at every stage of the criminal justice system. Rehearsing these statistics keeps the gaze firmly on Aboriginal bodies and excludes from the frame of consideration those of us who criminalise as well as other important contexts. In the absence of context, incarceration statistics stigmatise only those who are incarcerated and those most closely associated with them; for this reason, I do not rehearse them again here. Absent a nuanced, contextual account that at least includes a consideration of colonisation's impact on such communities, this amounts to racial stereotyping and can impede our capacity to make sense of the offence. 'Othering' indicates a failure to reflect on one's own 'standpoint'[62] or 'positionality'.[63]

[30] Acknowledging one's standpoint is not in tension with the need for courts to aspire to objectivity; in reality, it is not possible to be objective without first addressing one's subjectivity. Standpoint affects how one determines what material is relevant and then how one interprets that material. Judicial officers tend not to reflect on our standpoint (also called 'positionality' or 'perspective'). Acknowledging one's subjectivity is not condoned in the legal field. In this, we are a product of our training and enculturation at law schools and in legal practice, and we engage the methodology in which we have been trained. That is, we adopt a *faux* position of neutrality that keeps oneself out of the frame of consideration and, in a case such as the appellant's, we continue to maintain the gaze solely on the Indigenous Other. Maintenance of this *faux* objectivity requires numerous discursive devices, legal fictions, rules, and problematic methodologies that facilitate veiling (unconsciously or otherwise) colonisation's effects on us and our courts. There is now a significant body of scholarship by First Nations and other First Peoples on the harmful effects of not recognising one's standpoint. While judicial officers must strive for objectivity, we should not be complacent about our capacity to be objective in all cases and should remain vigilant about our susceptibility to bias, recognising the effect that colonisation has had on our society broadly and therefore on us as well. It is for these reasons that I set out my standpoint at the outset of this judgment.

[31] Acknowledging one's standpoint ameliorates to some degree the risk of bias arising in a sentencing hearing, as does requiring judicial officers to consider material that they might otherwise unconsciously exclude. Many people are

unconscious of the degree to which we normalise what is in reality racist.[64] Material that can offer insight into an Aboriginal appellant's background will include material that is particular to the appellant, as well as material that can help to understand the broader context and social forces that affect those whose status is also Indigenous. When the court omits such contextual material, the judicial officer's insight into complex issues is inhibited. Omitting contextual material creates a risk that the offence and its causes are left under-analysed and gives rise to unintended consequences that can include leaving potential victims vulnerable to the terrible harm of lateral violence. We do not protect society from future harm by not making sense of the present offence. Without context, one is left only with the coincidence of a criminal offence and the individual. If one introduces only a thin reference to the status of an offender and the struggles of his or her community, this has the potential to perpetuate harmful stereotypes and the offender's deviant conduct is conflated—misleadingly—with cultural difference. Demonising culture[65]—and other ways that groups of people are differentiated—diminishes our capacity to make sense of lateral violence, gender violence, and other socially destructive conduct.

[32] The profound effects of colonisation have continued over time and should be given full weight in the determination of the appropriate sentence in every case that concerns an Indigenous offender. In making sense of the individual case of an Aboriginal offender or appellant, the sentencing or appellate court must consider the intergenerational effects of colonisation on the collective experiences of Australia's First Peoples and contemporary structural discrimination. Considering material that offers insight into the unique experiences and perspectives of First Peoples would have helped the intermediate court to understand the particular circumstances of the appellant.

[33] This is not special treatment.[66] Rather, it ensures that we apply the principles of substantive equality and individualised justice to offenders who come from all social groups, including those with which the judicial officer is unfamiliar. This aspect of sentencing methodology is already practised unconsciously when a judicial officer is familiar with or has insight into an appellant's (or offender's) social cohort—whether this be class, education, culture, place of origin, ability, gender, sexuality, etc. Taking into account social phenomena that may affect only one social cohort is not a novel precedent.[67] Material that can only be relevant to some offenders does not become irrelevant because that material can never be relevant to other offenders. Unilaterally excluding it from consideration is both unfair and unreasonable, and a denial of individualised justice.[68] In the case of an Aboriginal offender such as the appellant, it is arguably racially discriminatory.[69]

[34] Structural discrimination means that an Aboriginal offender, such as the appellant, is unlikely to have been treated the same as other offenders.

Judicial officers have a duty to ameliorate unfair discrimination however it manifests in the cases that come before us. This is consistent with the rule of law and the principle of substantive equality. We can only do this if we have ameliorated the risk of our own bias. Structural racism influences individuals in our society; judicial officers are as susceptible to this influence as is any other member of our society, and so there is a risk that racist discourse, ways of thinking, and ideas could pollute legal reasoning and principles. The findings of the intermediate court in relation to the appellant's case raise such an apprehension. Such discrimination is socially destructive and the duty of this Court is to repudiate it.

Notes

1 Mary Spiers Williams.

2 *R v William David Bugmy* (unreported, New South Wales District Court, Lerve AJ, 16 February 2012).

3 *R v Bugmy* [2012] NSWCCA 223 ('*Bugmy No 1*').

4 *Crimes Act 1900* (NSW) s 60A; maximum penalty five years' imprisonment with no standard non-parole period.

5 Ibid., s 33(1)(b); maximum penalty 25 years' imprisonment for which the standard non-parole period is seven years (see *Crimes (Sentencing Procedure) Act 1999* (NSW) s 54D).

6 *Bugmy v The Queen* (2013) 302 ALR 192, [6]–[11] ('*Bugmy*').

7 Bugmy, 'Appellant's Submissions', Submission in *Bugmy v The Queen* No. 99 of 2013, 14 June 2013, [5.5].

8 *Elias v The Queen; Issa v The Queen* (2013) 248 CLR 483, 494–5 [27].

9 *Bugmy* (2013) 302 ALR 192, [42].

10 Sentencing judges only need 'material tending to establish that background' or context: *Bugmy* (2013) 302 ALR 192, [41], and do not require 'evidence'; *Olbrich v The Queen* (1999) 199 CLR 270; *Weininger v The Queen* (2003) 212 CLR 629, [24]; *Markarian v The Queen* (2005) 228 CLR 357.

11 We should have advanced considerably beyond the conservative recommendation regarding this set out in 1991 in Elliott Johnston, *Royal Commission into Aboriginal Deaths in Custody National Report* (Final Report, 15 April 1991), Recommendation 96:

> That judicial officers...be encouraged to participate in an appropriate training and development program, designed to explain contemporary Aboriginal society, customs and traditions. Such programs should emphasise the historical and social factors which contribute to the disadvantaged position of many Aboriginal people today and to the nature of relations between Aboriginal and non-Aboriginal communities today. The Commission further recommends that such persons should wherever possible participate in discussion with members of the Aboriginal community in an informal way in order to improve cross-cultural understanding.

12 See discussions of synthesis in *Weininger v The Queen* (2003) 212 CLR, [24]; *Markarian v The Queen* (2005) 228 CLR 357, [27].

13 Aboriginality and its relevance to sentencing was an issue in the hearing of this matter and was the subject of extensive discussion in oral argument before this court; Transcript of Proceedings, *Bugmy v The Queen* (High Court of Australia, 99 of 2013, French CJ, Hayne, Crennan, Kiefel, Bell, Gageler and Keane JJ, 6 August 2013) lines 475*ff*, 605*ff*, esp [635] ('Transcript 6 August 2013'). See also lines 784–91. There is dicta related to the appellant being 'aboriginal/Aboriginal': for example, the

NSWCCA quoted with approval dicta that 'the mitigating effect of being an aboriginal person loses much of its force where the offender has committed similar serious offences in the past'; *R v Ah-See* [2004] NSWCCA 202, [21]–[22], citing *R v Drew* [2000] NSWCCA 384, [21], cited in *Bugmy No 1* [2012] NSWCCA 223, [49]. See also *Bugmy* (2013) 302 ALR 192, [36] and *Munda v Western Australia* (2013) 249 CLR 600, [53] ('*Munda*'), citing *R v Fernando* (1992) 76 A Crim R 58 ('*Fernando*') and 'Transcript 6 August 2013', line 690.

14 *Bugmy No 1* [2012] NSWCCA 223, [20].

15 Ibid.

16 Ibid.

17 Ibid., [23].

18 Ruth McCausland and Alison Vivian, 'Why Do Some Aboriginal Communities Have Lower Crime Rates Than Others? A Pilot Study' (2010) 43(2) *Australian & New Zealand Journal of Criminology* 301, 313.

19 Martin Chanock, *Law, Custom, and Social Order: The Colonial Experience in Malawi and Zambia* (Heineman, 1998) 4, cited in Sally Engle Merry, 'From Law and Colonialism to Law and Globalization' (2003) 28(2) *Law & Social Inquiry* 569, 572.

20 The Uluru Statement, 'The Uluru Statement from the Heart' (May 2017) <https://ulurustatement.org/the-statement>.

21 Colonisation is not a single event of initial dispossession, it is ongoing and has been described as a 'structure'; Patrick Wolfe, 'Settler Colonialism and the Elimination of the Native' (2006) 8(4) *Journal of Genocide Research* 387. See also J Kehaulani Kauanui, '"A Structure, Not an Event": Settler Colonialism and Enduring Indigeneity' (2016) 5(1) *Lateral*.

22 *Bugmy No 1* [2012] NSWCCA 223, [23].

23 Ibid., [20], [21], [23].

24 Ibid., [20].

25 Ibid., [23].

26 Ibid., [21].

27 Ibid., [20].

28 Ibid., [21].

29 Ibid., [23].

30 Bugmy, 'Appellant's Submissions' Submission in *Bugmy v The Queen* No. 99 of 2013, 14 June 2013 [5.7]–[5.10].

31 See e.g. Chris Cunneen, *Conflict, Politics and Crime: Aboriginal Communities and the Police* (Routledge, 2001); Johnston (n 11); Ronald Wilson, *Bringing Them Home: The 'Stolen Children' Report* (Final Report, 1997). These reports indicate a significant sample size of cases that raise concerns about police–Aboriginal peoples relations immediately preceding and contemporary to the appellant's childhood and early adulthood.

32 *Bugmy No 1* [2012] NSWCCA 223, [23].

33 Cressida Fforde et al., 'Discourse, Deficit and Identity: Aboriginality, the Race Paradigm and the Language of Representation in Contemporary Australia' (2013) 149(1) *Media International Australia* 171.

34 Famously observed by Garfinkel; see Harold Garfinkel, 'Conditions of Successful Degradation Ceremonies' (1956) 61(5) *American Journal of Sociology* 420.

35 See e.g. Kate Seear, 'Sentencing Practices: On Assembling "Alcohol Effects" and the "Aboriginal Community" in Criminal Law' in *Law, Drugs and the Making of Addiction: Just Habits* (Routledge, 2019).

36 Herbert Packer, 'Two Models of the Criminal Process' (1964) 113(1) *University of Pennsylvania Law Review* 1, 11.

37 Harry Blagg, *Crime, Aboriginality and the Decolonisation of Justice* (Hawkins Press, 2008), 18*ff*. See also the reflections of Fitzgerald J in *R v Daniel* (1998) 1 Qd R 499, 530:

> [t]he criminal law is a hopelessly blunt instrument of social policy, and its implementation by the courts is a totally inadequate substitute for improved education,

> health, housing and employment for Aboriginal communities. Irrespective of race, the criminal justice system increasingly merely punishes those who are the product of deficient or failed social policies...While courts cannot entirely yield to the pessimistic belief that adequate punishment frequently does not act as a deterrent to violent offences, it is unrealistic to think that imprisonment is a wholly satisfactory response to behaviour based on anger, resentment, powerlessness and frustration related to deprivation and oppression, whatever the race of the offender.

38 *Bugmy* (2013) 302 ALR 192, [44].
39 *R v Fernando* [2002] NSWCCA 28, [64].
40 See e.g. Lawrence Bamblett, 'Rags to Riches: Aboriginal Identity as Deficit' in Lawrence Bamblett, Fred Myers and Tim Rowse (eds), *The Difference Identity Makes: Indigenous Cultural Capital in Australian Cultural Fields* (Aboriginal Studies Press, 2019) 141. Re: deficit accounts in pre-sentence reports, see Australian Law Reform Commission, *Pathways to Justice—Inquiry into the Incarceration Rate of Aboriginal and Torres Strait Islander Peoples* (Report No 133, 28 March 2018) [6.129]*ff.*
41 See e.g. Seear (n 35).
42 *Bugmy* (2013) 302 ALR 192, [44]; *Veen v The Queen* (1988) 164 CLR 465 ('*Veen No 2*'). The purposes of punishment may pull in different directions: *Elias v The Queen* (2013) 248 CLR 483, 494–5 [27].
43 *Fernando* (1992) 76 A Crim R 58.
44 See, for example, a review of problematic cases until that time in Janet Manuell (2009) 'The Fernando principles: the sentencing of Indigenous offenders in NSW' (Discussion paper prepared for the NSW Sentencing Council); Richard Edney, 'The Retreat from Fernando and the Erasure of Indigenous Identity in Sentencing' (2006) 6(17) *Indigenous Law Bulletin* 8. The analyses therein are wholly congruent with that in this judgment.
45 Ibid., 62–3.
46 See Johnston (n 11), which directs the reader to 99 reports on the deaths and other reports regarding 'underlying issues' investigated by the Royal Commission. The Royal Commission made 339 recommendations regarding the issues underlying the deaths. A common feature of many of those who died was the state separating them as children from their families and placing them into state 'care'. The 'Stolen Generation' was the subject of another Commonwealth sponsored inquiry soon after; Wilson (n 31).
47 Paul Keating, 'Year for the World's Indigenous People' (Redfern Speech, Redfern Park, Sydney, 10 December 1992) <https://www.youtube.com/watch?v=x1S4F1euzTw>.
48 'Wiimpatya' means 'person'; 'Paakantji' means 'of the Paaka/Baarka', a river that flows through western New South Wales.
49 'Person' in various first languages.
50 See e.g. Sophie D Hickey, '"They Say I'm Not a Typical Blackfella": Experiences of Racism and Ontological Insecurity in Urban Australia' (2016) 52(4) *Journal of Sociology* 725; Gillian Cowlishaw, *Blackfellas, Whitefellas, and the Hidden Injuries of Race* (Blackwell, 2004); Philomena Essed, *Understanding Everyday Racism: An Interdisciplinary Theory* (Sage, 1991).
51 Jacqueline Nelson and Jessica Walton, 'Explainer: What Is Casual Racism?' *The Conversation* (2 September 2014) <https://theconversation.com/explainer-what-is-casual-racism-30464>.
52 Daniel Simons and Christopher Chabris, 'Gorillas in Our Midst: Sustained Inattentional Blindness for Dynamic Events' (1999) 28(9) *Perception* 1059.
53 Judy Atkinson, Jeff Nelson and Caroline Atkinson, 'Trauma, Transgenerational Transfer and Effects on Community Wellbeing' in Nola Purdie, Pat Dudgeon and Roz Walker (eds), *Working Together: Aboriginal and Torres Strait Islander Mental Health and Wellbeing Principles and Practice* (Department of Health and Ageing, 2010) 135.

54 See e.g. Mick Gooda, 'Lateral Violence in Aboriginal and Torres Strait Islander Communities' in *Social Justice Report 2011* (Australian Human Rights Commission, 2011).

55 See e.g. William Jonas, 'Expert seminar on Indigenous Peoples—Issue 3: Recognising Aboriginal Customary Law and Developments in Community Justice Mechanisms' in *Submission to the Expert Seminar on Indigenous Peoples and the Administration of Justice, Madrid, Spain, 12–14 November 2003* (Australian Human Rights Commission 2003).

56 Cf. Donald Ritchie, who discussed the various theories in relation to the impact of imprisonment and finds that while there is some evidence to raise concerns about this, there is no simple, single finding about this; Donald Ritchie, *How Much Does Imprisonment Protect the Community Through Incapacitation?* (Victorian Sentencing Advisory Council Report, July 2012). See also Donald Ritchie, *Does Imprisonment Deter? A Review of the Evidence* (Victorian Sentencing Advisory Council Report, April 2011).

57 See e.g. Andrew McGrath, Allison Gerard, and Emma Colvin, 'Care-Experienced Children and the Criminal Justice System' (*Trends & Issues in Crime and Criminal Justice* No 600, 2020).

58 Re: synthesis see *Weininger v The Queen* (2003) 212 CLR 629, [24]; *Markarian v The Queen* (2005) 228 CLR 357, [27].

59 Cf. John Toohey, 'Sentencing Aboriginal Offenders' (Conference Paper, Second International Law Congress, 19–24 June 1988) 21–2, cited in *R v Fuller-Cust* (2002) 6 VR 496, 522 [86]–[87] in which former High Court Justice John Toohey asserted the need for 'Aboriginal sentencing principles' and stated that 'aboriginality as a factor in sentencing is readily understood and should be readily accepted'.

60 See e.g. John A Powell and Stephen Menendian, 'The Problem of Othering: Towards Inclusiveness and Belonging' (2016) (1) *Othering & Belonging*.

61 See e.g. instances of such a 'deficit' account in *Fernando* (1992) 76 A Crim R 58, 62–3 and *Bugmy* (2013) 302 ALR 192, [40].

62 See e.g. Dorothy Smith, 'From Women's Standpoint to a Sociology for People' in Janet L Abu-Lughod (ed), *Sociology for the Twenty-First Century: Continuities and Cutting Edges* (University of Chicago Press, 1999) 65; Aileen Moreton-Robinson, 'Towards an Australian Indigenous Women's Standpoint Theory—A Methodological Tool' (2013) 78 *Australian Feminist Studies* 331.

63 See e.g. Roni Berger, 'Now I See It, Now I Don't: Researcher's Position and Reflexivity in Qualitative Research' (2015) 15(2) *Qualitative Research* 219; Gawaian Bodkin-Andrews et al., 'Mudjil'dya'djurali Dabuwa'wurrata ('How the White Waratah Became Red'): D'harawal Storytelling and Welcome to Country "Controversies"' (2016) 12(5) *AlterNative: An International Journal of Indigenous Peoples* 480; Karen Martin, *Please Knock before You Enter: Aboriginal Regulation of Outsiders and the Implications for Western Research and Researchers* (Post Pressed, 2008).

64 See e.g. Chabris and Simons (n 52) 13: 'The idea that we can look but not see is flatly incompatible with how we understand our own minds, and this mistaken understanding can lead to incautious or overconfident decisions'.

65 Sally Engle Merry, 'Human Rights Law and the Demonization of Culture (and Anthropology along the Way)' (2003) 26(1) *Political and Legal Anthropology Review* 55.

66 Cf. *R v Ah-See* [2004] NSWCCA 202 and *Munda* (2013) 249 CLR 600.

67 E.g. the phenomenon of domestic violence does not require proof; *Munda* (2013) 249 CLR 600, especially [37], [126], [135]; also [19], [41], [45], [46], [129], [53].

68 Cf. the Plurality rejected the appellant's proposition of the potential relevance of the high rate of incarceration of Aboriginal people when sentencing an Aboriginal offender for this reason: '[w]ere this a consideration, the sentencing of Aboriginal offenders would cease to involve individualised justice'. *Bugmy* (2013) 302 ALR 192, [36].

69 Cf. *Bugmy* (2013) 302 ALR 192, [36], where the Plurality endorsed the principle of anti-discrimination.

17

REPORT OF THE INQUEST INTO THE DEATH OF MS DHU (PERTH, 16 DECEMBER 2016)

Commentary: Report of the Inquest into the Death of Ms Dhu (Perth, 16 December 2016)

Suvendrini Perera

> *The emergency department*
> *That she was*
> *Am satisfied that*
> *I am satisfied.*[1]

> *The questions considered at the inquest were not so much what happened, but rather why did events unfold the way they did?*[2]

The case of Ms Dhu, of the Yamatji Nanda family group on her mother's side and the Bunjima family group on her father's side, is probably the most infamous among instances of women's deaths in custody in contemporary Australia. The stark fact of a 24-year-old Aboriginal woman's death, within two days of being taken to prison for fine default, could not but provoke public outcry. In a campaign led by her grandmother, mother, and other family members, together with the Western Australian First Nations Deaths in Custody Watch Committee, Ms Dhu's death gained national attention. Her image was projected onto Perth's landmark buildings and, in an act of extraordinary symbolic significance, the demand 'JusticeforMsDhu' was beamed onto the state Parliament House. The case attracted support from the international Black Lives Matter movement and from Indigenous groups in North America. A song, featuring Indigenous children's choirs with Cat Empire vocalist Felix Riebl, was broadcast on national radio.

A fatal chain of events was responsible for Ms Dhu's arrest. Police were in fact looking for her violent partner, Dion Ruffin, who was wanted on charges relating to violence against a previous companion, when they knocked on her door. Under Western Australia's antiquated laws, a warrant had been issued previously for Ms Dhu on charges of fine default. The fines, accrued over the past three years, were for offences such as unpaid parking tickets, swearing in a public place, and disorderly behaviour, including waving her right finger in a police officer's face. She was required to spend four days in jail in order for the fines, amounting to about $3,600, to be acquitted. Instead, they cost Ms Dhu her life.

While words such as 'tragic' and 'unfortunate' are often used to describe Ms Dhu's death, her untimely and painful death is less a matter of fatal coincidence than the outcome of a clear racial logic. As the Office of the Inspector of Custodial Services Report concluded in 2016, 'Aboriginal women [are]...by far the most likely cohort to be in prison for fine default'.[3] Aboriginal women are disproportionately likely to be charged for 'disorderly behaviour' and they are more likely to be the targets of intimate family violence, as Coroner Hannah McGlade details in her revisionist judgment.[4] Miss Dhu was at 'a lethal intersection'.[5]

At the time of her arrest, Ms Dhu was suffering from a broken rib, caused by Ruffin, which was slowly turning septic. The pair were arrested together, and despite his known record of domestic violence, Ms Dhu was not afforded a safe opportunity to report his treatment of her or to disclose the true cause of her injury. They were put into adjacent cells at the Port Hedland police lock-up on 2 August 2014. CCTV plainly shows Ms Dhu moving with difficulty from the time of her arrival. Within hours of being locked up in the cell, Ms Dhu pushed the call button and reported to police officers that she was experiencing pain in her rib area.[6]

What followed over the next two days is well documented: as her injury continued to worsen, Ms Dhu repeatedly appealed for help, reporting ever worsening symptoms. In a sequence of interactions between Port Hedland police and medical staff at the Hedland Health Campus ('HHC') where she was taken for treatment, her cries for help were repeatedly discredited and discounted. She was stereotyped as a 'junkie' experiencing withdrawal symptoms.[7]

On 4 August, the day of her death, Ms Dhu reported that she could not feel her legs. Following her second return from the hospital the previous evening, where she was again issued with a 'fit to hold' certificate and some Panadol, it was noted that she 'had been screaming all night'.[8] Sergeant Rick Bond, the senior officer at the lock-up, repeatedly rejected any suggestion that Ms Dhu might need to go to the hospital again. He entered her cell around noon on 4 August to direct that she be taken to have a shower. Senior Constable Sue Burgess attempted to comply with this directive. According to the inquest findings, Burgess 'approached Ms Dhu who was still lying on her back and with her right hand grabbed Ms Dhu's right hand to pull her up into a sitting position. She then lost her grip of Ms Dhu who fell backwards, striking her head on the concrete floor'.[9]

This fall has now been viewed thousands of times after the family demanded public release of the footage of Ms Dhu's final hours.[10] Its impact is all the more horrific as it took place in silence because the cell's CCTV lacked audio:

> What does the law see? On a silent monitor, the impact of flesh and bone on concrete; the reflexive movement of recoil of a young woman's broken frame as it is 'grabbed', then falls backwards. Is there a small twitch in the arm that grabs, then 'loses grip'? No moans, cries or curses to be heard, but a slight turn of heads to the reverberation of skull on floor, a reverberation that seems to run through a current on the screen to a shudder in our own bodies.[11]

There is no visual evidence of the officers present reacting to Ms Dhu's fall with any sense of urgency or empathy. She was pronounced dead at 1:39 pm on 4 August, less than 45 hours after being taken into custody at 5 pm on 2 August.

The image of Ms Dhu's unconscious body being dragged across the floor on her third and final trip to hospital evokes a painfully ingrained memory in the communal archive on deaths in custody. In the case of the 16-year-old John Pat, whose killing at Roebourne jail was the catalyst for the national movement to end Aboriginal deaths in custody, a witness testified to hearing the phrase 'like a dead kangaroo'[12] used to describe the actions of police in flinging John Pat's inert body into their van. Even more horrific, following the discovery that John Pat had died, some police officers conducted what Commissioner Elliott Johnston describes in his report on the case as 'The Kangaroo Experiment'.[13] This experiment 'involved police officers dragging dead kangaroos from a police van and kicking them in the same conditions (insofar as the lighting was concerned) which were present on the night of John Pat's death'.[14]

In the minds of veteran activists such as Uncle Ben Cuimermara Taylor, the footage of the officers dragging Ms Dhu across the cell floor triggered the memory of John Pat's killing 30 years earlier. In both instances, the officers' actions can be situated within what has been described as 'the repertoire of gestural violence'[15] inscribed in the history of Indigenous deaths in custody. This store of evidence, via eyewitness accounts and CCTV, shows a repertoire of violence that includes dragging, kicking, and punching of unconscious or incapacitated Aboriginal bodies. Yet its lethal force remains mostly unacknowledged in coronial or legal findings. In the case of John Pat, in May 1984 a non-Aboriginal jury in Karratha acquitted all of the police charged with his manslaughter. This pattern has continued in inquests into Aboriginal deaths in custody since the Royal Commission triggered by John Pat's death. The findings overwhelmingly stop short of ascribing criminal culpability to the perpetrators, favouring instead terms such as 'unprofessional', 'inhumane', or 'error'. Thus, as Alison Whittaker powerfully puts it, 'Australia's legal processes after a death inside are brutal and inhumane in their own right. They drag those who die inside down their corridors like dead kangaroos'.[16]

Unsatisfied

Many of those who sat through the inquest for Ms Dhu experienced a sense of outrage and incredulity on reading Coroner Rosalinda Fogliani's findings. Cries of 'racism' and 'shame on you' arose from the gallery when it became clear that no charges would be recommended against police or medical staff for their role in Ms Dhu's death. Speaking outside the court, Ms Dhu's mother and grandmother called for accountability for her death: 'A human life and no-one got accounted for it, you know'.[17]

Former Human Rights Commissioner Gillian Triggs has described Coroner Fogliani's report as 'extensive and thorough' and points out that it criticised the conduct of a number of police and medical officers.[18] The coroner did indeed provide a meticulous reconstruction of the three occasions on which Ms Dhu was taken to hospital and of her interactions with several members of the police at Port Hedland jail, in particular Senior Constable Sue Burgess, First Constable Christopher Matier, and Sergeant Rick Bond. With regard to these three police officials, Coroner Fogliani found that they all failed to treat Ms Dhu as a 'human being'.[19] The findings abundantly use terms such as 'unprofessional and inhumane' (15 times), 'unfortunate' and 'unfortunately' (25 times), 'sadly' or 'very sadly' (12 times), and 'disturbing' or 'disturbingly' (five times) to describe the assumptions and actions that led to Ms Dhu's death. However, Coroner Fogliani failed to recommend legal proceedings or investigations against any of the officials, instead concluding that any necessary measures to address the failings in their actions had already been undertaken internally by the agencies concerned.

Crucially, Coroner Fogliani rejected any notion of 'conscious deliberations of racism' on the part of police or medical officials:

> I do not find that any of the HHC staff or police were motivated by conscious deliberations of racism in connection with their treatment of Ms Dhu, nor does Ms Dhu's family make that submission. It is important to be clear on this point.
>
> However, it would be naïve to deny the existence of societal patterns that lead to assumptions being formed in relation to Aboriginal persons. This is not a matter only for HHC, or its staff or the police. It is a community-wide issue and until there is a seismic shift in the understanding that is extended towards the plight of Aboriginal persons, the risk of unfounded assumptions being made without conscious deliberation continues, with the attendant risk of errors.[20]

The contradictions and gaps in this passage are important to draw out. The coroner dismisses the possibility of 'conscious deliberations of racism', an opaque phrase that suggests both intentional (i.e. *deliberate*) racism and discussions (i.e. *deliberations*) of a racist nature among staff. Yet this leaves open the question of unconscious, unspoken, or taken-for-granted beliefs and assumptions, which she describes as 'societal patterns that lead to assumptions being formed in relation to Aboriginal persons'. She states that 'it would be naïve to deny the existence' of these patterns, but concludes that no specific measures are called for on the part of institutions such as the HHC or the Western Australia Police to address them, as they are a 'community-wide issue and until there is a seismic shift in the understanding that is extended towards the plight of Aboriginal persons, the risk of unfounded assumptions being made without conscious deliberation continues, with the attendant risk of errors'.

This is a staggering statement of indifference. Coroner Fogliani shows no interest in exploring the role that institutions could or should play in bringing about the required 'seismic shift in the understanding that is extended towards the plight of Aboriginal persons'. Until that change is brought about, through unspecified means or magical thinking, the coroner contemplates with apparent equanimity the prospect that 'the risk of unfounded assumptions being made without conscious deliberation continues, with the attendant risk of errors'. Errors that include, in this instance, the painful and untimely death of Ms Dhu.

Perhaps the most pointed rejoinder to this section of the coronial findings is by Kalare Wiradjuri elder and Redfern Tent Embassy activist Jenny Munro: 'Why is it raised if it is a non-issue? Why then define and dismiss it, *when the dismissal fits almost word for word with the description of the institutionalised racism*, everybody is at great pains to ignore?'.[21]

As Auntie Jenny Munro points out, the coroner's description of 'societal patterns that lead to assumptions being formed in relation to Aboriginal persons' is almost a 'word for word description of institutionalised racism'; yet it is acknowledged only to be perpetuated through a rhetorical throwing up of hands on the grounds that a 'seismic shift' in thinking would be required to change it.[22] What Coroner Fogliani's findings neatly sidestep, between the distracting mention of 'conscious deliberations of racism' and the call for a 'seismic shift in the understanding that is extended towards the plight of Aboriginal persons', is precisely the responsibility of public agencies such as police or hospitals for addressing institutional racism.

Auntie Jenny Munro ends her commentary on Ms Dhu's inquest with an eloquent statement: 'All are culpable, but will any be charged? I think not, and that is the GREAT crime in this beautiful land and it is still called Institutionalised racism'.[23]

Through an Indigenous lens

All are culpable, but will any be charged? This is the question taken up in Coroner McGlade's revisionist findings. While Coroner Fogliani's findings evade the core question of institutional racism and consequently avoid reporting any belief that criminal offences had been carried out by any of the officials accountable for Ms Dhu's safety while in state custody, Coroner McGlade addresses the matter of accountability without equivocation. Her judgment is grounded in frameworks of both Indigenous truth-telling and the international human rights agreements to which Australia is a signatory.[24] Her findings speak directly to Indigenous people. Coroner McGlade's incisive conclusions can also be read in conjunction with two key documents that have appeared since Coroner Fogliani's report: the 2020 *Findings of the Inquest into the Death of Tanya Louise Day*,[25] and the *Final Report of the Canadian Inquiry into Missing and Murdered Women and Girls* released in late 2019.[26] I discuss each of these in turn below.

Naming institutional racism

Auntie Tanya Day was a 55-year-old Yorta Yorta woman who was travelling on a train from Bendigo to Melbourne to visit her daughter on 5 December 2017. When woken up by a ticket collector, she was unable immediately to produce the ticket which she had purchased at the station earlier, or to answer his questions. Noting that Ms Day appeared intoxicated, the ticket collector made the decision to call police for assistance, describing her as an 'unruly…Aboriginal'.[27] The train made an unscheduled stop at Castlemaine, where Ms Day was removed from the train by waiting police and taken into custody. She was placed in a cell at Castlemaine police station at approximately 4 pm. CCTV footage reveals that between 4 pm and 5 pm, Ms Day attempted to stand up at least five times, each time falling and hitting her shoulder and head against the wall and floor of the cell. Regular physical checks and verbal rousing are required as standard procedure for intoxicated or drugged prisoners. However, although the log-book entries indicated that these checks were performed, they were contradicted by the CCTV evidence. It was not until 8 pm that officials entered Ms Day's cell and discovered injuries to her head. She was taken to Bendigo Hospital and later transferred to St Vincent's in Melbourne where she underwent cranial surgery for traumatic brain injuries. Her death occurred on 17 December.

There are a number of inescapable similarities in the treatment of Ms Dhu and Ms Day. In both cases, officials responsible for their care failed to conduct basic monitoring procedures such as temperature checks, pain scores, or X-rays (in the case of Ms Dhu), and breathalyser tests, fall assessments, or coma scores (in the case of Ms Day). Both women were subjected to unwarranted assumptions of being a 'junkie' and a 'drunk' respectively, which informed their subsequent treatment. From the decision of the train officials to call in the police, to police at the Castlemaine lock-up who viewed Ms Day prone on the floor of her cell without performing the proper physical and verbal checks, to the ambulance paramedic who failed to take spinal precautions in moving her, the treatment of Ms Day was shaped by assumptions that she was 'a drunk'.

The destructive stereotypes through which Ms Dhu and Ms Day were perceived were compounded by laws by which they, as Indigenous women, were disproportionately targeted: in the case of Ms Dhu, WA's fine default laws (based on charges such as public disorder or insulting a police officer);[28] and in the case of Ms Day, laws on public drunkenness. The effects of such laws in contributing to

Aboriginal deaths in custody were noted 30 years ago by the Royal Commission, yet still remain in effect.

For both Ms Dhu and Ms Day, the campaign for justice and accountability for their deaths was shaped by grandmothers, mothers, and daughters connected in an unbroken chain of love and resistance. Just as Ms Dhu's grandmother and mother led the campaign in WA, Ms Day's children spoke in their mother's voice to address the coroner directly:

> Tanya Day is our mother. We need you to tell the truth about what happened to her. Our children need you to tell the truth, so that they can try to make sense of why their grandmother died. We want you to listen to her story, to hear and to understand her story. We are therefore going to tell her story using her voice, which speaks in us.[29]

In a submission that combines the voices of Ms Day with the voices of her children and grandchildren, the coroner is directly enjoined to address two matters:

> I. *What we want you to do*
>
> 38 The two most important things to us are:
>
> 38.1 That you notify the DPP under s 49(1) of the Act. As we talk about below, individuals are hardly ever referred to the DPP after an Aboriginal death in custody. There has to be accountability…
>
> 38.2 That you make findings about systemic racism and unconscious bias. These issues are almost never talked about in inquests and other court proceedings…You cannot properly make findings about what happened without considering them.[30]

The inquest into the death of Ms Day was historic in being the first in Australia to consider whether systemic racism was a causative factor, in response to the request by the family. In a Directions Hearing in June 2019, Coroner Caitlin English determined that a consideration of systemic racism was consistent with the scope of both the *Coroners Act 2008* (Vic) and the *Charter of Human Rights and Responsibilities Act 2006* (Vic).[31] The determination, described as 'momentous' by the Human Rights Law Centre (which represented Ms Day's family), raised a sense of hope among many.[32]

In her final report, handed down after much anticipation on 9 April 2020 via video link (due to the COVID-19 lockdown), the coroner ultimately did not find that systemic racism was a cause of Ms Day's death. Yet her findings did contain, in the words of Ms Day's family, 'sparks of justice'.[33] The coroner identified 'unconscious racism' in the behaviour of the train employee, as well as acts of 'cultural complacency' by police in the treatment of Ms Day. In describing the actions of two officers, she stated: 'Both Sergeant Neale and LSC Wolters thought at all times they were looking at Ms Day as a "conscious, breathing drunk" doing what all drunks do',[34] and found that their behaviour 'illustrates the power of stereotype and its resistance to correction'.[35]

Critically, Coroner English took the step of calling for the death of Ms Day to be referred to the Director of Public Prosecutions on the grounds that she believed 'an indictable offence may have been committed' to cause it.[36] Whittaker notes that in her research into 134 cases of Aboriginal deaths in custody, no more than five instances were referred to prosecutors, with only two of those five finally being 'taken up by prosecutors on the record'.[37] As the sixth instance in which a coroner has recommended referral to the DPP, the findings on the death of Ms Day represent an important milestone.[38] The inquest stands as a departure from the tradition in which 'the coroner's court is also where most investigations conclude' as, by a form of 'blameless fatalism', Indigenous deaths in custody are found to be the outcome of tragic misunderstandings or accidental errors.[39]

In their submission, Ms Day's family asked the coroner not to indulge in the clichéd phrases common to inquest findings, where words such as 'regrettable', 'sad', and 'unfortunate' abound.[40] Instead, they wrote: 'We ask you to look beyond what is "usual", and to look for the truth'.[41] The search for truth and accountability, looking beyond the 'usual', and a rejection of clichéd regrets in favour of the recommendation of indictable charges, links Coroner McGlade's revisionist findings on Ms Dhu's death to the findings regarding Ms Day.

Naming Indigenous femicide

Coroner McGlade's revisionist finding ends with a powerful call for the protection of Aboriginal women, and names the distinctive forms of violence to which they remain subject since colonisation. These remarks can be contextualised against recent attempts to document the forms of lethal violence to which Indigenous women are subject, both inside and outside formal state custody.[42]

A landmark achievement in recognising and theorising violence against Indigenous women is Canada's National Inquiry into Missing and Murdered Indigenous Women and Girls ('MMIWG'). In a supplement providing their analysis for their naming of this violence as a form of genocide, the report's authors argue that the 'The omission of Indigenous voices [from the UN's original definition of genocide] was more than mere oversight',[43] and reframe the term so as to include both gendered violence and violence against Indigenous peoples:

> Unlike the traditional paradigms of genocide, such as the Holocaust, the Armenian Genocide, and the Rwandan Genocide...colonial destruction of Indigenous peoples has taken place insidiously and over centuries. The intent to destroy Indigenous peoples in Canada was implemented gradually and intermittently, using varied tactics against distinct Indigenous

> communities. These acts and omissions affected their rights to life and security, but also numerous economic, cultural and social rights. In addition to the lethal conduct, the non-lethal tactics used were no less destructive and fall within the scope of the crime of genocide. These policies fluctuated in time and space, and in different incarnations, are still ongoing. Without a clear start or end date to encompass these genocidal policies, colonial genocide does not conform with popular notions of genocide as a determinate, quantifiable event.[44]

The MMIWG report identifies Indigenous genocide as characterised by slow and ongoing violence, rather than as a temporally contained event, such as the Holocaust. Furthermore, it is constituted by a composite set of policies and practices that operate in differential ways to produce specific gendered effects:

> Targeting victims in a gender-oriented manner destroys the very foundations of the group as a social unit and leaves long-lasting scars within a group's social fabric...Genocide is a root cause of the violence perpetrated against Indigenous women and girls, not only because of the genocidal acts that were and still are perpetrated against them, but also because of all the societal vulnerabilities it fosters, which leads to deaths and disappearances and which permeates all aspects of Canadian society today.[45]

The report argues that genocidal violence against Indigenous women may not always take directly lethal forms, but also fosters 'societal vulnerabilities' that, although non-lethal, work through a process of accretion in destructive ways that lead to the deaths or killing of Indigenous women. Such 'societal vulnerabilities' also lead to Indigenous women being placed in custody in prisons and hospitals, in conditions that too often prove lethal to them. In drawing attention to femicide and colonial genocide as underlying formations for the death of Ms Dhu in custody, Coroner McGlade brings to the fore another dimension of Indigenous women's deaths in custody that, like systemic racism, is denied or obfuscated in many coronial findings.

Walking with Ms Dhu

As much as Ms Dhu's death must be situated within the extensive catalogue of deaths of Indigenous women in police and prison custody and the broader context of Indigenous femicide that produces them, the activism following her death is situated in a parallel history of resistance led by Aboriginal women. Carolyn Lewis, an Auntie of Ms Dhu and co-chair of the First Nations Deaths in Custody Watch Committee, wrote on International Women's Day 2017: 'Women walking with Julieka have come together to fight for her, they've stood as one in solidarity and strength amongst each other, with care and love'.[46] The collective community efforts in response to Ms Dhu's death helped make visible the violence to which Aboriginal women continue to be subject in Australia's custodial and medical institutions. They also made visible the omissions, evasions, and refusals in the inquest finding into her death. The behind-the-scenes work of a coalition of long-term activists, researchers, journalists, and anti-racist campaigners following that inquest doubtless played a role in the very different findings reached in the case of Ms Day's death in custody. The latter shows us that the coroner's court does not have to be the place where investigations are brought to an end with ritual declarations of sadness and regret. Together with Coroner McGlade's revisionist judgment, and the continuing efforts of those walking with her, it points the way to future justice for Ms Dhu.

Notes

1 Alison Whittaker, 'Exit Tab' in *Blak Work* (Magabala Books, 2018), Stanza 3. This poem is composed of the 49 most common three-word phrases in the Western Australia Coroner's findings on the death of Ms Dhu, ranked.
2 *Findings of the Inquest into the Death of Tanya Louise Day* (Melbourne Coroners Court, Deputy State Coroner English, 9 April 2020) ('*Tanya Day Inquest*').
3 Office of the Inspector of Custodial Services, *Fine Defaulters in the Western Australian Prison System* (Report, April 2016) ii.
4 Coroner Hannah McGlade rewrites the original findings from Ms Dhu's inquest.
5 Michelle Bui et al., 'At a Lethal Intersection: The Killing of Ms Dhu' *Deathscapes* (Case Study, 2017) <https://www.deathscapes.org/case-studies/ms-dhu/>.
6 *Report of the Inquest into the Death of Ms Dhu* (Perth Coroners Court, State Coroner Fogliani, 16 December 2016) ('*Ms Dhu Inquest*').
7 Ibid., [501].
8 Ibid., [27].
9 Ibid., [134].
10 Sebastian Neuweiler, 'Ms Dhu's Family Renews Plea for CCTV Footage to be Released after Four Corners Program' *ABC News* (online, 27 June 2016) <https://www.abc.net.au/news/2016-07-27/ms-dhu-family-renew-plea-for-cctv-footage-to-be-released/7664910>.
11 Suvendrini Perera and Joseph Pugliese, 'What the Law Saw' *Researchers Against Pacific Black Sites* (30 December 2016) <https://rapbs.org/index.php/2016/12/30/what-the-law-saw/>.
12 Elliott Johnston, *Royal Commission into Aboriginal Deaths in Custody* (Report of the Inquiry into the Death of John Peter Pat, 30 March 1991) [13.1].
13 Ibid., [11.3].
14 Ibid.
15 Perera and Pugliese (n 11).
16 Alison Whittaker, '"Dragged like a Dead Kangaroo": Why Language Matters for Deaths in Custody' *The Guardian* (online, 6 September 2018) <https://www.theguardian.com/commentisfree/2018/sep/07/dragged-like-a-dead-kangaroo-why-language-matters-for-deaths-in-custody>.
17 Nicolas Perpitch, 'Ms Dhu Inquest: Coroner Criticises "Inhumane" WA Police Treatment before Death in Custody' *ABC News* (online, 16 December 2016) <https://www.abc.net.au/news/2016-12-16/ms-dhu-inquest-coroner-slams-police-over-death-in-custody/8122898>.
18 Gillian Triggs, *Speaking Up* (Melbourne UP, 2018).
19 *Ms Dhu Inquest* (n 6) [454].
20 Ibid., [859]–[860].

21 Jenny Munro, 'Statements for Ms Dhu, Survival Day, 26 January 2017' *Deathscapes* (8 March 2017) <https://www.deathscapes.org/engagements/statements-for-ms-dhu/> (emphasis added).

22 Ibid.

23 Ibid.

24 See Department of Foreign Affairs and Trade, 'Treaties' (Database) <https://www.dfat.gov.au/international-relations/treaties/Pages/treaties>.

25 *Tanya Day Inquest* (n 2).

26 *Reclaiming Power and Place: The Final Report of the National Inquiry into Missing and Murdered Indigenous Women and Girls* (Final Report, 3 June 2019) ('*MMIWG*').

27 *Tanya Day Inquest* (n 2) [184], [206].

28 See Office of the Inspector of Custodial Services (n 3).

29 Day Family, Submission No A1 to Inquest into the Death of Tanya Day, <https://static1.squarespace.com/static/580025f66b8f5b2dabbe4291/t/5e966dca03a960031c0a4f9d/1586916819951/Inquest+into+the+Death+of+Tanya+Day+-+Day+Family+submissions.pdf>.

30 Ibid., [38].

31 *Inquest into the Death of Tanya Day* (Melbourne Coroners Court, Deputy State Coroner English, 25 June 2019).

32 Human Rights Law Centre, 'Coroner to ask whether Racism Played a Role in Tanya Day's Death' (News Article, 27 June 2019) <https://www.hrlc.org.au/news/2019/6/27/coroner-to-ask-whether-racism-played-a-role-in-tanya-days-death>.

33 Madeline Hayman-Reber, 'Tanya Day Inquest: Coroner Recommends Victoria Police Officers be Referred to DPP' *NITV* (online, 9 April 2020) <https://www.sbs.com.au/nitv/article/2020/04/09/tanya-day-inquest-coroner-recommends-victoria-police-officers-be-referred-dpp>.

34 *Tanya Day Inquest* (n 2) [529].

35 Ibid., [530].

36 Ibid., [645].

37 Whittaker (n 16).

38 On August 27, 2020 Victoria Police announced that no charges would be laid in the case of Ms Day, following advice from the Office of Public Prosecutions. In their response Ms Day's family pointed out: 'In the last 30 years, hundreds of Aboriginal people … have died at the hands of the police, yet no police officer has ever been held criminally responsible. Aboriginal people will keep dying in custody until the legal system changes and police are held accountable'. See Stephen Schubert, 'Tanya Day's family "devastated and angry" no police officers will be charged over the Indigenous woman's death' *ABC News* (online, 27 August 2020) <https://www.abc.net.au/news/2020-08-27/victoria-police-officers-not-charged-over-tanya-day-death/12600798>.

39 Ibid.

40 Day Family (n 29) [50].

41 Ibid., [55].

42 Tess Allas et al., 'Indigenous Femicide and the Killing State' *Deathscapes* (Case Study, 2018) <https://www.deathscapes.org/case-studies/indigenous-femicide-and-the-killing-state>.

43 *A Legal Analysis of Genocide: Supplementary Report of the National Inquiry into Missing and Murdered Indigenous Women and Girls* (Supplementary Report) 7.

44 Ibid., 9.

45 Ibid., 8.

46 Carolyn Lewis, 'Statements for Ms Dhu, Survival Day, 26 January 2017' *Deathscapes* (8 March 2017) <https://www.deathscapes.org/engagements/statements-for-ms-dhu/>.

Report of the Inquest into the Death of Ms Dhu

Perth

16 December 2016

Inquest—Death in police custody—Aboriginal women—Systemic racism—Human rights violations—Intersectionality.

Coroner McGlade.[1]

[1] All across Australia, the Aboriginal cultures, the oldest living cultures in the world, teach us that the truth must always be told. This includes truthful accounts of colonial violence and racial violence, the killings of Aboriginal men, women, and children in times past and today. We all have a responsibility to speak truthfully about Australian history and what continues to be done to Aboriginal people in this country. This record of the death of Ms Dhu is intended as an act of truth telling, recording the killing of Ms Dhu by the state of Western Australia in 2014. It is also a call for justice and healing.

[2] Ms Dhu was a member of the Yamatji Nation. There is no doubt she died as a result of cruel and inhumane conduct by officers of the law and members of the medical profession.

[3] Indigenous femicide, a severe human rights violation, has a long history in Australia. It has also been normalised and excused by state authorities. This record calls for state accountability and an end to impunity for both individuals and systems that engage in abusive and violent practices towards Aboriginal women to this day.

[4] Aboriginal people were and remain First Nations peoples, having sophisticated systems of lore and governance, and deeply spiritual relationships to land. This was violently disrupted in 1788 when the British unlawfully appropriated the lands as terra nullius, meaning an empty land for the taking, violating the international law of nations in doing so.

[5] Incarceration was used as a key tool of colonisation, to subdue and overcome Aboriginal resistance. Aboriginal women and children were not exempt from frontier violence, or in any way shielded. Instead, they were violated and degraded, including through massacres and sexual exploitation. The colonists faced no consequences for taking the life of any Aboriginal man, woman, or child, and they knew that only their lives mattered under British laws. Genocide is a part of this nation's history and Aboriginal people say the Killing Times, as this history is known, have never ended.

[6] Ms Dhu was only 22 years old at the time of her death in police custody on 2 August 2014. She had been detained in Port Hedland by the local police for the offence of non-payment of fines. On the morning she was arrested, Ms Dhu was attempting to seek medical assistance in relation to injuries sustained from an assault on her by her partner. Like many Aboriginal women and girls, she was experiencing family violence, or intimate partner violence ('IPV'). Aboriginal women and girls often experience violence at the hands of Aboriginal and non-Aboriginal men; in a great many cases this results in their hospitalisation and often death.

[7] Ms Dhu was a young woman who had not yet been a mother. Had she become a mother, Ms Dhu would have been 17.5 times more likely than a non-Aboriginal woman to be a victim of homicide. Across Australia, Aboriginal women are estimated to make up a quarter of all homicide victims. The risk of hospitalisation is conservatively estimated to be 35 times more likely for an Aboriginal woman. Aboriginal women and girls are also at greater risk of sexual assault and rape. The Australian state has a positive duty to address this violence, to act with Aboriginal women in doing so, and to respect Aboriginal women's right to self-determination. Disturbingly, Aboriginal women's lives have not been valued; instead, they are routinely dismissed as non-consequential and unworthy of protection. Ms Dhu is one of many Aboriginal women who has died in police custody in Australia.

[8] Indigenous women experience intersectional discrimination. Gender, poverty, and disability also influence the discriminatory treatment that is experienced, often on a daily basis. Aboriginal women have always been leaders in their communities, but the imposition of white patriarchal culture disrupted Indigenous cultures which valued Aboriginal women's own systems of lore and governance. The denial of Aboriginal women's self-determination and other human rights by the state acts to facilitate the high levels of interpersonal violence against women seen today. Very often Aboriginal people are blamed for this violence, even though perpetrators include non-Aboriginal men. Furthermore, institutions such as police and courts discriminate against Aboriginal women and systemically fail to provide equal rights and protection of the law. Australia still remains unwilling to work closely with Aboriginal women to address this violence, convinced of its own failed responses.

[9] Discrimination, marginalisation, punitive policing, poverty, homelessness, poor health, trauma, family violence, and substance abuse are interrelated and contribute to a situation that can be described as mass incarceration. Aboriginal women comprise the largest prison population group in the country, and in fact, may represent the most incarcerated group of people in the world. While the federal government commits to 'Close the Gap' on inequality, the incarceration of Aboriginal women continues to widen, along with the removal of Aboriginal children. This is a prison complex with Aboriginal women's bodies used in an extractive manner.

[10] Words struggle to convey the inhumanity and violence of those involved in the killing of Ms Dhu. These people have all denied that her identity as a young Aboriginal woman was relevant, but they are not at all convincing. The evidence shows their actions and behaviour and the casual dismissal of her life were clearly underlined and driven by their prejudice and racialised set of beliefs, unconscious or otherwise. It was not, however, aberrant behaviour, as stereotyping and racial bias are deeply ingrained in Australia, albeit rarely acknowledged. Aboriginal people instead experience deficit discourse, where Aboriginality is constructed as dysfunctionality and acts as an excuse for racism and denial of human rights.

[11] Ms Dhu and her family, including her grandmother, Carol Roe, who has long campaigned for justice in her granddaughter's name, are entitled to a truthful account of the circumstances of her death. They are also entitled to justice. As such, this record will provide facts, describing the circumstances of her death and also naming those responsible for her death. This is required because those involved in Ms Dhu's death, who participated in her killing, have never been held to account for their actions. Too many Aboriginal women have been killed with impunity, as the circumstances of their deaths are denied by the state despite overwhelming evidence to the contrary.

[12] These are facts that are uncontroversial. Ms Dhu was arrested at 5 pm on 2 August 2014 by Port Headland police who determined that she would be incarcerated for four days at the lock-up, as neither Ms Dhu nor her family had the means to make payment for outstanding fines. Her grandmother, Carol Roe, informed police of her concerns that her granddaughter's partner had been abusive and violent to her. The police also knew from their own records that he had breached a violence restraining order from a previous partner, for which he was also apprehended at the same time as Ms Dhu. And yet they refused to recognise her as a victim and gave no weight to her vulnerability or legal rights as a victim.

[13] After her arrest, Ms Dhu had difficulty walking from the police van to the cells, and requested medical help, advising of her injury and pain. She was subsequently taken to the Hedland Health Campus ('HHC') for a medical assessment, where she was seen moaning and crying in pain. CCTV footage from the police station and hospital record Ms Dhu having difficulty walking, and moaning and crying in pain. Prior to her apprehension, Ms Dhu was herself attempting to travel to the HHC to seek medical assistance for her injuries.

[14] Nurse Glenda Lindsay could see that Ms Dhu was moaning and crying in pain, but she made a nursing assessment indicating that she was not very sick. Ms Dhu was next seen by Nurse Samantha Dunn who turned away from her, 'rolling her eyes' in disrespect and disbelief. The police told Dr Annie Lang that Ms Dhu became unwell when told she would spend the night in the lock-up, inferring that she was faking illness. Dr Lang undertook a physical assessment of Ms Dhu that lasted several minutes, although

she denied in evidence that she only spent that long with Ms Dhu, claiming her notes recorded differently. The CCTV footage, however, clearly shows that Dr Lang only spent a few minutes with Ms Dhu and her claim to the contrary was not credible. Dr Lang noted Ms Dhu's injury caused by the previous assault on her but concluded Ms Dhu had 'behavioural issues'. I find that Dr Lang made a hasty and prejudiced assessment as she considered and felt entitled to treat Ms Dhu as unworthy of medical attention, thereby showing racialised conduct towards Ms Dhu.

[15] Dr Lang later claimed she did make a diagnosis that Ms Dhu had a 'musculo-skeletal' condition and also that she was an 'angry' patient. No other witness supported this claim and the CCTV footage shows Ms Dhu walking slowly, bent over, quiet, and subdued. On questioning, Dr Lang admitted she 'exaggerated' her claim that Ms Dhu was an 'angry' patient. The evidence from Dr Lang shows she was not a witness of truth. Ms Dhu was returned to the lock-up on the night of 2 August, being declared fit to be held in custody.

[16] The following day, 3 August, Ms Dhu was recorded hunched over and shuffling still in pain. She called for help from her cell many times, telling police of her pain. By late afternoon, she was taken again to the HHC for medical assistance. Nurse Heatherington, however, also made no record of her pain and failed to record her temperature. She gave her a low triage score which indicated she did not consider her presentation or health issue serious. Nurse Heatherington's medical notes indicated that she was sceptical when Ms Dhu told her she couldn't breathe properly. Nurse Gitte Hall also examined her, although she advised she did not look at the triage form completed by Nurse Heatherington. Nurse Hall did not take her temperature either. Even though they failed to record her temperature, both Nurses Hall and Heatherington formed a view that Ms Dhu's pain was a result of drug withdrawal.

[17] More than two hours passed before Ms Dhu was seen by a doctor, even though she was still in pain. Dr Naderi undertook an examination of Ms Dhu next, and like Dr Annie Lang and the nurses, his diagnosis of Ms Dhu was also drug withdrawal and 'behavioural issues'. Dr Naderi did not take Ms Dhu's temperature, nor did he undertake an X-ray, even though Ms Dhu told the hospital staff of her fractured rib injury. She also had an elevated pulse rate. Ms Dhu was very ill at this time and in the process of dying from septicaemia and pneumonia. These simple established medical processes would have indicated her infection, the severity of her illness, and the necessary course of medical treatment which could have saved her life.

[18] As she was again declared fit to be held in custody, Ms Dhu was returned to the lock-up where police officers continued to maintain, on the basis of medical advice, that she was 'faking it'. The CCTV footage is *profoundly disturbing* as it shows Ms Dhu was treated by officers as an *object, as invisible, as a person unworthy of basic human dignity*. They acted as if they were not aware that she was even *another human being*. Notwithstanding the CCTV footage

which records Ms Dhu in an advanced state of dying, Senior Constable Bond told officers on duty on 4 August that Ms Dhu was a 'junkie' who was 'faking' her illness and who had twice been seen at the hospital.

[19] Senior Constable Burgess, with Aboriginal Liaison Officer Edwards, entered Ms Dhu's cell at 12:06 pm. Ms Dhu told her that her legs were numb and she called out to them saying, 'Help me, I can't feel my legs'. They realised they could not shower Ms Dhu as instructed by Senior Constable Bond and told him so. Senior Constable Burgess returned to Ms Dhu's cell where she grabbed roughly at Ms Dhu's arm, and then released her so that her head fell and struck the concrete floor. Ms Dhu, who was dying in pain, did not cry out or break her fall.

[20] Senior Constable Bond decided to have Ms Dhu assessed for a third time at the hospital, but he waited another 25 minutes to do so. First Class Constable Matier entered her cell and handcuffed her, somehow considering her as a flight risk, even though she was now dying. He dragged her around the cell, telling her to walk as she told him, 'No, I can't move my legs'. Along with Senior Constable Burgess, they dragged and carried her through the cells by her arms and legs back to the HHC. At the hospital reception, Constable Matier told Nurse Jones, 'She's just putting it on. She's faking it'. Ms Dhu was now in a wheelchair; her head had fallen backwards completely. The CCTV footage shows the officers acting in a nonchalant and indifferent manner as if they were completely oblivious to what was happening in front of their very eyes.

[21] The HHC medical staff failed to undertake basic and appropriate medical procedures, such as taking a temperature and chest X-ray, and yet declared her to have 'behavioural issues'. At the inquest, the medical experts described the conduct as 'premature diagnostic closure'. But this analysis fails to recognise the social context and the way that the identity of Ms Dhu as an Aboriginal woman made her vulnerable to discriminatory decision making which had a lethal impact. This 'colour-blind' explanation proffered by non-Aboriginal medical experts acts as a diversion from the true circumstances of death: Ms Dhu died because of the colour of her skin, the prevalence of racism in Australia today, and the violent manifestations of racism towards Aboriginal women, including by the legal system and health profession.

[22] Racist violence, racial bias, and discrimination are prohibited under the *International Convention on the Elimination of All Forms of Racial Discrimination*, which Australia agreed to abide by before the United Nations several decades ago. More than 30 years ago, the national human rights institution documented the prevalence of racial hate and racial violence in Australia and towards Aboriginal people, including by the police.[2] And yet in Australia, racism remains rife and Aboriginal deaths in custody continue. There is evidence that the criminal justice system discriminates against Aboriginal people at every stage possible. Hospitals and medical staff, doctors and nurses are witnessed behaving in a racist manner towards Aboriginal people, at times

even causing death. While governments have established institutions to uphold the principle of non-discrimination, these bodies typically exclude Aboriginal people, lack independence from government, and serve to function as an illusion for racial equality. The country will remain diminished until racism, racial violence, and discrimination against Aboriginal women are unequivocally denounced.

[23] None of the persons named in this record of investigation, who are responsible for the death of Ms Dhu, have been held accountable for their conduct, even though it proved fatal. Ms Dhu's family, notwithstanding, have ensured that all around the country, Aboriginal people learnt the truth of the violent circumstances of her death and called to account all those responsible for her death. Aboriginal people across the nation shared the pain and suffering of her family and community, holding protests and rallies in her name and speaking when told to be quiet in the face of erasure of the true circumstances of her death. In a song made in her memory, 'Aboriginal Girls of the Pilbara', Australia has been reminded that Ms Dhu did not 'die for nothing', and this will always be Aboriginal land: 'We're not going away, this is our home'.

[24] As Aboriginal people know, Australian laws have long protected the perpetrators of racism and state violence, a grave human rights situation. The persons named in this record should be held to account. I therefore recommend that they are criminally prosecuted for their conduct and the way in which they deprived Ms Dhu, who was a victim entitled to legal protection, of her dignity and her life. As a nation, we must begin to equally uphold the human rights of everyone, especially those vulnerable to multiple forms of discrimination and inequality. We must acknowledge that Aboriginal women give life to their community and nations; their lives are sacred and must always be protected.

Notes

1 Hannah McGlade.
2 *National Inquiry into Racist Violence in Australia* (Report, 1991).

INDEX

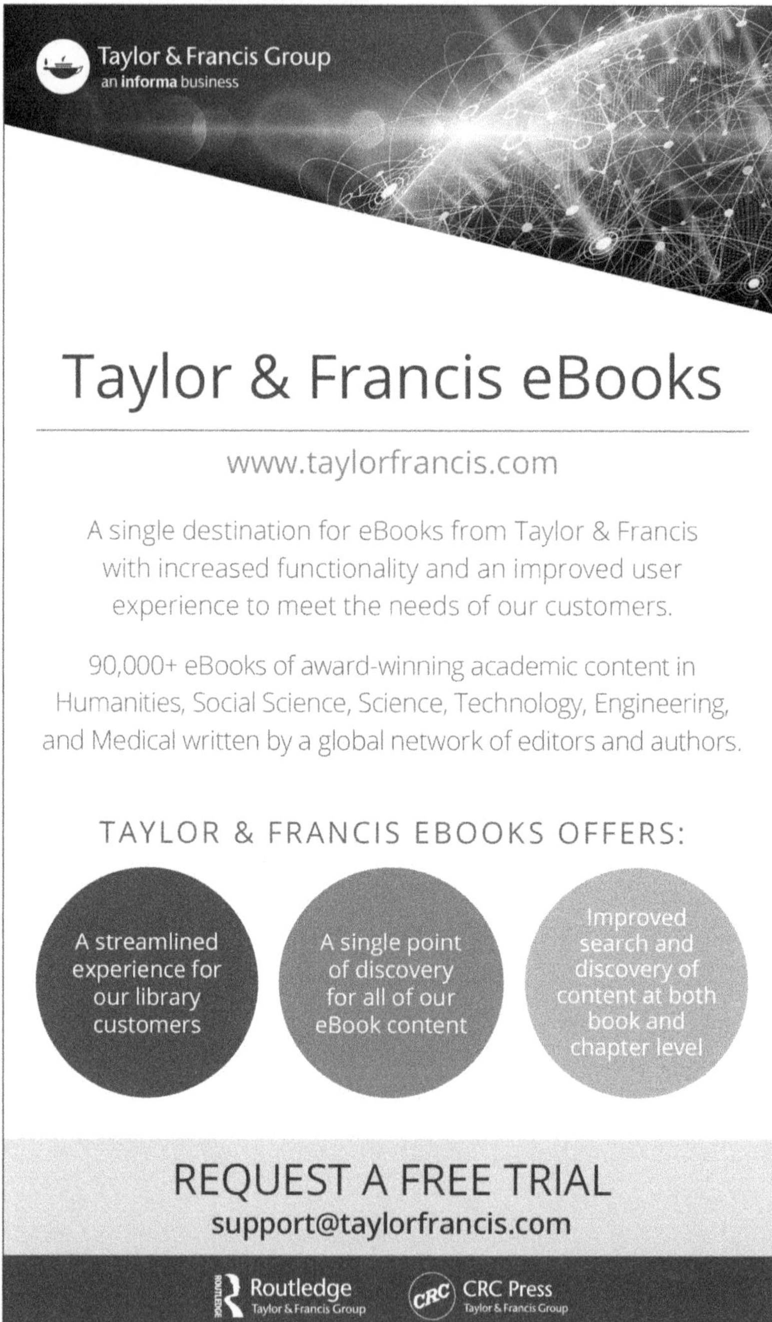
Taylor & Francis Group
an informa business
Taylor & Francis eBooks
www.taylorfrancis.com
A single destination for eBooks from Taylor & Francis with increased functionality and an improved user experience to meet the needs of our customers.
90,000+ eBooks of award-winning academic content in Humanities, Social Science, Science, Technology, Engineering, and Medical written by a global network of editors and authors.
TAYLOR & FRANCIS EBOOKS OFFERS:
A streamlined experience for our library customers
A single point of discovery for all of our eBook content
Improved search and discovery of content at both book and chapter level
REQUEST A FREE TRIAL
support@taylorfrancis.com
Routledge
Taylor & Francis Group
CRC Press
Taylor & Francis Group

For Product Safety Concerns and Information please contact our EU
representative GPSR@taylorandfrancis.com
Taylor & Francis Verlag GmbH, Kaufingerstraße 24, 80331 München, Germany

www.ingramcontent.com/pod-product-compliance
Ingram Content Group UK Ltd.
Pitfield, Milton Keynes, MK11 3LW, UK
UKHW022009180926
475701UK00003B/277

* 9 7 8 0 3 6 7 4 6 7 4 5 6 *